TO: Bob
Birthday - aug. 22, 1977
                Mother

Kentucky Basketball's
BIG
BLUE MACHINE

Kentucky Basketball's
BIG
BLUE MACHINE

by
Russell Rice

THE STRODE PUBLISHERS, INC.
HUNTSVILLE, ALABAMA 35802

Photographs Courtesy Of
University Of Kentucky
Department Of Athletics

Copyright 1976
By Russell Rice
All Rights In This Book
Reserved Including The Right
To Reproduce This Book Or Parts
Thereof In Any Form — Printed In U.S.A.
Library Of Congress Catalog Number 75-32110
Standard Book Number 87397-078-0

Contents

Foreword
Preface

1. The Beginning 15
2. "A Prince Of A Fellow" 19
3. A One-Man Operation 27
4. How "Sweet" It Was 31
5. Champions Of The South 40
6. Kentucky's First All-American 47
7. "March Madness" 58
8. The "Submarine" Attack 64
9. Time Out: Adolph Rupp 74
10. Rhapsody In Brown 84
11. A Serious Matter 92
12. A Whirling Dervish Job 99
13. Ride 'Em, Cowboy 107
14. Nothing's Wrong 116
15. Echoes From The '30s 125
16. The Beardless Wonders 137
17. Time Out: Alex Groza 148
18. Echoes From The Early '40s 156

19.	An Era Begins	162
20.	The "Fabulous Five"	170
21.	The Olympic Games	183
22.	Weep No More	191
23.	Echoes From The Late '40s	200
24.	The Impending Storm	209
25.	Time Out: Bill Spivey	218
26.	The Darkest Hour	226
27.	Time Out: Cliff Hagan	235
28.	Return Of The 'Cats	242
29.	An Upsetting Situation	249
30.	A Highly Competitive Business	258
31.	Time Out: Johnny Cox	264
32.	The Fiddlin' Five	269
33.	Letter From A "Preacher Man"	276
34.	Echoes From The '50s	282
35.	Only At Kentucky	289
36.	"King Cotton"	297
37.	The "Katzenjammer Kids"	306
38.	"Rupp's Runts"	315
39.	A Cruel Blow	327
40.	Time Out: Dan Issel	333
41.	Echoes From The '60s	339
42.	The Last Hurrah	346
43.	In The Shadow Of Rupp	356
44.	Gentleman Jim	365
45.	Time Out: Kevin Grevey	373
46.	Something To Prove	381
47.	The Slaughterhouse Five	390
48.	A New Identity	398
	Appendix	413

Foreword

This is the first complete history ever written about basketball at the University of Kentucky, and what a glorious story it is. Due to the fact that its high schools have always played a high brand of basketball, Kentucky has always been known for excellence in the sport. During the days of the old Stagg tournament in Chicago, when high schools from many states met to decide the national championships, Carr Creek gave an excellent performance the same year that Ashland won the championship of this tournament. The Carr Creek team almost to a man went to Eastern Normal College while some of the Ashland boys came to the University of Kentucky and played for me there.

I think we are safe in saying that until 1970 the history of basketball at the university has to a large extent been dominated by Kentucky players. The game really started moving at the university when it won the 1921 championship of the South over many of the teams that are now in the Southeastern, Atlantic Coast, and Southern conferences, all once part of the old Southern Conference. From then on, Kentucky had winning years.

Kentucky received its greatest national recognition in 1934 when it played NYU as part of a doubleheader at Madison Square Garden. The game was played under Eastern rules that were considerably different from those of the South. Rules then were interpreted sectionally, not nationally, and the play of that game attracted much attention. The Wildcats also received recognition by playing doubleheaders in Buffalo and in Philadelphia and by visiting Boston, Creighton, and other spots out of the Southern realm of competition.

But the "glory road" for UK really started when the 1945 Wildcats won the NIT. Many of the Kentucky boys went away to war. Five of them never returned. When the remainder returned, it was a team composed of players of excellence, with two All-Americans sitting on the bench. They won the NCAA tournament in 1948, went on to help win the Olympics, and then repeated in 1949. For some unknown reason they were not invited back in 1950, although they had an excellent team with an excellent record and practically all of them were veterans. In 1951, the university was invited to again participate in the NCAA and won the championship. They repeated with the "Fiddlin' Five" of 1958. So far, Wildcat teams have participated in more NCAA tournaments than any other school in America. They have been great and glorious years for the university.

Russell Rice spent six years in research to help prepare this book. I remember him visiting libraries in New Orleans, Atlanta, Chicago, and many other cities where we played to dig up long lost and interesting facts. He went to Lawrence, Kansas, with me when I was honored by the alumni there, and he also went to Lawrence and Topeka another time on his own and then another time to Freeport, Illinois, where I coached high school basketball. Three hundred pages could easily be added to this story, but the accuracy of what is written in these pages cannot be disputed.

As I completed reading the galley proofs of this immense, well-written, and interesting volume, I was thankful that Russell spent so much time on what must have been a labor of love for him. I also wish to thank all those who have helped build basketball not only at the university, but in the South, in the nation, and perhaps in the world. I thank them for their loyalty during these years that they have enjoyed watching Kentucky march down the "Glory Road."

Adolph Rupp

Preface

On the night of a University of Kentucky basketball game in Memorial Coliseum, ceiling lights, juiced to 250 candlepower for the benefit of color television cameras, would beam onto a highly waxed 50' x 94' wooden floor as more than eleven thousand faithful followers suddenly became silent and awaited the magic moment when their blue and white-clad warriors would run onto the floor of battle.

In the northwest corner of the arena, men wearing blue coats and blazers of the "Committee of 101" would place a large roll of blue carpeting in front of an opening leading to the stadium catacombs and let the heavy strip of acralon play out to the corner of the floor. Cheerleaders in scanty blue and white uniforms would prance nervously at the end of the carpet while uniformed police shielded it from a pushing, surging group of youngsters and oldsters.

While the drama unfolded inside, hundreds of hardy souls would be standing in the cold on the Avenue of Champions, hoping some students would not claim seats. On rare occasions when there were such unclaimed seats, the first person in line would eagerly pay the price, hustle through the east door, and head up a ramp leading to a seat high in the XX section. En route to his seat he would pass recessed wall panels containing the names of more than nine thousand Kentucky dead of World War II, but he would pay them no heed. His mind was on living heroes fighting the continuous fight to keep Kentucky supreme in the world of basketball.

After the Coliseum was completed in 1950, a steady stream of kith and kin had visited the magnificent structure to pay homage to their fallen heroes. Four years later the names of

1,159 Kentuckians killed in the Korean War were displayed on the west ramp of the structure and were equally honored by the citizenry. However, as the Veterans Day parades and various other patriotic functions lost their appeal and as time thinned the ranks of visitors and dimmed the memory of past war heroes, the Coliseum became what many Kentuckians had suspected all along—a monument to the game of basketball—and the basketball trophy cases along the east and west concourses far outshone the memorial plaques on the walls.

Enshrined in these trophy cases are such basketball memorabilia as retired jerseys worn by past UK stars, silver cups denoting four NCAA championships, and trophies and plaques representing more than two dozen SEC crowns won or tied since the league was organized in 1933, seventeen UKIT trophies, and National Invitational, International Universities, and Olympics crowns.

Reigning over all this is a large color portrait of Adolph Frederick Rupp, who for more than four decades guided the destiny of Wildcat basketball teams and who became known throughout the world as the "Blue Grass Baron of Basketball." His accomplishments included more victories than any coach in the history of the game, and his honors were seemingly endless.

Although it seemed that Rupp had been the UK basketball coach forever, Wildcat basketball predated him by more than a quarter of a century. The first UK teams began playing in Buell Armory in 1903 and then moved to Alumni Gym twenty years later. The new gym, considered a white elephant at the time it was built, was already overcrowded and outdated by the time Rupp arrived on the scene in 1930. His teams won so many championships and created so much interest that Memorial Coliseum was constructed immediately after World War II, becoming a showcase for the Wildcats and many of the nation's finest teams and players.

Although the march of time finally caught up with Rupp in 1972, the Coliseum still rang out the echoes praising his accomplishments as the Wildcats, under successful new head coach Joe B. Hall, played their last games in the structure and prepared to move into a new 23,000-seat downtown arena for the 1976-77 season. Among those who bade a fond goodbye to the Coliseum were many of Rupp's former players, ones who would remember particularly how he would sit alone in the team training room just before sending them into warm-up for battle, a solemn, solitary figure bearing the responsibility of perpetuating the tradition that was and is Kentucky basketball.

Although he had fought more than a thousand such battles, he would always feel the same fears and anxieties—"like having lye on your stomach"—that he felt when he first started coaching. Sitting alone, with his players quietly occupying nearby bunk beds, he was convinced that it mattered much whether you won or lost; otherwise, why keep score? He could not imagine thousands of spectators coming from all corners of the state to see his teams play basketball and then returning home not interested in the score. His ambition in life was simple—"I just want to win every basketball game my team plays"—and his sole purpose in participating in sports was to succeed. Defeat and failure to him were enemies, and basketball without victory had little meaning.

After the players had warmed up and returned to the dressing room, they would sit silently while he gave them the numbers of the men they were to guard, told them the plays he thought would work, and passed on what he had observed. There were no pep talks. He did not care for rah rah or tears-in-eyes stuff. He wanted baskets. He would discuss offensive and defensive plans, starting lineups, and other such sensible things. He wanted them to go onto the floor of battle poised, cool of nerve, and keen of judgment, not nervous and excited.

The players would silently return to the arena for a ritualistic introduction of starters. As each player's name was called, he would run onto the blue "K" in center circle, face the TV camera on the student side, shake his partner's hand, pat his partner's rear, and then all would return to the bench, huddle, and interweave hands with the coach. Players, coaches, and Coliseum dwellers thus would be united in the activity. So would Wildcat fans throughout the nation, who would be tuned to UK Radio Network as Cawood Ledford, "Voice of the Wildcats," started his play-by-play account.

An eastern Kentucky group would gather atop tall Pine Mountain for better reception on their automobile radio; a couple in Dayton, Ohio, would circle the block before parking their car where experience had taught them that the signal bounced down strongest; in far-off Watervliet, New York, the radiocast would take precedence in a tavern operated by Bob Sherlock, who had tuned in a UK broadcast in 1945 and had been a UK basketball fan ever since. Throughout Wildcat basketball land, women would wash dishes, mop, iron, sew, wax, and shine while their nervous spouses would pace, smoke, flip coins, play cards, or do a variety of other things to ease the tension. Throughout the Commonwealth hardly a radio would be tuned to a station other than those on the Wildcat Network.

When the Wildcats took their first possession of the ball, knowledgeable fans would watch for a pet pattern that, according to tradition, the Wildcats would execute. The nationally famous saying attributed to Rupp was "Star Spangled Banner and then No. 6," stemming from his strategy after the opening song of running the guard-around play to tell immediately if the opposing team was playing a zone defense. After the preliminary skirmishing, action would quicken and Rupp would squirm on the bench, yelling, "Go, dammit, go! Get up on those boards!" Like a computer programmed to obey its master's commands, the team would respond.

Pit-pit-pit-pit. The ball would flick from one eager pair of hands to another. An opening in the defense would yawn, the ball would swish through the net. Many minutes later the demoralized visitors would trudge off the court. Though the home team had won by 26 points, Rupp would grunt, "We need to work on that defense."

When the Wildcats won, all would be well, and radio listeners would settle back for Rupp's game comments delivered in a homespun Kansas twang and embellished with metaphors and alliterations. The tone was more somber, however, on those rare occasions when the team lost, and the Old Man's disappointment would fairly crackle over the airwaves. There would be no joy in the land and lights would burn late in many homes as the faithful played and replayed the games.

This was and is Kentucky basketball, and nowhere is the game placed on such a pedestal. Wherever the Wildcats travel, fans young and old alike come out to see the game at its finest. Telegrams, letters, and telephone calls follow them on the road. Good luck messages come from such sources as the Western Union employees in Lexington and the "Wildcat Club" of Wilmore, Kentucky. One telegram, signed by 101 fans, was received prior to the Alabama game in 1966 and marked the beginning of the "Committee of 101," a booster organization that now boasts a 500-member branch in Austin, Texas, and a smaller "subsidiary" in Tokyo, Japan.

Approximately one hundred members of the Austin

branch, consisting mainly of International Business Machines Corporation employees, make an annual pilgrimage to Baton Rouge to see the Wildcats play Louisiana State University.

The problem in the past had been an inability of fans to purchase tickets to Wildcat games in Memorial Coliseum. Other than the traditional allotment for students, all seats were purchased by holders of priorities. These priorities were so treasured that they often became points of contention in divorce settlements and wills and have been known to entice persons to enter the political arena where a winning effort meant two season guest tickets in the bleacher section at the south end of the Coliseum playing floor.

With the opening of the new Rupp Arena, hope flared that at last tickets would be available for everyone. However, demand so far exceeded the supply that all applications from the general public for new priorities were dumped into one huge pile from which were drawn the names of those who would be permitted to purchase those priorities. Which simply meant that Kentucky basketball had outgrown one of the biggest arenas in the nation...before that arena's doors were open.

To an outsider the foregoing preface may seem too enthusiastic. All I can say is, that is the way it looks from inside the Wildcat's lair.

Russ Rice

The Beginning

Kentucky at the turn of the century was a predominantly rural culture where winter entertainment consisted mostly of corn huskings, spelling bees, and church-related affairs. The menfolk, a hard-drinking, hard-living lot, took pride in their skill with horses and firearms. Match races and turkey shoots were big events. Feuds were common in the eastern mountains, and violence by gunfire pervaded the entire Commonwealth, including the Capitol grounds in Frankfort.

During the long winter months most Kentuckians were isolated, and nearly all rural activities had to cease. Due to the Fourth Constitution in 1891, which prohibited the state from establishing highway funds, there were no good roads except short stretches here and there that had been kept privately. Sometimes even schools could not be reached until mud holes were filled or bridged. Country churches were called off in winter, and a visit to the neighborhood grocery was a tedious chore.

The winter doldrums also extended throughout the nation for sports fans desperately in need of a great indoor game comparable to the outdoor games of that era. Students had become bored by the mass calisthenics, marching, gymnastics, and other traditional body-building exercises they were forced to turn to when winter drove them indoors. It was also a time of great change in sports tastes. Since 1870, baseball and football had become increasingly popular, and students preferred a game flavor to their indoor recreation.

The center of higher education in Kentucky, then and now, was Lexington, where the Agricultural and Mechanical College of Kentucky, established in 1865 as a result of the

Morrill Act in 1862, was located as a part of Kentucky University. The connection of the two schools was severed in 1878. The A&M college remained temporarily located at Woodland and Maxwell Streets until 1882, when it was moved to South Limestone Street at the present site of the University of Kentucky. Kentucky University continued on North Broadway and is now known as Transylvania University. By 1881 the A&M college was beginning to be called Kentucky State College. The name of the institution was officially changed to Kentucky State University in 1908 and to the University of Kentucky in 1917.

The most popular winter events at the colleges in those early years were oratorical contests held in the Opera House on North Broadway in Lexington. Enthusiasm was so wild that KU de-emphasized the sport because oratory interfered with studies; the students drank too much at the contests and they also gambled on the outcome.

Relations between the town and State College students were strained due to overzealousness, and the Legislature sent a committee to investigate the college. When the time came to go back to town, committee members discovered the students had stolen the horses and wheels from their carriages.

The *Kentuckian*, annual student publication, saw no harm in the antics. "The boys of Kentucky State College do things to startle the world," it reported, "and while they are mischievous, they compel others to admire their wonderful strength and originality."

In those early years of statewide civil disorders, feuds, general violence, and a lack of respect for law and order, the State College students were mostly men—girls were not admitted until 1890—and they reflected the times. Football was the big game, and the "Immortals of '98" were the toast of the town after giving the school its only undefeated football team.

James K. Patterson, president of the university from 1878 until 1910, loathed football and all other sports, and was almost continuously troubled by problems arising from the increasing emphasis on intercollegiate athletics. His opinions were expressed in 1901 to the trustees: "From the end of November 'til about the middle of March, when the baseball season begins, there is a comparative lull and during the interval, the serious work of the year is done. I do not speak of broken noses, legs and arms, but of the time wasted, idleness encouraged, and a heritage of demoralization carried over to the succeeding year. This is a serious matter and deserves your careful attention."

At that moment in time, forces were at work polishing a game that would fill the big sports lull that Patterson spoke of, and little did he realize that one day Kentucky would be recognized as the biggest name in the collegiate game.

That game was basketball, which had its beginning in the autumn of 1891 at the International YMCA Training School in Springfield, Massachusetts, where a 30-year-old gym instructor named Dr. James A. Naismith nailed two peach baskets onto the lower rails of 10-foot balconies at the end of the school gym, tacked a set of 13 rules to the gym bulletin board, rolled out a soccer ball, and let the fun begin.

In Kentucky, basketball was played in YMCAs and on an exhibition basis at some schools before the turn of the century. Years ago a Louisville architect named Hugh Nevin recalled playing in the first organized basketball game in that city. It was played in 1895 at the old YMCA at Fifth and Walnut streets.

"We had been playing the game two or three years at the 'Y,' but just in gym classes and in no organized manner," Nevin said. "There might be 50 in the class, and we'd split up 25 on a side to play. In 1895, though, we organized the first league and team at the 'Y.' I was on the Black team that won the championship. All the teams were named after colors.

"The game was more like indoor football. The referee's biggest job was separating two opponents who got entangled wrestling for the ball. It was a rough game. You couldn't dribble the ball. You could pass by rolling it, though. Bushel baskets were used for goals set on shelves. We drug out the stepladder to climb up and get the ball out of the basket.

"We thought cutting a hole in the bottom of the basket was a pretty neat trick, but it took them three years to think about it. Every time we made a basket, we had to get a pole and poke the ball out through the hoop. The net got torn several times, but we carefully sewed it back up. Fortunately, we weren't good shots."

The first basketball game in which collegians in Kentucky competed against someone other than match games within their own school was played February 4, 1901, when teams from the Art, Bible, Law, and Medical schools of Kentucky University selected a squad to represent that institution the following night against the Lexington YMCA. KU was also trying to schedule

Georgetown College and the Louisville YMCA, but there is no record of those games having been played.

During the ensuing year there were some Friday night games at the YMCA, while KU played some exhibitions for fun and amusement. A picture of its basketball team was featured in the 1901-02 school yearbook, which reported, "Basketball was very popular with both the young men and the young women. The boys made a Northern trip and met one of the best teams in the country. They did not expect to win, and though defeated, everybody felt the team made a very creditable showing on the trip."

There were three match games that year between the College of Liberal Arts and the College of the Bible, and the young women also organized first and second basketball teams. The KU girls lost that year to Hamilton College, a division of KU, in what was probably the first match game between collegiate girls in the Blue Grass. There were also match games that summer between school and playground teams in Lexington. The *Leader* reported, "Basketball seems to be the favorite mode of amusement at present, and the game is getting to be quite popular not only in college but also among the YMCAs." A movement was started to organize a Blue Grass Basketball League that would include teams from the YMCA, KSC, KU, and Georgetown as charter members. It was just a matter of time before the game would sweep the city and the state.

"A Prince Of A Fellow"

Walter W. H. Mustaine, the new physical director at Kentucky State College, awakened to a busy schedule on Friday, February 6, 1903.

In addition to his well-attended morning classes he would oversee a "volunteer army of indoor athletes" that afternoon in the new gym. He would have the "preps" participating in graceful movements with Indian clubs; freshmen and sophomores doing stunts on the bars or mats; juniors boxing, wrestling, or fencing; and seniors "adding the final embellishments to the bodies as well as their minds."

Lean, hawk-faced with protruding ears and hair parted in the middle, he was described by the local press as "an athlete of no mean ability." A sharp dresser and good mixer, he fitted right into the spirit of the times, managing the glee club, giving toasts at annual smokers for the football team, maintaining an active membership in the YMCA, teaching classes in dance to prepare the juniors for their prom, and later playing the part of a college president in "The Halfback," a musical play in three acts.

His hang-up, however, was gym work, and interest manifested in that phase of the curricula was the best in the history of State College. In fact, he was eagerly looking forward to March 7, when the first annual Gym Tournament, under his direction, would prove a pronounced success. But on that February 6 his nonclassroom thoughts centered around the Eighth Annual Intercollegiate Contest, which he considered a truly big event, to be held in the school chapel and, of lesser importance, a basketball game to be held in the gym.

The *Herald* did not think enough of the basketball game to mention it in its edition that morning, but the *Leader* recorded the event as follows:

> The first intercollegiate basketball game in the history of State College will be played this afternoon in the State College gym. The Cadets will play Georgetown's crack team.
>
> The students are taking a great deal of interest in basketball. Mr. Mustaine has gotten the boys interested in the sport. With such football players as Wurtle (H. J. Wurtele), Guinn (J. White Guyn), (William) Goodwin and (Joe) Coons and others like Amet (Harold Amoss), (Ed) Pierce, Andrews (Leander Andrus) and little "Monty" (apparently G. C. Montgomery), it is thought that a team can be selected that will give their opponent a hot time to land the ball in the basket.
>
> The match game between the girls will be played at 3 p. m. Saturday.

Although Mustaine had gotten the boys interested in basketball, that first game had no special significance to him, other than to heighten his growing concern that athletics took so much student time away from glee club practice and other more important functions. He had organized the basketball team simply by calling together some students, taking up a collection totaling $3 for the ball, telling them to elect a captain, furnish their own shoes and uniforms, and start playing, and that was the extent of his concern.

"I remember chipping in to help buy the ball," said Thomson R. "Tommie" Bryant, who had just turned 90 in January of 1975. "It was one of those you inflated with a foot pump and then laced. If something had happened to it, we couldn't have played."

Bryant came to Lexington in 1903 from nearby Nicholasville and enrolled in the KSC prep school. At six-foot he was considered a big boy at the time and had played a little unorganized and somewhat crude basketball during his two years in high school.

"None of us knew much about the game," he said. "We knew what jump-center was and that's about all. Mustaine let us preps cavort with the varsity, but we weren't allowed to play on competing teams, even if we were better than some of them. It was a college rule.

"Mustaine was a prince of a fellow. He had a wonderful team of tumblers and taught a class in swinging Indian clubs, but he didn't know or care much about basketball."

Bryant would earn his basketball letters in 1905-06-07 and eventually spend a career as an agricultural specialist with UK.

During his undergraduate days KSC had no coach, but a gymnasium had been provided- apparently with no such spe-

Walter W. H. Mustaine did not pose with the UK basketball team in 1904, but he was more than happy to surround himself with members of his fine gym squad. Indian clubs and tumbling were more important to the father of UK basketball than was the roundball game.

cific purpose as basketball in mind—when Barker Hall was erected and placed in use in 1902. The structure was three stories high in the center with broad lower wings on each side. The south wing housed what has since become known as Buell Armory, where cadets drilled on a dirt floor. In the other wing was the shiny new gym, described by the school annual as "a splendid room with a good floor, an elevated running track and all the apparatus necessary for complete gymnastic training." Spectators sat on the circular mezzanine track, where three rows of chairs were installed on game days.

State lost that first game to Georgetown, but the big story in both newspapers the following day was about State's Allan Higgins Rhodes winning the Intercollegiate Contest amid the flaunting of banners and the deafening roar of college cheers... before the largest and most enthusiastic audience ever in attendance at such a meet. When the winner was announced, Rhodes was carried away on the backs of his supporters. The story rated more than a full column in the *Herald*, which did give a brief writeup of the basketball game, as follows:

GEORGETOWN
Defeated State College In
Basketball Match

The basketball game between Georgetown College and State College, played in the gym of the latter college yesterday afternoon, resulted in a decisive victory for Georgetown, the score being 17-6.

The players for Georgetown were: Stockton, center; Parrigan, guard; Abernathy, guard; Lovelace, forward. (Omitted by the newspaper was a player named Browning.)

State College Players were (J. White) Guyn, guard; (Joe) Coons, forward; R. H. Arnett, guard; (Lee) Andrews (Andrus), guard; (H. J.) Wurtle (Wurtele), center.

The larger part of the score was run up in the last half. At the end of the first half, the score stood at 7-1 in favor of Georgetown. During the latter part of the game, State College weakened appreciably. This is the second time this season Georgetown has defeated a local team. KU was defeated by the same team some weeks ago to the tune of 22-8.

The 1904 team: (left to right) R. H. Arnett, J. White Guyn, Joe Coons, C.P. St. John, H.J. Wurtele, and H.H. Downing with ball.

The *Leader*, giving the score as 15-6, reported:

When the game began at 4 o'clock, the gym was packed with rooters for the two teams who continually applauded the brilliant plays of their respective colleges. The initial game was a success in all particulars. The game was very interesting and both teams gave an excellent exhibition of basketball playing.

Georgetown had the advantage on account of having been in training since last fall and having played a number of games while the local team only had a few days practice.

The State boys defeated the Lexington YMCA, 11-10, and closed their season with a 42-2 loss to KU. As part of a double bill in the latter game, the KSC girls defeated the KU girls in the first basketball game between girls from those two schools. The KSC boys had scheduled three games with the YMCA that year, but only the one game is recorded as having been played.

The KU yearbook, noting that KU was state champion by virtue of two victories in three games with Georgetown and the victory over KSC, reported, "This was the first season that basketball contests were ever held between Kentucky colleges, since it is comparatively new as a college game. Every game was attended by large and enthusiastic crowds. The intense interest taken by the public in the games makes it assured that from now on basketball will become a prominent factor in college life during the winter months."

State played its first game out of Lexington at the beginning of the 1904 season, losing to Georgetown, 26-11. The *Leader* reported, "State's team was also handicapped by playing under different rules from those they have been accustomed to, and this caused a calling of many fouls by Kline, the Georgetown official, which assisted materially in piling up that team's score."

Before playing a rematch with Georgetown during the 1904 season, manager Leander Andrus took his team across town to watch a scheduled game between Georgetown and KU in what perhaps could be classified as State's first basketball scouting mission. However, the game was called when the teams could not agree on a referee. Georgetown players contended that Kline should act as referee. The KU team, which had lost a previous game to Georgetown after permitting the Tigers to have a referee for one half of the game, proposed that Kline referee one half and a KSC man, probably Andrus, referee the other half. When neither side would yield, the Georgetown team went home. State offered to play KU and lost, 12-5. The State boys also lost their game to Georgetown, 22-10, later that week.

While the State boys finished the 1904 season with two losses each to Georgetown and KU and a 25-21 victory over Cincinnati, the girls won both their games and got an "All Hail" from the *Kentuckian*, which said, "Successful from the start—two years ago—basketball as played by girls caught not only the student, but the public favor as well, and every game played drew an enthusiastic house which packed the standing room to the doors—an appreciative crowd of fellows—mad—riotously mad, over contests abounding in snappy spectacular play."

That year a student named Herman Scholtz dressed as a girl and went to Georgetown with the State co-eds, obviously with their connivance. The heavily veiled Scholtz watched much of the spirited contest, forbidden to all males except those in an official capacity, before the girls noticed his feet and started giggling. Scholtz, ejected from the gym, had to be punished, but the faculty was at a loss since neither of 180 specific rules covered the incident. He received a general reprimand.

State opened the 1905 season with a 14-9 loss to Georgetown in a game that "got somewhat rough." The newspaper quote was probably an understatement; basketball had become so rough that a 1905 guidebook warned that a manager must have a team physically fit to withstand the hard knocks of the game. For many years early teams were divided into lightweights and heavyweights to keep the combatants at a more competitive level. The first official uniform, suggested by the Spalding Co. in 1901, consisted of knee-length padded shorts or tights, sleeveless or quarter-length shirts, and long woolen stockings. The suction-cup, rubber-soled shoes were introduced in 1903, and knee guards were soon found to be necessary.

"We were just as dirty as smut," said Tommie Bryant. "There was ugliness that showed its head. We didn't play for championships but for bloody noses. I remember when those guys from KU came onto the floor wearing football pads while we came out in our jerseys and basketball panties. I've still got a tender ankle that I inherited when J. Franklin Wallace, a 6-foot-3½, 250-pound football tackle, stepped on it during the game. He poked me with a left jab, and I came back with a haymaker to the face. They threw both of us out."

That was apparently in 1907, when renewal of the KSU-KU series resulted in a game described by a local newspaper as more like a football battle—hurdling, forward passes, end runs, and slugging.

"A good fight was the expected thing," Bryant said. "Cincinnati's playing floor, located in a basement, had padded iron posts at the ends and on the sides. They always roughed us up, especially around those posts. We put up with a lot from them one night, but when they rammed our smallest man deliberately into a post, there wasn't any more basketball. It ended in a fist fight."

Since the home officials often favored the local players, visiting teams brought along their own referee and timekeeper. In addition, different goals, boundaries, and other factors entered the picture. For example, State, after losing to the Cincinnati YMCA in the second game of the 1905 season, defeated KU, 30-29, and then went across town and lost to the same KU team, 22-1.

"One fact that made the goal shooting difficult was the arrangement of the baskets, which were placed differently from those in their own gym," the *Leader* reported. Playing in its own gym for the state championship in February of that year, State lost, 33-23, to KU.

In its first three years of basketball competition, KSC won only three of 13 games, but the game itself was fast becoming the center of interest in college and athletic circles around Lexington.

A One-Man Operation

Wylie B. Wendt was all things to all people in the Kentucky State College basketball camp in 1906. A slender, 6-foot-1 engineering student, he had cut his basketball teeth in a playing arena located on the top floor of the Newport, Kentucky, city hall, just over the jail. Although he was a good player, he chose the lot of an administrator and was named the KSC team manager for that 1906 season.

While entertaining a visitor in his room at Wesley Manor in South Louisville in December, 1974, the 89-year-old retired teacher of engineering let his mind travel back to those pioneer days of basketball at KSC.

"No, there was no such thing as a coach back then," he said. "We just practiced. I was a one-man operation. I made the schedule, printed the tickets, collected money, paid the bills, was in charge of the team on the road, and sometimes swept the floor.

"We printed our own cards to advertise the games, and classmates would take care of the ticket sales. We charged 25 cents a game and were allowed $25 expenses on the road. That included overnight rooms and meals. We tried to sleep as many in a room as we could, sometimes all eight of us that made the trips.

"Still, we always seemed to be running out of money. I made a little (money) playing trap drums at the Opera House, and I sometimes made up the basketball deficit with that.

"I was referee for all our games away from home and some of them at home. It was the custom for the visiting manager to referee while the home team had the umpire. The umpire was the one who controlled the game, the one who threw people out."

While officiating a game in the Armory in 1906, he tried to break up a fight between two players and ended up on the bottom of a pile, with his back pressed against three hot steam pipes. "I yelled and they let me up," he said, "but I carried the imprints of those pipes on my back for 25 or 30 years."

Wendt was the first person connected with basketball at the university to purchase a scorebook—"I think it only had pages for the home team." He also talked the Faculty Athletic Committee into purchasing jerseys for the team and arranged the school's first out-of-state basketball trip.

"We were scheduled to open the season against KU," he said, "but the athletic committees of both schools had canceled all contests after a fight at a football game. The KU manager and I agreed to play at the YMCA and list the State opponent as

1906 KSC Team—Front row, seated left to right: Dick Barbee, D. P. Branson, Stanley Baer. Back row, left to right: J. M. Wilson; Wylie B. Wendt, manager; and T.R. Bryant.

the YMCA. That was crooked, of course, but that's how we got around it. State won the game, but we didn't record the score, as you can imagine why."

After three straight losses at home in midseason, the team went on that first road trip, losing to the New Albany, Indiana, YMCA and defeating Vernon College and Moores Hill before losing to Christ Church and the YMCA in Cincinnati and Miami at Oxford. At Moores Hill they played by the light of lamps placed up and down both sides of the court.

State center Tommie Bryant would long remember the Christ Church team and its big center, Harry Box. "He was about a foot taller than me, and his arms were a yard longer than mine," Tommie said in 1975. "We all spent a good deal of the time climbing on Harry's frame, and most anything went in the way of elbows but we couldn't cope with him. They'd beat the thunder out of us and then take us out on the town, which was quite a treat for a group of country boys."

All the cadets were required to drill, and the basketball players were among a contingent that paraded at the dedication of the new Capitol building in Frankfort. "We marched and then went to Louisville to play a game," Wendt said. "The new jerseys that we had ordered way ahead of time didn't come in until that day. We unpacked them on the train. We thought we looked pretty sharp."

Those jerseys were blue and white. The original school colors of blue and yellow were chosen in 1891 at a meeting of students, who selected blue because it was typical of the Blue Grass State and light yellow because it represented the richness of the land. However, those colors did not stay around long, and the UK teams were being referred to as Blue & White by the turn of the century. These colors would be adopted officially in 1910.

The Kentucky State teams in those days were referred to as "Cadets," "Colonels," "Corn-Crackers," and "Thoroughbreds." It seems as though each newspaper or periodical had a different name for the team. The current nickname of "Wildcats" apparently had its origin in 1909 in a speech made by Commandant Corbusier, then head of the school's military department, who told a chapel audience of students that the Kentucky football team "fought like Wild-Cats" in defeating Illinois, 6-2.

Basketball at State was crude but certainly not dull,

despite a combined record of 12 wins and 21 losses in 1906-07-08. The daily press reported that a very commendable feature of a loss to Miami of Ohio at home in 1906 was the perfect fairness dealt out to both teams by the referee and umpire. Wendt placed seats on the gym floor to accommodate a large crowd during a loss to Cincinnati YMCA, a game "noted for warm contentions." The trend of "honest" journalism and righteous indignation continued as "State suffered heavily from the rocky decisions of the referees" during a home loss to Georgetown.

Contesting a referee's decision in those days was considered part of the game. A real rhubarb developed in the State gym in 1907 when Georgetown captain Harry Herrick made a free throw that was not seen by the referee, Carmack, of Georgetown. Herrick tried again and missed. Georgetown naturally contended the goal should be counted since the team should not be made to suffer from failure of a referee to see a play, but State was given the decision, 16-15.

Other highlights of the season included music by the college band, a three-round pugilistic encounter at halftime of a game with Central, renewal of the KU-State series, and cancellation of a game with Georgetown, which sent word just before tip-off time that two of its players had been disabled. State also played its first sudden death overtime, losing to Central, 25-23, that season.

The *Kentuckian* pointed out that the "slow development of our basketball team from year to year was not due to lack of material interest, but to lack of time for practice. As a matter of fact, our gymnasium is too small," it said. "Too many different organizations were sought to be accommodated in one building, hence its inadequacy for any one of them. Only a few more years should find us with a new commodious and modern gymnasium, adequate for the development both of physical education and of athletes. Not withstanding this handicap, however, our basketball teams enlivened the winter season."

One year later the yearbook reported, "There is one thing to be borne in mind. It takes time and a maximum amount of practice to produce a championship team. Now, we have the facilities, the men and the experience season, and when the time comes play the game for all it's worth. 'Clean game' is the watchword of State, and may she never forget herself so far as to gain a victory in any other way."

How "Sweet" It Was

The appointment of E. R. Sweetland as Kentucky State University's first basketball coach was a popular move that resulted directly from his success with the 1909 Wildcat football team (9-1) and indirectly from a faculty move to abolish basketball at the institution.

The antibasketball move was reported as follows in the November 19, 1909, edition of the *Kentucky Gazette*:

> The faculty committee on athletics at State University passed a resolution abolishing basketball at that University. The cause of this action was the view that things are better never done than half done.
>
> The gymnasium building is so over crowded with the required work that there is absolutely no time for the team to practice and as this matter has been threshed over and over again with no solution, the faculty decided the best way out of the difficulty was to do away with the sport entirely.

The armory was floored in early December and the resolution abolishing basketball rescinded. The student newspaper was up in arms because State, with about $2,400 clear money in the treasury, would not hire a basketball coach. The men were coming out, but there was no one to coach them.

Naturally all eyes turned to Sweetland, a big, square-built man who had arrived on campus in the spring of that year after coaching stints at Hamilton College, Colgate, Syracuse, back to Colgate, and then to The Ohio State University. Colleagues described him as a man of high character, intellectuality, and scholarship. A rival coach said he was that rare combination of trainer and coach and was every inch a gentleman, a person with complete control over every man on the team and one of quiet field manners, no bad habits, and a simplicity and thoroughheartedness. Some called him an eccentric.

He became ill shortly after the KSU-Central football game on Thanksgiving Day 1909 and was hospitalized until late January, when the college offered him the new post of director of athletics, with the understanding that he would be in charge of all schedules, financial arrangements, etc. One week later he signed a three-year pact as director of athletics, also assuming the post of basketball coach.

During his hospitalization the basketball program had been under the direction of Prof. R. E. Spahr, who accompanied the team to Winchester, where the Wildcats defeated Kentucky Wesleyan, 14-12, in overtime. State defeated Georgetown on the weekend that the position of director of athletics was created; lost to DePauw, 24-11; and then fell to Central, 87-17, at Danville. Sixty-five years later the 70-point differential would still stand as the worst defeat ever suffered by a UK team. The *Leader* headline and story put it bluntly:

THIS IS AWFUL

State University Basket Ball
Five Beaten By Central 87
to 17—Revenge For Foot-
Ball Defeat

DANVILLE—The State University basket ball team of Lexington was overwhelmed here tonight by the Central University aggregation, 87-17. At the end of the first half the score was 51-3.

The game was fast and furious, but the superior strength and team work of the blue and cardinal was too much for the visitors, who had little team work and were outclassed in every part of the game. The Seelbach brothers were the stars for Central. In the second half Captain Mason of the local team was put out of the game for disputing a decision of the referee.

Sweetland took over the team and brought back into the

roundball fold such football players as Dick Barbee, Wayne Plummer, and William "Red Doc" Rodes; however, those players and some of the front-liners were forced to stay home and catch up on their school work while he took a "scrub" team on a road trip north and lost to Cincinnati, 47-17; DePauw, 28-10; and Rose Poly, 52-11. UK defeated Tennessee, 20-5, in Lexington that year to begin a series that would develop into one of the most interesting and bitterly contested rivalries in the nation. The Volunteers did not score a field goal, getting all their points from J. D. Welcker, who hit five of 24 free throw attempts.

State lost the championship of Kentucky to Central, 31-13, defeated Georgetown by one point, and closed out the season with a 51-9 loss to Central at Danville. During the second half Central piled up an overwhelming score and gave UK's Rodes a clear road on a field goal attempt. He shot three times before making the goal.

The unpredictable Sweetland left State after the 1910 football season to coach the boat crew at the University of Wisconsin, where he was granted a one-year leave of absence and spent most of the time with his brother, who was a physician in Constantine, Michigan. In a letter to a friend in Lexington he said his greatest desire was to return to Kentucky. He would get that wish one year later.

While Sweetland was on leave from Wisconsin, H. J. Iddings, track and field coach at Miami University (Ohio), was hired as State basketball coach. He started practice January 9, 1911, in the Armory, which had been used the preceding week for a corn show. After the team opened with consecutive losses to Lexington High School, Transylvania (formerly Kentucky University) and Kentucky Wesleyan, Iddings began operating day and night shifts on the Armory floor in search of candidates for the varsity squad. The extra duty apparently paid off as new recruit R. C. Preston led State to a 24-11 victory over Bethany, Indiana. The Wildcats lost to Ohio Wesleyan at Delaware, where they were "introduced to the dribble," and to Otterbein and Christ Church before returning home to win their last four games. The final game with Transylvania was characterized by whistles, bells, horns, and yells which caused players at times to hold hands over ears in the crowded gym.

Iddings' team finished with a 5-6 record, which the *Leader* called a remarkable season, considering the late start of practice and the use of ILL instead of AAU rules on the northern trip.

Sweetland arrived back in Lexington shortly before the 1912 basketball season and coached State to its first undefeated slate, which the *Kentuckian* described as "one glorious march from start to finish." In sweeping a nine-game schedule, the Wildcats were never behind in a game. The victims were Georgetown, Central, Lexington YMCA, Miami, Central, Tennessee, Vanderbilt (twice on successive nights to inaugurate the series), and Georgetown. It would be 42 years before a UK team would again finish a season undefeated.

Earning varsity letters that year were Brinkley Barnett, H. L. Farmer, J. H. Gaiser, D. W. Hart, W. C. Harrison, R. C. Preston, William Tuttle, and manager Gils F. Meadors. Manager Meadors was credited with securing a fine schedule, although some teams broke their contracts with State, and for making the season such a success through his able management.

Barnett, selected as captain of the 1913 squad, would teach electrical engineering at the university and remain in Lexington after retiring in 1959. Sixty years after playing his last game he would remember Sweetland as "a very restless fellow, but a good coach."

"No dribbling was allowed," he recalled. "You had to pass the ball. You could bounce it one time and shoot. We played in football pants, with the padding taken out. We had to buy our

The undefeated 1912 Wildcats, left to right: Brinkley Barnett, D. W. Hart, W. C. Harrison, R. C. Preston, and Jake Gaiser. Gils Meadors (front) was team manager.

own shoes. Sweetland was the football coach, and he just sort of supervised us. I was only 5-9 and weighed 130 pounds when I played, so I wouldn't stand much of a chance today."

The *Kentuckian* said that Barnett was "fast as a jack rabbit...plays the floor well and is a dead shot at a basket... mighty little but awful loud...slippery as a varnished snake and can crawl through an opposing guard's defense without the slightest trouble and shoot from any and all angles, played the floor in classy fashion and his throws from fouls averaged three in five."

"I shot all the foul goals, but I wasn't any star at all," he said. "Harrison easily was the best center in the state and in the South. He had a reach of about half a mile on the jump and generally did what he pleased with his opponents."

Barnett played his high school basketball at Somerset, where the team always practiced outdoors and played games in a small gym "where the ceiling was so low we sometimes banked the ball off it." He attended KSC on some type of academic appointment obtained through the superintendent of schools in his county.

"The main thing I remember is beating Vanderbilt twice," he said. "We got them good (28-17) in the first game, but they almost beat us (22-18) that second game. After it was over, Sweetland treated us to a big dinner."

After that all-winning season, the *Kentuckian* said: "The whole season bears the impress of the magical hand of Coach Sweetland. To him, if to any man, the credit for this most successful season must be given. He filled the boys with confidence, trained and instructed them, as only he can, and, as is his invariable custom, turned out a championship team."

The student newspaper, the *Idea*, said, "We had always been weak in basketball. We had no basketball coach until Mr. Sweetland first came and there was practically no interest taken in the sport by the student body. The basketball season lost money for the Athletics Association, and it was proposed and seriously considered that this line of sport be eliminated. All this has now changed. Instead of being looked down upon contemptuously as in the past, basketball will from this time forward be one of the chief sports at the University."

During the next seven years, a steady procession of coaches would compile a record of 50-32-1. They were for the most part men involved primarily with the football teams. The most prominent figure in that group was Dr. J. J. Tigert, who succeeded Sweetland as director of athletics on a temporary basis at the beginning of the 1912-13 school year.

A tall, handsome man with thinning blond hair; an honest, pleasant face; and a fine background both in the world of athletics and academia, he came to State in the fall of 1911 to fill the chair of philosophy. He also coached the girls' basketball team two seasons.

At Vanderbilt he was All-Southern halfback and captain of the 1902 championship football team and captain and center on the Commodore basketball team that lost only once in three successive years. At Oxford, on a Rhodes Scholarship, he earned a silver cup with the rowing crew and was a sensational first baseman on the championship baseball team of Great Britain.

He spent two years in the chair of philosophy and as head football coach at Central College, Missouri; two years as president of Kentucky Wesleyan College; and later would serve as U.S. Commissioner of Education and president of the University of Florida.

J. Ed Parker, who entered UK in 1916 and was a 5-foot-7, 130-pound guard-forward substitute (except in 1919, when he was team manager), remembered Tigert "well and fondly." "He'd show us how to run plays, which I guess by today's standards would look pretty crude," the retired Fayette County farm agent said in January 1975. "We usually didn't have enough players for the practice sessions and Dr. Tigert and his assistants would practice against us. Most of us couldn't play very well at all. We were just out of high school and had had little experience and what games we had played were played in dance halls, YMCA's, and mostly on outdoor courts."

Due to the confusion created by the resignation of Sweetland and related events, the 1913 basketball season did not get underway until January 24. The Wildcats lost their opener to the local YMCA, 27-25. A two-point victory over Cincinnati in the Armory was spiced by boxing at halftime and wrestling after the game, indicating that perhaps the game still was not considered a major attraction. They easily defeated Marietta and then held Louisville to a single field goal in a 34-10 victory in the first basketball game between the two schools.

Vanderbilt visited Lexington for the second straight year and split two games. The Commodores would return for back-to-back games in 1915 and 1916 and single games in 1919 and

Wildcat coach John J. Tigert is pictured with the 1914 UK faculty basketball team.

1921 before a Wildcat team would finally visit Nashville in 1922.

The abbreviated season ended with a victory over Miami and a loss to Christ Church for a 5-3 record. While Tigert tried and failed to schedule more games, students circulated a petition to get Sweetland back as football coach. The move failed, and Alpha Brumage, a Kansas graduate who was physical director and head coach at Virginia Military Institute, was secured as director of athletics and professor of physical education. Tigert would continue to coach the girls' basketball team and serve as backfield coach for Brumage.

The new coach found immediate favor with the student body after his 1913 football team won six of eight games. He was greeted by approximately 30 varsity basketball candidates when practice began in early December, and the afternoon sessions in the Armory drew large crowds. Optimism was high, and he justified the confidence by molding a team described in the school annual as "clothed in class." Led by Capt. William Tuttle and high-scoring Ralph Morgan, the team christened the new Woodland Auditorium on East High Street on January 31 by romping over Louisville YMHA, 59-12, and won six more games, including two over Tennessee, for an 11-2 record.

The 1915 season at State, beginning with a 37-17 victory over Maryville in Woodland Auditorium, was considered successful despite a 7-5 record. Tennessee, with one of the strongest teams in the SIAA, defeated the Wildcats twice in February and was undefeated when the two teams met later in Lexington. The Wildcats defeated the Vols on two successive nights as enthusiastic fans stood in the balcony during the greater part of the game.

On the trip to Tennessee the Wildcats had defeated Maryville by one point for their fourth win in a row, but they had a 4-3 record after losing to the Vols and splitting two games with

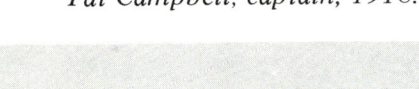

Pat Campbell, captain, 1918.

Vanderbilt at home. They closed the season with losses on the road to St. Andrew's and Louisville, teams they had defeated early in the season at Lexington. Their record at home was 6-1 as opposed to 1-4 on the road.

Brumage left Lexington to return to school, and Dr. Tigert once again assumed duties as athletic director. His assistant in charge of basketball was James Park, who supervised practice sessions and other team activities. Tigert accompanied the team to Cincinnati and Georgetown, where it won before large crowds. Georgetown lost to State two weeks later before a frenzied crowd in Woodland Auditorium, where all State home games were played that year. A few fans braved the dangers of a trolley ride in a blizzard to see the home team defeat Maryville. State lost its last two games at home to Marietta, Ohio, whose "Dribbling Kids" claimed the world championship after defeating the famous Buffalo Germans the preceding week. State finished the season with an 8-6 record.

J. A. "Tony" Dishman of Louisville, who was captain of both the football and basketball teams at UK in 1919, would remember S. A. Boles, UK basketball and football coach who would later become athletic director, as a lovable character who knew little about coaching. In 1918, Andy Gill, who played at Indiana, was brought in to coach. Dishman said Gill contributed little to the development of material and had a hard time controlling the boys.

The only team coached by Gill finished the 1919 season with a 6-8 record. The school was closed three months during a flu epidemic at the beginning of the school year and did not resume its work until the middle of January. After opening with a 46-5 victory over Wesleyan, the Wildcats dropped a two-point decision to Georgetown, their first loss to the Tigers since 1910. The Tigers defeated them again later in the season.

They lost twice to Centre, split games with Cincinnati and Tennessee, lost to Vanderbilt and Miami in single encounters, and beat Chattanooga and Cumberland.

Gill's replacement, George Buchheit, would serve five years, longest tenure for a Wildcat basketball coach until Adolph Rupp would come along in 1930.

Champions Of The South

Tuesday, March 1, 1921, was one of those mild Kentucky winter days that gives just a hint of spring while at the same time threatening to dump rain, snow, or even hail on a populace long accustomed to the unpredictable.

The thermometer began a slow rise to a peak of 62 by mid-afternoon and then dipped slowly to a rather pleasant 50 degrees, enough to make the sap rise and start Lexington out of its cold weather doldrums.

In addition to the first sign of upcoming spring, the city was still astir over events of the preceding night, when President-elect Warren G. Harding had stopped in Lexington en route via the northbound Royal Palm to his home in Marion, Ohio.

Tanned by the Florida sun and clad in dark suit and leather cap, Harding, who was to be inaugurated on Friday, stepped from the Southern Railway System's crack passenger train and greeted the local gathering with such stock questions as:

"How big is Lexington? This is where all the horses come from, isn't it? And whisky? How's the tobacco this year?"

He was informed that Lexington was a city of 40,000 souls, that the thoroughbreds for which the Blue Grass is famous were still in the Commonwealth, but prohibition had taken its toll of bourbon whisky, and burley tobacco was in such short demand that "lots of us are trying to give it away and can't."

After the president's departure, the sporting element of the town gathered at the Phoenix Hotel on East Main Street to check on another Kentucky product, basketball, which someday would take its name alongside horses, burley, and bourbon as trademarks of the Blue Grass.

The big news was Kentucky's 28-13 victory over Mississippi A&M in the semifinals of the Southern Intercollegiate Athletic Association Tournament. An air of excitement permeated the entire city during that long, exciting Tuesday, when the final game would be played on a rattling, temporary court in the Atlanta Auditorium.

Making the trip South with Coach George Buchheit were the allotted eight players, all Kentuckians. The play-making captain, Basil Hayden, and defensive guard Robert Lavin had been teammates at nearby Paris High School. Forward William King was a product of Lexington Senior High. Paul Adkins of Williamsburg attended Cumberland College two years and earned a letter before joining the Wildcats as a center. Sam Ridgeway, standing guard from Shepherdsville, completed the starting five. The substitutes were guard Gilbert K. Smith of Lexington, center James E. Wilhelm of Paducah, and forward William L. Poynz of Covington.

Buchheit, a big, timid man, came to Kentucky the preceding school year from the University of Illinois, where he was an All-Western end and star of the basketball and track teams. He served as football assistant at State in the fall of 1919 and then began a five-year basketball stint in rather unimpressive fashion, winning only six of 14 games as influenza took a toll of the squad in late season.

He took to Atlanta an offense described by the Georgia press as one of the most peculiar attacks yet uncovered on a basketball court. Baffling the Southerners was the switching of guards to forwards by the Kentuckians. In addition, King, Hayden, and Adkins immediately impressed the Atlantans with their shooting.

Possibly half a dozen persons from Kentucky followed the team to Atlanta, and they were not very hopeful. But their spirits soared when Kentucky opened with a 50-28 victory over Tulane and then routed Mercer, 49-24. By the time the Wildcats defeated Mississippi A&M, the unorthodox shots of Adkins and the fine all-round play of the Wildcats were the talk of the basketball South.

In Lexington, hundreds of university students, alumni, and rooters crowded the balcony and mezzanine of the Phoenix, where a telegraph operator stood by to receive news of the game. Shortly before tip-off time booster Albert E. Hukle, flushed face matching his red hair, stretched his slender 6-foot-5 frame, looked down at the crowded lobby, took a deep breath, raised a megaphone, and read the first message:

"Game ready to start. Boys in fine shape."

As tension mounted, the noise built to a crescendo and then suddenly stopped as Hukle once again spoke from the balcony. It was 9:40 p.m., and the first news of game action dot-dashed into the hotel:

"Adkins makes first goal. King second. Outclassing the Georgians. Adkins repeats. Georgia scores three on fouls; score 6 to 5 in favor of Kentucky."

Once again the Kentuckians cheered and shouted; then, at 9:50 p.m., a final wire came through on the first half:

"Georgia substitutes forward. Adkins makes goal. Georgia scores. Score end of first half Kentucky 9 Georgia 7."

During a long 30-minute wait for more news, plans for a welcoming celebration, including a parade and banquet, were announced.

"Ridgeway shoots foul. So does Georgia. Georgia makes another on foul. Score Kentucky 11 Georgia 10."

The shouts drowned out Hukle's excited voice. After a couple of minutes he finished the message:

"King makes goal on foul. King makes long goal."

During another long lull between messages, an enterprising representative of a book publishing company started a spiel about his business. The crowd, in no mood for encyclopedia or dictionary talk, shouted him down.

"King makes goal. Georgia makes goal. Georgia makes another score. Kentucky 17 Georgia 16. Georgia makes goal. Georgia scored on foul."

Here is how "Fuzzy" Woodruff described the remaining action in the *Atlanta Journal*:

> More red-blooded stuff was crowded into one brief minute last night, when Kentucky State University defeated the University of Georgia, 20 to 19, for the Southern Intercollegiate Athletic Association's first basketball championship, than comes to most men in a lifetime.

The 1921 Wildcats, left to right, front: Sam Ridgeway, Paul Adkins, Basil Hayden, Bill King, and Bobby Lavin. Back: Coach George Buchheit, Jim Wilhelm, Bill Poynz, Gilbert Smith, and Athletic Director S. A. Boles.

There's less than a minute left to play. Georgia is leading by the scant margin of 19-17. Both teams are desperate. The Kentuckians are fighting with the courage born of despair. The throng watching the Homeric struggle is raving. Men are shouting in the hoarse combativeness of a struggle in which no mercy is expected or desired. Women are screaming in the fierce staccato battle-cry of motherhood defending its young. The athletes on the broad floor have aged a lifetime in a few brief minutes. They are no longer carefree, clean-limbed college boys. Their faces are drawn. Their eyes are dull. They are fighting, but they are not fighting with the joyous lust of the charge. They are fighting the grim fight that men wage when their backs are against the wall, when hope seems just a mirage, fooling weary travelers into useless exertion of already spent bodies. But they still fight.

Georgia, for the second, forgets the tactics that so far have carried it to the lead. All through the tournament Hayden, the Kentucky captain, a blond Apollo, a Kentucky thoroughbred, if one ever stepped on the turf, has been the thorn in the side of Kentucky's opponents.

Coach Stegeman of Georgia has watched all the Kentucky games. He knows that danger lurks in Hayden's race horse anatomy. He has instructed his men to guard Hayden as they would guard their good names. And throughout twenty minutes of the first half and nineteen minutes of the second half, Hayden is kept as closely covered as the grand fleet kept the Kiel canal when civilization's future was the stake.

But Georgia forgot. The failing is human, and with less than a minute to play and with the palm of victory almost extended to the Athenians, their forgetfulness gives him the opportunity for freedom.

He sees it and seizes it. He is down the court like a streak. He sweeps across the floor with the fleetness of a meteor. He is under the basket and the ball is hurled to him. All five of the Georgia players are now charging him. They are late by the merest fraction of a split second. The ball hardly pauses in Hayden's hands. His shot is fast but accurate. It drops through the basket without hesitating. The score is tied. Georgia is 19. Kentucky is 19.

Possibly forty-five seconds of playing time are left. The ball is tipped off. Little Lavin of Kentucky is on it with the swiftness and surety of a cat leaping for an elusive mouse. He sends it hurling down the court to King. Adkins, Kentucky's center and surest goal shooter in the tourney, is back down the court and he is uncovered. The ball reaches him.

"Buck" Cheeves, Georgia's captain, sees the danger. Adkins must not shoot. Cheeves throws himself on him to intercept his throw. Adkins is bowled over right under the basket. The referee's whistle sounds—he had declared a foul. Little King of Kentucky takes the ball as the players group themselves about the basket. "This decides the game," a thousand whispers say. The great building is suddenly stilled. No one talks. No one even breathes. No one dares to think.

Bang! It's the timer's signal that the twenty minutes of playing time has expired. The rules permit the attempt at goal, however. King takes a new stance. The crowd takes another breath, a deep one. King is coolness personified. He hasn't been particularly good on foul goals all night, and Georgia has hopes, though it fears for the worst. The ball leaves his hands, and King's eyes do not even follow it to the basket. It strikes a rim and then slowly falls over to the right through the network. In a second he is in the arms of his comrades and is being hoisted to their shoulders.

The telegraph in the Phoenix Hotel relayed the good news:
"King scores one point. Final score Kentucky 20 Georgia 19. Bring home cup tomorrow."

Nobody heard Hukle's final report: "Greatest game we ever played."

Never had there been such a victory celebration in Lexington. Wildcat fans stayed up throughout the night praising the team, planning a gala reception, and discussing a drive for funds to build a new basketball court.

The team arrived in Lexington at 6:30 p.m. Wednesday, exactly 24 hours after the president-elect's visit, and was met by a large delegation of students. A parade downtown through driving rain ended at the Phoenix Hotel, where the UK band struck up "My Old Kentucky Home" as hundreds applauded, cheered, and blew "victory" whistles that had been passed out wholesale. In the ballroom every available seat was filled, and many persons were turned away.

Led by Hukle, the 350 persons present lustily cheered the guests of honor. Boles paid tribute to Buchheit as a person "who doesn't write long articles in the papers and doesn't make flowing addresses, but does deliver the goods."

The *Kentuckian* said the student body had become "an aggregation of hero worshipers, and the Blue and White quintet became the acme of things basketball." However, there were more concrete benefits to be realized from the championship. During the tournament, representatives from Kentucky, West Virginia, Washington & Lee, Virginia Military Institute, North Carolina, North Carolina State, Clemson, Georgia Tech, Georgia, Alabama, Tulane, Alabama Polytech, Mississippi A&M, and Tennessee met and formed the Southern Athletic Conference along the lines of the Western Conference.

The new conference was not meant to replace the 27-year-old SIAA, but merely to have an organization composed of the larger institutions so they could play by rules which otherwise would handicap smaller institutions. It also would pave the way for interconference athletic contests with the universities of the Midwest.

Kentucky's victory also had spurred public clamor for a new court, and a drive for solicitations soon got underway in Lexington. Basketball until that time had been an individual game, but drastic changes were in the making, and UK was primed for the revolution.

Kentucky's First All-American

Basil Hayden, Kentucky's first All-American basketball player, looked out the front door of his home in Paris, Kentucky, in late December, 1974, and pointed toward the town square, which was glittering with Christmas decorations.

"When I was in the sixth grade, we started out playing on a cinder floor in an area under the city auditorium," said the 75-year-old retired banker. "They had six padded posts holding up the place. We also played in a tobacco warehouse. They built a new YMCA and we played in that. It had a small floor with a nice, tall ceiling.

"I graduated from high school here just as we were getting into the First World War. There wasn't much going on in athletics at UK, but we did play some good games after Christmas. When the war was over, we got a good schedule.

"I was a 5-11, 165-pound, play-making guard, and I was ahead of the others because I had the experience, and they hadn't played much. We played then with a center under our goal and a big backguard under the opponent's goal. Three men brought the ball down the floor. You threw the ball always to the man running toward you.

"We didn't fool with dribbling. We didn't even practice it, so none of us were any good at it. The floors were smaller than they are now, and you could keep everybody guarded better. And the refereeing wasn't as close. Fouls they call now for reaching over backs and things like that weren't called then.

"My responsibility was to get the ball to Bill King or Paul Adkins. I got most of my points following their shots and pushing the ball through the basket.

"Sam Ridgeway was the backbone of that team. He was a big fellow and quick as a cat, a good jumper with enough weight to push through. I always told him that he made me an All-American."

Buchheit had high hopes for the 1922 season, but they went down the drain as Hayden received a knee injury before the first game, and Ridgeway was out for the season with an illness. The Wildcats lost to Georgetown, defeated Louisville, and lost to Vanderbilt before Hayden returned to action against Louisville in Lexington. The *Leader* explained his contribution to the 29-22 victory:

"Basil Hayden, the crippled, started the game Saturday night, and it was the same Hayden who made the second goal of the fray when he jumped high in the air and converted King's foul failure into two points. He was forced to retire at the close of the initial period, but replaced his substitute near the end of the game and played a prominent role in the belated rally."

Hayden was replaced at the start of the fourth quarter against Mississippi A&M, but was sent back into the game after two goals in succession were scored over his substitute.

"Hayden is to the Kentucky team what pork is to beans," the *Leader* said. "When he is on the sidelines the team seems to have lost its punch and becomes careless in its play."

"The games with Centre naturally stick out in my mind, because they were our big rival then," Hayden said. "I particularly remember that Bo McMillin—he was coaching Centre at the time—was pretty upset at a referee's call near the end of the first half of our game at Danville."

The decision occurred when a Centre forward made a goal beneath the basket with 10 seconds to go, and the official ruled that he had stepped out of bounds. McMillin protested vehemently, and the official admitted that he might have been at fault.

"They had both the out-of-bounds line and a chalk line that had been put down to keep spectators back," Hayden said, "and the balconies over the ends of the playing floor were filled with yelling spectators who sometimes interfered with the ball when you shot it. It was hard to tell anything about what was going on."

However, the referee refused to change his decision, insisting that the matter be taken to the National Basketball Rules Committee. After a 30-minute delay, Buchheit and McMillin

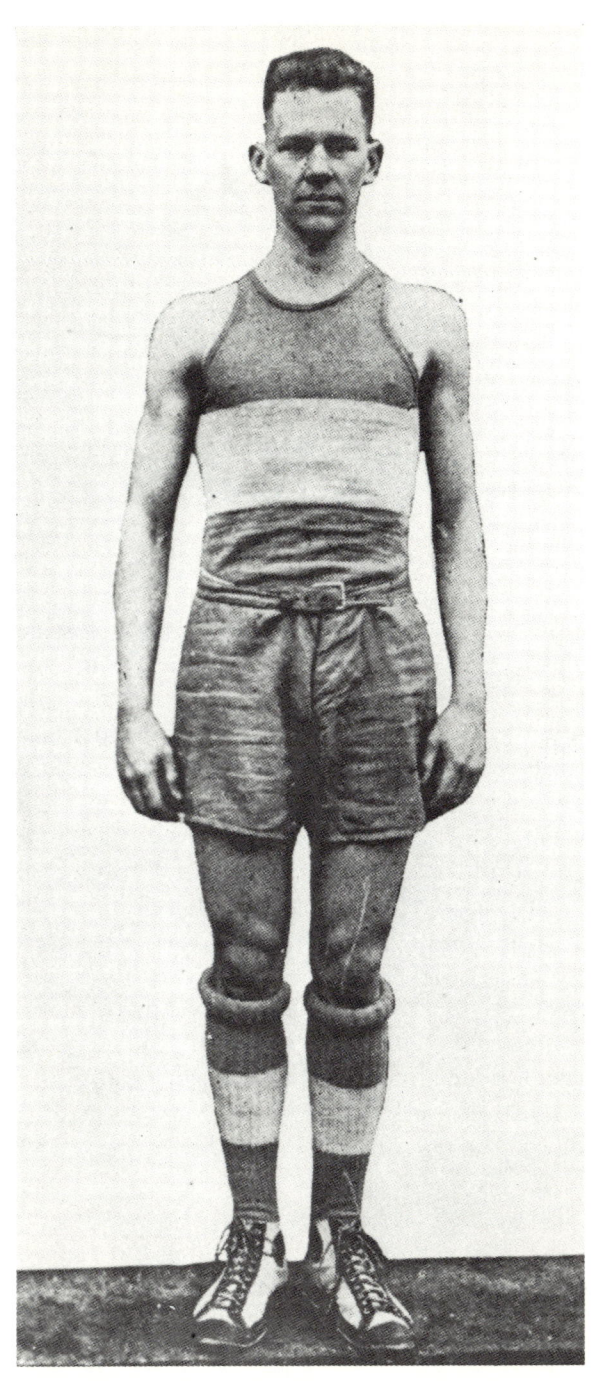

Kentucky's First All-American, Basil Hayden.

decided that in case the game was won by Kentucky by two points or less, the decision on the play in question would rest with the committee. However, they also agreed that if UK were ahead by two points at the end of the game, they would go ahead and play a five-minute overtime. UK won by six points. It was the first time in four years they had defeated Centre in Danville.

They lost consecutive road games to VMI, Georgetown University, and Virginia. Four of their five regular season losses were on the road while four of their 10 victories were away from home.

During Hayden's three varsity years the Wildcats were 28-14. They outscored their opponents 1,266-902, won one tournament championship, and lost in the second game of another. In addition to Hayden there were other fine players on the squad. Adkins was a consistent performer whose forte was scoring goals from different and difficult angles. King had a good eye for the basket and an unusual ability on the floor. He saw the most playing time and perhaps was the most important member of the teams on which he played. Lavin, the running guard, was the smallest performer and team captain in 1922.

In those days, when the roughest, toughest defensive guard was stationed permanently under his own basket to ward off the enemy, Burgess Carey was the closest thing in basketball to an immovable object. He would plant his bulky 6-foot, 195-pound frame firmly on two big, flat feet and inflict punishment on any enemy who tried to penetrate his domain. When you speak of old-time backguards in Lexington, you start and end with him.

"He was just the best there was in his time," said Buchheit during a visit to Lexington in 1971. "Of course, people today probably can't understand how a man can make All-American honors without scoring a lot of points, but that wasn't his role. His job was to stop the other team from scoring, and he did it well."

Nobody worried about how many points Carey scored, because backguards seldom scored anything but free throws or an occasional long shot from behind the center line. His game high was five points against Tennessee in 1925 out of a team total of 51. He finished the season with 29 points in 18 games. He became Kentucky's second All-American simply because he was the right man at the right time at the right position.

His path to UK was paved with bruises, taken and given, and with hurrahs and accolades. As team captain and defensive bulwark, he led the 1922 Lexington Senior High School team to state and national championships, collecting many honors along the way.

"The first time I saw Burgess he had a patch over one eye," his widow of 13 years recalled while talking to a visitor in her Lexington home during the 1974 Christmas holidays. "That was during my first year at UK. No, I don't know how he got it, and I didn't ask.

"I remember he loved the free-for-all, rough type of game. When he stood in front of the basket, nobody could budge him. And he couldn't stand to see a team lose or make a lot of mistakes. And all those new rules coming along made him sick. I didn't even know he was an All-American until somebody told me. I've never known a man with so many friends."

Joining Carey on the 1923 Wildcat freshman squad were fellow Senior High starters Jim McFarland, Will Milward, Len Tracy, and Lovell "Cowboy" Underwood, along with substitute Foster Helm. Charles "Turkey" Hughes, of Repton, Kentucky, was the only non-Lexingtonian on the squad.

"That was a fine freshman team," Buchheit said. "The varsity had a bad season (3-10) that year, and I was really looking forward to having them move up."

The 1923 record, bad as it sounded, was deceptive. Playing without Ridgeway, who had a broken ankle, the Wildcats opened with an expected victory over Georgetown, but lost a close, 30-26, decision to Tennessee at Knoxville. They defeated Chattanooga, 25-18, at home and then lost nine consecutive games, longest losing streak in the school's history, before closing with a 30-14 victory over Sewanee. But they were outscored only 348-289 by their combined opponents, with Georgetown (48-21) and Centenary (38-21) enjoying the widest victory margins.

"I was naturally disappointed when Burgess didn't return with his freshman teammates the next year," Buchheit said. "He had enrolled at Washington & Lee in September, but he returned to Lexington in January and was unable to compete because of a conference one-year residential rule. We still had a pretty good group of boys, and we had what I thought was a real fine season."

Led by Capt. A. T. "Chuck" Rice, the Wildcats opened

with a 33-13 victory over Vanderbilt and defeated a group of Mexican students who were on a 6,750-mile tour of 16 states and Havana. That was the first foreign team to play the Wildcats.

"They really weren't a bad ball club," Buchheit said. "They had some speed and we had a fine crowd at the game. We only beat them by 11 points."

The Wildcats defeated Georgetown and sandwiched a 50-15 victory over Sewanee between losses to Mississippi A&M and Tennessee. After scuttling the criss-cross offense, they defeated Chattanooga, 24-23, to start a nine-game streak that included victories over West Virginia, Centre, Georgetown, Clemson, Virginia, and first-time foes Virginia Tech and Georgia Tech. The 13-2 season on record was UK's best since the 1921 team lost only one of 14 games.

"We lost to North Carolina in the Southern Tournament," Buchheit said, "but we weren't dissatisfied with the season. In addition, we returned home in time to see the high school tournament played in the newly finished Alumni Gym. It seemed like a mighty fine place at that time."

The movement for construction of the gym had rolled into high gear more than a year earlier after members of the Athletic Council complained to the Board of Trustees that the old gym was unsafe even for the small number of people it could accommodate, that large crowds had to be turned away, and that the popular state high school tournament might be moved to Louisville if the university did not provide better facilities. The plan for a gymnasium to seat 2,800 persons was approved, and the Alumni Association immediately started to raise $100,000 for the building to be located on Winslow Street, west of Stoll Field. Upon completion the new arena was considered a white elephant by many Lexingtonians who thought such a spacious building would never be filled for a basketball game.

The university hired Fred J. Murphy as football coach that year and asked Buchheit to remain as basketball coach, but he chose to move to Trinity College in Durham, North Carolina. The 1925 and 1926 Wildcat basketball teams were coached by C. O. Applegran and Ray Eklund, respectively, who came to UK as assistants to Murphy. Applegran, a former University of Illinois star, coached the first UK team to play in the new facility. The Wildcats beat Cincinnati, 28-23, in that game.

Indiana, defending champion of the Western Conference,

Burgess Carey, All-American 1925.

featuring aggressive dribblers utilizing a short-pass offense, came to Lexington eight nights later and employed a five-man defense that formed a barrier around the foul line and forced the Wildcats to shoot long. The Kentuckians, slipping and sliding on the slick floor, fell behind, rallied, and then lost by two points after switching from the criss-cross to an open floor attack. Carey was easily the best Kentucky player on the floor, repeatedly fighting back the Indiana attack and controlling the defensive board whenever a Hoosier shot missed the mark.

Michigan's Wolverines showed Lexingtonians how the short-pass game should be played, advancing the ball down the floor principally by use of the dribble and, when challenged by a defender, pivoting sharply and making a timely short pass to a teammate going full speed down the floor. Early in the second half Applegran instructed his men to forget their sputtering criss-cross and use a combination short and long pass. Michigan won, 21-11.

After the holiday break the Wildcats took a three-day trip North. During a 24-20 loss to Cincinnati four Kentucky goals were nullified by the official, who ruled he had blown the whistle before the shots were made. Next came the first meeting

UK's Alumni Gym.

between Kentucky and Illinois. Led by Capt. John Mauer, the Illini displayed a criss-cross offense that was all too familiar to the Wildcat defenders. Applegran received a fine ovation at half time, but the Wildcats lost, 36-26, and traveled to Crawfordville, Indiana. Weakened by the absence of Captain McFarland and A. T. Rice, who were sent home to rest, they were stomped, 57-11, by Wabash.

Returning home they won 13 of their last 15 games, all against schools south of the Mason-Dixon line. After defeating Centre, 39-10, for the state championship before the largest crowd of the season in Alumni Gym, they beat Mississippi A&M in the opening round of the Southern Tournament. Then they lost by one point to Georgia as Bulldog captain Wiehr scooted outside a teeming mass of red and blue jerseys, picked up a loose ball, and feebly tossed the winning basket with 28 seconds remaining.

Eklund drilled his 1925-26 squad along the same lines as had Applegran and Buchheit and rewarded them with two sets of uniforms, a first for a Kentucky basketball team. One set consisted of white woolen jerseys with "Kentucky" spelled in blue letters across the chest while the breeches were solid blue with a white border. The other set had solid blue jerseys and breeches with a white border and white letters.

The nattily attired Wildcats opened against DePauw, only northern invader on the schedule, and held their own until Carey fouled out with three minutes remaining. DePauw won, 38-29. The Wildcat passing attack was erratic, and the offense did not score a crip shot against the Tigers' man-to-man defense.

After losing to Indiana, 34-23, Eklund junked the crisscross and, following the pattern of the preceding year, won 15 games in a row against Southern schools before losing to Mississippi A&M in the semifinals of the Southern Tournament.

That season had many high points, including a 25-24 victory over Georgia Tech and 6-foot-7 "Tiny" Hearn, who stood a head taller than the tallest Wildcat. When the ball went in Tiny's direction, Jenkins, McFarland, Carey, and Gayle Mohney would surround the "giant" while Underwood leaped high in an attempt to knock the ball from his possession.

In what the *Lexington Herald* termed "no game tonight, merely an exhibition," the Wildcats defeated Tennessee, 51-17, in Knoxville. "The Kentucky offense, employing Capt. Carey at stationary and the four ponies racing over the court, with Carey feeding them the ball, broke through for crip shots galore and were never forced to attempt long shots," the newspaper said. "The Kentucky defense, however, forced the Vols to resort to long heaves and these met with little success." In a reversal of the home court advantage, the Volunteers, in Lexington six nights later, played a fine game, losing to the Wildcats by only six points.

Against Alabama, Kentucky nursed a lead in the final three minutes and held the ball while the Tide players waited patiently for them to do something. The Wildcats did nothing and won the game.

The 1926 season's biggest surprise came just before noon February 5, when the Washington & Lee team walked into Athletic Direcor Boles' office and announced it was ready to play. Neither Boles nor Eklund knew of such a game. The Washington & Lee manager produced a contract, which Boles recalled signing a year earlier. A game between University High School and the Kentucky Institute for the Deaf was moved from Alumni Gym to another site, and the Wildcats defeated the unexpected visitors, 44-34.

That UK team lost to Mississippi A&M in the third game of the annual tournament and finished with a 15-3 record.

Basil Hayden returned to UK as basketball coach in 1927, a move brought about by the sudden resignation of Eklund. Hayden had coached at Stanford High School and at Kentucky Wesleyan after leaving UK. He was in the insurance business two years before returning to UK and was out of touch with the rapid developments in the game.

"I came back to the University because they asked me," he said 48 years later. "They asked me to coach until they could get somebody else. I knew all those good players, including members of Senior High's national championship team, had graduated, and it was going to be tough.

"We had to play Cincinnati one week after the Council called me. I started the game with a lineup of football players. They were Paul Jenkins and Ray Ellis at forward, Elmer Gilb at running guard, Clair Dees at back guard, and Foster Helm at center. We hadn't had time to put anything together."

Ailing with tonsillitis on the day of that first game, he directed the team by penciled messages to Jenkins, but the instructions were of little use as "Red" Bolton, the Bearcats' big center, consistently out-jumped the shorter Helm. Cincinnati rolled to a 28-7 halftime lead. The Bearcats outscored the Wildcats 20-3 in the second half for a 48-10 victory, worst defeat UK had suffered since falling to Wabash by 46 points in 1925.

That loss would prove the first of four consecutive setbacks as Indiana, Cincinnati, and Princeton beat the Wildcats, although the Bearcats' final margin in the second game was 10 points less than at Cincinnati. The Wildcats beat Florida at home and then lost to Wesleyan, Vanderbilt, Tennessee, and Georgia Tech before taking a two-point decision over Centre. They lost four more in a row, beat Centre again, and then dropped their finale to Tennessee.

"I couldn't get a very good effort out of them all season," Hayden said. "They had no incentive, except against Centre, which had beat them in football. I remember in that second game the Centre coach didn't let his boys shoot until they were in close to the basket. By the time he changed his mind, it was too late."

Throughout the season the Wildcats displayed a remarkable ability to miss crip shots, walk with the ball, step on opponents' toes, and commit personal fouls. Described as a comedy of errors by the local press, the team compiled the worst record (3-13) in UK's basketball history, one that was still standing when Hayden reminisced about old times a half-century later.

"March Madness"

The "March Madness" that descended upon the UK campus during the first two decades of the Kentucky High School Athletic Association tournament laid the foundation for a Wildcat basketball program that was to become one of the finest in the nation.

Beginning as an invitational affair at Danville in 1916, the tournament was moved to Lexington in March 1918, under the auspices of the newly formed KHSAA. The university managed it until 1938, paying the bills and turning the remainder over to the KHSAA for division among the teams as partial payment. The event would remain in Lexington a few years after the KHSAA assumed management responsibilities, move to Louisville, back to Lexington, and then to Louisville as each city built a bigger arena.

However, it was on the UK campus that the character of the tournament was molded. During those early years it gained so much in popularity that all eyes in Kentucky would turn to Lexington when the "Sweet Sixteen" finalists finally emerged through a series of district and regional eliminations.

Lexington Senior High won the 1918 tournament and repeated as champion in 1920, 1922, and 1924. Other large schools won their share of the tournaments, but the big "Dribble Derby" gained much of its flavor from a steady procession of fine players and teams from little-known hamlets in all reaches of the commonwealth. The most famous of these teams was a group of "barefoot" youngsters who came out of Carr Creek in the winter of 1928 and blazed a trail of glory all the way to the big national tournament in Chicago.

The "Creekers" first displayed their basketball prowess before a regional audience at Richmond and then advanced to Lexington to meet Ashland, another mountain powerhouse. The confrontation was classic—Carr Creek from an isolated, rural area; the Tom Cats from the industrial northeast.

The Carr Creek roster consisted of starters Gurney Adams, Ben Adams, Gillis Madden, Shelby Stamper, Zelda Hale, and three substitutes. They were all related to each other, averaged 155 pounds per man, had no matching uniforms, and played most of their games outside. The settlement, not on a map and 20 miles from the nearest railroad, was identified by a sign on a tree. It had a population of 140, no post office, and a school with an enrollment of 18 boys and 13 girls.

After they finished the season undefeated and accepted a bid to the regional tournament, the Creekers went by log wagon to Sassafras, by boat to Jeff, and then to Richmond on their first train ride. Friends and relatives chipped in to purchase pants and cheap jerseys, but there was not enough money left to outfit the eighth fellow. Fans in Richmond raised enough money to purchase a new set of white uniforms for the entire team to wear to the state finals.

The best all-around athlete on the Ashland team was Ellis Johnson, who had never played in a losing football game and whose high school basketball team had won 44 straight games over a season and a half before losing to Portsmouth, Ohio. He and teammates Darrell Darby and Jack Phipps already had committed themselves to attend UK.

Although the Creekers planned to attend Eastern Normal at Richmond, UK went all out to make them feel at home. When they came onto the floor attired in the same color jerseys as their semifinal foe Lawrenceburg, UK loaned them eight blue Wildcat jerseys.

Prior to the championship game, Athletic Director Boles seated the Ashland band on one end of the floor and placed the UK band on the other, to even things up. The 1,000 fans who accompanied the Tomcats to Lexington far outnumbered Carr Creek's "home folks" section—three substitutes, the coach, and a school benefactor—but the other 2,000 fans who braved sleet and snow to attend the game were pro-Carr Creek.

"We were all looking forward to that tournament," Ellis Johnson would recall 47 years later. "It was always sorta like homecoming...an affair everybody wanted to see. And that

particular one was something special. I'd heard it said that Carr Creek couldn't play, but they wouldn't let you play either, and that's just the way it seemed to me."

The game was called the greatest high school battle ever fought in Alumni Gym. A defensive battle, Carr Creek used a man-to-man attack that paralyzed Ashland's scoring territory, while the Tomcats retaliated with a zone that forced the Creekers to hurry their shots.

Carr Creek led, 2-0, at the end of the first quarter and 4-3 at halftime, but Ashland forged ahead, 8-6, during a third quarter that featured Carr Creek's first time out of the season. The break came when Hale hurt a foot. Back in action, the Creekers cut the margin to 9-8 with 30 seconds remaining. Stamper made a free throw to send the game into the first of four overtimes. Neither team scored until the fourth overtime, when Ashland got the tip, and Strother made a crip shot. Ashland again controlled the tip and worked the ball to Johnson, who twice "dribbled all over the floor" as time elapsed.

"There was no 10-second rule then and you could also tip the ball and catch it yourself on the jump," Johnson recalled. "I had Hale guarding me the latter part of the game. I don't remember about his foot being injured, but I would dribble around and let him tie me up, and then I'd get the tip, catch it myself, bring it down, pivot, dribble around some more, and let him tie me up, and then do it all over again. I was taller and could outjump him. The clock was running all the time."

Although they lost that championship, the Carr Creek boys generated more enthusiasm than any team in the history of Kentucky basketball and gave the tournament a kind of color it had never before achieved. Joining Ashland in the national high school tournament in Chicago, they were an immediate hit, causing writers there to dig out their geography books and spread the story of Carr Creek.

The annual tournament had drawn interesting teams in the past and other crowds had cheered their favorites, the *Tribune* said, "but no town anywhere ever had a team which has captured the imagination and hearts of basketball fans everywhere as have these lithe sharpshooters whose uniforms were overalls and whose school is a barn-like structure with its front porch digging into a mountain side."

After the Creekers defeated the U. S. Indian School of Albuquerque, New Mexico, almost 4,000 fans filled Bartlett

Gymnasium while an equal number lined the street for a chance to see the "team from nowhere." They defeated Bristol, Connecticut, 22-11, and lost to a veteran team from Vienna, Georgia. Ashland won the tournament, giving Kentucky the distinction of having both the best and the most colorful teams in the nation.

Carr Creek got more publicity than all the teams combined, but there was enough glory to go around. Johnson was named captain of the National Interscholastic Basketball All-American team by sportswriters, and Carr Creek's Stamper was also placed on the first team. Darby and Phipps of Ashland were on the second team, and Gene Strother was an honorable mention.

Carr Creek was just one of several small towns that caught the fancy of Kentucky basketball fans throughout the years.

The Ashland national champions of 1928. Front row, left to right: Gene Strother, Darrell Darby, Jim Barney, Jack Phipps, Ellis Johnson. Standing: Mgr. Gordon Kershner, Bill Hemlepp, Bud Fullerton, Eck Allen, Kermit Riffe, and Coach James Anderson.

Almost perennially a team from some small, obscure community would fight its way to glory in the State Tournament. The teams, representing schools big and small, featured a steady array of fine players, many of whom cast their lot with UK. In addition to the 1922 Senior High champions, who attended UK as a group, the Wildcats secured the services of such outstanding local boys as Bill King, who sank the free throw to win the 1921 Southern Championship, and Carey Spicer, All-American forward and captain-elect of the 1930-31 UK team.

The list of other outstanding high school performers of that era who wore the blue and white of UK includes Yates of Elizabethtown, DeMoisey of Walton, Little of Crab Orchard, Lawrence of Corinth, Tucker of Cynthiana, Kreuter of Newport, Davis of Hazard, Anderson of Covington, Lewis of Jeffersonville, and Goforth and Hagan of Louisville.

The crack Manual team of 1923 sent Paul Jenkins to UK. Jenkins made All-Southern in 1926. His mother was equally famous in her own right as a fan. She attended her first tournament in 1923 and had a long attendance streak that included only one miss, when a broken ankle kept her home in 1929. She would correctly predict that Midway would win the championship in 1937, Sharpe in 1938, Brooksville in 1939, and Hazel Green in 1940.

Sharing the spotlight with Mrs. Jenkins was Mrs. Rhoda Kavanaugh, founder of the famous (now closed) prep school at Lawrenceburg that sent Paul McBrayer, Aggie Sale, and Ralph Carlisle to UK. In addition to being her team's No. 1 rooter, she sometimes helped coach the team and became somewhat of a legend. At most games she would position herself under the basket armed with a long umbrella and was not above flailing one of her boys who did poorly.

Another "super fan" was A.B. "Happy" Chandler, whose political career would include two terms as governor of Kentucky, U. S. Senator, and commissioner of baseball. After presenting the championship trophy for the fourth consecutive year in 1939, he would compliment the capacity crowd for their patience in the face of inconveniences produced by the inadequate old UK gym. "You will have a new field house in which to see the tournament when you come back here next year," he promised, but Kentucky would not get that field house until after World War II.

The "Submarine" Attack

An air of secrecy shrouded the entire University of Kentucky basketball operation in the winter of 1927 as new coach John Mauer wasted no time indoctrinating his charges into an intricate new system.

The mystery was baffling, but not silent, as Mauer's shouts resounded throughout Alumni Gym:

"Talk it up! Get some enthusiasm! Snap out of it!"

Neville Dunn of the *Herald* told a curious public, "The Illinois system is the same in basketball as it is in football—drive and hard work, topped with a line of chatter that would make a pack of monkeys hide their faces behind coconuts in shame. No Illinois coach thinks much of a player who goes about his work with tight lips and tied tongue."

There was no mistaking the Illinois influence throughout the entire Wildcat athletic operation. Harry Gamage was football coach, Bernie Shively was line coach, Fred Major coached the freshmen in basketball and football, and Mauer coached varsity basketball, freshman baseball, and the football backfield.

"That's right, practically the whole Illinois staff came here then," Mauer would recall while scouting a UK football game in Lexington almost a half-century later. "In those days, we worked at all different sports, but I guess my primary interest was football."

"And what about those closed practice sessions?" he was asked.

"I did no different than most other coaches," he replied. "I knew we had to do one of those new things when we came here. Well, it wasn't exactly new to me, because I had seen it and used it a lot prior to coming here. Let's say it was new to the South."

He spoke of a pretty set type of basketball, a five-man offense with guards as important to the attack as centers and forwards. The slow-break attack featured a steady procession of bounce passes that had the players operating from bended positions and working persistently for the good shot.

He had received his basketball indoctrination at Batavia High, where he was an all-sports star, and at the University of Illinois, where he was an All-Western Conference forward. Mauer had played halfback in the same backfield with the immortal Red Grange. Just under six feet, with a shock of dark, wavy hair, he was described as a taciturn individual who was very set in his ways.

"We had some pretty good players returning," he recalled. "There was Paul Jenkins, the captain, and Lawrence McGinnis, Paul McBrayer, Stanley Milward, and Cecil Combs. And there were some football players who came over too, guys like 'Baldy' Gilb, Leonard Miller, Clair Dees, June Lyons, and Ray Ellis. I used that crew as my substitutes, and that's what most teams did in those days."

At the time there was much skepticism throughout the South about his "submarine" attack, but the disbelievers would begin to take notice after the Wildcats defeated South Carolina and Georgia and lost only to Mississippi in the 1928 tournament. Ed Danforth of the *Constitution* would call them "just about the sweetest bit of basketball mechanism of the age." One year later Ben Cothran of that newspaper would describe the offense as a "weird sort of dribble-pass that keeps the ball almost rolling on the floor." The Wildcats would lose in the second round of the 1929 tournament and advance to the semifinals in 1930.

Mauer remembered that the players he inherited were "pretty green." "I started five sophomores (Combs, Owens, Milward, McGinnis, and McBrayer)," he said, "and all were Kentuckians. They had a lot to learn. They had trouble catching and holding onto passes, and sometimes they would forget the plays and completely miss the ball or get hit in the back with it. But we beat Clemson (33-17) pretty good in that first game, and I guess that sent the fans home happy."

The local newspapers reported that the game drew one of the largest crowds ever to attend a Wildcat opener, but that it was devoid of thrills. The Wildcats would have their good and bad moments throughout that season as they sought to master Mauer's intricate system of passing and feinting. They would fumble away a game to Miami of Ohio, defeat Centre in a game cited for the referee's knack for ignoring football tackles and wrestling, defeat Vanderbilt 43-23, lose to the Naval Academy on an asphalt playing surface in Annapolis, and then become so confused by Maryland's five-man defense the following day at College Park that they would score only one field goal in 48 attempts en route to a 37-7 loss.

"I remember inserting Irvine Jeffries into the lineup and he responded with a lot of points (22), and we beat Tennessee rather easily (48-18)," Mauer would recall. "We beat them later in the season at Knoxville and also beat Vanderbilt on the road."

Among those joining the varsity in 1929 was Louis McGinnis, who was nicknamed "Little" because he was one inch shorter and three years younger than his brother, Lawrence "Big" McGinnis. Sitting in his office at the W. R. Milward Mortuary in Lexington in the spring of 1975, "Little" McGinnis would not remember his first varsity game, other than the fact that the Wildcats beat Eastern pretty handily. However he would recall a three-overtime victory over Miami and a losing effort against a North Carolina team that had won four southern championships in six years by using what Neville Dunn of the *Herald* called "that flip and run stuff that nearly makes you crazy with the sheer speed and excitement of it."

Although they were coming off losses to Butler, Ohio State, and Louisville, the Tar Heels had no trouble stopping the vaunted UK submarine attack. They defeated the Wildcats, 25-15. That would be UK's lowest scoring production of the season and third lowest during Mauer's stay in Lexington.

"Little" McGinnis would remember a UK victory over Notre Dame (19-16) at South Bend in the first meeting between Wildcat and Irish basketball teams. "We traveled by train in those days, riding a sleeper all night," he said. "We got lost going to South Bend and had to backtrack. I don't remember if we got there in time for practice. We played on a temporary floor in the fieldhouse. There was a small crowd in attendance. They thought we would be a pushover. Out-of-bounds plays were not common then, but we had practiced hard on them, and we worked two of those plays to perfection, actually getting crip shots at the end of each. I think that's what won for us."

It would be 14 years before the Wildcats would beat the Irish again.

The roughest game that year was in New Orleans, where the Wildcats lost to Tulane in the Greenies' box-like gym that had big square pillars along each edge of the floor.

"The spectators sat right at the out-of-bounds line," Louis McGinnis said. "If you went out, they wouldn't help you back; they would throw you back. The game got so rough that Coach Mauer sent in his 'wrecking crew' and that's how it ended, like a football game."

The Wildcats also lost on the road to Georgia Tech and at home to Alabama that year. They defeated Tulane, 29-15, in the opening round of the Southern Tournament. They were trailing Georgia, 26-24, when Louis McGinnis shot what looked like a sure basket, but the ball rolled around the rim, dipped down, and then rolled off the hoop just as the final gun sounded.

Captain of the Wildcats the following year was Paul McBrayer, who had joined the UK freshman team as a 6-foot-3, 155-pound guard after playing two years at famed Kavanaugh Academy in Lawrenceburg, and had two years experience with the varsity before being elected team leader.

He told the *Courier-Journal*, "Even as a kid when I first played basketball, I wanted, some day, to captain the UK team."

On the starting unit with McBrayer in 1930 were "Big" and "Little" McGinnis, Combs and Milward, all of Lexington. Two other Lexingtonians, Carey Spicer and Hays Owens, were the chief substitutes.

That UK team was a sensation wherever it played, displaying a floor game polished to the finest degree and a defense hard to penetrate. In victories over Georgetown, Miami, Berea, and Clemson, the Wildcats utilized what the local newspapers called "legal blocks" to spring men open time and time again for easy crip shots.

The biggest event of the season was a two-night series with Creighton, which featured 6-foot-7 center Brud Jensen, considered a giant in those days. When Willie Worthing scored from 50 feet in closing seconds of the first game to put the Blue Jays

The 1929-30 Wildcat squad. Front row, left to right: Leonard Wenkley (manager), Stanley Milward, Cecil Combs, Paul McBrayer, Lawrence (Big) McGinnis, Carey Spicer. Middle row:

Coach John Mauer. Jake Bronston, Ercel Little, Bill Trott, George Yates. Back row: Hays Owens, Larry Crump, Milton Cavana, Bill Kleiser, and Louis (Little) McGinnis.

ahead by one point, Jensen rushed into the game, got the tip, and preserved the victory for Creighton. UK won by four points the following night.

Although the turnout was tremendous at both games, the athletic department did not make money. Athletic Director Boles said there were approximately 50 unsold box seats, and no reserved seats in the lower portion of one section were sold. The university could have realized something like $300 more on each game had there been capacity attendance. Expenses came to almost $1,000, with the breakdown as follows:

Creighton $700; Referee Lane $110; printing of tickets $114; ushers, ticket-takers, and ticket-sellers $30; advertising placards $2.14; basketball $15; plus some minor items.

Ticket sales at the door totaled $775. Receipts from downtown ticket sales made up the deficit.

Creighton officials invited Kentucky to play in Omaha the following season, but the Wildcats, like most other teams, were unable to afford the high costs of long travel. They would not be ready for intersectional play for three more seasons.

The other team to beat them that year was Tennessee, which took a 29-26 decision in Knoxville to avenge a 23-20 loss in Lexington. The Wildcats closed the regular season with an exciting 28-26 overtime victory over Washington & Lee.

In Atlanta they defeated Maryland, 26-21, doubled the score, 44-22, on Sewanee, and lost to Duke, 37-32, in what Ed Danforth of the *Constitution* called "one of the most brilliantly played games the conference has ever produced and was a neck-to-neck race down to the final wire."

Although they lost the championship, the Wildcats received a royal welcome upon their return to Lexington. They were met at the station by a mob of boosters who shoulder-carried them through the terminal.

The school newspaper described Mauer as the "Moses" of Kentucky basketball, a roundball prophet who had led the game out of its slambang hit-and-miss style of former years and developed it along the lines of the machinelike precision of football. He had changed the Wildcats from doormat to drawing card, the newspaper said, and his influence had become felt throughout the South, where coaches had begun to adopt his style of play.

Paul McBrayer, All-American 1930.

He seemed destined to go down in Southern basketball annals as the pioneer of a new system, the father, so to speak, of Dixie basketball.

Less than two months later, after the Athletic Council gave him a token raise, Mauer resigned as UK coach and accepted a similar position at Miami University in Ohio.

"Well, you know how people are," he said years later. "They're just used to winners, and that's what they expect. I spent two terms coaching at Tennessee, and they aren't so different. They want to win. I went to Miami and stayed there nine years. I was at Tennessee eight years and at West Point four years and then to Florida for 10 years and back to Tennessee. I was out of basketball then and stayed in football and then I went with the pros. Vince Lombardi hired me and I went to work for him.

"I've been a lot of different places, and I often thought wouldn't it be nice to stay in one place? But I tell you I don't regret it because I've been to some very fine schools in different localities and made a lot more friends than if I had stayed in one place.

"I know we made a good impression (at UK). We played real good ball and of course everything is relevant and the development has been tremendous, but you have to think in terms of what it was when you were playing and I thought we did real good."

With so much interest in basketball in Lexington and with a wealth of talent in his own backyard, it is surprising that Mauer left UK. However, he was a sensitive man, and he felt he deserved better treatment than was being accorded him by the athletics board.

The job did not go begging. Within days after Mauer's resignation 70 persons had applied. The list was narrowed to a man from Indiana and to a high school coach whose Freeport, Illinois, teams had won most of their games. The man from Freeport was Adolph Rupp, who reputedly told the board it should hire him because "I'm the best basketball coach there is."

Rupp accepted the UK job on the same day that Mauer left town. The school newspaper duly recorded each story in its March 23, 1930, issue, saying goodbye to the submarine offense and hello to Rupp.

"Mr. Rupp will face the handicap that all new coaches

must face—the critical eye of the students, alumni, and fans who are skeptical to a high degree," Vernon Rucks wrote. "He will realize that unless he makes good he runs an excellent chance of losing his job at the end of the two-year contract, and producing winning teams when so many of the coaches of other schools have a head start by knowing their school and their material will be difficult. We are not trying to be pessimistic for we firmly believe we have the material and Mr. Rupp the ability. Good luck to him."

Time Out: Adolph Rupp

As with many American heroes, Adolph Rupp, the man who was to become the winningest collegiate basketball coach of all time, was of humble background and had to work long hours and burn midnight oil to reach his pinnacle of success.

Born on a 120-acre homestead near Halstead in central Kansas, he was the fourth of six children of Heinrich Rupp and Anna Lichti, who came to this country from Austria and Germany with the first wave of Mennonites who settled in frontier Kansas in the 1880s.

After the father died of stomach cancer in 1910, the oldest son, Otto, dropped out of school and took over the farming operation. The other children—Henry, Theodore, Adolph, Elizabeth, and Albert—assisted with the chores and attended District 33 elementary school and Halstead High School.

Theirs was the usual story of hardships, dawn-to-dusk toil in the fields, and a close family relationship that resulted from the battle for survival on the prairie.

But we are interested in what brought Adolph Rupp to the University of Kentucky, and we glean that from interviews tape-recorded by the writer in the summers of 1971 and 1972:

"I was about four years old when basketball really made its inroads in our section of the state. Halstead had fine teams, without any coaching. It won the state championship and repeated the following year. That meant a great deal. We were just a little community of 1,200 people. All that the teams that wanted to compete had to do was simply go to Lawrence, have a drawing, be assigned a bracket, and play all week until a champion was crowned.

Adolph Rupp, 1930.

"The state championship ignited a spark in our community. Everybody talked basketball. We finally got the school board to get two posts, build backboards, and put baskets up in the yard at District 33. I don't remember if we had any nets. I don't think so, but the board did give us a basketball. It cost four dollars. It had a bladder and a little tube. We'd blow up the bladder, tie the tube, lace her up, and away we'd go.

"At home we had a basketball made of a gunnysack. It was round and filled with rags and hay. Mother stitched it together. The nice thing about that basketball was that you couldn't dribble it, so there was no such thing as individual play. You couldn't have had an Oscar Robinson in those days. You had to pass or shoot. We four brothers would get together before and after dinner and shoot at that basket. My oldest brother and I would play against the two middle brothers.

"We were in the Arkansas Valley League with Reno County, Hutchinson, Newton, Wichita, Wellington, Winfield, and Arkansas City. Halstead dominated that league for quite a while. Then Reno County at little old Nickerson dominated the

Young Adolph Rupp shoots at a goal in the yard of District 33 school at Halstead, Kansas, about 1915.

league. Then Newton came along under a coach named Lindsey and dominated the state for a long time because he knew something about screening that other coaches didn't know. We were the first to drop out of the league, because we couldn't finance the deal against those bigger schools. We organized another league with Moundridge, Sedgwick, Burrton, Valley City, all smaller towns comparable in size and population with Halstead.

"During my sophomore year we had possibly the lowest spot in the history of basketball at Halstead. We won only three games. I didn't play that year. The following year we started moving; by the time we were seniors we had a fine basketball team. We were conference champions. We gave Newton a fine game before they eliminated us from further competition.

"Those gyms were not great affairs. We played in the Halstead City Hall. The ceiling was only three and one-half feet above the goal. You couldn't arch the ball much. The gas lamps were covered with wire wastepaper baskets. We later got electric lights, which had the same cages over them for protection. Burrton played in a garage; on game nights they moved out the cars, swept the floors, and went to it. Moundridge played in an old church. Sedgwick played in an old store, which had a back end elevated higher than the street. One night one of the boys went in for a crip, hit the door, and went outside. Since there were no steps, he had to run around the front of the store to get back in.

"In my first high school basketball game I played the pivot position. I got ten field goals. We beat Sedgwick, 67-17. We won the championship that year and the following year. Records will show that I averaged 19 points a game the two years that I played.

"We didn't have much trouble with those teams. The crowds turned out nicely. We always packed the old city hall. We had all that hoopla, rah, rah, rah, and at the end of the year we held a big banquet. That consisted of roasting wieners and marshmallows over a bonfire in Chappie Master's pasture at the edge of the town. We sang a few school songs, and that was our banquet. We had our fun. We learned some fundamentals in life that perhaps the boys and girls aren't learning today. Halstead High continued to have good teams and won some championships. A new high school was finished in 1970-71. The gym was named after me. A very fine painting of me is in the hall.

"One thing I remember about the University of Kansas are

The Halstead, Kansas, City Hall, where the Halstead High School teams played basketball when Adolph Rupp was a student there.

the pep rallies we had. For some reason or another you can't get a pep rally started around a school anymore. We used to get together and hold the rallies on the campus. We had men cheerleaders. There weren't any pompon girls or girl cheerleaders. We used to give the 'Rock Chalk, Jayhawk, K. U.,' some riproaring sounds; you could hear us all over town. I believe we had more school spirit then than they do now, although I can't kick about the school spirit at our University of Kentucky basketball games.

"Robinson Gym seated about 1,500 downstairs. They would add chairs there and on a running track upstairs, swelling the crowd to about 3,000. That was adequate in those days, about as big as anybody's.

"My old coach, 'Phog' Allen, was a strict disciplinarian and a health addict. He believed everybody should exercise. His exercises were tough. He would make us do push-ups on our fingertips, not letting the heel of the hand touch the floor. That was supposed to strengthen the fingers to such an extent that when we shot a basketball, our fingers would have a lot of snap.

They would have a lot of strength, also, so we wouldn't strain them. I had a sprained finger every year I was there, so those exercises didn't help me a great deal. It seemed every time that finger started to get well, bang, there it would go; a ball would hit it, or something like that.

"He took pride in his personal appearance. He always had to look his best. Whenever a team photograph was taken, everybody had to have a haircut; everything had to be just so. He would not put up with any sloppy business at all.

"Dr. Allen was a great crank on eating. He did not believe in feeding too much. On the morning of a trip, he would feed us some oatmeal or corn flakes, toast, and a glass of milk. In the four years I was there I didn't have but one steak. Our standard piece of food during the basketball season was roast beef. With it we would have some kind of fruit, mashed potatoes, and a little ice cream. At five o'clock he would get us up, give us a half slice each of canned peach, and a little juice with a lot of sugar, to give us energy, he said. I finally got so I wouldn't show up. I could go to the Jayhawk Cafe, where I worked, and eat anything I wanted.

"That first day of practice at Kansas was just about as brutal as anything you could get. Phog was great on practice. We would practice and practice, pivoting and pivoting and all those things, until the blisters would be on our feet the size of a dollar. He didn't hesitate to work twice a day, but we never worked three times a day. He did a lot of things that I consider not worthy, simply because we don't do things like that anymore. We would spend 10 or 12 minutes on hook passing. We would throw a hook pass probably once a year, and that usually went out a window.

"He did a lot of other funny things. We practiced in Omaha during one holiday season because he felt the change of scenery would do us good. We would get up early in the morning and make an eight-mile trip in the country. We would run one-half mile, walk, jog, run, walk, jog, run. We would be completely pooped out by the time we got back to the hotel. He made us go to bed early in the afternoon. Some of us would get together and play cards. In the evening we would have a real workout.

"We finally played Creighton. We held them without a field goal until the last minute of the game, when one of their boys threw one in from about twenty-five feet.

"In addition to Dr. Allen it was my privilege to be associated for five years at Kansas with Dr. James Naismith, who invented the game of basketball. I met him many times after that at national conventions and when I went back to Lawrence.

"He was not a difficult man to find. He was always in the gym early and late. He was a hard worker, interested in developing the youth of the land. That was right after World War I, and he was chiefly concerned in seeing that the boys home from the services maintained a good physical condition.

"The first class I had with him was a class in hygiene. He was a very interesting teacher, seldom using notes and drawing from his vast store of knowledge. He lectured interestingly, talked plainly with just a little hint of a Canadian accent, and

The young Rupp.

didn't hesitate to call a spade a spade. He told me many times that he did not believe the game of basketball would ever draw national attention, or would ever grow to the point where admission would be charged to see the game played. I wish it were possible for Dr. Naismith to see the way the game has developed.

"I played on two national championship teams at Kansas. I was a member of what Phog called his 'meatpackers,' which meant that we got in the game when things were pretty well settled, one way or the other. I had the misfortune of playing behind two fine All-Americans, Paul Endacott and Charlie Black. When we had a class reunion many years later and were lining up for a picture, I told Paul, 'Let me hold that ball. I never got a chance to hold it while I was playing.'

"George Rody was captain of our team my senior year. Other players were John Wulf, Armin Woestemeyer, and Byron Frederick, along with my fellow meatpackers Andrew McDonald and John Lonborg.

"I embraced much of my basketball philosophy from Allen and Naismith, including my personal belief in regard to how I should conduct myself with my teams, the public, and others.

"I had my sights set on going into banking, and the coaching of basketball was the furthest thing from my mind. But times were pretty hard, and I returned to the university to work on an advanced degree after walking the streets of Topeka and Wichita.

"I finally took a job as teacher and coach at Burr Oak High School in western Kansas. Imagine my surprise when the football players showed up in overalls, saying there was no equipment at the school. The principal and I finally rounded up some uniforms, but they were substandard and I ended up paying for them.

"The basketball court was located in an old barn renovated for a skating rink. Well, I went home for Thanksgiving, and when Bryan R. Miller, principal at Marshalltown High School in Iowa, said there was a teaching and coaching job open I jumped at the chance to get away from Burr Oak.

"Instead of being basketball coach I discovered I had accepted a job as wrestling coach. I had never seen a wrestling match in my life. I didn't know one hold from another.

"I bought a book on wrestling and solicited the services of

The national champion University of Kansas team of 1923. Back row, left to right: A. F. Rupp, Bob Mosby, Tus Ackerman, Verne Wilkins. Second row: John Wulf, Dr. F. C. "Phog" Allen, Dr. James A. Naismith, Charlie Black, Byron Frederick. Front row: George Glaskin, Waldo Bowman, Paul Endacott, Andy McDonald.

Allie Morrison, who had been a fine wrestler for Marshalltown the year before. We won the state championship.

"I went to Freeport the next year. They had a new gymnasium seating 1,500, and they were really enthused about basketball. Our teams won 66 games and lost 17. We won two district and one sectional title and ranked third in 1929 among Illinois high schools. We had the high scorer in the league three times. The only guy I couldn't beat regularly was Jim Laude of Rockford. We split even. During the summers he and I attended Columbia University, where I got my teacher's certificate and master's degree.

"Many times at Freeport I went over to Madison to see

Wisconsin play basketball. The coach there was Dr. Walter O. Meanwell, who had compiled an excellent record at the University of Missouri and the University of Illinois. He was kind enough to let me sit up in the pressbox with his team. Substitutes had to climb up and down the ladder. He would be up there hollering at his boys, and I was amazed at some of the things he said. I got some of my vocabulary from him.

"I considered him the first of the modern coaches to come up with the screening-type offense that really makes the game what it is today. It .was not as complicated then because, goodness knows, there are hundreds and hundreds of coaches today who have contributed to the game of basketball.

"It was during my second year at Freeport that I bought me a fine-looking new blue suit to replace that old brown thing I had been wearing all the time I had been there. When we lost the game that night, with me wearing that new suit, I said, 'Hey, this blue won't get it done.' From then on I wore nothing but brown to my teams' games.

"The guest speaker at our annual basketball banquet in 1930 was Craig Ruby, who told me about the coaching job being vacant at Kentucky. He said he would not recommend one of his men, but he agreed to recommend me. A few days later I got a telegram from S. A. Boles, asking that I come to Lexington and discuss the situation.

"I wasn't impressed with Lexington. First, as I was driven from the train station to the university, I noticed an unsightly slum area known as Pralltown. Next, we arrived a little late for lunch in McVey Hall, and I had to settle for one piece of cold fish and some cornbread. Finally I was taken to Alumni Gym. I saw this little old peanut-huller of a gym, and I just couldn't get steamed up. Besides, I saw about a half-hundred little shanties across from the stadium, and I wasn't a bit impressed.

"They offered me exactly the same salary at UK as I was making at Freeport, but I figured that was a golden opportunity to get into college coaching, so I accepted. I remained in Freeport, selling securities, until late in August, when I shipped a trunk full of clothing and other articles by train and got in my car and headed South, wondering all the time if I was making a big mistake."

Rhapsody In Brown

Rupp came to UK at a time when Wildcat teams had completed their best year. Although no championships were won, not one season of sport had been a failure. Boles flatly stated that the 1929 football team (6-1-1) was the best UK ever had, and the 1930 team should be even better. The basketball and track teams were also among the best in the state.

While football fans dreamed of an invitation to the Rose Bowl, the basketball camp moaned the loss of such outstanding players as Captain McBrayer, "Big" McGinnis, Combs, and Milward. Everyone felt that the new coach would get the most of his material, but that the nucleus of second string holdovers and new men did not give much cause for optimism.

Describing the upcoming season as one big question mark, the *Kernel* said, "If Coach Rupp does come through with a winning team, he will be hailed as a miracle man and he might do that very thing."

In reality he inherited a pretty good squad. Aggie Sale, a high school All-American, was among the record 50 candidates who reported for the first varsity practice session while Carey Spicer, who was an All-American the preceding year; Jake Bronston; and Ellis Johnson were among the football players joining them later.

Speculating on the new system the *Kernel* said, "It is generally supposed that the idea is to put the ball through the hoop and the team that does it most will win...whether the guards will stand around and talk it over or give someone else a chance to make a basket will be a secret for the time being. At any rate, basketball fans are expecting a new style of play."

"I called Captain Spicer in when I first got there and told him my plans to run a fast-break type offense," Rupp said. "He got the word around to the others. They got a little confident that maybe the new coach was going to give them a better opportunity to shoot and score."

"My first impressions of the new coach are very clear," Sale would say four decades later. "I saw in him a man of intelligence, great leadership, and personality, and all the other splendid qualities he has shown down through the years. One of the many very important lessons I learned from him that proved most useful to me in my 31 years of teaching and coaching was the way practice sessions were conducted. By this I mean they were so well-planned and conducted that instead of being dull,

Carey Spicer, All-American, 1929, 1931.

burdensome, and tiresome they were exciting with variations of many drills, exercises, scrimmages, competitive games, etc. This was not only helpful in my coaching but also in my teaching of academic classes."

Dan Bowmar, sports editor of the *Leader*, promised UK cage fans they would see plenty of action and get their money's worth. Neville Dunn, sports editor of the *Herald*, described Rupp as a person with a gloriously developed sense of humor, a droll, witty man who knew his basketball, made a friend out of every new acquaintance, and was, in all the popular meaning of the phrase, "a good sport."

They wrote of a freedom of movement and the racehorse quality of a new system of play that should thrill everyone in the Blue Grass. The system, built around the screens developed by Meanwell, consisted of a set of 10 plays centered around the pivot-post, with the players instructed to run and fast break whenever the opportunity afforded itself.

He cut the squad by more than half and relentlessly stressed fundamentals, particularly goal-shooting. His impatience with anything less than perfection resulted in a verbal barrage against the varsity for letting the freshmen score so many points in their first scrimmage, which the varsity won, 75-21. After long hours of work on defense, the varsity won the next scrimmage, 75-9.

"Fans don't appreciate good defensive players, but you must have them," Rupp said. "It's just like on a farm. Fertilizer must be spread. Nobody likes to spread it, but it just has to be done. That is the way with defense. A lot of boys just want to shoot, but you have to have defense."

On offense he used five or six standard plays based on outside screening. "They were very kind to us because the South still had not caught onto the screen," he said. "We didn't use the inside screen until five or six years later, when we discovered it in an accidental way. We were running spring practice when I saw the thing developing one day on the court. 'Wait a minute,' I said. 'Run that thing over just exactly the way you ran it before.' They didn't run it quite so smooth as the first time, but I told them to set it up again. I thought they had something.

"We got out on the floor and talked about the proper footwork that we thought would be essential to the setting of an inside screen. Utilizing that inside screen we won 48 consecutive games in the conference before we were defeated, all due to the fact that teams in the South did not know what we were doing. That was Kentucky's big contribution to basketball."

The December 18, 1930, debut of his first UK team rated five inches in the *Leader*, which reported that the Wildcats were not expected to have much difficulty with Georgetown. His starting lineup would consist of Spicer, McGinnis, Yates, Trott, and Johnson.

Capt. Harry Lancaster of Georgetown started the scoring with a field goal, but Johnson matched it, scoring the first UK goal for Rupp. The UK offense then went into high gear, and the Wildcats won, 67-19. "Georgetown used a man-to-man defense," the *Herald* reported, "but the speed with which Kentucky broke for the goal often left the (Chester) Dillon men behind, and easy short shots under the basket resulted. Then again, if Kentucky had no opportunity for a fast break, it employed blocks with such deception Georgetown floundered in its efforts to break them up."

"If the Wildcats failed to show anything else in their initial contest on the waxed hardwood, they demonstrated that the fast break system of play used by the new coach...has scoring potential," the *Leader* said. "On the few occasions that the Kentucky offense moved smoothly, the Cats kept the scorers working at a rapid pace and several times scored as many as six points in less than it takes to tell about it."

In addition to the starters 12 other Wildcats saw action in that game. They were Kleiser, Lavin, Bell, Sale, Krump, Richards, Congleton, Skinner, Bronston, Cavana, Little, and Worthington.

"Then we played a benefit game for the Unemployment Fund," Rupp recalled. "I don't know why we did that. Eight hundred people paid one dollar each to see it. We gave Marshall $155 and the rest went to the Unemployment Fund. I guess that money lasted longer than it does today. Anyway, it didn't help the Athletic fund a bit. We beat Marshall.

"When Bobby Dodd and the Tennessee team came to town, we packed our gym. I remember some 50 or 60 people got in wearing freshman caps, and those faces looked pretty old. Now, you've got to have an I.D. card. I even had trouble getting into Memorial Gym, and I was coach of the team.

"We beat Berea, Clemson, and Chattanooga and finally got around to taking our first trip. At the depot a bunch of boys

Rupp's first UK team. Front row, left to right: Ercel Little, George Yates, Carey Spicer, Aggie Sale, Bud Cavana. Second row: George Skinner, Allan Lavin, Bill Trott, Jake Bronston,

Louis McGinnis, Cecil Bell, Morris Levin, manager. Back row: Rupp, Bill Congleton, Bill Kleiser, Ellis Johnson, Charles Worthington, and Darrell Darby.

showed in knickers, which was all right because that was the style of the times. What got me was that some of them had sweat shirts on. 'Why in the world are you guys showing up in clothes like that?' I asked. 'I'm taking around a bunch of university students, not a bunch of bums. I'm packing around the finest boys from the finest university. You've got time to go home and get your clothes on. I want you to get on a shirt, a tie, and a coat and get back here. This sloppy business isn't going to get by as long as I'm coach. Let's get some class in this organization.'"

When the Wildcats had a poor first half in Nashville, Rupp asked Bronston, "What were you thinking of when you were going bad out there?" "I was wondering if you had on brown socks," Bronston answered. Rupp pulled up his trousers to reveal brown socks. The Wildcats won, 42-37.

They defeated Tennessee by four points in overtime in Knoxville and returned home to lay their seven-game winning streak on the line against Washington & Lee. Before playing the Generals, Rupp visited the Joseph E. Widener Farm in Lexington with Elmer Hoffman, his house guest from Freeport, Illinois; referee Dick Bray; and *Herald* sports editor Frank K. Hoover. When they saw a black cat, Rupp yelled, "Boys, it's in the bag," and proceeded to cross over and follow in the footsteps of the cat. The Wildcats defeated the Generals, 23-18.

"As we kept winning, the papers were very delighted with my brown suit because they thought it was a good thing," Rupp said. "They kept talking about it. We kept going very good. We won 10 straight before we went down to Athens and lost to Georgia in Woodruff Hall. I'll never forget that old place. They should have given it to Carnegie Institute. Harry Mehre, a football coach who substituted as basketball coach that day, tells the story of the game as well as anybody. He had two sporting goods salesmen referee the game."

After UK lost to Clemson two nights later, Neville Dunn wrote that maybe it was because Rupp's brown socks were in the laundry, or because he left his brown suit and brown tie at home, or because he had broken his rhapsody in brown by using it during a freshman game, or because the game was played on Friday the Thirteenth.

The Wildcats defeated Georgia Tech, 35-16, and returned home to beat Vanderbilt, 43-23, a week before they left Lexington for the Southern Tournament in Atlanta. Rupp showed up at the railway station attired in a freshly pressed brown suit, newly shined brown shoes, a brown hat, brown tie, and brown socks.

McGinnis, Spicer, and Yates shared scoring honors with 10 points each in a 33-28 victory over North Carolina. McGinnis scored 18 of UK's points in a 35-30 victory over Duke, and Spicer scored 11 points in one two-minute stretch en route to a 22-point performance in a 56-36 victory over Florida.

The stage was thus set for a championship game between UK and Maryland that would be called one of the most exciting games played in the South all season. Trailing 18-7 at halftime the Wildcats rallied behind McGinnis, Yates, and Bronston to tie the score and take a 27-25 lead on a sideline shot by McGinnis with less than a minute to play. Maryland came right back to tie the score on a layup by "Bozzy" Berger. As the final seconds ticked off, Berger made his third field goal of the half and 12th point of the game, firing a long shot to give the Terrapins a 29-27 victory.

"I'll always to this day, not as an alibi or as a cheap sport, question the time," Rupp said, "because the clock continued to run from the time the ball went in our basket until we went back to the center jump with that minute left. We took our time walking back, but there were still 15 seconds to go when we lined up for the center jump. They threw the ball up, Berger got it, and shot from the middle of the floor."

Despite the defeat the Wildcats were the talk of Atlanta. Spicer broke the tournament scoring record and was voted on the All-Tournament team with McGinnis and Yates. After the final game, Rupp wired the *Herald*:

"Getting away to a bad start and fighting an uphill battle all the way then forging to the front only to be denied by a long shot from mid-court with ten seconds to go, was a little too much for the Wildcats tonight.

"The boys from old Kentucky staged the greatest comeback of the tournament, and their loss to Maryland is no disgrace. I only wish that the people at home could have seen the battle, for the fight they put up in the last half will live in my memory forever.

"We'll be home Wednesday evening at 8 o'clock."

A Serious Matter

"When a Kentucky baby is born, the mother naturally wants him to be president, like another Kentuckian, Abraham Lincoln," Rupp once said. "If not president, she wants him to play basketball for the University of Kentucky."

There was some truth in that overstatement in the early 1930s, but the best players did not just walk uninvited onto the UK campus. They had to be recruited, and Rupp was a master of the art.

And while other Southern schools were searching for football talent, he was making a concentrated drive for basketball players. A boy had to be an outstanding basketball player before he could get a scholarship for his effort in places other than UK. Consequently, there were few Northern preparatory stars on the basketball rosters as compared to football rosters in the South. As late as 1941, there were no basketball scholarships given at Mississippi, only two at Tennessee, and a few at the other conference schools. Lack of playing space was also a big handicap in the South, with secondary schools, where the game was nurtured, having to play on outdoor courts.

"The South did not have big places to play in," Rupp said. "As a result I did not like to go there. When I was coaching in high school at Freeport, every school had a nice place to play. The Joliet Field House seated some 5,500, and we'd fill that when we'd go there to play. Rivalry in that conference was extreme.

"I came to UK and we'd go down there to Georgia Tech and play in that little old wooden building. It finally burned down. They accused me of doing it, but that wasn't the truth.

But they didn't even fill those little shacks.

"The coaches in the North felt that the Southern basketball just wasn't up to par. When they took on a Southern team, it was just a win for them, and I wasn't going to put up with that kind of arrangement. And so we went up there to Notre Dame, and they beat us seven times in a row before we finally beat them. I kept going back, because if they were better than we were, I was going to find out what made them better, and I found out some of the answers by getting beat by some of those teams."

From the moment he stepped onto the UK campus he was involved in recruiting fine players. The Athletic Department had no money set aside for recruitment, but he did comb the state for talent.

"Nowadays, coaches subscribe to possibly 10 or 15 papers from Detroit, Pittsburgh, Indiana, St. Louis, Kansas City, and places like that," he said in the spring of 1975. "We didn't do that because we found about what we wanted in the *Courier-Journal* and the Lexington papers. We did not go out and recruit where we stayed overnight. If we went somewhere we went on our own. My assistant coach would look over some boys, naturally, and we'd see the boys play in the State Tournament, which was held in Lexington.

"When I first came to UK, I heard about this boy from Walton named 'Frenchy' DeMoisey who was about 6-6 and had scored 50 points in a game against Butler High and 45 in a regional game against Paris. That got me interested.

"I visited him and he was working on a road gang. We sat in the shade on a creek bank, and I asked if he would like to attend UK. He told me he was making plans to attend Trinity College because he was a minister's son and entitled to free tuition there. They had also promised him a job.

"I went back home, and when I visited Frenchy again I told him that tuition for the first semester was $31.50 and that I would try to find someone to pay for the second semester or find some way he could work it out. When he came out for the varsity as a sophomore in 1931, he told me he had paid tuition, room, and board through Christmas and would make the team or go home. There wasn't any doubt in my mind about him making the team.

"I remember Birkett Pribble and I drove up to Corinth to

see Dave Lawrence. He was working on putting a ditch in the road under a railroad track. He was down in the mud digging around, and we talked to him and asked him to come to UK. There were some fences on the campus that needed painting, and that sounded better to him than fooling around with that dynamite, which gave him headaches, and digging in the mud.

"The entire interview was not over 15 minutes. We just watched him work there, that's all the contact there was. He said he had two brothers that attended Western, and he didn't want to go down there because he'd just be in their shadow. He didn't realize at the time that he was not the shadow but possibly the best of the Lawrence brothers. That was the only time I ever saw the boy until he came here the first day of school.

"'Andy' Anderson played in the State Tournament here. He was a very fine guard, but he couldn't shoot. We didn't know that at the time. But he was a hustler and always got in there and set up plays nicely. I didn't even contact Jack Tucker. In fact I didn't even know he was in school until he came out for basketball, and we'd pick our talent from those.

"Little Billy Davis came down here from Hazard and was also a product of the tryouts. I had never seen Leroy Edwards play either, but I heard how good he was, so I went up to Indianapolis. It was quite a thrill for him to come here, the farthest he had ever been from home. I did see Russell Ellington of Manual and Jim Goforth of Male play in the old Knights of Columbus gym in Louisville."

In the summer of 1975 Ellington would recall how he came to attend UK:

"Adolph sent Porter Grant to see me and Goforth at Sutcliffe's Sporting Goods store in Louisville. Grant explained to me that because I had played freshman football at the University of Louisville I would have to wait two years to play football for UK.'Meantime they put me on a basketball scholarship and then transferred me to a football scholarship after the two years. I went there under a full scholarship, but like other freshmen on scholarship Jim and I had to work in a restaurant at noon to earn our meals. After one semester, a trial period so to speak, we didn't have to do that anymore."

One of the best athletes in Louisville at that time was Joe "Red" Hagan, who starred at both Male and St. Xavier high schools and was in the football camp at Cincinnati Xavier for a week before returning home on a Friday night to get his clothes and belongings. UK alumnus Reed Miller came by his house and said, "Get in the car. We're going for a ride."

"Where are we going?"

"Up the road a piece."

They ended up on the UK campus. Hagan decided to stay on a football scholarship. He went out for basketball without an invitation from Rupp and would earn three varsity basketball letters (1936, '37, '38) and would be team captain his senior year.

Warfield Donohue of St. Xavier was an excellent tennis player whose basketball exploits were overshadowed as a college prospect by several other players in Louisville, notably Ellington, Goforth, and Hagan. He went out for the UK basketball team on his own without an invitation from Rupp and would become a three-year starter and team captain in 1937.

Bernie Opper was a high-scoring guard at Morris High in New York and later at a New York prep school. He wanted to attend school away from home and to play for a strong team. "I knew Rupp always had a good record," he told Tev Laudeman of the *Courier-Journal and Times*, "and I saw Kentucky play in 1935 against NYU in Madison Square Garden. I didn't talk to Rupp at the time, but I wrote him a letter and told him I'd like to attend UK. I had recommendations from Clair Bee (LIU coach) and Nat Holman (CCNY coach). Rupp wrote back and said to come on down."

Layton "Mickey" Rouse (1938, '39, '40) of Ludlow, Kentucky, was a 6-foot-1 guard who came in contact with Rupp when the UK coach spoke at the Ludlow basketball banquet. "I recruited myself for Kentucky," he told Laudeman. Rupp invited him to Lexington for a tryout. Playing against the varsity he hit three of four shots and was offered a partial scholarship with the assurance that if he proved himself he would get a full ride. He would make All-SEC in 1940.

Lee Huber (1939, '40, '41) was the best schoolboy tennis player in the state, winning the state high school singles titles as a sophomore and senior (the matches were rained out his junior year). He was also a member of the 1937 St. Xavier basketball team that lost to Midway in the finals of the 1937 State Tournament. His specialty was a two-hand set shot.

"The partial scholarship consisted only of tuition and food," Huber said. "In those days Rupp had a lot of players on the team. He thought he had a fine team my sophomore year,

Layton Rouse, Bernie Opper, Marion M. Cluggish, Jim Goodman, Elmo Head.

so he put me on the 'Z' squad, which was what he called the redshirts. I actually played my last year as a graduate student, and I was captain of the team."

Other names that would become familiar to Wildcat fans during those years preceding World War II were Walter Hodge of Paris (1937), Homer "Tub" Thompson (1937, '38, '39) of Jeffersonville, Jim Goodman (1938, '39) of Paris, Marion Cluggish (1938, '39, '40) of Corbin, Carl "Hoot" Combs (1940) of Hazard, Waller White (1940, '41, '42) of Lawrenceburg, Marvin Akers (1941, '42, '43) of Jeffersonville, Indiana, and Milt Ticco (1941, '42, '43) of Jenkins. Most would receive some type of assistance from the university.

"Some we gave meals, some we gave tuition, some we gave rooms," Rupp said. "I think the first aid came as a result of (Harry) Gamage finally convincing the Athletic Department if they didn't give help of some kind there was no way for us to maintain a program here. They did allocate a little money. The boys stayed at a rooming house on Maxwell Street for about three years for about $3 a week, room and meals, all they could eat. I went up there and ate with them several times, but I don't remember how that thing was financed. I think tuition was an

Lee Huber, Harry Denham, Homer "Tub" Thompson, Keith Farnsley, Fred "Cab" Curtis.

easy thing to give because it didn't cost us anything."

Carl Staker, who would serve as team captain in 1942, came to UK from Maysville, where he was a fine defensive player for one of Earle Jones' State Tournament teams.

"In those days you had to be 'sold' to come to UK," he recalled while attending a K-Men's golf outing at Paintsville, Kentucky, in June, 1975. "Coach Jones had got me an interview with Rupp through Paul McBrayer, so I hitchhiked to Lexington in the summer of 1937 to get in school. After meeting with Rupp and McBrayer at Rupp's house, I was offered a partial scholarship as a freshman. He asked me what I wanted to do, and I said I thought I'd like to be a basketball coach. He and McBrayer looked at each other and he said, 'Staker, you don't want to be a basketball coach. The salary is so small you couldn't live on it.' Since I was a fairly good student in math and science, I told them maybe I'd take engineering, and that's what I did."

"I remember the first aid we gave," Rupp said. "We had a filling station at Euclid and Upper. Pribble was in charge. He was a part-time coach and a full-time insurance man. His job was to find places where these boys could work. We decided to go into the filling station business, providing employment for some of the boys, but that didn't work because there were times when Pribble would come by in the evening to close the station and there was very little cash in the drawer. We were pumping more gas than we were getting money for.

"When the conference came out in December 1935 and said it was okay to give aid, that was just getting it above the table. We knew they were giving aid anyway. It was by outside people and things like that."

During that year, Ralph McGill of the *Constitution* observed, "Kentucky has gone ahead and taken the game seriously. When any sport is taken seriously, it becomes a serious matter; now that Kentucky has developed superior teams it will likely have the other boys taking their game seriously. It is a vicious cycle. But it gets results."

Left to right: George Yates, Aggie Sale, Dave Lawrence, Darrell Darby, and Ellis Johnson.

A Whirling Dervish Job

Wildcat basketball teams during Rupp's first four years at UK compiled a 64-9 record and placed four players—Carey Spicer, Aggie Sale, Ellis Johnson, and John "Frenchy" DeMoisey—on All-American teams.

This was an era spiced by such exciting UK developments as:

DeMoisey's revolutionary hook shot.

Formation of the Southeastern Conference.

A national collegiate record for most consecutive wins (23 from February 6, 1933, to February 24, 1934).

Rupp's opposition to the annual tournament.

Near riots as fans struggled to get into Alumni Gym for home games.

In his first year at UK, Rupp had displayed such intelligence, wit, humor, fine coaching ability, and a general awareness of what the public wanted that he made UK fans forget about Johnny Mauer and other Wildcat coaches up to that time. With the storytelling and superstitious aspects of his nature established, he got down to the business of developing a basketball powerhouse.

It was in March 1931 that he announced his first spring practice, teasing everyone by saying the Wildcats were working on a revolutionary new shot. Four decades later he would not remember any such announcement, but it is a matter of record that DeMoisey's hook shot came to the forefront at that time.

"I wasn't successful in teaching that shot to any of the other boys," Rupp said. "Frenchy was the only one able to make a go of it. It made him an All-American."

Captain-elect George Yates was scheduled to play center that season, but he hurt a shoulder in the UK-Tennessee football game and would not rejoin the squad until the following season. However, Frenchy was still so far down the list that he wondered if he would survive past the Christmas holidays. He got his chance when Rupp called to him in practice one day and said, "Frog, get in there at center against Sale." After Frenchy scored 12 points in 10 minutes, Rupp said, "Move over, Sale. I think I have me a new center."

After Capt. Jake Bronston was declared ineligible for having played four or five minutes against Centre during one season, Johnson was elected captain, becoming the third player that year to have been so designated before the season began. Worthington was the other guard; Sale and Darby were at forward to complete the starting lineup with DeMoisey.

They easily defeated Georgetown, which was coached by Carey Spicer. National recognition of a sort came to the Wildcats when they defeated Carnegie Tech, 36-34, with DeMoisey and Sale combining for 28 points. Berea and Marshall were easy victims and UK had a perfect slate entering the holidays.

DeMoisey was declared ineligible for a brief spell due to a deficiency in sociology. While bringing up his grades in that subject, he learned to shoot his hook shot with his left hand.

Sale shifted to the pivot, and Howard Kreuter moved to forward. Sale scored 17 points in a home win over Clemson. The Wildcats then beat Clemson, Sewanee, and Tennessee on the road and Chattanooga at home. At Knoxville, Sale had what Rupp called his greatest performance, blocking five shots as the Wildcats won by one point. The team was undefeated when DeMoisey rejoined it prior to a game with Washington & Lee on January 30. UK won, 48-28.

Ellis Johnson remembered when he and Frenchy came in late from a movie the night before the game. "Rupp was waiting for us," he said. "He blasted Frenchy mostly. Although we were playing W&L, he told him, 'We don't need you against Vanderbilt,' which was an important upcoming game. I told him if he would let us alone, we would get 30 points against Vanderbilt."

At Nashville, Frenchy scored 29 points and Johnson added a free throw, allowing them to keep the promise to Rupp. A Nashville writer called Frenchy's hook shot "a whirling dervish job that looked like an accident, but wasn't." UK won, 61-37.

The Wildcats were one game shy of a perfect season when

the Commodores defeated them by one point in Lexington. DeMoisey and Sale were ailing with flu at the time and were still slightly under the weather when they played North Carolina in the Southern Tournament. With one minute remaining, Worthington put UK ahead, 42-41, but the Tar Heels scored in the waning seconds to win the game. Here is how Ed Miles of the *Journal* described the action:

> Then a tremendous scrambling under the North Carolina basket—a wild leaping to bat the ball in; a wild lick that caused the ball to bound backward toward the foul line, when inrushing Virgil Weathers spanked it handball fashion and into the basket it went for the greatest victory in the history of the Southern Conference basketball meet.
> The bounding ability of the Kentucky players and the sure dexterity with which they handled the ball and the remarkable accuracy of their goal-shooting on shots made from the most difficult angles conceivable, made them appear the much better team even in defeat.

The Southeastern Conference was formed prior to the 1932-33 season. Charter members were Kentucky, Georgia, Georgia Tech, Alabama, Alabama Polytech (now Auburn), Mississippi, Mississippi State, Louisiana State, Tulane, Tennessee, Sewanee, Vanderbilt, and Florida.

Rupp designed a set of charts that season for designation of shots attempted, shots made and missed, bad passes, intercepted passes, fouls attempted, and fouls committed. They would be the forerunner of the extensive statistical basketball charts in use today. He also instituted a system of scouting foes that he would refine over the years.

Returning veterans were Sale, Johnson, DeMoisey, Darby, and Yates. They were joined by sophomores Davis, Tucker, and Lawrence. Davis started in the backcourt with Johnson; Demoisey was at center, Darby and Sale at forward.

Prior to the tipoff against Georgetown, Rupp walked to the press row, pirouetted, and said, "Look, new from head to foot and all brown." The Wildcats easily defeated Georgetown, Marshall, and Tulane before taking on Chicago on the road and Ohio State at home.

In Chicago, DeMoisey asked sportswriters, "What's the scoring record for this gym?"

John DeMoisey, All-American, 1934.

"Twenty-four points," a writer replied. "Why?"

"Because I'm going to break it."

The partisan crowd sat in amazement as he hit his whirling pivot shots from all angles to lead UK to a 58-26 victory. Rupp took him out after he scored his 24th point.

"I wasn't worried about Frenchy breaking any records," he said. "I'm just concerned that Chicago scored so many points."

Prior to the Ohio State game a mob formed in front of the Alumni Gym entrance, making it impossible for ticket holders to enter. Several persons received minor injuries, and the danger was heightened by boys attempting to climb through the transoms. A woman was knocked down inside the building, and the second half was delayed five minutes while the crowd was cleared from the playing floor. The problem would be solved later by moving the ticket booth away from the gym entrance, roping off that part of the street in front of the gym, and assigning football players to keep order. Students would be admitted through the basement doors, and all doors would be closed after a capacity crowd was admitted. The need for a new field house was evident.

Led by Wilmer Hosket, a 6-foot-5 center who scored 14 points and dominated the boards, the Buckeyes won, 46-30, inflicting on Rupp his worst defeat up to that time in high school or college coaching. Thirty-four years later Hosket's son Bill would make a crucial play to give the Buckeyes an upset victory over the Wildcats in Lexington in a game to decide who would play in the national finals in Los Angeles.

They split two games with Missouri Valley champion Creighton at Omaha, and lost only one other game, to South Carolina, before entering the first annual Southeastern Conference Tournament with a 17-3 record. In Atlanta, Rupp had a student manager go to the auditorium long before gametime and take possession of the left-hand bench, where the team had sat when it won the first game the preceding year.

Sale scored 17 points and DeMoisey 16 in a 49-31 victory over Mississippi. Sale scored 20 in a 48-24 romp over Florida, then outscored Jack Torrance, 20-2, in a 51-38 win over LSU. Rupp cleared his bench as DeMoisey and Sale scored 29 points between them for a 46-27 victory over Mississippi State and UK's first championship in 12 years.

Those 1933 Wildcats outscored their opponents, 1,073-630. Sale set a new individual scoring record for the tournament, and UK set a team high of 48.5 points a game. Sale, DeMoisey, and Johnson were named to the all-conference team, and Johnson was selected on Frank Lane's All-American team. Lt. Gov. A. B. "Happy" Chandler presented Kentucky Colonel commissions to Rupp and all members of the squad, the first time in the history of the Commonwealth that such an honor had been bestowed on an athletic squad and its coach.

They opened the following season with easy victories over the Alumni, Georgetown, and Marshall. Their wins were overshadowed, however, by the resignation of Harry Gamage and the appointment of Chet Wynne, highly successful coach at Auburn, to a three-year term as head football coach and athletic director, with all coaches under his direct supervision.

The basketball team ran its two-season victory string to 17 by the end of January, but attendance at the games experienced a steady drop, due mostly to the fact that football was a main topic of conversation. This irritated Rupp, who entered the New Year with the following suggestions from Neville Dunn:

Now if Snapshots were Coach Rupp, he would resolve:
1. To equip my chair on the sidelines with a friction-proof pillow so as to save the seat of my pants from wear and tear when the score is too close for comfort.
2. To remain silent on the sidelines and not once shout instructions to my team, thus keeping the letter and the spirit of the rule regarding sideline coaching.
3. To speak more kindly to the coaches whose teams defeat mine and not tell them, at least to their faces, that I think they were lucky and that their teams are the poorest aggregations I ever saw.

The Wildcats won their 15 regular season games and were credited with avenging football defeat after football defeat. Anderson was the lone sophomore in a veteran lineup that included DeMoisey, Davis, Tucker, and Lawrence. Their toughest game came at Birmingham, where they rallied in the last five minutes to beat Alabama, 33-28. DeMoisey had his best game in the home finale against Vanderbilt, scoring 25 points in 27 minutes. The 'Cats won, 47-27.

In the opening round of the annual SEC tournament UK was paired with Florida, a team that had been invited only because some of the Ole Miss players were ailing. Florida had lost to some of the weakest teams in the league. Kentucky was such a prohibitive favorite that when the Wildcats left their hotel for the gym, Tucker said, "We'll run out to the auditorium, beat Florida by about 20 points, and hurry back to a big steak supper."

Rupp attempts a "basket in one" during basketball coaches meeting in Atlanta in 1934. From left: Carey Spicer, former Wildcat All-American then coaching at Georgetown; G.N. Amiott, Massachusetts; and A. D. Kahler, Brown.

Florida scored the first four points, but nobody seemed excited; it was just a matter of waiting for the Wildcats to explode. When the Gators scored the next basket, however, the crowd suddenly came alive and began to yell and scream for them. Each foul called on Florida was booed, and the noise was deafening when a Wildcat stepped to the line for a free throw. Florida increased its lead to 18-8, and UK was in trouble. The 'Cats cut the margin to 33-31, but lost 38-32, in an upset of monumental proportions.

When DeMoisey was asked what happened, he replied, "We just came down here to play in the finals. That was our main trouble. We were wondering all along whether it would be Alabama or LSU that we would meet Tuesday night."

Rupp was irritated because the tournament signaled the end of each basketball season. "I see no reason why a basketball team should end its season in February or early March just to permit some of the other schools to start spring football practice early," he said.

His opposition to the tournament had not helped his standing with the SEC coaches or the Atlanta fans and sportswriters. When it was disbanded for one year in 1935, Ed Danforth, of the *Georgian*, in an open letter to UK president McVey, said that Rupp's attitude of victory first and championships above all was a very unwholesome influence on intercollegiate sports, and that Rupp stood alone in that archaic attitude.

Rupp replied that he was interested in scheduling teams that would give UK fans the type of game to which they were entitled. To prove his point he had scheduled a game with NYU the following season in Madison Square Garden. Kentucky basketball was ready to sprout its wings on a nationwide scale.

Ride 'Em, Cowboy

Around the Indianapolis high school circuit, they called 6-foot-5, 210-pound Leroy Edwards the "East Side Terror." At the University of Kentucky he was known as the "Hoosier Horror," "Big Ed," "Big Boy," and "Cowboy."

He thought of himself as "Beefsteak Man."

"I can't do my best on the tea and toast Coach Rupp gives us before a game," he explained after scoring 22 points in an 81-12 UK victory over Oglethorpe in the second game of the 1934-35 season. "Why, if they would give me a couple of beefsteaks before a game, I could really play. It takes a couple of beefsteaks to carry you up and down the floor."

How about that, Adolph?

"He forgot about those two scrambled eggs we gave them with the tea and toast. I guess he just gulped them. He could eat. In fact, he was the second best eater I ever had. And also the strongest player."

Who was the best eater?

"A kid named Steve Schmitt." (Schmitt, a 6-foot-10 center, would leave UK after playing his freshman season in 1968.)

And the second strongest player?

"Dan Issel, then Mike Pratt, and Pat Riley." (Issel would be a UK All-American in 1970, his three-year teammate Pratt would enter the coaching ranks in 1975, while Riley would be an All-American in 1966.)

That's pretty Herculean company. Just how strong was Edwards?

"He could bust the cable over the Golden Gate Bridge."

Come now, let's have something more realistic.

"Okay, he walked up to newspaper reporter Ed Templin, who was a pretty big fellow, before that Oglethorpe game, picked him up from his seat at the press table with one hand and asked, 'Now, what was that you wrote about me not playing a good game last Saturday?'"

Was he serious?

"Edwards? No. He was a non-conformist. I remember when he first came down here. He woke me up at 12:30 at night. I told him there wasn't room and sent him next door to a fraternity house. He stayed eight or 10 days there and wouldn't do anything they said. We finally got him relocated, and the fraternity sent me a bill for his keep. It came to $6."

What did he do in that opening varsity game?

"Oh, he scored 18 points against the Alumni, guys like DeMoisey, Spicer, Settles, McBrayer, Milward, Kleiser, and Krump. We beat them, 61-10. I guess people expected more from him."

Why did they expect more?

"Well, he had scored more than 400 points in 16 games with the freshman team that didn't lose a game. He came up to the varsity with Ralph Carlisle and Warfield Donohue, and I started them most of the games that year, along with Lawrence and Tucker and then Andy Anderson after Tucker broke his hand against Michigan State."

Did he give them more?

"He sure did. He scored 34 points in 34 minutes against Creighton and broke DeMoisey's Alumni Gym record, but he complained after that game."

About what?

"He said he missed too many shots under the basket. That he never played a good game when he shot that much. I encouraged him to shoot whenever the occasion arose."

How good a shooter was he?

"One of the best, and he would tell you so. After he scored 21 points in our victory over Alabama in Birmingham, a woman walked up to him and said, 'You were wonderful. You never missed.'"

What did he say to that?

"He said, 'Listen, I'm not supposed to miss.'"

How did you get him in the first place?

Leroy Edwards.

"I don't know about the standards at Purdue or those other Indiana schools at the time, but none of them seemed interested in him. Perhaps it was because he was so happy-go-lucky that they thought he wasn't interested in higher education. George Keogan, my friend who was coaching at Notre Dame, told me Ed was as big and tough as they come, if we could just get him in school and keep him there. Recruiting wasn't a problem in those times. They didn't have to sign anything. I visited him one time, and he agreed to come down here."

How did you keep him here?

"Well, I didn't for too long. Two years, to be exact, before he turned pro. When he came down, he brought a little fellow (Jack Cronin) with him. We called him 'The Shadow' because he went everywhere Ed went. He carried Ed's books, did his studying for him, and kept Ed in line for me. Ed was in love and always homesick."

How was he as a player?

"Way ahead of his time. A great rebounder with excellent body balance. He could rebound the ball completely over the goal, get it on the other side, and score. He had a fine hook shot. Said he learned it from a bunch of touring pros from Texas who came through Indiana while he was at Tech High in Indianapolis. He went over to Martinsdale to see them play."

When your 1935 team left to play a two-game series with Tulane in New Orleans, you told the press it was Edwards' first train ride. Doesn't that seem rather odd since he was from a metropolitan area?

"No, he did his traveling before that by auto, interurban trains, and street cars. I remember when we went on our first overnight trip down South, and Ed came and said he planned to sit up all night because he was kind of confused by the rows of upper and lower berths. Figuring that he might grasp the idea if he were to watch the other players go to bed, I suggested that he do that. It was some time later that night that a long arm reached into my berth and shook me. I rolled over and looked up into his smiling face. He said, 'Think I got 'er now, coach,' and he went happily off to sleep."

It made a good story?

"A better story was the way he helped us handle Tulane. He scored 10 points in the first game, and we held them to three field goals and beat them, 38-9. In the second game he got

18 points, and we beat them, 52-12. We were leading, 18-0, with 10 minutes gone when they scored their first point."

In your 42-16 victory over Chicago that year, Edwards scored 26 points. A newspaperman said Chicago used everything but lariats, bludgeons, harpoons, and blackjacks in an effort to stop him.

"They were plenty rough, but that was mild compared to what 'King King' Klein and 'Slim' Terjesen would try to do to him in Madison Square Garden."

That was Kentucky's first visit to the Big City?

"So it was. They had started doubleheaders in the Garden the week before. Ned Irish, then a newspaper reporter, started it all when he talked the folks there into renting the building to him for college games. He got the idea when he tore his pants trying to climb through a window to get into a ball game in a packed auditorium. I knew Ned well, and he never denied the story. He invited us to come up and play, and we accepted. It introduced our boys to Eastern fans."

There was quite a controversy surrounding that game?

"It has been reported dozens of times, and is reported here, as possibly the roughest game that has ever been played. NYU knew that Edwards was big, strong, and a deadly scorer under the basket, and they would not permit him to get under the basket."

How did they stop him?

"The way those two centers kicked each other around, shoving, pushing, holding, and all those things, both should have been thrown out of the game in two minutes."

You had another problem?

"Our attack was built around some screens that were perfectly legal in the South and Midwest. Lo and behold, as our boys attempted to set up their plays, they were called for screening. Naturally they were thrown off their game, and I was at a loss to understand the interpretation of the rule.

"At the half I went to the official (Jack Murray) and politely asked him what we were doing that we should not have been doing. The only answer I got was, 'You know what you're doing. It isn't legal.'"

How did NYU win the game?

"With eight seconds to go and the score tied, 22-22, Murray called Edwards for setting an illegal screen. They made the free throw to win the game. We felt bad about this. As far as I

knew, everything that I had taught them was perfectly legitimate and was also being taught in every section of the U. S. outside of the New York City area."

What were the repercussions?

"When movies of the game were shown at a meeting of the Rules Committee, the play of the pivot men under the basket was so rugged that it shocked the coaches who saw it. The three-second rule was put in that year to force the pivot man away from the basket, and the screening rule was given its first long session of housecleaning."

Were you satisfied then?

"The screening rule has never been cleared up to my satisfaction even to this day. It varies according to the section of the country where you go. If you play on the Pacific Coast, you get called for some things you don't get called for someplace else. In NCAA tournaments they swap officials around, section to section, in order that you don't get any 'homers,' guys who favor the home team.

"When we draw a Pacific Coast Conference official, the Southern teams really get blistered because we just don't play the way they play out there. We played Southern California one time out there and, if I am correct in my memory, they called fifteen fouls on us before they called the first foul on them. Our game was practically shot by that time, and our boys were under such a severe handicap that they were afraid to even move. We lost that ball game."

You said there was no use taking a team to New York until they changed the rules on screening, but you would be back there the following year?

"Yes, and Murray was officiating again. I objected, but to no avail. We got the opening tip, and Carlisle was called for blocking on our first offensive play. Our Captain 'Red' Hagan later got into an argument with Murray that held up play for more than a minute in the second half after Red was called for blocking. They beat us, 41-28, and we didn't return to the Garden until three years later. We would lose to Long Island and then beat St. John's in 1943 for our first victory there, beat Long Island in overtime the following year, and then beat St. John's again in 1945. So we weren't doing badly."

You could have done better with Edwards?

"No doubt about it. His loss was a big blow, because at that time he was a bonafide All-American, not one of these southern breeze All-Americans that you pick up if you don't make the AP or UPI. It was the Edwards team that gave us our first national publicity."

Did you have any idea that he wouldn't return from Indianapolis?

"Naturally I thought he was coming back in his junior year, but a rubber company had a team—they called it AAU

Three coaches' opinion on the pivot play, left to right: F. C. Allen of Kansas, who would outlaw the play entirely; Rupp, who approved the play; and Nat Holman of City College of New York, who would modify the play.

since there was no such thing as the pros then—and they talked him into staying."

Was that hard?

"Well, they paid him $200 a month, which wasn't a bad job. That's $2,400 a year. I was only making $2,800 to coach the team here, so he decided to just lay out and play ball up there and support his wife."

Were you for the marriage?

"I remember I was violently opposed to it. In those days an athlete just didn't get married. There is no use kidding anybody. When these kids have to have scholarships to go to school, how are they going to support a wife? I've just never been able to figure that out."

How do you compare him with other centers you've coached and played against?

"I was asked that same question, but in another manner, by reporters after Jacksonville beat us in the 1970 Mideast Regional at Columbus. They asked me if Artis Gilmore was the greatest pivot man I had ever seen?"

Was he?

"I told them 'No!'"

Then they asked who was?

"That's right."

And you told them?

"Leroy Edwards."

What did they say?

"Some of them laughed. Others looked puzzled. That shows you how much some so-called experts know about the game."

Nothing's Wrong

From the time the University of Kentucky helped usher in the modern era of basketball (1934-35) until the advent of World War II, Wildcat teams compiled a record of 112 wins and 36 losses. They were 58-15 against teams in the Southeastern Conference, 54-21 against teams outside the conference.

Six of the nonconference losses were to Notre Dame, two to NYU, and one each to Detroit, LIU, Nebraska, and Indiana in the only games the Wildcats played against those teams during that period. Kentucky was 3-3 vs. Michigan State, 4-2 vs. Creighton, 12-2 vs. Xavier, and 2-1 vs. both West Virginia and Cincinnati. The Wildcats held the edge over Marquette (3-0), Pittsburgh (2-0), Kansas State (2-0), Butler, Akron, St. Joseph's, Ohio State, and Chicago, playing one game each with the latter five teams.

Rupp had first exposed his "pore li'l mountain boys" to the Chicago area during the 1932-33 season, beating Chicago, 58-26. Chicago returned the visit in 1935, losing to the Wildcats, 42-16, in Lexington only three days before UK made its debut in Madison Square Garden. The losses to NYU and to Michigan State at East Lansing were the only blemishes on the Wildcat record that season. Both teams were first-time foes for UK.

One of the fine teams UK met early in the 1935-36 season was Pittsburgh, which featured a "figure eight" offense that Dr. H. C. Carlson, the Panther coach, had made famous nationally. The object was to keep the entire team in perpetual motion, giving the defensive men no time to get set, and striking with what was considered furious speed in those days. There were

Jim Goodman of Kentucky and Art Hillhouse of Long Island at Madison Square Garden.

times when Pitt kept the ball moving at top speed for as long as 15 minutes without taking a shot.

"Doc wrote me and said they'd like to pick up a game on the way to the Sugar Bowl," Rupp said. "I didn't know a thing about that 'Figure Eight,' but I did know that Pitt was regarded right up there with Notre Dame, Indiana, Wisconsin, Purdue, Kansas, and other outstanding teams in the nation. It was a chance for us to 'break the barrier,' so we gave them $300 to come here."

En route to New Orleans, Carlson also scheduled games with Butler and Xavier. After watching the game in the Butler Field House, Rupp had his assistant Len Miller drive him back to the hotel where they were to spend the night.

"Pitt absolutely tore Butler apart," he recalled. "I told Len, 'Get the car. I'm not going to sleep after that game. I've got my work cut out for me.'"

They arrived in Lexington about 4 a.m., and Rupp still could not sleep. Finally he came up with the idea of virtually zoning the cutter on the Figure Eight. When Pitt sent a man out to screen, and the cutter went around the screen, Rupp temporarily abandoned his man-to-man defense and had his defender make an automatic switch on the cutter.

The move worked so well in the first half that Pitt only scored two points while UK was tallying 22 points. Rupp cleared his bench in the second half, holding the final margin to 35-17.

"I didn't want to crush Doc," he said. "It sure wouldn't look good to go to the Sugar Bowl with a whipping like we were inflicting on them in the first half."

The next day he and Mrs. Rupp took a box of oranges, bananas, and cookies to the train station for the Pitt players. Carlson had purchased 10 little elephant pins and attached one to each boy's shoulder. After he took a picture of Rupp and players, he told them, "An elephant never forgets. I want you to never forget the humiliation you got here in Lexington. I'm going to make each of you a copy of this picture to be sure you won't forget."

Two years later the Wildcats made their first appearance in the Sugar Bowl, meeting Pitt in a two-team affair. When the Pitt players could not get layups off their Figure Eight, they refused to shoot. UK held a 28-13 halftime lead.

Pitt's Ed Spotovich and Bob Johnson started hitting in the second half, but Hagan kept UK out of danger. Hagan finished with nine points and was presented the game ball. After the game, Carlson gathered up a bunch of sweat clothes, rushed up to Rupp and dumped them at Rupp's feet. "Here, take these," he said. "You've taken everything else."

After their 1935 victory over Pitt, the Wildcats made their second appearance in Madison Square Garden, losing to NYU. They defeated Tulane (twice), Michigan State, and Tennessee before losing to Vanderbilt at Nashville, their first regular season conference loss in four years.

Notre Dame more than doubled the score on them (41-20) in South Bend, although Keogan pulled his regulars early. Tennessee beat them at Knoxville, and Creighton surprised them in the second game of a two-night stand in Lexington. The Bluejays were an easy (68-38) victim the first night, but Eddie Hickey, in his first season at Creighton, shuffled his lineup to

Donohue tries crip for UK vs. NYU in Madison Square Garden in 1935.

get more height and revamped his style of play, resorting to a slower attack. Creighton won, 31-29, inflicting on the Wildcats their first loss at home in 40 games.

"He just slowed the game down completely," Rupp said. "He did exactly what his old mentor (A. A. Schabinger) had taught him—don't run with Kentucky." Many other coaches through the years would realize the folly of running with the Wildcats.

UK finished with a 15-6 record after losing to Tennessee, 39-28, in the conference tournament, which was revived and held in Knoxville that year after a one-year absence. The record was Rupp's worst in six years at UK.

The following year the Wildcats won five straight games, including a 28-21 conquest of Michigan State. Then they lost to Notre Dame, 41-28, before 6,352 persons in the Jefferson County Armory, largest crowd up to that time to see a basketball game in Kentucky. It was the first appearance of a Rupp-coached team in Louisville.

After a victory over Creighton at home and a loss to Michigan State, 24-23, at East Lansing, the Wildcats won four in a row, split two games with Tulane, defeated Mexico City, lost to Alabama and Tennessee, and ended the season with victories over Vanderbilt, 51-19, and Xavier. They were 14-5 entering the conference tournament, and UK fans were asking, "What's wrong?"

"I don't know if there was anything wrong," Rupp said. "It was just that Michigan State and Notre Dame had good basketball teams, and these other teams (in the South) were beginning to catch up. Hank Crisp was coaching at Alabama at the time. We usually played them in Birmingham. They had a place in Tuscaloosa that was awful. After we beat them so many times, they put up Foster Auditorium, which was a fairly nice place, but it wouldn't do in these days at all.

"Hank told me he was going to beat me if it was the last thing he did. So he got himself in some basketball players. I remember he had a great big center named Jim Whatley. He was a football player and just too big for us, and they beat us."

The Wildcats beat LSU, Georgia Tech, and Tennessee for the championship of the conference tournament, giving them two championships in the four tournaments held since the SEC was formed. They had also shared a championship in 1935, when no tournament was held.

The victory over Pitt in the 1937 Sugar Bowl gave them a 4-0 slate in December of that year. They went north in early January and lost three games in a row, a first for a Rupp-coached team, falling to Michigan State (42-37), Detroit (34-26), and Notre Dame (47-37).

In the summer of 1975 Fred "Cab" Curtis of Nashville, Tennessee, would remember those losses. "After we got beat we had one of those meetings," he said. "Paul McBrayer was the chairman of the board. If you had anything to say, you had to stand up and say it. Adolph just wanted to know what was the cause of all the troubles. If you're not passing me the ball, I'm not passing you the ball, and all that stuff. It was just one of those heart-to-heart talks.

"Finally it got around to 'Tub' Thompson. He said, 'Coach, I think you're calling us too many s.o.b.'s.' Adolph said, 'Well, I'm going to say this. If you don't like it, you can turn in your uniform and go back where you came from.' We only lost one of the next 10 regular season games. Then Tulane beat us in the conference tournament."

One of those games was the first meeting between athletic teams from UK and Marquette. A capacity crowd turned out to witness the event in Alumni Gym. The game boiled down to the final seconds with the score tied, UK in possession, and time out on the floor.

"I told the boys we were going to take the last shot and win, or go into overtime," Rupp said. "After they went back onto the floor, they all got in a huddle together. The official blew the whistle, and they all got up and went to their positions. There was 'Red' Hagan, kneeling on the floor, praying. He crossed himself and he was completely unaware of the whistle being blown, but he got up, ran to his position, and when they threw the ball to him, he hit the longest shot ever made in Alumni Gym up to that time. It measured 48 feet 2¼ inches."

"I thought it would take 1,000 years to come down," Hagan said. "Then I saw it go through the hoop. Next thing I knew, Happy Chandler was on the floor with a nail and hammer. He drove the nail through the floor at the spot I took the shot."

The 'Cats were 4-0 the following year when LIU beat them, 52-34, behind the fine shooting of Irving Torgoff, in Madison Square Garden. They beat St. Joseph's in Philadelphia and gave Notre Dame a tough battle before falling, 42-37, in Louisville. Back-to-back losses to Alabama and Tennessee gave Rupp three defeats in a row two years in a row. They got back on the winning track by beating Vanderbilt, 51-37, and then came home to meet Marquette, which was playing in Lexington for the second year in a row.

"Adolph played only seven men in that game," Lee Huber said. "I remember Don Orme came in and hit four or five long shots in a row, and we upset Marquette, 37-31. Adolph was so happy that for the first time he let us go out and do what we wanted."

After the three back-to-back losses, the Wildcats had put together an eight-game winning streak before entering the SEC tournament. One of the late season victories was a two-point decision over Tennessee on a shot by Farnsley from the foul line midway of a second overtime.

In the championship game of the annual tournament, Opper scored three baskets to get UK moving after Tennessee took an 18-11 lead in the early going. Opper scored 13 points to spark the 'Cats to a 46-38 victory. He was an almost unanimous choice for All-SEC and would be named All-America that year.

The flu bug would hurt the Wildcats in 1940, but not before they had won six of their first seven games, including a 36-30 victory over powerful Ohio State in the Sugar Bowl. Notre Dame beat them, 52-47, behind Ed Riska's 17 points at South Bend. They defeated Tennessee in Lexington, but lost to Alabama and Vanderbilt on the road. Although Huber was ailing with the flu, they beat a good Marquette team at Milwaukee.

They bowed to Tennessee and Georgia Tech on the road before closing the season with a win over Vanderbilt at home. They beat the Commodores in the first game of the annual tournament and were leading Tennessee by two points in the closing minute when Huber and Rouse rebounded a shot into the basket for the Vols.

"My hand hit the ball just as Mickey went up," Huber would explain later, "and I tipped it in to tie the score and send the game into overtime. I remember Adolph saying, 'God, now you're making it for them.'

"I remember taking the ball out of bounds on a play designed to go to either of two people. Farnsley was open over on the side, and I threw it to him. He made a long hook shot to win the game."

"The tournament finale against Georgia was merely an anti-climax," the *Kernel* reported, "and so certain were Knoxville partisans that Kentucky had the game in the bag that fewer than 600 customers paid to boo the Cats and see them win by 51-43."

Rouse was voted a guard position on the Associated Press all-conference team. Farnsley rated a second team berth, while Cluggish, Allen, and Carl Combs, who so ably filled in for Huber in the latter stages of the season, received honorable mention.

Huber would become UK's seventh All-American in 1941, a year in which a UK team would make its longest trip West, traveling to Lincoln, Nebraska, and Manhattan, Kansas. On the tour they would encounter two innovations—semicircular backboards and the molded ball—both standard equipment in the Big Six.

Prior to the journey the 'Cats had defeated the Alumni, West Virginia, and Maryville. They lost to Nebraska, 40-39, and Creighton, 54-45, before salvaging some prestige by downing Kansas State, 28-25. Nebraska hit 14 of 22 free throws; in the Creighton game, 23 fouls were called against UK, 14 against the host team. The Wildcats returned home to defeat Centenary, 70-18, before meeting Indiana in the Sugar Bowl.

With the Hoosiers' Herm Schaefer and Bill Menke threatening to make the game a runaway in New Orleans, Huber started hitting from the outside and pulled UK within three points (48-45) of IU before time ran out. A New Orleans writer said Huber received a bigger ovation than did the Indiana team when post-game honors were distributed. Huber later would be named to the all-time Sugar Bowl basketball team.

Trailing Notre Dame, 36-19, in Louisville, UK thought it had a 47-47 tie when the final gun sounded. Both teams were still on the floor and ready for an overtime when the official scorers informed them that the Irish had won by 48-47. A check of the official scorebook showed that the boys on the scoreboard had overlooked a Notre Dame free throw near the end of the game.

After that game the Wildcats defeated Xavier and lost to West Virginia and Tennessee. They defeated Georgia Tech in Atlanta and returned home to end January with a loss to Xavier in Alumni Gym. Throughout that loss, Rupp, dogged by a chest cold, sat wrapped in a big overcoat. At that point in time the 'Cats were 6-7, worst record in his coaching career. He was con-

Mel Brewer goes up for a tip in UK's contested 48-47 loss to Notre Dame in Louisville in 1941. He was killed in World War II.

fined to bed in the Good Samaritan Hospital and did not accompany the team to Vanderbilt. The 'Cats defeated the Commodores, 51-50, to start an 11-game winning streak that did not end until Tennessee beat them, 36-33, in the conference tournament, which was moved to Louisville that year.

Kentucky's Huber, Akers, and King were named to the All-SEC team that year, but so were Tennessee's Bernie Mehen, Frank Thomas, and Gil Huffman. It appeared that at least Tennessee was beginning to gain on UK just as World War II approached.

Echoes From The '30s

(In the world of thoroughbred racing practically everybody knew Allan "Doc" Lavin, who as director of racing for Churchill Downs annually put together the field for the Kentucky Derby. Doc died in 1974. The author received the following letter from Doc in 1970.)

Dear Russell:

I have quite a few plaques and awards in my den here at home, and they were received mostly in the 'thoroughbred world'—but also hanging there is the picture of Rupp's first team, including *me*.

Although I did play in his first game, I also probably hold two records: (1) at 5-7 ¾ I claim to be the shortest man to have ever worn a uniform for Rupp and (2) I challenge anyone for minutes spent on the bench.

I was cut off of the freshman team early in the season as Coach Peter Potter said the squad was too unwieldy and I had no chance to go any place anyway. I guess he knew that I came from Athens High School (Fayette County) which did not have a gym or coach and all we learned of the game was from a book by Craig Ruby, coach at the University of Illinois.

When I was game enough to go out for the varsity and see the list dwindle from an original 125 (approx.) to 100-75-50-25 and a final 16, I was still there. I dropped out of school in 1931 (junior year) due to the fact that I liked to eat, and if you think everybody was eating during the '29-31 era ask some old fogey like me.

My impression and association of His Holiness—The Baron? I will be ever grateful to him because of a short time around him I have gotten many miles of publicity from coast to coast and of one comment which was picked up by AP and UPI. I was often asked what kind of a player I was, and I said I was a situation player. When I was put in a game we were too far in front for the opposition to catch us—or too far behind for us to ever catch up.

I spent much time out of Kentucky the past 40 years, and the mention of Kentucky and basketball or the fact that you are a Kentucky Colonel will immediately create an interested audience. A current Kentucky Colonel card is just about as valuable as a BankAmericard—if you are about four states distance from the Commonwealth.

When Rupp arrived at Lexington, he had lost the figure he had when he was performing for Phog Allen at Kansas. In several of his ball handling operations for the benefit of us rookies it showed that he had not been taking his daily dozen push-ups during the previous few years. He got his points over well just the same.

Rupp as I knew him had a touch of "Patton" in him, and when he arrived at UK he was presented with one All-American (Carey Spicer), and two (Ellis Johnson and Darrell Darby) who played on the Ashland High School National Championship team—plus "Aggie" Sale, another gifted sophomore who was a high school All-American if there ever was one.

I don't think that any coach ever walked into a greater wealth of talent. Rupp knew what to do with the material when he did get it, which helped make him great. I know several players which thought he was a great guy—while I knew several who hated him with a passion. This is perhaps natural on all teams when everybody can't be in the starting five.

           Doc

Forest Sale (1931, '32, and '33)
Harrodsburg, Kentucky

Dear Russell:

In January of 1933 we were playing South Carolina at Columbia. I had been eating too much and drinking too many milk shakes and consequently had accumulated a few extra pounds and was not playing as well as I should have been playing. In fact, on this particular night my playing was terrible. At the half, when Coach Rupp was saying a few words to us, he looked directly at me and said, "Sale, I guess you have your newspaper clippings with you tonight."

We made all our trips by train, arriving at a small railroad station some three or four miles from the college (Clemson). After our games we would eat in the college dining hall and then go back to our sleeping car waiting for us on a side track. Much later, after we had all gone to bed, the Pullman car would be hooked onto the main train for our return trip to Kentucky. Meanwhile Coach Rupp would remain outside in an automobile talking with the Clemson coach while we were supposed to be sleeping. One night some of the boys began throwing paper cups full of water. After taking all the nonsense I could take, I joined in the fight. It so happened just as I was crawling down the aisle with a cup of water, Coach came in and stumbled over me. All the other boys were quietly sleeping in their berths, and I was the only one to receive the blame and the resultant tongue-lashing. However, Coach Rupp readily realized what had been going on—that there were others involved besides me."

Sincerely,

Aggie

Jack Tucker (1933, '34, and '35)
Paris, Kentucky

Dear Russell:

During the 1933-34 season—my first year as a regular varsity player—we were playing the University of Cincinnati in old Alumni Gym and, as the game progressed, I was fouled and went to the free throw line and missed both of them. A little later on I was fouled again for two shots, and I knew I had better make these because Coach Rupp was breathing down my neck. I stepped up and got the ball and behold!...I missed these too.

Although we beat Cincinnati—and after the game Coach Rupp told us we played a nice game—I was still very uncomfortable about missing those four free throws. This was on Saturday night. The following Monday we reported to practice and, as usual, Coach Rupp had us sit down around the center circle while he reviewed the Cincinnati game with us.

After the review he told us to start running some drills. I took my place and he yelled, "Tucker, come here and get that chair and place it on the foul line and you sit there the rest of the afternoon and look at that goal"...which I did...with much embarrassment while the other players came by and made remarks to me which did not help matters. My foul shooting percentage the rest of the season was quite good.

During the 1934-35 season when big Leroy Edwards was our center, we were playing Tulane at New Orleans and in those days we played both Friday and Saturday nights. On Friday night "Big Ed" did not have a very good game and did not have too many points on the record book. Coach Rupp was not happy with his playing at all.

The next night Rupp called Ed over and told him if he scored 25 points he would buy him the best pair of Florsheim shoes in Lexington.

The game was up to about four minutes to play, and Ed had 22 points when Rupp took him out. Ed was working hard on that pair of shoes, which he needed very badly. He was sitting on the bench thinking that he would not have a chance to get his 25 points. With two minutes left to play, Coach put him back in the game.

I knew that Ed needed three more points to get his shoes, so I called time out and we went into our huddle, where I told the other members of the team that Ed needed three points to get a pair of shoes.

The team worked the ball down and passed it to Ed so that he could score. As soon as he got his 25 points, he took himself out of the game and went to sit on the bench with Rupp to discuss the shoes.

    Jack

    Fred Curtis (1937, '38,
      and '39)
    Nashville, Tennessee

Fred "Cab" Curtis wanted to play basketball for UK, but the year was 1935 and he was reluctant to give up a good job in a shoe factory. Rupp had called Jimmy Armistead, Cab's coach at East Nashville High School, to see if Cab was going to accept his scholarship offer. (Armistead called Fred "Cab" because he was from Nashville's Cab Hollow.)

Dear Russell:

I was working at Carter Shoe Factory and playing basketball and softball for them. The job paid 35 cents an hour and that was good money. So when Armistead called me about the scholarship, I told him, "I don't know if I ought to give up this job for an education. I'm making 35 cents an hour, and that's a dime more than folks who've been here 10 years."

My job was bed-lasting shoes, where your hands get so sore you can't even scratch. (He gave that up to play for UK. When his girl friend, Nell Jones, who would later become his wife, put him on a midnight bus for Lexington, he was attired in a new $10 suit and a new pair of Friendly Five shoes.)

> I got all cleaned up at the hotel and went to see Adolph. He looked at me and said, "Hell, Armistead said you need help. You got better clothes than me."

Curtis was 6-foot-3 and a teammate of Marion Cluggish, a 6-foot-8 center who would later play for the New York Knicks. J. Rice Walker was the UK captain.

> Before the game started, we always dribbled the ball the length of the floor, and Cluggish would stuff it through the hoop. Adolph said such showmanship would win over a critical crowd.
> We were playing LIU in Madison Square Garden. So when we dribbled down the floor, J. Rice passed the ball off to Clug to stuff. Clug was nervous and missed the basket, and we got the thunder beat out of us (52-34).
> Adolph warned Clug, "We'll be playing (St. Joseph's) in a new place in Philadelphia, son, and it'll be a critical crowd. Now, by gravy, Walker's gonna dribble down the floor and give you a good pass before the game. I want you to jam your arm through that basket, or I'm going to ship your tail back to Corbin." Clug made the basket. We won, 41-30. I got 19 points.

Cab also remembered when UK was in Baton Rouge for a tournament.

> Adolph gave us two dollars a day for meals. He'd always say, "Now, boys, lay off the girls and the booze." We didn't do any drinking, but we'd spend the dime for milk and 15 cents for a po-boy sandwich and keep the rest for girls.
> When we ate together as a team, he wanted us to eat all we wanted—if it didn't cost more than 45 cents. We ate the regular lunch, and I also bought a salad that cost 45 cents. When he saw the two meal checks I had signed for a total of 90 cents, he sent the team manager to get me.
> "Well, Mr. Curtis," he said, waving the checks in the air, "I see your eyes are bigger than your belly again. You can't eat like the rest of us. Well, Mr. Curtis, if you don't

play me some basketball and make me some points tonight, I'm gonna ship your tail back to Cab Holler."

Sincerely,

Cab

Ralph Carlisle (1935, '36, and '37)
Lexington, Kentucky

Ralph Carlisle was so excited over the prospects of playing NYU in Madison Square Garden in January, 1935, that he did not discover until two minutes before the train was to leave Lexington that he had forgotten his basketball uniform. While he made a headlong dash to Alumni Gym, some five or six blocks away, C&O officials generously agreed to delay the departure of their fastest train.

When Carlisle arrived back at the station and boarded the train, he remembered that he had left his suitcase in the Union Station waiting room. With another mad dash he retrieved the bag; a few seconds later the train, with Carlisle and teammates aboard, pulled out of the station.

Rupp & Ready

In New York, Rupp told Paul Gardner of the *American* that some of his boys had never seen a train before they came to the Big City and that some had never tried basketball before they got to Kentucky. When another writer asked if he could suggest some changes in the game, Rupp replied, "Sure, put the center jump back, take the backboard and net off—just leave the hoop on—and raise the hoop five feet."

"You don't really believe that, do you, Coach?" one of the Wildcats asked later.

"Hell, no!" Adolph replied, "But anything for a column."

When asked what happened against NYU in his team's first appearance in Madison Square Garden, Rupp replied, "I was heading for home the next morning, a Sunday, and I saw on one of their church signs where the sermon topic that day was, 'I was a stranger and they took me in.' That's all I know about it."

> Joe Hagan (1936, '37, and '38)
> Louisville, Kentucky

After UK defeated Alabama for the second time in a row in Lexington in 1936, Joe (Red) Hagan grabbed the game basketball and ran to the locker room with it. He wanted it for shooting practice, but Rupp also wanted it, and he followed Hagan and demanded the ball. When Hagan handed it to him with a little more force than necessary, Rupp said, "That will be all for you," and had Athletic Director Chet Wynne suspend the player.

When the Wildcats prepared to leave on Sunday for a Monday game with Notre Dame, Hagan accompanied teammates Ellington and Goforth to the station. Rupp asked, "What are you doing here?" Then he added, "Well, as long as you're here, you might as well make the trip because it'll be the last one you'll make anyway."

When UK fell behind 14 points in the first half, Rupp pulled a piece of paper from his pocket, waved it down to Hagan, who was sitting on the end of the bench, and said, "I just got a telegram. Your suspension has been lifted, and you can go in now."

Hagan scored six field goals, but UK lost the game, 41-20.

ON THE AIR

The first radio broadcast of a Kentucky basketball game was held March 7, 1935, at the season finale against Xavier in

Alumni Gym. Earlier that season several simulated accounts of out-of-town games were broadcast from the studios of WLAP. Ed Ashford re-created the play-by-play from wire reports while an engineer provided sound effects. The State Tournament also was broadcast for the first time that year, with Rupp and A. B. "Happy" Chandler assisting Ashford at the microphone.

Dear Bernie:

In the mad scramble following the game I did not get a chance to express to all the Kentucky boys my congratulations on their fine victory. You have a fine team and one that adds further prestige to our fine type of ball played in the SEC.

Your own performance in the tournament was the best I have seen, and you have been a fine leader and player. I hope that all future games between Kentucky and Tennessee are as well played and that the keen rivalry and good feelings between the boys will continue in years to come.

I hope that you will convey these sentiments to all members of the squad, coaches and friends of Kentucky, and that you continue to be as successful in whatever you do as you have been in basketball.

Sincerely,

Johnny Mauer
Basketball Coach
University of Tennessee
March 5, 1939

Dear Coach Rupp:

The boys on the basketball team here at State have asked me to write you and compliment you and your team upon the splendid exhibition of sportsmanship which you displayed during our game here Feb. 13 (1935).

We want you to know that we are proud to have played against as fine an aggregation as you have turned out this year, and that we appreciate the splendid way in which your boys took the outcome of the game (UK lost, 32-26). We sincerely believe that we are expressing not only our own opinion but that of the entire student body and the hundreds of fans who watched your team play.

Our midwestern basketball is usually a case of "dog eat dog," and it is a real treat to play as cleanly a fought game as was ours. We begin to understand much better the expression "Southern gentlemen."

We are extremely sorry that Mr. Tucker was hurt in our game, and hope that his services will not be lost to the team for long. We would like to express our admiration for Anderson, who, we understand, played the entire game with a painful toe injury. In conclusion it is our opinion that your team is the finest in every respect we have seen in action this year, and believe that in Edwards you have a true All-American.

>Sincerely,
>
>R. C. Herrick
>(Michigan State star guard)

>Pat Harmon
>Sports Editor
>The *Cincinnati Post*
>*and Times-Star*

Dear Russell,

Adolph had a positive attitude about matters that concerned him. I once asked a former member of the UK athletic board how the board had happened to hire Adolph, a mere high school coach, in 1930. The board member said, "Because he told us, 'I'm the best damned basketball coach in the United States,' and he convinced us he was."

The fact he won so many conference championships

plus four national championships leads me to believe he was right when he said he was the best coach anywhere.

Sincerely,
Pat Harmon

Frank Lane, a noted baseball executive, was also a nationally known basketball official who "called" many games involving UK teams. He told the following story about a game involving the University of Kentucky in the early 1930s:

I believe the oddest decision I ever witnessed in any kind of a contest occurred in a basketball game in which Kentucky participated and, possibly, ultimately resulted in the Wildcats losing a very important contest. Because it is only human to err and the fact that the chap officiating that game is a very high-class gentleman, I refrain from mentioning in which particular game this rather dubious decision was made as it might identify him. However, it did not occur at Lexington so but a few of the Wildcat adherents witnessed the faux pas in question.

During this exciting and hotly contested game wherein any single play might have been the margin of victory or defeat, a Kentucky try for goal late in the game missed, and Aggie Sale and "Dutch" Kreuter "followed up" the unsuccessful shot. Sale was just a trifle ahead of the Newport Dutchman and was actually trying a shot for the basket when Kreuter's big mitts, in a belated attempt for the ball, slammed across "Aggie's" arms. "Hacking—two shots," rang out the official's voice, synchronizing with a shrill blast from the protesting whistle.

Sale perched himself on the foul line preparatory to pitching the fouls when the captain of the opposing five, awakened to the situation that neither he nor his teammates had fouled, asked who committed the infraction. The referee, still expectantly waiting for Sale to start the foul-throwing, casually pointed out the offender—Krueter!

The referee then quickly realized the fact that he had awarded two free throws because of a Kentucky player fouling (?) another teammate—of course, he knew this could not be. But the argument ended, which no one in the audience ever has gotten the straight of, with the referee calmly but firmly walking to the other end of the floor and giving Kentucky's opponents a free throw— which was made! Quite likely Kentucky's amazed team said something untoward as to the official's eyesight or judgment that may have caused this penalty, but just the same the Wildcats lost the game by one point. No, this was not in the last few seconds or minutes of play when the odd decision was made—there still was about 10 minutes to play—but this point, the margin of the Wildcats' defeat, was certainly very pertinent no matter when the weird ruling occurred.

The Beardless Wonders

On the afternoon of December 7, 1941, Kenny Rollins and Mulford "Muff" Davis walked out of a picture show and into a war.

"It was about 2:30 or 3:00, and newsboys were running up and down the streets of Lexington announcing the news that Japan had attacked Pearl Harbor," Rollins recalled in the summer of 1975. "It shocked us both. We didn't know what would happen."

At the time Rollins and Davis were freshmen basketball players at UK, two of only five who had been chosen from about three dozen who had tried out for Rupp four months earlier.

"I was leading scorer and two-year captain on my high school team at little Wickliffe in Western Kentucky," Kenny said. "We never went to the regional or state tournament. The only recognition I got was in the final game of the 1941 district tournament, when I played exceptionally well."

Some people who saw that performance contacted both Ed Diddle of Western and Rupp about the possibilities of Rollins receiving a scholarship.

"Even in my wildest dreams I never dreamed of coming to Kentucky," Kenny said. "I went to Bowling Green and tried out for five or six days for 'Uncle Ed.' He finally told me, 'Kenny, you have the talent, but you're a little small for my style of basketball, and I don't have any more scholarships available for small men.'"

Diddle then asked him to attend Western at his own expense and try out for the team. If he made it, he would get a scholarship.

"I was crushed," Kenny said. "So were mom and dad. We had just about given up any thought of me getting a scholarship in basketball when I got a letter from Rupp inviting me to UK.

"Adolph had called in 35 boys from all over the U. S. He sat on one side of the floor, and Paul McBrayer sat on the other side. After five or six days of intense scrimmages and workouts, I was one of those he selected. I don't know that I've sensed any greater feeling than when he told me I was one of the five. Perhaps winning a gold medal in the 1948 Olympics equaled it."

While Rollins and Davis were leading McBrayer's freshmen to a clean sweep of their abbreviated four-game schedule, Rupp was having trouble finding a starting varsity combination. He finally settled on Allen and White at forwards, Brewer at center, and Akers and Staker at guard. During the season King would draw several starts at center, England at guard, and Ticco, Ramsey, and Splane at forward.

On the eve of Japan's attack on Pearl Harbor they defeated Miami of Ohio, 35-21. Ticco was high-point man with nine points in a 43-41 loss to Ohio State at Columbus, but he missed a shot under the basket near the end of the game, causing Rupp to sarcastically suggest that Ohio State award him a varsity letter.

They defeated Nebraska, South Carolina, Texas A&M, and Washington & Lee at home before journeying to Cincinnati for a game with Xavier. With eight seconds to go Xavier led by one point and had possession of the ball. A Musketeer was called for traveling, Allen took the pass on the throw in, missed a shot, and was fouled with four seconds left. He made both shots, giving Kentucky a 40-39 victory.

"It was like sitting in the electric chair, strapped and ready for the executioner to throw the switch, and then having a fellow dash in and yell, 'Hold it, we got a reprieve,'" Rupp said. "That boy doesn't have any blood in him; it's all ice."

A slick floor at Knoxville handicapped the fast-sprinting Kentuckians, who fell to the Volunteers, 46-40, as forward Bernie Mehen scored 13 points. Tennessee officials offered their apologies for the condition of the floor, explaining that it had been waxed for a dance held there the previous night.

Alabama beat them, 41-35. They were leading Notre Dame, 27-21, in Louisville when Staker fouled out, and the

Irish rallied to win, 46-43. They got revenge for the Alabama and Tennessee losses, but the Vols finished first in the SEC standings and were favored to win the annual tournament. However, Alabama upset the Vols, and UK edged the Tide, 36-34, for the championship. Ermal Allen was named to the All-SEC team.

After losing to the Great Lakes team in a benefit that raised $5,800 for navy relief, Kentucky made its debut in NCAA tournament play, meeting Illinois (18-4) in the Eastern Regional playoff in New Orleans. Penn State and Dartmouth were paired in the other game.

The Illinois team, known as the "Whiz Kids," featured five sophomore starters, including Ken Menke, Andy Phillip, Jack Smiley, and Gene Vance. Coach Doug Mills preferred to house them in a hotel apart from the other three teams in New Orleans, which got under the Kentuckians' skin a little. However, the fact that Illinois represented the aloof conference

Returning home with the 1942 championship to their credit are, left to right: Wildcats Carl Staker, Ermal Allen, Waller White, assistant coach Paul McBrayer, Mel Brewer, Adrian Back, Rupp, Milt Ticco, Lloyd Ramsey, Jim King, Kenny England, and manager Billy Evans.

north of the Ohio River was incentive enough for Rupp and his "pore li'l mountain boys." With Ticco scoring 13 points, Staker nine, and Akers eight, they edged Illinois, 46-44.

The 'Cats were rather listless the following night and fell, 47-28, to Dartmouth, for a 19-6 record. Stanford beat Dartmouth by 15 points the following week for the national championship.

Rollins and Davis were sophomore starters on the 1942-43 team, along with seniors Ticco, Akers, and Brewer. The main reserves were freshmen Paul Noel, Midway, at forward; Ed Lander of Lexington Lafayette, center; and Clyde "Ace" Parker, Chrisney, Indiana, and Bill Barlow, North Vernon, Indiana, guards. King, Staker, White, and Allen had graduated, and England and Ramsey had entered the service.

"We beat Cincinnati (61-39) and Washington of St. Louis (45-38) at home and then played our first game away from home," Rollins recalled. "It was in the Armory at Louisville, and I was scared to death. It was the largest crowd I'd ever played before. I remember that Indiana's coach Branch McCracken employed the fast break and they ran it tremendously well. I keep trying to place Ralph Hamilton's face, but I'll never forget what a fine game he had. (Hamilton scored 18 points as the Hoosiers won, 58-52.)

"That was two days before Christmas and I rode a bus to Wickliffe. I returned to Lexington, and we played Ohio State there the day after New Year's Day. They had a football fullback named Gene Fekete and another football player (Jack Dugger) on the team. We couldn't seem to do anything right. Rupp kept trying all kinds of combinations, pulling guys in and out. Of course we were aware of the war situation, especially since we had just come from home. Maybe that affected us. We lost (45-40).

"That game was my non-claim to fame. It was the last game UK would lose in Alumni Gym and the last home defeat until after the 1949-50 season, when Georgia Tech broke the string at 129 straight. During that period of time everything concerning home wins was measured back to that loss to Ohio State."

Rollins got his indoctrination into Knoxville's famed "Heckler's Row" that year. "They were mostly football players," he said, "and they sat behind the bench and rode all of us,

Rupp talks to Notre Dame players Johnny Dee, left, and Billy Hassett prior to UK-Irish game in Louisville in December 1943.

especially Rupp. He stood it, and we took it, and we beat them, 30-28. I think it was Clyde Parker who hit the winning goal in the last minute."

Nineteen fouls were called against Kentucky, 14 on Tennessee. Rupp was booed loudly for protesting the clock operation. As the final gun went off, he threw up his hands and shouted.

"I remember he turned to the Hecklers, smiled, and pointed to the scoreboard," Rollins said.

"The only other place worse than that was the Notre Dame Field House at South Bend. They'd pinch you, shove you, and pull the hair out of your legs when you took the ball out of bounds. Their band was right in your ear.

"I was glad we played them in Louisville that year, but I didn't do so well there either. My parents came to see me play, and I never played well when they were at a game. My floor game was all right, but I don't think I made a point. Thanks to 'Big Train' (Marvin Akers), who was bombing them from 30 feet out, we beat them."

In that biggest win of the season UK fell behind by 10. Then Akers hit a two-hand shot from midcourt and Ticco connected from the side to start a rally that tied the score, 49-49, with nine minutes remaining. Although Akers, Ticco, and Rollins had been whistled out on fouls, UK outplayed the Irish the rest of the way and won, 60-55. Akers had 17 points in what he considered his finest hour as a Wildcat.

In conference action they lost to Alabama at Tuscaloosa and were defeated by Tennessee, 33-30, in the final game of the conference tournament. Before entering the tournament they got a lesson in batting the ball away from the basket by George Mikan, 6-foot-8 DePaul center. Holding UK without a field goal in the first six minutes, the Demons built up a first half lead and coasted to a 53-44 victory. Akers, who scored 18 points for UK, called Mikan a one-man show.

Rollins got his draft notice shortly after a 53-39 loss to Great Lakes in a postseason game. He would play for Great Lakes the following season and return to UK after a three-year absence to serve as captain of the "Fabulous Five."

By the beginning of the 1943-44 season the war had begun to take its heavy toll of manpower, leaving Rupp with a squad that was to become known as the "Beardless Wonders" or the "Five F Formula—four 4 F's and a Freshman."

"You'd start to build a team, and the first thing you'd know a boy would be drafted and away he'd go," Rupp said. "That left us with Jack Tingle, who was rejected because of a broken arm that was set crooked; Wilbur Schu, who had bad knees; Ken Campbell, who had a nervous condition; and Jack Parkinson, who would be drafted later."

Filling the gap at center was Bob Brannum, a 6-foot-5 native of Winfield, Kansas. "I was visiting my mother in Halstead when I heard about Bob and his twin brother Clarence," Rupp said. "I invited them to Lexington for a tryout."

The twins arrived in Lexington on May 28, 1943, a few days after their 17th birthday. During a half-court game they were being shoved around when Bob stopped play, walked over to Clarence, and said, "Look, there's nobody calling fouls out here. Let's go."

As Bob told Tev Laudeman years later, "We started cleaning house. We bounced those other guys around good. I looked over at Mr. Rupp, and he was smiling."

"Sure I was smiling," Rupp said. "He was the closest thing

to 'Cowboy' Edwards I had seen. The rougher it got, the better he liked it. I offered them both scholarships." Bob accepted, but Clarence would not attend college until after the war.

The squad consisted of 15 freshmen and two sophomores. The players were so young that Rupp said, "It's like running a kindergarten." He had Don Whitehead (6-foot-0) and Schu (6-foot-3) at forward, Moseley (6-foot-3) and Johnson (6-foot-0) at guard, and Brannum in the middle. After a few games, Tingle (6-foot-3) replaced Whitehead at forward. Whitehead and Johnson were both called into the navy before the season was over. Parkinson (6-foot-0) moved into Johnson's spot.

The Wildcats had no trouble beating Fort Knox, 51-18, but Berea's naval trainees put up a good battle before falling, 54-40. Rupp took special note of Joe Holland, Berea star from Benton, Kentucky, and would have a scholarship waiting for him after the war.

They beat Indiana, 66-41, for UK's first win over an IU basketball team and then defeated Ohio State, 40-28, for the first time in Columbus. The Buckeyes would win the Big Ten title that season. Cincinnati was No. 5 in a row, but the string ended at Champaign-Urbana, where Howie Judson (a major league pitcher after the war) hit a looping basket shot with 40 seconds left to play to give Illinois a 43-41 victory. Parkinson, Moseley, and Johnson fouled out of that game.

The Kentuckians then completed the most successful Eastern trip ever taken by a Wildcat team. They set a defensive record in the auditorium at Buffalo by holding Carnegie Tech to 14 points while scoring 61 themselves, and defeated St. John's, 44-38, for UK's first victory ever in Madison Square Garden. After the turn of the new year, they defeated Notre Dame, 55-54, the third time in the series that a Kentucky team had emerged victorious.

Prior to the Notre Dame game the UK players dressed at the Kentucky Hotel and headed across the intersection at the Armory. Don Whitehead laughed aloud. Rupp turned and said, "Don't you realize we're playing Notre Dame?" With the score tied, 52-52, Irish center Mark Todorovich got the ball and wheeled around Brannum for a layup. Seconds later Brannum intercepted a pass from Johnny Lujack (the football quarterback) and dribbled the length of the court for a layup. He was fouled on the play by Todorovich and sank the game-winning free throw. In the locker room Rupp got after him for the

Southeastern Conference Champions—1943-44. Front row, left to right: Nathaniel Buis, Rudy Yessin, Jack Parkinson, Buddy Parker, Tom Moseley. Back row: Manager Allan Abramson, Wilbur Schu, Truitt DeMoisey, Bob Brannum, George Vulich, Jack Tingle, Coach Adolph Rupp.

defensive lapse that allowed Notre Dame to tie the score.

In early December seven teams, including Xavier and Georgia Tech, canceled games with Kentucky, leaving the Wildcats with only three games in January. After defeating Notre Dame, they won easily over Wright Field and the Fort Knox Army Reserve Corps. They avenged their only loss by defeating Illinois, 51-40, in Alumni Gym, and a "tired but happy Rupp calmly smoked his traditional cigar," the *Kernel* reported.

In Cincinnati's gym, a crackerbox affair with a low ceiling and a 40 x 78 floor, the Wildcats hit 14 of 92 shots for a miserly .152 percent. Cincinnati hit 10 of 49 shots. The Wildcats won, 38-35. The following week Rupp had everyone who missed a crip shot jogging around the court twice for each miss. After defeating Ohio University in the final game of the regular season, they waltzed over Georgia, Louisiana State, and Tulane for the championship of the Southeastern Conference Tournament in Louisville, and accepted an invitation to play in the National Invitational Tournament in Madison Square Garden.

Parkinson scored 20 points and Brannum hit 11 in a 46-38 victory over Utah, a team UK and the nation would hear more about in the future. The Wildcats led St. John's twice by eight points in a game that was tied eight times. They were trailing the Redmen by one point with less than two minutes to play when referee Pat Kennedy awarded the ball to St. John's after Kennedy blocked Tingle out of a play that prevented the UK forward from getting the ball. Don Wehr scored on an easy crip for a 48-45 St. John's victory.

In the consolation game Oklahoma A&M's seven-foot Bob Kurland stationed himself under the basket and batted Brannum's shots away so effectively that the UK center was content to pass off to his teammates, who had practiced banking the ball to avoid Kurland's "rejections." Although Brannum was scoreless, UK won, 45-29.

Brannum became the youngest player ever named a consensus All-American. After the tournament he and his wife boarded a train for Kansas. He would serve in the Army and return to UK for a brief spell after the war.

For his part in molding a championship contender, Rupp became the 10th coach elected to the Athletic Foundation Collegiate Basketball Hall of Fame. The citation read:

Attending the 1944 All-American dinner at Toots Shor's in New York are UK freshman Bob Brannum, left; Adolph Rupp; Oklahoma A&M coach Hank Iba; and Aggie center Bob Kurland.

"Rupp took a group of freshman players just out of high school, and directed them to nineteen victories in twenty games this year. It was one of the outstanding achievements of the 1944 basketball season."

Time Out: Alex Groza

Alex Groza was one of four brothers whose athletic exploits were a constant source of conversation in their father's tavern, above which they lived, in Martins Ferry, Ohio.

First, there was John, who had the distinction (at St. Thomas, now Scranton University) of being the first of the brothers to play basketball in Madison Square Garden.

Then came Frank, who was an outstanding basketball, football, and baseball player at Martins Ferry High. He played one year of Class D baseball.

Next was Lou, who played football at Ohio State and was a fine offensive tackle and record-setting place-kicker for the professional Cleveland Browns.

Last in size and age, though certainly not least in accomplishment, was Alex, who as a freshman played with Lou, a senior, on the 1942 Martins Ferry High basketball team.

Alex always credited Frank with teaching him how to play basketball. Alex was playing in grade school and after basketball practice he would hurry home in time to go with Frank to the high school to pick up Lou. While Lou was showering and dressing, Frank would get a basketball and teach Alex fundamentals.

Alex was the leading scorer his last two years at Martins Ferry, an Ohio River town of 16,000 on the eastern border of Ohio. He twice made All-State and scored 628 points as a senior to set a state record. At the end of his senior season, he was a slender 6-foot-5, 165-pounder who wanted to play at Ohio State, but had no offers from them or anyone else.

On the morning of UK's game with UCLA for the 1975

national championship, he sat in his office at the San Diego Arena, where he was president and general manager of the San Diego Conquistadors, and discussed his early days at UK:

"I didn't know whether I had the size, stature, or physical ability to go to a big school. I was hoping at the time to get a scholarship to Ohio State. Lou was there and I hoped to go along, my dad being a coal miner and tavern operator. My high school coach Floyd Baker called Adolph and asked him to come up and speak at our banquet.

(Baker gave Groza a big buildup to Rupp. Realizing he might need a new center to replace Brannum the next season, Rupp invited the skinny Ohioian to Lexington for a tryout.)

"I was invited with two kids from the Wheeling area to go down there for the tryouts, which they held every weekend. The players they cut would be picked by other Kentucky schools, which was why there was good basketball in colleges throughout the state.

"Adolph met us at the train and took us to the Phoenix. I'll never forget it was the first time I had southern fried chicken. There were 25 or 30 of us—some big ones, some tall ones, some short ones. We went through the drills, shot crips, passed the ball, ran up and down. I was somewhat worried, and lo and behold I was one of the few Adolph invited to come back.

"I'll never forget when I first went to Kentucky. Adolph called me into his office and was telling me about the schedule. When he said, 'We'll play in Loo'l-vul,' I thought that was in Massachusetts or somewhere. I had never heard it pronounced the way he pronounced it. In Ohio, we called it Lou-eeville. To me, the way he said it, it sounded like a city in another state, a long road trip.

"Adolph was young and aggressive. I was greatly impressed with his vast knowledge of all aspects of the game. You normally find that a coach who had played forward or guard has a hard time coaching centers, but he was thorough in his teaching of everybody...individually as well as team. He knew the things to show you.

"The hardest part of practice was after the opening shooting drills, when the guards went to one end and the forwards to the other end and the centers to a corner of Alumni Gym. We would go one-on-one and two-on-two. I mean *we worked*. I recall battling with (Bob) Brannum and (Ken) Campbell. You moved against each other and Adolph would stand there and watch you. He would put you in the proper position and if you walked, he told you you walked. What impressed me most was not that he had the best material, but that he could take the material he had and mold it.

"On the No. 6—second guard around—I can still see me handing the ball to (Ralph) Beard and him scoring and Adolph blowing the whistle as we started back down court and telling 'Wah' Jones he was out of position and telling Ralph to run it a little big tighter. We would then do it four or five or six more times and then start playing again.

"He always said, 'I don't have a zone offense or a zone defense. We'll run this thing against anything they'll throw at us. If we run it perfect, *nobody* is going to stop us.' He seemed to have two eyes in the back of his head and one eye on each side. He's forgot more basketball than most coaches know today.

"He wore that khaki uniform every day, and I often wondered if he ever washed it. Then I found out that he had a whole supply.

"I'll never forget when I first realized how serious the coach, players, and people of Kentucky took basketball. When I took my physical, I pranced into the dressing room singing, 'I'm in the Army now.' Jack Tingle said, 'Hey, cut that out. We've got a basketball game to play. Let's get serious.' Then I heard Adolph come in and ask, 'Who the hell's making all that noise?' I sneaked through the row of lockers, went outside, and came back all serious like. I thought if this is the atmosphere and this is the way it's going to be, then it's also the way I'm going to be. It was the first time I realized basketball was a very serious business there.

"I remember that before playing Notre Dame in Louisville, Adolph had Harry scout them twice and Ed Landers scout them once. We were going over the scouting report and he (Adolph) looked at his watch and said, 'It's 27½ minutes of, let's go.' I don't care if he was in the middle of a sentence, he would always say, 'It's 27½ minutes of, let's go.' It might be 25 till or 29 after, but he always said 27½.

"When he said he wanted you in at 7 o'clock, he meant 7 o'clock. I'll never forget the time we went to a Perry Como show in New York and did not get back to the hotel until one minute after 7. 'Where in the hell have you been?' he asked.

When told we had been to see Perry Como, he asked, 'Who in the hell does he play for?'

"He demanded things his way and he got them his way. Once we sat down to eat a steak in New York, and one of the guys asked the waitress for ketchup. 'Hey, you take that back,' he told her. 'If I'd wanted them to eat ketchup, I'd have ordered it.'

"From the time you walked in the gym until you left, you were there to play basketball. He said if you wanted to do other things, then get out and do them. He wanted none of that joking around and hollering. If he couldn't get it done in two hours, he wouldn't keep you, figuring you were too tired to get it done by then.

"I remember the time we beat somebody real bad, and we thought we had played a good game. He told us, 'I want you to tell your wives and girl friends good-night because we are going to practice. Manager, get the practice gear.' After the gym was empty, we practiced 45 minutes because in his mind he thought we had played a very poor basketball game.

"In my senior year, when Barker, Beard, and I were picked to represent Kentucky in an All-Star game and Adolph was coach, we assembled and scrimmaged little St. Francis of Brooklyn. We didn't do too well. Adolph gave us two or three plays and we scrimmaged them three days later, beating the same team 54 points.

"Adolph really stressed defense. He made you work your fanny off. He was a firm believer if your offense let you down, the defense would win a lot of games for you. He always said if you were going to foul, make it an aggressive foul, a good one, none of those YMCA fouls. He had a knack of getting a ball club fired up.

"We were going to play Notre Dame in Louisville (1949), and he had scouted them three times. He was telling us how tough this club was. He had us so high nobody in the world was going to beat us. We won, 62-38.

"I appreciated from the standpoint that when you played bad, he got on you; when you played good, he didn't compliment you, because he figured that was what you were there for.

"We were very, very sound fundamentally; set pick, roll, set pick, etc. He spent a lot of time teaching basic fundamentals. You could always tell basketball players who went to Kentucky. You never had to worry about them being sound fundamentally."

The success of the 1944-45 season depended on Groza. Four starters—all except Brannum—were back from the 19-2 team of 1944. Sophomore Jack Parkinson of Yorktown, Indiana, and junior Tom Moseley of Lexington were back at guards; sophomore Jack Tingle of Bedford, Kentucky, and junior Wilbur Schu of Versailles, Kentucky, were at forward. Moseley was dismissed from the squad for failing to report one night for extra practice, and Johnny Stough of Montgomery, Alabama, a freshman, moved into a starting role.

"I almost passed up that season entirely," Groza said. "I had passed the Army exam and I decided to spend the remaining three weeks with my parents. My mother said, 'No, you owe those people something. They took you when no one else would.' I went back to school in September and played in nine games."

Kentucky's Alex Groza drives against Georgia.

In the first four games, he scored nine points twice, then 11, and then 15 against Indiana. The Wildcats were undefeated, as was Ohio State, when the two met in Alumni Gym.

"I remember playing Ohio State," he said, "because I was ready to show them they were wrong about not wanting me. Arnie Risen (a future pro player who was from Williamsburg, Kentucky) was their center and he was experienced and about three inches taller than me."

The matchup was about even in rebounding, and Groza had a 16-14 edge in scoring. UK won 53-48 in overtime. Tingle and Parkinson each scored 15 points for UK while OSU's Don Grate, a hustling forward, was the only other big Ohio State scorer, with 14.

Later in the shower area near the basement, Coach Harold Olsen walked up to Groza and asked, "Son, why didn't you come to Ohio State?"

"Nobody asked me," Groza replied. "If you want me now, it's too late."

Groza got his induction notice in the latter part of December and reported to his draft board. Rupp got his papers transferred to Lexington. Alex joined the team on an eastern swing, scored 14 points against Wyoming at Buffalo, hit 27 in a 45-44 win over Temple at Philadelphia, and followed with 25 as UK beat LIU 62-52, in Madison Square Garden. With UK trailing by 15 points, Buddy Parker came off the bench to spark the team. Alex scored 25 points against Ohio University in Lexington and then went home for a visit while the Wildcats trounced Arkansas State, 75-6.

"I'll never forget my train back to Lexington was a few minutes late," he recalled. "They picked me up, rushed me to the gym, brought me out at halftime, and presented me with a key to the university and farewell gifts. That was probably the nicest thing that had ever happened to me up to that time. I knew then I was a Kentuckian for life."

He had arrived at the gym only two minutes before that game against Michigan State. The opening half was 10 minutes old by the time he dressed and entered the game. He scored only two points in the half, and UK trailed. He came back in the second half with 12 points as UK won, 66-35. The Wildcats were 11-0 when he reported to the Army two days later.

Five days after Groza's departure, the Wildcats traveled to

A happy Rupp welcomes Alex Groza back from army service during World War II.

Knoxville which, as usual, was prepared for them. Joining the hecklers in seats directly behind the Wildcat bench was the Tennessee band, which blared each time Rupp tried to give instructions to his players. Rupp said he did not mind the band so much as the chant, "Miss it! Miss it!" each time a Wildcat prepared to shoot a free throw.

The action was spiced by two fights on the floor, which the Kentuckians lost, and some in the bleachers. The first flare-up of tempers occurred midway of the second period when a Tennessee player grabbed Parkinson and started twisting his neck. When another Kentucky player intervened, both teams took up the fight, with the substitutes and Tennessee fans joining in the melee. The game got away from the officials near the end of the first half, when the racket was so loud the timer's buzzer went unheard as Tennessee scored a basket that was counted by the referee. Near the end of the game, Tingle was called for a technical foul when he protested an out-of-bounds call—"Hell, friend, it hit that guy on the head." The free throw proved the winning margin for Tennessee.

Knoxville newspapers reported after the game that virtually all the Kentucky players jumped two smaller Volunteers while Rupp looked on and laughed.

"The truth is," Rupp said, "I was in a telephone booth at the time, phoning for reinforcements, a cab."

"Let it go, boys," he advised his squad. "Talk like that does no good. Of course, the papers were in error. We may not be the brightest lads in America, but I know we're smart enough not to go to Knoxville and start a fight. Let's not speak unkindly about those folks down there. Just let it be said that sportsmanship, gentlemen, is at the lowest ebb in Knoxville."

Commenting on UK's loss of Groza, Johnny Mauer jokingly asked, "Why should Rupp miss one player when he has 30?" With Dutch Campbell, a 6-foot-4 freshman from Newark, Ohio, moving into the starting lineup at center, the Wildcats defeated Georgia Tech, 64-58, and then lost, 59-58, to Notre Dame in Louisville. Vince Boryla, a future Olympian, and Johnny Dee, a future Alabama and Notre Dame coach, each scored 16 points for the Irish. Kentucky lost one other game, to Michigan State at East Lansing, in regular season play; swept through the Southeastern Conference, beating Tennessee, 39-35, in the final game; and lost to Ohio State, 45-37, in the Eastern Regional of the NCAA Tournament.

The Wildcats defeated Tufts for third place and finished with a 22-4 record. With Groza in the lineup, it is conceivable they would have done better. He would return after the war to become the anchor man of the "Fabulous Five."

Echoes From The Early '40s

Carl "Hoot" Combs (1940)
Lexington, Kentucky

Dear Russell:

During the 1939-40 season we headed north to play Marquette, a team then regarded as the best team in the country. By the time we got to Cincinnati just about everybody was ailing. We left one guard in the hospital there and another one at Chicago. They were Lee Huber and Carl Staker as I recall. By game time we had only two able-bodied guards left, Mickey Rouse and I.

In the dressing room Adolph was very relaxed and he told us to just go out and have some fun. He told me I would be guarding a fellow who had already been All-American twice and this was his senior year. We tied into Marquette pretty good and at half time we were only a point or two behind. Adolph came charging into the dressing room at half and said, "By God, don't forget this is a Kentucky team and I am the...coach. What I said before the game is out. We are going to beat these bas...s and there will be no more †*†&! fun this trip." We did beat them 51-45 and went on to win the SEC title and he never did tell us again to just have some fun.

Sincerely,

"Hoot"

Vince Splane (1942)
Ft. Lauderdale, Florida

Dear Russell:

The Coach Rupp of thirty years ago was a different man than the Coach Rupp of today. I say this in regard to his temperament, not to his desire to win or his desire for perfection. Sarcasm was a trait he had developed to a razor's edge and when it came to a caustic remark, he knew no master. His temper control went out the windows of the old Alumni Gym on more than one occasion. I remember several instances where I was on the receiving end and received the full brunt of one of his broadsides.

We were playing Georgia Tech in Atlanta. The game was close, and Moore, a guard for Tech, had already scored 18 points when Adolph sent me in to guard him. I promptly fouled him on a shot which went in and he made the free throw awarded also. Adolph took me out pronto, and when I reached the sidelines to confront him, his face was purple with rage and that blood vessel in his forehead was pulsating wildly. He screamed at me, "Splane, what the...is the matter with you? Have you gone crazy?"

In the fall of 1941, my grandmother died. I had to attend the funeral in Paintsville, Kentucky, and I received Coach Rupp's permission to do so. A few days after my return, during practice, Coach Rupp blew his whistle and called the squad into a circle for a talk. We received the usual lambasting, "My God, boys, we're just not going to continue playing like this. We're not playing girls' rules. This is **WAR!**" Then he singled me out, "And another thing, boys, we're not going to have anymore of this grandmother dying business."

There was always the sarcasm present at practice sessions or the caustic remark, e.g., "Splane, your...is dragging sparks!" Another, "Manager, oh, manager, go ask Buster if he has a dress for Weber and Boehler. They're playing girls' rules. Hell, they might as well dress like one."

The search for perfection and a winning combination by Coach Rupp produced many night sessions for us. We would practice all afternoon, then eat and be back on the floor by 7 p.m. for a few more hours of drills and scrimmage with attention given to the minutest detail in ball handling, footwork, shooting, and timing on the guard around series. Repetition, repetition, repetition, we could run those drills blindfolded. Even today, thirty years *later*, I believe I could go out on the floor and go through that guard around series with *very few* mistakes.

When we would return to Lexington from our out of town games, many is the time when we would go immediately to the gym and practice all Sunday afternoon. More practice, practice, practice, more drills, drills, drills.

Around this time (1939-1941) Coach Rupp had purchased some farmland around Lexington along with a few head of cattle. We had several boys on the squad who were in the school of Agriculture and I remember a trip to South Bend to play Notre Dame. We traveled in private autos in those days and, on this trip, I was in Coach Rupp's auto along with a couple of boys who were in Ag school, one of whom was Ken England who was later killed in World War II. We didn't discuss basketball, we discussed livestock, i.e., raising, feeding, breeding, etc. Coach Rupp picked those boys' minds as clean as a plucked chicken in all fields of knowledge pertaining to his "farm." His genius for detail was not confined only to the basketball court.

Seven years ago, Boehler, Ticco, and myself met in Lexington and visited Coach Rupp in his office in the Coliseum. We asked him about his retirement to which he replied, "When I reached 65 I thought they might ask me to retire. They didn't so I just kept on going. When I reach 70 if they don't say anything, I guess I'll just keep on going. Hell, I can't think of a better way to die than just fall off that bench some night."

Sincerely yours,

Vince Splane

Lee Huber (1939, '40,
and '41)
Orlando, Florida

Dear Russell:

Several years ago at the Centennial banquet Adolph was master of ceremonies and invited all ex-basketball players to a special practice he was having on Saturday morning before the football game. About twenty of us showed up and Adolph sat with us in the stands while the team went through their drills. After they made about fifty lay-ups there were three straight misses. Adolph jumped up, blew his whistle, and had them all line up in front of us. Next came a speech that all of us had heard twenty-odd years earlier—they would be out there all afternoon and even at night if they did not shape up. After about two minutes he dismissed them to return to their practice drills. As he turned around to sit back down with us he winked and said, "Same old Stuff." I might mention that I cleaned up his remark.

After an important Saturday night win, Adolph presented the game ball to me, a rare occurrence. The following Monday before practice I was called in to his office. He had heard that I was out on the Friday night before the game after training hours. Coach gave me a lecture and said that I did not deserve the game ball since I broke training and he wanted it back. There was quite an explosion when I told him I had sold the ball to one of the fraternities. To the best of my knowledge I never received a game ball again.

Several years after I graduated I ran into Dan Tehan, whom I regarded as one of the finest referees when I was in school. In our discussion Dan told me about an incident in a game he had recently worked at Kentucky. In the last few seconds of the game Kentucky was leading by 25 points. Dan gave the opponents the ball out of bounds before Kentucky was set-up defensively, in Rupp's estimation. The opponents threw the ball in and got a fast basket. In Dan's words, "Adolph came charging out like a mad bull." Dan pointed to the scoreboard and told Adolph he was ahead by 25 points. Adolph replied that "without your bonehead call it would have been 27."

Sincerely,

Lee

Ermal Allen (1940, '41,
    and '42)
Dallas, Texas

Dear Russell:
   Coach Rupp really believes in what he is teaching and has great confidence in it. On one occasion, he took me out of a game and told me to run Play No. 5. I went back in and saw the defense was sagging and I called some other play. He took me out and asked why I didn't run No. 5. I tried to explain why I thought the play wouldn't go and he said, "Look, Allen, these plays will go. I don't care if we're playing the University of Jerusalem, they will go."
   On another occasion, we were playing Xavier. They were one point ahead with five seconds left and I had two free throws and shot them very fast. I made both of them. He congratulated me and wanted to know why I would shoot so fast. I told him if I had a four-foot putt for one dollar that I wouldn't stand over it. He said, "That's just for one dollar. These free throws are for my job."

Ermal

Ken Kuhn
U.K. SID
(1948-69)

Dear Russ:
   On the academic scene, Adolph taught a class in advanced basketball which he insisted was invaluable for athletes who intended to become coaches. Moreover, he

proclaimed himself the best professor at the University because all of his students got A's.

"What kind of professor gives failing grades?" he asked. "It just proves he didn't teach his students anything."

When all of the students except one had attended classes faithfully one semester and were entitled to A's, he asked Harry (Lancaster) to find out why the one student had been absent. Harry replied that the boy had a broken leg.

"Well, in that case, he'll have to be satisfied with an A-minus," Rupp said.

In the early 1940s, Rupp was accused by a Big Nine coach of raiding the North for basketball talent. In his denunciation of the Baron, the Big Nine mentor included an old Southern expression, "carpetbagging." A short time later, Rupp was invited to speak at a banquet in Ohio, deep in Big Nine territory, and the banquet chairman, eager to have Rupp's name on the program, asked him what his subject would be.

"My text," the Baron replied, "will be: A Carpetbagger in the Holy Land."

Once, when drilling a freshman group in fighting for the ball under the basket, Adolph exhorted them: "Beat the other fellow to the charge. Hit hard; remember the Bible says, 'It is better to give than to receive.'"

"But coach," countered one of his players, "I always thought the Bible said, 'Love thine enemies.'"

"That's the old version of it," Rupp snapped back. "But the rules committee changed it."

Rupp's method of player selection was a mystery to everyone but himself. He would simply point to the top of his office door—six feet, two inches high—and say, "If they don't bump their heads when they came in, I don't even bother to shake hands."

"They're like a bunch of quails," Rupp said of one of his teams. "Somebody shoots and they all scatter."

Sincerely,
Ken

An Era Begins

What was to become collegiate basketball's "Era of the Wildcats" had its beginning in the 1946 season, coinciding with the arrival on campus of Kentuckians Wallace "Wah Wah" Jones of Harlan, Ralph Beard of Louisville, and Joe Holland of Benton.

Wah Wah was the key that first season. A high school legend, he had established a national scholastic record in basketball by scoring 2,398 points during his career at Harlan High. He was also a two-year All-State football choice and a fine baseball player.

He and his brother Hugh had led Harlan to the state tournament in 1942 and 1943. After Hugh was graduated and in the navy, Wah Wah led Harlan to the state tournament two more years.

At one time Wah Wah planned to attend the University of Tennessee. He and Humzey Yessin, a guard on the Harlan team, visited the campus and were just about sold on the "Big Orange." When they said they had to go home for their belongings, a Tennessee booster let them use his car. En route to Harlan, they stopped at Middlesboro to see Edna Ball (the future Mrs. Wallace Jones), who was a sophomore at UK. She would have no part of Wah Wah attending UT. He and Yessin enrolled at UK. Yessin had to drive the car back to Knoxville.

By the third game of that season, Jones was the starting center, teaming with Beard, Parkinson, Holland, and Tingle. Wilbur Schu was a sometime starter in place of Holland.

They won their first seven games before losing to Temple, 53-45, in Philadelphia. They had put together six more consecu-

Ralph Beard is fouled (above) and Wallace Jones (below) ties up the ball as UK whips Western Ontario early in the 1945-46 season.

tive wins before losing to Notre Dame in Louisville. Irish Coach Elmer Ripley, knowing Beard's remarkable speed and fondness for leaving his defensive assignment to seal an opponents' pass, set a trap for him. On the first Notre Dame offensive pattern, a guard faked a pass to All-American Billy Hassett, who was being guarded by Beard. When Beard left Hassett and jumped between the guard and Hassett to intercept what he thought was an obvious pass, Hassett reversed direction, took an easy "backdoor" pass, and had a clear path to the basket for a layup.

Realizing that he had been "suckered" before the home crowd, Beard tightened up and for the rest of the night was unable to recover his customary poise. Rupp told him he had to learn how to relax, to learn to lose his pregame tension, and "to go out and break training, miss practice a few days, do something drastic." Tingle and Parkinson allegedly spotted Beard in a downtown cafe, solemnly following orders by stuffing himself with pie, ice cream, and Coca Cola.

Rupp diagrams a play for Wallace Jones (left) and Ralph Beard, outstanding freshmen on the 1946 Wildcat team.

In winning all their remaining games, the Wildcats avenged one of their losses by beating Temple, 54-43, in Louisville; breezed through the SEC tournament; and accepted a bid to the National Invitational Tournament.

They easily disposed of Arizona in the first round, but had trouble with West Virginia, which tied the game 14 times before UK scored eight consecutive points in the final two minutes to win, 59-51. They were matched point for point by Rhode Island until the final minute, when Beard, with thousands of spectators screaming and shouting in an effort to rattle him, made a free throw, giving Kentucky a one-point victory and the championship. The players carried Rupp to the dressing room.

Rupp predicted there would never be another Kentucky basketball team that would equal the record of that squad: 28 victories in 30 games, conference and National Invitational titles, and a new team scoring record of 1,821 points. The secret was a reserve squad on par with the starters.

Returning the following season was the finest group of basketball players assembled at UK up to that time. Lettermen Tingle, Davis, Holland, Campbell, McMullen, Beard, Parker, Jones, and Yessin were joined by veterans Groza and Brannum, who were teammates on the Camp Hood, Texas, team; Jim Jordan, a two-time All-American on North Carolina Pre-Flight; Cliff Barker, who had spent 16 months in a German prison camp; and Kenny Rollins, who would be elected team captain in mid-season.

There were so many fine players reporting to Alumni Gym that they were divided into two squads, with 19 on the "A" squad and 23 on a "B" squad coached by Lancaster, who was named a full-time assistant after his discharge from the navy that year. Later in the season four members of the "B" squad were promoted, and the others were told to pursue their studies uninterrupted by basketball.

"To say that I was coming back to a great big surprise would be an understatement," Kenny Rollins said, "because when I saw all the ball players that walked on that floor for the first time in the fall of 1946, I said to myself, 'Kenny, you've come to the wrong place.'

"There were four All-Americans—Beard, Jordan, Parkinson, and Brannum—and three of them were guards. When they hit the floor for the first practice, it was quite some session. Not only did these fellows play the game well, but they were excellent people along with it. To my surprise, I was on the first five when we started the season."

Other starters in an easy conquest of Indiana Central were Beard at guard, Groza at center, and Tingle and Holland at forward, with Barker as the No. 1 substitute. Freshmen Jim Line and Dale Barnstable started the second half, along with Brannum, Rollins, and Beard. Others seeing action were Parker, Davis, McMullen, Jordan, Campbell, and Cummins.

After they defeated St. John's, 70-50, in the Garden for their 24th straight victory over a two-season span, Joe Lapchick

Rupp gets a ride after his 1946 team wins the NIT championship in Madison Garden. From left to right are: manager Humzey Yessin, trainer Frank Mann, "Muff" Davis, Elmer Gilb (head down), Buddy Parker, Ken Campbell, Ralph Beard, Jack Parkinson, and Bill Sturgill.

called them the greatest team he had ever coached against. The Associated Press said they were "the greatest aggregation to visit the Eighth Avenue arena."

Rupp called it a "dream team," but insisted it did nothing differently from others: "It plays straight basketball, but it is equipped to do a little better than some. This team is composed of players adapted to the positions in our style of play. We can rebound and we have speed. We have a bunch of clever kids, and they possess a fine spirit."

The Wildcats, ranked No. 1 in the nation, returned home from New York and defeated Baylor and Wabash before a 37-31 upset loss to Oklahoma A&M in the Sugar Bowl.

After that Sugar Bowl game, someone said to Rupp, "Tough luck, coach."

"Coach?" Rupp screamed. "Don't call me coach. A team that makes only 12 points in the last half has no coach."

"We had made great progress, and we sold the coaching staff on letting us go home for a couple of days before the Sugar Bowl," Rollins said. "That was a great, great mistake. We went home and filled ourselves with turkey, dressing, cranberry sauce, rolls, and pie. We reported back to take a train down to Louisiana, and we only had about three practice days. We didn't recover our edge."

After that Sugar Bowl game, Rupp asked some of his more mature players what was wrong. They replied that more leadership was needed. Rollins was elected captain to replace Tingle, who had been chosen by the coaching staff before the season began.

The Wildcats put together a 10-game winning streak, including a 60-30 victory over Notre Dame in Louisville. Beard scored 17 points and held Irish star Kevin O'Shea to two. They lost to DePaul in Chicago, 53-47, and closed the regular season with six victories.

Prior to the annual conference tournament, Rupp cut his squad to the 10-man limit, choosing Line and Barnstable ahead of Brannum and Jordan. The Wildcats easily won the tournament and once again dominated the All-Tournament team, with Tingle, Beard, Rollins, Jones, and Holland—all products of Kentucky high school basketball—on the first team, and Groza, whose action was limited by a lame back, on the second team.

Before defending their NIT crown, they defeated Temple, 68-29, in a postseason game in Louisville. Holland and Beard

Five Wildcats, all native Kentuckians, were named to the 1947 All-Southeastern Conference basketball team. They are, left to right: Wallace Jones, Jack Tingle, Joe Holland, Ralph Beard, and Kenny Rollins. Rupp smiles in left background.

were hospitalized with the flu, marking the first time Beard had failed to start in the 63 games since he joined the squad as a freshman. He rejoined the team in time to make the trip to New York. Conspicuous by his absence was Brannum, who planned to transfer to Michigan State.

When a writer at a press luncheon asked Rupp why Brannum was left home, he sharply replied that Brannum "just wasn't good enough to make the team; and if any of you coaches are interested, his telephone number is Lexington 682."

Upon hearing about Rupp's statement, Brannum said, "Maybe I'm not as good as the boys he took in my place, but I made my plans some time ago to leave the university and go to another school." He later said the incident was as much his fault as Rupp's. "I didn't put out like I should," he said. "Mr. Rupp and I never had words. I was unhappy that I wasn't playing. He was unhappy with my performance. You don't just walk in at Kentucky and take a position, no matter who you are."

Rupp suddenly was no longer the darling of Gotham sportswriters. They accused him of erring in not using some of his touted reserve strength in a one-point victory over LIU and wrote of alleged dissension among some of the players who did not see enough game action.

The United Press quoted Line as saying, "I will not transfer from Kentucky this year, but I can't say for sure what I will do next year. I do know that I would like to play more basketball." (Line sent statements of denials to Lexington newspapers the following day.)

"We won 34 of 36 starts with boys who are unhappy," Rupp said. "Imagine what those guys would have done if they had been happy."

They defeated North Carolina State and lost, 49-45, to Utah in the final game of the tournament. Utah guard Wat Misaka, Utah-born of Japanese parents, held Beard without a field goal, and the Utes' Vern Gardner and Arnold Ferrin scored 15 points each in the slowdown game.

"If you weren't hitting in those days, you didn't keep on shooting," Beard explained. "Adolph would tell us to give it to somebody else. There wasn't anybody hitting for us but Jim Line."

The 'Cats finished with a 34-3 record, scored 2,533 points, and placed Beard and Groza on All-American teams. Beard also was selected as the outstanding player to perform in the Garden that year. Crushed by the loss to Utah, Ralph refused to remain in New York to receive his cup. He asked Rupp how to improve his game and was told he would have to learn to shoot long shots from the floor. In order to do so, he would have to change his entire technique on two-handed push shots, since every shot he took revolved to the right because of too much right-hand pressure.

Six hours after the team arrived home, he was on the gym floor practicing his long shot. He practiced it at least three days a week all summer long, taking approximately 500 shots each session. He would return to competition the following season as one of the deadliest shooters in the nation.

The "Fabulous Five"

The University of Kentucky's "Fabulous Five" basketball team of 1948 was one of the finest sports units of all times. Perhaps never before had a series of world events occurred so as to bring together players of such fine caliber.

Patton's Third Army freed Cliff Barker from a German prisoner-of-war camp; a national ruling allowed Wallace Jones and Ralph Beard to play four straight years together; the army nurtured and developed Alex Groza into one of the finest pivotmen ever to wear the Kentucky colors; and the navy matured Kenny Rollins into a fine floor leader.

Beard was perhaps the most idolized of the group. In training all year round, he was described by the school annual as "the perfect Wheaties ad, the All-American boy." His mother said he started shooting baskets when he was a baby, with his potty serving as his first hoop. Almost from the minute he was able to walk, a basketball goal was attached to the wall of the family garage at Hardinsburg, Kentucky. When he reached the age of 14, his family moved to Louisville. During his last year at Male High School, the Purples won the state championship.

Jones was dubbed "Wah Wah" because as a child a younger sister could not pronounce his name. He was an all-conference choice in both football and basketball during his freshman year at UK. Due to football commitments he turned out late for basketball the following year and had to fight Groza and Bob Brannum for his position at center. He eventually ended up at forward and was one of those rare three-letter athletes, winning monograms and all-star honors in football, basketball, and baseball. His main role with the Fabulous Five was to provide the

Rupp poses with members of his Fabulous Five. They are Ralph Beard (12), Kenny Rollins (26), Wallace Jones (27), Alex Groza (15), and Cliff Barker (23).

inspirational spark necessary to pull the team through tough situations.

Groza was a devout Catholic who attended services regularly and was vice-president of a campus religious organization. He was unofficial team spokesman during his senior year and was president of the K-Club for letter winners at UK. Due to his background of living over a tavern and having three rough, tough, athletic brothers, he was a very positive and forceful young man with much influence over his teammates.

Groza's excellence as a basketball player was due to his remarkable speed for a man of his size and an uncanny ability to control both the offensive and defensive backboards. Rupp termed him one of the best rebounders the game had ever known.

Barker was the old man of the group. He became 27 in January of that year of the Fabulous Five. The least publicized but not the least spectacular player of the group, he left school after his freshman season at UK and eventually entered the Army Air Corps. Shot down while serving as an engineer and gunner aboard a B-17 bomber, he was taken prisoner and had plenty of opportunities to play basketball during his first six months of imprisonment. "We could play about all we wanted," he said. 'We'd go from one camp to another, playing other teams."

However, it was while fooling around with a volleyball during his long period of confinement that he developed the ball-handling skill that was to earn him the reputation of a true "Houdini of the Hoops," "Basketball Banshee," and "Super Magician." He was used primarily as a spot player after his return to UK in 1946, but he eventually would win his way into the starting lineup.

Rollins was the team captain, the glue that held it all together. He recalled one point in that fantastic season when the pressure became so heavy that the coaches began riding the team and some of the players indicated they had had it.

"They were ready to throw their hands up in despair," Kenny said. "We called a meeting. I personally felt I needed to say something to get us back on the right track."

In essence, he pointed out that most of them planned to play professional ball, and the best record they made in college basketball would mean the best money they would make in the pros. He asked them to carry on for themselves, not the coaches. They got the message.

In addition to the advantage of age and maturity, the veteran stars were under the tutelage of the nation's most successful coach, a person they would all remember as a strict disciplinarian; one who was aloof, quick to criticize, and easy to anger.

Due to increased enrollment and the unprecedented popularity of the basketball team, all but one of the 11 home games that season were played before students only. The other game was limited to faculty and staff members. No student was allowed to see more than five games.

When that season began the starting lineup consisted of Beard and Rollins at guard, Groza at center, and Barker and Holland at forward. Jones was in the process of making the change from football to basketball; in addition, he had received a foot injury in football.

The Wildcats had dispatched six foes in routine order when they stopped off at Philadelphia to play Temple while en route to meet St. John's in New York. The Owls won, 60-59, as the second of two free throws by Rollins missed the mark at the end of the game. Beard had an injured hip and played only 10 minutes as a substitute. Jones' sore foot kept him out of the game entirely.

Kentucky disposed of St. John's and Creighton before Jones broke into the starting lineup against Western Ontario. However, Beard was still ailing and did not start that game. Jack Parkinson started in his place.

Two nights later, on January 5, 1948, the Wildcats defeated Miami (Ohio), 67-53, as all the pieces fell together to form what was to be known as the "Fabulous Five." In the dressing room before that game, Rupp announced a lineup consisting of Rollins and Beard at guard, Groza at center, and Jones and Barker at forward. They would become a yardstick by which all future UK teams would be measured.

That new combination took an 11-game winning streak into South Bend, but a fine Notre Dame team and a vociferous student body proved too much for the Wildcats, who fell, 64-55. UK would lose no more collegiate games that season.

A late season highlight came against Tennessee in Alumni Gym when Beard hit a shot from 52½ feet with one second remaining in the first half. That beat the previous long shot of 48 feet, 2½ inches set by Joe Hagan in 1938, but Hagan's shot had beat Marquette in the closing seconds while Beard's shot

173

Captain Kenny Rollins drives a nail to mark the spot where Ralph Beard made a 52½ foot shot against Tennessee in 1948. Beard watches the ceremony, along with, left to right, standing: Rupp, Cliff Barker, Joe Holland, Alex Groza, and Wallace Jones.

was of no great significance in a 69-42 win over the Vols.

In the opening round of the NCAA playoffs, UK defeated Columbia, 76-53, and then prepared for Alvin "Doggie" Julian's fine Holy Cross team. Rollins drew the assignment of guarding Bob Cousy, proclaimed on a large banner as "Best Player in the World."

"We studied his moves and Barnstable and I talked about what we would try to do," Kenny said. "We never knew which way he would go. Some players prefer to go one way. If they're right-handed, they might like to drive to their right and you can overplay them that way. But with Cousy, it didn't matter. So we made a concentrated effort to keep him in the center of the floor because he did most of his scoring from the sides of the floor."

When Rollins was relieved by Barnstable near the end of the game, Cousy had three points, all on free throws. He got a field goal and another free throw. Meanwhile, Groza controlled the boards over George Kaftan and scored 23 points. UK won, 60-52. After the game someone brought the scoresheet to Rollins as a souvenir.

In the collegiate final the Wildcats built up an early 13-1 lead over Baylor and coasted to a 58-42 victory. Groza was named the tournament's most valuable player.

Calling that squad "the greatest team ever assembled in college sport," Rupp, eyes filled with tears, locked the dressing room door and said, "You've done everything you've been asked to do. You won your own SEC tournament, you won the NCAA championship. You've kept training and made many sacrifices to do these things and for all of it I thank you from the bottom of my heart."

To Groza, who scored 26 points in the first half and seven in the last half against Baylor, he said, "You undoubtedly played the greatest game at center that has ever been seen in the Garden."

The trials championship game, played before 18,475 fans, was described as a dream game and lived up to all advance billing. With Kurland holding Groza to one field goal, the Oilers neutralized Beard's 23 points and won, 53-49.

The Oilers were stretched out on benches and tables when Rupp entered their dressing room and said, "Boys, you have a great team. You beat us fair and square and deserved to win. Congratulations."

Turning point of the game, he said, was midway of the first half, when Barker received a broken nose.

"If they had beaten us 20 points," Rupp said, "it wouldn't have been so hard to take, but we practically had it—and let it get away. It looked like I could have done something when we had them 47-45 there right at the last, but I can't think what it was I should have done or could have done.

"It hurts to lose, but we lost to a great team tonight—the greatest team we have faced this season. I guess fate decreed that Kentucky shouldn't win tonight."

1948 University of Kentucky NCAA champions. Front row: Coach Adolph Rupp, Johnny Stough, Ralph Beard, captain Phil Rollins, Cliff Barker, Dale Barnstable, assistant coach Harry

Mike Lee of the *Long Island Press* said, "It was poise and experience that told the story. There may have been greater individual performances in the Garden than the one by Beard, but I doubt it."

Lou Effrat termed it the "greatest game of all times. Five

Lancaster, Back row: Manager Humzey Yessin, Garland Townes, Jim Jordan, Joe Holland, Alex Groza, Wallace Jones, Jim Line, Roger Day, trainer Wilbert (Bud) Berger.

words that cover a lot of years, and a lot of thrills were heard all over the Garden, undisputed by anyone...an exciting, tense, spectacular contest in which fortunes rose, sagged and rose again...basketball at its very best, sharp, smart, daringly aggressive."

Carl Lunquist of the United Press said the Oilers, "playing like mad men because they had to, won...over a magnificent Kentucky team that lost no stature in defeat...It was one of the most bitterly fought contests in Madison Square Garden annals and a thoroughly thrilled throng of 18,475 sat limp at the finish, too exhausted even to give a cheer to the superman-sized winner."

Before the Olympic Trials got underway, the U. S. Basketball Committee had voted that the 14 members of the Olympic squad would be chosen in the following manner: five players from the winning team in each bracket, two from the other three teams in each bracket, the coach of the winning team as head coach, and the coach of the second place team as associate coach.

The squad members were UK's Beard, Rollins, Groza, Barker, and Jones; Phillips 66's Bob Kurland, Jesse Remick, Gordon Carpenter, R. C. Pitts, and Lew Beck; Vince Boryla of the Denver Nuggets; Don Barksdale of the Oakland Bittners; Jack Robinson of Baylor; and Ray Lumpp of NYU.

Rupp waves to the crowd during parade welcoming Fabulous Five home from NCAA championships and Olympic Trials.

The Wildcats were met in Lexington by an estimated 15,000 fans, who mounted them on a city fire truck and paraded them through the crowded streets to the university campus. Banners proclaimed them the greatest collegiate champion basketball team of all time, and classes at the university and at many elementary, junior, and senior high schools were excused. The festivities were broadcast on radio and recorded by Warner Brothers' *Pathe News,* and the two local newspapers published editorials lauding the team.

The lone serious note was sounded by Rupp's old coach, Dr. Allen, guest speaker at a banquet sponsored by six local luncheon clubs. Stressing a need for a high commissioner of basketball, he said gamblers throughout the country were seeking to control the outcome of football and basketball games, and that colleges and college athletic conferences were not doing one thing to protect their athletes from the gamblers.

The Wildcats and the Oilers played three exhibition games that summer to raise money for the Olympic Fund. Barksdale led the Oilers-dominated group to a 60-52 victory in the first game, witnessed by 6,000 persons at the Fairgrounds Pavilion in Tulsa. Trailing by one point in a second overtime in Kansas City, Rupp told Holland and Rollins to two-time whoever had the ball. Rollins chased the Oiler in possession and the ball was batted into the hands of Holland, who was halfway to the goal when a firecracker went off in the stands. He went ahead and scored an easy layup shot. The Kentucky-dominated squad won, 70-69.

So elated was Phog Allen that he grabbed a microphone after the game and said how proud he was of Rupp and how delighted he was to see Rupp at the top of the heap of great champions.

"Rupp was my pupil in 1923," he said, "and I am thrilled to death at his great success. The Kentucky boys fought their hearts out, and I never saw a greater exhibition of basketball in my life."

During an open practice session in Alumni Gym prior to the final game of the series, several hundred central Kentuckians turned out to watch the Oilers and the Negro star Barksdale. The "rubber" game of the series, won by the Oilers, 56-50, represented a longtime ambition for Rupp as more than 14,000 persons witnessed the event, played on a temporary floor on

Stoll Field.

"They said Larry McPhail was crazy when he was president of the Cincinnati baseball team and suggested night baseball," Rupp said. "Well, sir, his craziness made attendance five times greater. When I suggested a couple years ago that basketball could draw at night in summer as well as winter, a lot of sportswriters and others said I was crazy. If that's so, we had 14,000 crazy people at Stoll Field last night. Maybe it would be better for promoters if they made a play for those crazy people."

In addition to the benefit game, Kentucky fans raised more than enough money to send team members Holland, Line, and Barnstable to the Olympic Games.

1948-49 Wildcats. Front row, left to right: Adolph Rupp, Jim Line, Cliff Barker, John Stough, Ralph Beard, Joe B. Hall, Garland Townes, Harry Lancaster. Back row: Dale Barnstable, Walt Hirsch, Wallace Jones, Alex Groza, Bob Henne, Roger Day, and manager Humzey Yessin.

The Kentucky delegation arrived in New York the following day, and was welcomed by the Olympic Committee, which, according to Rupp, asked:

"Coach, you had a good game last night?"

"No, I'll tell you, fellows. I've got some bad news for you. We had a rain last night and could not play. We had to call the game off."

"You mean you didn't bring any money up here then?"

"No, we haven't got any money."

"We thought sure you'd have some, with the advance sales you had."

"We have got to give all that money back. We could not play in a driving rainstorm."

"I kidded them along a little bit more," Rupp said. "Then I handed them a check for $25,000. I said there'd be more coming later, but we had not been able to balance the books. We could not tell at the time exactly what the expenses were, how much it was going to cost to take up the floor and move it back to Louisville, and all those other things.

"I thought they would treat us nice, but, after receiving that check, they said, 'Well, we can take the women's track team then.' Of course, women's track was not too important and wrestling was not too important, but they said, 'We can take the wrestling team, too.' I said, 'Fine,' and, by George, when we got on that ship, we were on the sixth floor, down below the water line. Those wrestlers were down about the third floor and I think the women's track team was on the second floor. I can understand why they did not put the women down in those holes. When you turned the lights off down there where the basketball team stayed, you could not see a thing. It was really dark. I thought they would have treated my boys better than they did those wrestlers."

The Olympic Games

The role of associate coach to Bud Browning was an unaccustomed one for Rupp, but, all in all, a spirit of harmony existed when the U. S. delegation sailed for London aboard the U.S.S. *America* in the summer of 1948.

Before settling down at Uxbridge, a Royal Air Force camp, the basketball players toured Scotland by bus, playing exhibitions wherever a court, usually an ice hockey rink, could be found. Lou Wilke served as spokesman for the Americans, with the help of Rupp and Browning.

The tour included stops at Paisley, Glasgow, Perth, St. Andrew, Kilcarney, and the capital city of Edinburgh, where the Americans had a good scrimmage on the first wooden floor they had seen in Scotland.

Edinburgh's official welcoming ceremony for the visitors reeked with tradition, as did other stops along the tour. Rupp, appointed to make the American response to lengthy and flattering welcoming addresses at the customary high teas given by the lord provost of each city, ran out of souvenir tokens before the Edinburgh tea. Digging into his suitcase, he found a large tin key with a thermometer on it. He told of the wonderful treatment he and his boys had received in the small towns, the ancient inns, and the metropolis of Edinburgh. In appreciation he presented to the lord provost a key to Lexington, Kentucky. With tears in his eyes, the official accepted the key.

The Americans played their farewell exhibition game in an open air arena in Princess Park at the foot of Edinburgh Castle, where they were cheered by more than 12,000 Scots and escorted by police through a mob of autograph seekers in order

Members of the 1948 U. S. Olympic basketball team are kneeling left to right: Bud Browning, Ralph Beard, Jack Robinson, Cliff Barker, Ray Lumpp, Kenny Rollins, Lew Beck, and

Adolph Rupp. Standing: Wallace Jones, R.C. Pitts, Don Barksdale, Bob Kurland, Lou Wilke, Alex Groza, Gordon Carpenter, Vince Boryla, and Cab Remick.

to get to the station in time to catch their train to London.

That the Kentucky and Phillips 66 players made a favorable impression on the people of Scotland during the exhibition tour was indicated in a letter received by Lexington mayor Tom Mooney from the lord provost of Paisley:

> When the American Olympic Basketball team visited Paisley on Thursday, July 22, I had the pleasure of extending to them a civic reception. On that occasion their coach, Mr. A. F. Rupp, on your behalf presented me with a golden key to the city of Lexington.
>
> In the course of his speech he remarked that it was also the key to the hearts of the City. May I thank you for your generous gift and also for your kind thoughts which accompanied it.
>
> The Paisley people took a keen interest in the basketball team, and I hope they will be very successful at Olympia.

The basketball and wrestling championships were held in Harringay Arena in London. The building seated approximately 10,000 persons, but crowds were meager during most of the basketball games. "I guess we only had about 53 people at one of the games," Ralph Beard said. "But most of those teams were no better than a good YMCA team back home."

The U.S. defeated Switzerland, 86-21; Czechoslovakia, 53-28; Argentina, 59-57; Egypt, 66-28; and Peru, 61-33, to place in the final elimination with Brazil, Uruguay, the Philippines, China, Mexico, France, and the Czechs. Argentina had led the U. S. by seven points at halftime as the U. S. boys passed badly, time and time again lost the ball on a sure-scoring, fast-breaking situation, and generally were not alert in defensive play. They came back better in the second half and avoided what would have been the biggest upset of the tournament.

In addition to overconfidence, the Americans were bothered by the fact that they were using a "unit" system of offense and defense for the first time in the Olympics, and that they had weakened that system by eliminating two Wildcats and two Oilers in the selection of units. The starters were Groza, Jones, Rollins, Lumpp, and Boryla. They held a 14-9 lead when relieved by Carpenter, Pitts, Beck, Barksdale, and Robinson. The relief crew fell behind seven points at the half.

The starters returned and tied the score, 37-37, in the second half; but adjustments had to be made due to personal fouls, and the score seesawed. Rollins scored a free throw to put the U. S. ahead with three minutes to play. Robinson scored a crip and Carpenter a foul point to make the score, 59-55. Argentina scored on a long looper just as the gun sounded.

"Many times basketball fans have talked with me about the practice of scouting opponents, something I have always considered highly advisable," Rupp said. "If I hadn't been convinced before about the wisdom of scouting future foes, I certainly would have been made a believer by one of the things that happened during the Olympic tournament in London. The U. S. team and its coaches simply didn't go to the trouble to scout Argentina before our game with that team. After that struggle, we scouted every team we had to play."

Immediately after the game, Rupp and Browning decided they would use the regular Phillips 66 offense when the Oilers were on the floor and the Kentucky offense when the team was made up mostly of Wildcats. In exhibitions in Scotland and again in the first three games in the Olympics, it had become apparent that it would be difficult to get a team to work smoothly by mixing up players from the AAU and collegiate ranks. They decided to let the Kentucky quintet and Boryla and Lumpp operate as one of the units and the Oilers, together with Barksdale and Robinson, as the other.

With five UK players starting, the U.S. defeated Uruguay, champion of South America, in the first round of the championship elimination. Like many other South American players, Uruguayans were much better at acting than playing basketball. They argued every point and overemphasized every incident and injury. When one of their better players fell to the floor after a brush with Kurland, stretcher-bearers carried him off the court; a short while later he recovered "miraculously" and returned to the game.

In the semifinals with Mexico, Browning started the entire Kentucky team. The contest was rough all the way. Early in the first half Barker zipped under the nets for a loose ball and struck his face on a poorly padded support for the basket. A bloody nose forced him to leave the game, but he returned for later action. Kurland also left the game, but for another reason. He and Gudino Goya came together under the net and as Kurland turned around his leg caught Goya and sent him sprawling.

The official, Ashri of Egypt, banished the surprised Kurland from the game.

"Not only were the teams and players amateur," Kenny Rollins said, "but the officials, timekeepers and scorekeepers also had to be. As a result, we could not take any American officials because they were paid to officiate games in the U. S. and therefore were classified as professionals.

"We might find ourselves playing with a Japanese official and one from Switzerland. If we tried to question a foul, we couldn't make any sense from what they were trying to tell us, and they didn't understand us.

"At the scorers' table, we would find a man from France and one from Yugoslavia. It just made the situation worse. We threw up our hands in despair and didn't question anything."

The Americans also could not understand at first why they were booed by the English fans.

"We asked why," Rollins said, "and it boiled down to the fact that they thought it was unsportsmanlike for us to have bigger players than the other teams and for our substitutes to yell and scream from the bench.

"We couldn't do anything about shrinking guys like Kurland and Groza, but after the first game we sat quietly on the bench throughout the rest of the games. I think we finally captured the fancy of the English people."

Other than the one close call with Argentina, the U. S. had a rather easy time winning the championship. The teams from many countries that competed with them in the Olympics were handicapped by a scarcity of good equipment, lack of indoor courts, and a lack of height. Rupp felt that if Peru or Brazil, for example, had some tall players on their squads, big men like Groza and Kurland, to help control the ball off both boards, they certainly would have given much better accounts of themselves in the London tournament.

Every team in the Olympics that summer employed the

Ralph Beard (12), U.S. guard, heads one for the basket during Olympic basketball competition with Mexico in Harringay arena, London. Louis Beck (11), guard, and Ray Lumpp (24), forward, of the U.S. wait for a possible rebound. Mexico players are Lizana Acuna (9) and Herrara Rojas (14). The Americans won easily, 71-40.

fast break, with the teams representing Europe, Egypt, Iran, Iraq, China, and the Philippines using what was commonly known as the "freedom offensive" pattern, in which the players were free to make their own play situations. Teams from the South American countries and those from Mexico and Canada used set plays whenever the fast-break situations were stopped.

Almost every team in the Olympic tournament used a zone defense except the U. S. The others usually presented a 2-1-2 pattern, with the front line dropping back to about the depth of the free-throw circle. Rupp said the zone operated rather well, possibly because no team presented a real long-shot artist. Even the team from the United States, which included some good long-shooters, could not hit very well in Harringay arena with the heavier ball used in the Olympics.

The U. S. team used two styles of defense, one the pressing pick-up defense employed during the regular season by the University of Kentucky and the other the retreating defense used by the Oilers. The two combinations generally employed the fast break on offense, scoring many baskets through its use, partly because the U. S. could control both backboards.

In retrospect Rupp was surprised that the early basketball games were not better attended. Attendance was a little better in the championship rounds, but still far below what he expected the sport to draw in Britain.

"The poor attendance for our games might have been foreseen because Great Britain has never cared much for basketball, or at least has never paid it much heed in the past," he said. "The game has not been greatly developed there, and the first broadcast on basketball ever made to the British Empire was the one presented as the Olympic tournament began.

"However, the sportswriters in England came around to where they liked the game, and many of them were highly enthusiastic about it before the tournament was over. All of their comments printed in the newspapers were most favorable, and England in the future doubtless will have much more and better basketball."

The basketball champions received their Olympic medals in traditional Olympic style at Wembley Stadium.

"It was the biggest thrill of my life," Rupp said, "to see five of my boys stand on the podium while the National Anthem was being played and get medals as world champions."

Weep No More

On February 24, 1949, Rupp stepped onto the podium of a downtown civic club meeting and was honored as the outstanding citizen of the City of Lexington. Presenting the annual Optimist Club award was Dr. A. D. Kirwan, university dean of students and former UK football coach, who said:

"Like Alexander the Great, Rupp can weep because he, too, has no more worlds to conquer. He's conquered them all in the basketball world—Southeastern, National Collegiate, and Olympics."

Kirwan enumerated not only Rupp's achievements in building up Kentucky basketball teams, but also his activities in other fields—farming, writing, and the Shrine, describing him as a master advertising man, selling Lexington and the university all over the sports world—a messenger of friendship and ambassador of goodwill.

Only a few weeks earlier, Rupp had been soundly booed by 14,000 fans in Boston Garden after he and Holy Cross coach Buster Sheary had rushed onto the playing floor when Cliff Barker and Bob Cousy started to fight. An official waved the coaches off the floor. At game's end, with UK ahead by three points, an irate fan hit Wallace Jones with a wadded paper cup. Jones hit the fan, knocking his shirt completely off, leaving only a tie around his neck. Another fan rushed toward the departing Rupp as a nearby police officer made no attempt to stop the melee. Lancaster knocked the fan down and received, in turn, a kick that left imprints on his stomach.

Two nights later they held St. John's to nine field goals and won, 57-30, before 18,481 fans in Madison Square Garden.

Former Wildcat football coach A.D. Kirwan presents the Optimist Club Cup to UK coach Adolph Rupp, named Lexington "Outstanding Citizen" by the club for the year 1949.

The New York writers praised them as a team of tremendous savvy, rebounding strength, and defense.

The Beard-Groza–Barker-Jones combine was backed solidly that season by proven performers Line, Barnstable, and Howe. Al Cummins transferred to Michigan State, noting, "I sat on the bench for the best team in the country. The best ball game you would see was when we were playing each other. Adolph was good to me, but I wanted to go somewhere where I could play."

Sophomore Joe B. Hall talked to Rupp about going where he could see more action, and Rupp arranged for him to attend Sewanee. Sophomores who remained were Walt Hirsch, Bob Henne, Roger Day, and Garland Townes. The squad was small numerically, but an abundance of quality made up for a lack of quantity.

Rupp entered that season with an 18-year record at Kentucky of 353-70 for a winning percentage of .834. Already a member of the Helms Athletic Foundation Hall of Fame (1944), he was selected in 1948 as "Coach of the Year" by a national sports magazine, polling more votes than the total of all the rival nominees for that distinction.

The secret behind such a long and successful career? "Why, that's easy," he said. "It's been good coaching."

His only regular season loss that year was a two-point setback by St. Louis in the Sugar Bowl. The defense-oriented Billikens of Ed Hickey, led by Ed Macauley, throttled the Wildcat fast break, forcing them to change offense, and slowed the game down to a walk. The Wildcats were leading by two points when one of their guards looked up at the clock and dribbled the ball off his foot. St. Louis took the ball out of bounds and scored a basket while the Kentuckians just stood around. When the Billikens were awarded a foul shot with seconds remaining, Rupp told his boys to be sure that St. Louis did not tip in the ball if the shot missed. A Billiken, standing in the No. 2 position, tipped in the winning basket as the gun went off.

As Rupp left the playing arena and started up the steps to the dressing room, Burgess Carey, former Wildcat All-American and a friend of his, stormed up to him and said, "Coach, you just cost me $500."

"By God, I didn't lose any $500 for you," Rupp replied.

He entered the dressing room and said to Barnstable, who had missed a crucial shot in the game, "You just cost my friend Burgess Carey $500."

There were rumblings among the gambling element that maybe everything was not on the up-and-up, but Rupp turned deaf ears to such gossip.

"The percentage caught up with us," he said. "You know, the object of the game is to put the ball through the hoop. We didn't do that. It's just like your dead grandmother. You know—she just died."

Another interesting game was at Cleveland, where the Wildcats defeated Bowling Green by two points in what the newspapers called the greatest game ever played there. The Cleveland writers, unlike their counterparts in New York, apparently saw no cause for suspicion in the below-par play of the Kentuckians.

In the season finale at Lexington, Barker made a shot from 65 feet out on the floor, beating the record of 52½ feet set by

Ralph Beard. As the shot dropped through, Dr. Donovan ran onto the playing floor and dropped his hat on the spot.

In an unprecedented move, Rupp accepted invitations to both the NIT and NCAA tournaments that year, explaining that he wanted a chance for a revenge meeting with St. Louis.

There was much suspected in the Wildcats' 67-56 loss to Loyola of Chicago in the opening round of the NIT. An air of indifference engulfed them from start to finish. Groza did not seem to be trying to block Alex Kerris' pivot shots, preferring to back away and let the Loyola pivotman hook them up unmolested; if they missed, Groza took the rebound; if they hit, he took the ball out of bounds. On offense he did not try to get in front of Kerris; consequently, Beard and Barker did not get the ball to him. Jones fouled out midway of the second half, and Groza and Hirsch soon followed suit. With only two points in the first half, Beard tried desperately to spark his team, hitting several long shots and finishing with 15 points.

Writers intimated that maybe the Wildcats had pulled their punches, for mysterious reasons, and let the game get out of hand. Such talk was discounted by Kentuckians, who blamed the loss on a variety of reasons, including overconfidence, too much traveling, failure to play as a unit, and poor officiating.

"It had to happen sometime," Rupp said. "It's a damn shame it had to happen here. We have no alibis. They outhustled us, that's all. I knew the jig was up when Jones and Groza fouled out."

Asked why his team was so far off form, he managed a wry smile, almost as if in sympathy for the interrogater:

"Well, sir, I can't figure that out...I never could figure why teams go flat. You go out and get the answer to that and you'll get the Academy Award, or whatever they give for basketball."

"But why didn't they feed the ball to Groza in the second half, when Jack Kerris was playing with four fouls and it seemed logical that Groza would shoot and try to foul him out?"

"That's another question I'd like answered."

"You mean you instructed the boys to feed him the ball?"

"Good Lord, man, didn't you hear the whole bench yelling for the boys to do just that?"

"I was so darned mad at the boys that I just took them home the next day," Rupp said. "I practiced them like the dickens. I'm telling you, we went through some bloodthirsty practices. Then I took them back to New York for the NCAA."

With Line replacing Barnstable in the starting lineup, they defeated Villanova, 85-72, and then unleashed a devastating attack that left Illinois helpless and on the ropes—a thoroughly defeated and stunned aggregation. The final score of 76-47 did not begin to indicate the sharpness of the Kentucky game. The writers were generous in their praise.

The championship between Kentucky and Oklahoma A&M was billed as a contest between the contrasting styles of "Red Hot Rupp" and "Deep Freeze" Iba. Before a capacity crowd of 12,500 at the University of Washington Pavilion in Seattle, UK slowed the game down to the Aggie pace and controlled it so artistically that for one 12-minute stretch A&M failed to score a single field goal. Groza fouled out with five minutes to go, but his 25 points and fine all-around play had kept Kentucky in the lead. The Wildcats stalled for a 46-36 victory.

During the first hectic moments after the game, Rupp kicked up his heels and did a jig as the players shouted and thumped each other on the shoulders and cavorted in a manner befitting the occasion.

"Look, Alex!" said a surprised Beard. "Adolph's dancing."

There was ample reason for rejoicing. In winning the tournament, the Wildcats set 22 NCAA team and individual records. Groza scored 82 points in three games and was again named Most Valuable Player. The season went on the record books as the greatest in the illustrious history of UK basketball. Groza, Beard, Jones, and Barker, billed as the "Fabulous Four," had led the team to such major marks as:

Thirty-two victories in 34 games, a percentage of .941, best in the modern history of the school.

Sixth straight SEC championship.

Number One ranking in the nation by the Associated Press.

First team ever to compete in the two major tournaments in one season.

Only school other than Oklahoma A&M to win two NCAA national championships.

Beard and Jones were accorded All-SEC honors for four consecutive years, a distinction also held by Jack Tingle. Groza and Beard twice before were chosen on prominent All-American teams. Groza, Beard, and Jones all scored greater point totals than any predecessor in a Kentucky uniform. Groza practically rewrote the SEC record book on scoring; that final season, he scored 696 points, an average of 20.4 in 34 games, and boosted his four-season total to 1,742. Beard added 372 for a total of 1,519, and Jones 300 for a total of 1,151.

Lexington had honored its basketball heroes with large celebrations in the past, but "Wildcat Appreciation Day," April 4, 1949, was the largest and most enthusiastic of them all. Twenty-five thousand persons turned out for the occasion, which brought a part holiday to most of the city and to all the schools. The morning had a chilly tang, but the sunlight helped pep things up as a 37-unit parade formed for a march through an eight-block downtown area and then to the campus. Main Street was a solid mass of humanity. Every store window from the first floor to the top was filled with faces; some of the more

Kentucky Victory Dance—Adolph Rupp staged this victory dance in dressing room after his Wildcats defeated Oklahoma A&M 46-36 to win NCAA basketball title for second straight year. His star center, Alex Groza (15), and Dale Barnstable, right, were happy, too.

hardy souls climbed to dizzy perches to get a good view. Two men sat on a ledge atop the highest building, their legs dangling over the side. One shiny car had as its attraction the "NCAA Victory Ball" used in the game against A&M.

"Can you imagine how I'd have felt coming back to this celebration if we hadn't brought this hardware with us," Rupp said. "Until today, I had been a bit skeptical about the profession of teaching, but, after seeing all the school kids on Main Street, I decided there must be a wonderful future in school teaching."

Even in that, his finest moment, he managed to alienate several people by issuing monograms to seven players—the four seniors, and Barnstable, Line, and Hirsch—and slighting five players who had accompanied the team to both tournaments in New York. He retired the jersey numbers worn by Barker, Beard, Groza, Jones, and Rollins, with the stipulation they were never to be worn again by a Kentucky player. The designation of those players as the "Fabulous Five" resulted from retirement of their numbers. (The numbers, however, would be worn by UK players again in later years.)

The four seniors organized a barnstorming team and then joined Joe Holland and former Lexington sports editor "Babe" Kimbrough to form the Indianapolis Olympians professional team. They owned all the common stock; in addition, Indianapolis businessmen purchased 30 shares of preferred stock at $1,000 a share. It was the first time in the history of professional basketball that five players from one school had made up a unit, and the first time the players themselves had owned a team.

That year the UK football team won eight games and accepted an invitation to the Orange Bowl. Also scheduled to participate in the basketball portion of the Sugar Bowl festivities, UK was the only college in the nation having two teams in bowl games. The university was certified by the National Collegiate Athletic Bureau as the nation's most successful major college in the combined basketball-football campaign of that year.

The university's rise to such a position of prominence was in direct contrast to the recommendations of Griffenhagen and Associates, an independent fault-finding firm that had declared four years earlier that athletics at UK, as in other universities, had become professionalized, though still considered amateur. In a report to Kentucky governor Simeon Willis, the firm coldly

Lining up for the tipoff of their last game in Alumni Gym are Wildcat seniors Ralph Beard (12), Cliff Barker, Alex Groza (jumping center), and Wallace Jones, right. Dale Barnstable is No. 18. The Wildcats defeated Vanderbilt, 70-37, in that game.

advised that the UK sports program be put on an "amateur" standing.

In essence, the report said that educationally and in terms of the ultimate welfare of the university, it would be better if football and basketball were just sports played for the fun of playing rather than for the fun of spectators. The report conceded, however, that UK had acted "realistically" in answering demands of alumni, other fans, and sportswriters for winning teams.

Donovan said the report showed that UK was making the best of what the Griffenhagens considered a bad situation. He said the university, realizing it could not reform sports in general, intended to continue its present course, because that was what the public demanded. That decision would prove costly to the university.

Echoes From The Late '40s

Wallace Jones (1946, '47, '48, and '49)
Lexington, Kentucky

Dear Russell:

I don't remember too many times when Coach Bryant and Coach Rupp had a disagreement over me, or over which team I would play for. I think the only time that happened was when I came down with appendicitis during one football season.

Coach Bryant and Coach Rupp wanted me to go to different doctors. Coach Rupp's main interest was getting me back in playing shape for basketball. Coach Bryant wanted me to be ready for the football game with Tennessee.

I had the attack coming back from a football game against Michigan State. I guess that Coach Bryant won the battle, because I went to his doctor for the surgery. I missed one game, against Alabama, but I was back to play in the Tennessee game.

I remember once when we were playing Alabama down at that old gym, Foster Auditorium, that they had in Tuscaloosa. There was a balcony that ran around above the playing floor, and the fans used to throw coins down on the floor when things didn't please them. And they had a stuffed owl up there. When they'd shoot the gun to end the half or the game, somebody would throw that bird down on the floor, like it had just been shot.

Before the game, Adolph got us in the dressing room. He told us, "Now, I don't want to see a damned one of you paying any attention to that crowd. When they throw that money on the floor, you ignore it." We were playing along, and then a decision went against Alabama that the crowd didn't like, and here came the money piling down on the floor, most of it pennies and nickels and dimes.

Bernie Shively was our athletic director then, and basketball teams didn't have as much money to operate on as they do now. Anyway, here came all these coins and finally a big half-dollar rolled right by Shively, who was sitting at the end of our bench. It was too much for him, and he just reached out, picked it up, and put it in his pocket. This was after Coach Rupp had warned all the players to ignore it.

Adolph just looked down at the end of the bench and said, "Well, Shive, I see they met your price."

       Sincerely,

       "Wah"

       Dale Barnstable (1947, '48,
        '49, and '50)
       Louisville, Kentucky

Dear Russell:

During the 1944-45 season, Coach Rupp came into the locker room at the Alumni Gym at half time with his squad leading Arkansas State 34-4. He bolted through the door and said, "Give me the scorebook." He looked at it, then eyed the team, which I am sure was thinking, "How in the world could he possibly be critical of us when we're leading 34-4?" One Arkansas State man had all his team's four points. Rupp looked around at his squad and then shouted, "Who is guarding No. 12?" Jack Parkinson looked up and said, "Coach, I am." "Well get on him because he is running absolutely wild," Rupp said. The final score was 75-6, so obviously in the second half not only Parkinson got on his man but so did everyone else because Arkansas only scored two points the last half. This was my first introduction to perfection on defense at UK. When I was told this story by a former player, I said, "I can't believe that that could happen." He said, "You just wait and see."

People have asked me how I got to UK and I tell them that when I was in the war in Germany in 1945, a former UK player, Milt Ticco, wrote Coach Rupp and said, "Dear Coach, I have been playing with a boy who I think could help the UK basketball program." Ticco gave him my name, age, accomplishments, etc., and then said, "P.S. My basketball shoes are worn out; could you please send me another pair?"

Rupp wrote Ticco a very gracious and kind letter and basically stated that he would like to have me write to him when I got out of the Army and possibly visit UK to look at the facilities and campus. He ended up with a P.S. to Ticco, "Milt, don't you realize there has been a war going? As a result, it has created a severe rubber shortage and therefore I'm unable to send you the shoes. However, I am interested in you sending me the boy."

In 1946, I drove my car from Northern Illinois down to the bluegrass country and on into Lexington. Coach Rupp asked me if I would like to try out and I replied that I would. When I finished, he asked me to come in to talk with him in his office. He said, "Nobody is returning." I found out that he was right because everyone was coming back and that nobody he was referring to was me. He only had six All-Americans coming back plus four All-SEC players. I would call this a lesson in salesmanship.

It got kinda rugged one day in practice and Bill Spivey and Roger Layne were going at it hot and heavy. Bill became a little perturbed with Roger and let a hook shot and an elbow fly simultaneously. The ball went in the basket and Roger went to the floor.

Roger had his hand over his mouth and Coach Rupp asked, "What's wrong?" Roger went "sput" and three white, hard objects flew out on the floor. Rupp asked, "What in the world are those?" Humzey Yessin, the manager, said, "Coach I think those are three teeth that belong in Roger's mouth."

"Are you all right?" Rupp asked.

"Hell, yes," Roger said. "Let's play some ball."

Rupp said, "All right, Humzey, throw her up and let's get back to work." Then he turned to Harry and said, "Now, that's what I'm looking for—a fellow that will lose three teeth and still say let's get back in the game. That's determination."

Everyone knows of the man in the brown suit, but there are very few people that know of the drinking cup. I always marvelled at how Rupp would get a Dixie Cup full of water at Convention Center, which was the old armory in Louisville, take a drink and then walk a few paces over, reach up as high as he could and place that Dixie Cup on a rafter. He would then get it down at half time and he'd get it down after the game. It was as if that paper cup was the most valuable thing in the world, when in reality, it was just a ritual and I suppose one of his superstitions. Another ritual was that we never took the floor before a game unless it was 27½ or 28¾ minutes, nothing like 20, 25, or 30 minutes.

We made some great bus trips back in those days. We most assuredly did not have the modern traveling conveniences such as jet planes, swanky motels and so on. We were fortunate enough to stay in the old Farragut Hotel in Knoxville.

In 1946, we were going over the scouting report—one of the most serious moments of the day—on the University of Tennessee. Rupp wanted to impress upon all of the war veterans how tough and cantankerous Knoxville could be and of course, how the Big Orange was going to treat us. Barker had been a prisoner of war and several of us had fought the Germans. Rupp, being a very quick thinker, followed up the scouting report by looking at Barker and saying, "If you think Anzio or North Africa were tough, you haven't seen a thing, wait until you get on this floor tonight, then you'll find out how tough war really is."

Line, who did not have the fastest shot in the West, was sitting in the back row with about a half-smile on his face. Rupp looked at him and said, "Laugh, you son-of-a-gun, you'll see what I mean when these guys fill your whole mouth with an entire basketball." I believe on that evening, Line speeded up his shot more than he had ever done before.

                        Sincerely,

                        Dale

                        Bob Roesler
                        Sports Editor
                        The *Times Picayune*
                        New Orleans, Louisiana

Dear Russell:

    My most memorable contact with Coach Rupp was my first. I don't recall the year, but it was in the glory days of the Sugar Bowl basketball tournament and the Baron's team won it in what might be considered a mild upset.

    I was assigned to interview The Great Man and, frankly, I was a bit nervous. You know, something like a commoner meeting the King of England.

    When this cub reporter met Rupp, I stuttered desperately trying to ask a probing and proper question.

    But all I could come up with was, "How do you feel, Coach Rupp?"

    He seemed eight feet tall as he looked down on me and said, "There is a Santa Claus."

    That gave me a lead and also relaxed me.

                        Regards,

                        Bob

                        Joe Holland (1946, '47,
                            and '48)
                        Charleston, West Virginia

Dear Russell:
    You know that in the late forties we took quite a few

trips by car and I shall always remember riding on occasions with Coach Rupp at the wheel, going through the bluegrass farmland which he loved so much. He very seldom looked at the road, but was constantly pointing out barns, tobacco crops, cattle and other points of interest to his passengers and most of the time he was doing the pointing with both arms. It was most exciting how he managed always to keep the car on the road.

There is a conversation which I had once with Coach Rupp which I wish could have been taped. It showed his foresight clearly. We thought ours was a great team with good size and all other attributes that it takes to make a great team. And I will add that I'm sure everyone agrees that is a true statement. But some of us were saying that there probably wouldn't be another like that team because of the World War II bringing it together, etc. Coach Rupp made a very wise statement to this effect. "There will be in years to come and I'll probably have them here, men that will be bigger, faster, will jump higher and shoot better than even this great team." I think what has happened since confirms his thinking, although I'm sure most of our bunch and many others still feel that we would have done okay as a college team in any era.

We were in Chicago to play DePaul and after the game some of the boys decided to see the bright lights. It so happened that my roommate was one of them. I noticed the next morning that his bed was untouched. I dressed and headed down to breakfast and coincidentally Rupp was waiting for the same elevator. To my dismay when the elevator stopped, my old roomie walked right off, quite bleary-eyed and ready for a little sleep. I immediately asked him what he forgot in the room and he caught on saying that he would be right back. He was and joined us for breakfast. I still don't know for sure whether we sold Coach on that one, but I doubt it.

The records will show that I was not a noted high scorer while in college. The following incident shows Coach Rupp's great sense of humor and quick wit at its best. I have a son who is a junior at UK this year.

About nine or 10 years ago, we were in Lexington and went by to watch the team practice. Joey was 10 or

11 and had been playing real good in the YMCA League. I introduced him to Coach Rupp and proudly told Coach that the kid had just recently scored 21 points in a game. With no hesitation and not even a smile Coach Rupp said, "Hell, that's a new high for the Holland family." My wife and Buddy Parker were standing there and it broke them up. I didn't think it was so funny.

                        Sincerely,

                        Joe Holland

                        Furman Bisher
                        Sports Editor
                        Atlanta Journal

Dear Russ:

    One story always pops into my mind when I think of Adolph. It happened several years ago when I stopped in Lexington to do a magazine story on him for *Sport*. We had gone out to look at his farm and were driving around the pasture with Chester Jones, his foreman. Adolph was admiring the bovine lines of the herd as if it were a basketball squad when we came upon this heifer lying on the ground.

    "What's wrong with her, Chester?" he said.

    "She just lays down and coughs all the time. I can't find a thing wrong with her."

    "Get rid of her," Adolph said abruptly. "She is not a credit to the place. She's like a sub sitting on the bench cheering for the other team. Get rid of her."

    I know you've read of the time he took little Herky, then 12, on a road trip and was treating him to dinner with the squad at Antoine's in New Orleans. And in this French gourmet atmosphere Herky ordered a bowl of chili and a Pepsi Cola and got mad as hell when Adolph told him he couldn't get it.

                        Best Regards,

                        Furman

Ralph Beard (1946, '47, '48, and '49)

Dear Russell:

As a freshman at UK, I had become discouraged and homesick, as a lot of immature 18-year-olds do sometimes, and I had decided to transfer to the University of Louisville. I went in to tell Coach Rupp and we had a chat about everything. He pointed out why he thought I was making a big mistake, but he said one last sentence that has stuck with me all these years: "Son, I can't keep you from going to UL, but I will tell you one thing. We here at the university will not cancel our schedule."

One of Coach Rupp's pet peeves was a guard who walked the ball up the floor. He called it "Tom-Tomming." Parkinson was walking up the floor with the ball. Coach stood up—it seemed like everything got quiet—and he said, "Quit that...around out there." A lady stood up and slapped him across the back with a purse or umbrella. Rupp never batted an eye, but said to Harry, "See who hit me."

Sincerely,

Ralph

Larry Boeck (deceased)
The *Courier-Journal*
Louisville, Kentucky

Dear Russell:

It was after a tournament in New York and Rupp called Beard and Jones to the hotel desk as the team checked out before returning to Lexington. "You boys have radios in your room?" Adolph asked. When they replied in the affirmative, he said, "Well, boys, you each owe one dollar a day for the three days you had the radio. That's three dollars each you owe the university."

I also remember a bus trip to East Lansing, where the Wildcats played Michigan State, and then to Athens to play Ohio University. After paying my bill, I was about to enter the bus when I heard several players calling my name. Beard finally reached me and, with a wry smile, said, "Mr. Rupp wants to see you. He's at the desk."

When I got to the desk, Rupp said, "Larry, there are three telephone calls from your room charged to the team's bill. You owe the university eighteen cents."

Sincerely,

Larry

Adolph Rupp

"When I get this business organized properly, you'll see something. I'll have a squad of ten centers, twenty-six guards and thirty forwards. I'll have a coach for the guards, one for the centers and one for the forwards, and a scout to go around and look over the opposition. I'll be the head coach. We'll have two ball teams—one for home games and one for the road. We'll pack the field house every night at two dollars a head. At the end of the season, we'll win the NCAA tournament with one team and the Metropolitan Invitational with the other. Then we'll throw the two together at Soldiers Field in Chicago for the national championship. That'll draw eighty-seven thousand people at ten dollars a head."

The Impending Storm

Replacing the Barker-Beard-Groza-Jones combine was an awesome task indeed, but Rupp still had such veteran performers as Barnstable, Hirsch, and Line around which to build a new team as UK entered the 1950s.

Loss of the four seniors had resulted in a sudden urge on the part of many teams to play UK, but the university refused to oblige those teams that had steered clear of the Wildcats in the past.

In addition the conference had adopted a new rotating system that required each team to play 14 league games, enabling the championship to be determined by the results of regular season play.

The teams were divided into three sections: North—Kentucky, Tennessee, Vanderbilt, and Georgia Tech; East—Auburn, Georgia, Alabama, and Florida; West—Mississippi, Mississippi State, LSU, and Tulane. Each school would play one game as a visitor with each team in another section and would be visited for home games by each of the schools in the third section. The visiting procedure would be reversed the following season. The setup left UK with 12 games scheduled outside the conference.

The UK sophomore "Mutt & Jeff" combination of that season consisted of 7-foot Bill Spivey of Warner Robins, Georgia, and 5-foot-10 Bobby Watson of Owensboro. After Harry Lancaster had suggested to Watson that he come out on his own, Bobby had decided to accept a scholarship offer to Alabama. He boarded a train for Tuscaloosa, but returned to Lexington after no one met him at the station, and he had difficulty finding out where to go. He played so well as a freshman at UK that he was elected captain of the yearlings and placed on scholarship the following season.

Other newcomers on the varsity team were guards Guy Strong of Irvine, Kentucky; Len Pearson of Chicago, Illinois; Lucian "Skippy" Whitaker of Sarasota, Florida; and forward C. M. Newton of Ft. Lauderdale, Florida. Junior college transfers Shelby Linville, a 6-foot-6 forward from Middletown, Ohio, and Read Morgan, a 6-foot-4 forward from Milwaukee, Wisconsin, would be eligible the second semester.

There was much anxiety and curiosity as the Wildcats lined up for their opening game against Indiana Central in Alumni Gym; however, what doubts the faithful entertained were soon dispelled as Line bombed the nets from the corner, hitting 13 of 16 field goal attempts and 11 of 12 free throws for 37 points, one shy of the conference record held by Groza. When Jim fouled out with almost two minutes remaining in the game, the capacity crowd gave him such a long ovation that the game was delayed five minutes. UK won, 84-61. Western Ontario was another "breather" on the Wildcat schedule, falling, 90-18, a week later in Lexington.

The Wildcats traveled to New York that season for their 31st appearance in the Garden, more than any team outside New York had made. They lost, 69-58, to St. John's, but bounced back to beat DePaul and Purdue on the road. After that victory over Purdue on Christmas night, someone wished Rupp a Merry Christmas.

"I've had my Christmas tonight," he replied. "The boys gave me a present I wanted."

Paul Arizin had a good game against Spivey in the Sugar Bowl, but the Wildcats defeated Villanova, 57-56, in overtime. Whitaker scored two goals and Line one in the extra period. Against a heavily favored Bradley team that featured Gene Melchiorre, Bill Mann, and Paul Unruh, the Wildcats got fine scoring from Spivey (22), Line (19), and Whitaker (13) to defeat the Braves, 71-66.

"I'm proud of you," Rupp told the Wildcats. "You've done something the 'Fabulous Five' never was able to do. We've been riding around since before Christmas with a bunch of kids in diapers and winning games."

Art Burrus outscored Spivey, 28-12, at Knoxville to lead the Vols over UK, 66-53, and snap a seven-game Wildcat winning streak. It was their first loss in the conference since UT

UK booster Jere T. Beam adjusts the new sign designating that portion of Euclid Avenue between the Coliseum and Stoll Field as "Avenue of Champions" after the Wildcats won the 1950 football Sugar Bowl and the 1951 NCAA basketball championship. From left are UK athletic director Bernie A. Shively, football coach Paul "Bear" Bryant, Lexington Mayor Ralph Looney, and Rupp.

beat them, 35-34, on the same floor January 20, 1945. They defeated Georgia Tech and then lost to Georgia at Athens as 6-foot-8 Bob Schloss outscored Spivey, 28-8. It was the first time since 1942 that UK had dropped two conference games. They beat DePaul, lost to Notre Dame, and ended the regular season by winning the next 11 games. Spivey outscored Burrus, 34-12, and Schloss, 18-4, in rematches with Tennessee and Georgia. Against Georgia Tech, he scored 40 points to break Groza's SEC single-game record of 38.

Trailing Vanderbilt by 12 points in the last game to be played in Alumni Gym, Rupp told his players at halftime, "Boys, a man spends a lifetime compiling a record, and in one given night a bunch of bums like you are about to tear it down. If it looks to me like we're going to go down in defeat tonight, I want you to know that I am personally going to do something to this facility before the game is over and before you get out of this gym."

The Wildcats won that game, 70-66, preserving the gym record of 84 consecutive victories and ending an era that saw Wildcat teams win 262 games and lose only 25 times in the facility.

Although Spivey scored 37 points in a 95-58 victory over Tennessee in the final game of the SEC tournament to tie Groza's one-game SEC tournament record, he was placed second to Burrus on the All-Tournament team. However, the Associated Press selected Spivey on its All-SEC team and to third team All-America.

Rupp felt that the Wildcats, with their 24-4 record and the conference championship, deserved to represent District 3 in the NCAA playoffs; however, the Selection Committee chose North Carolina State after UK stubbornly refused to play the Wolfpack for the honor. The NCAA would end such internal squabbling by doubling the tournament field the following year, automatically including 10 major conference champions, and filling the other berths with members-at-large, a total of 16 teams.

The Wildcats accepted a bid to the NIT, meeting City College of New York for the first time. The CCNY team, which included superstar Ed Warner and two other black starters, defeated the Wildcats, 89-50, pinning on Rupp his worst defeat in 24 years of coaching. UK had not been whipped so badly since losing to Centre, 87-17, in 1910.

"I'll say this for Rupp," CCNY coach Nat Holman said. "He was a gentleman in defeat. He came over and congratulated us in a very gracious manner."

Rupp was less gracious in the dressing room.

"I want to thank you boys," he said. "You get me selected coach of the year, and then bring me up here and embarrass the hell out of me."

At that point in time, Madison Square Garden, with upward of 18,000 vociferous fans basing their cheers and jeers on the point spread rather than the eventual winner, had become an awesome, sometimes cold, and threateningly evil place to take a basketball team. Some coaches flatly refused to let their teams play there. Rupp felt differently.

"Imagine what going to the big cities means to my boys," he said, "and it's all poppycock about them being contaminated by the gambling element at the Garden. In the first place, they're always under my wing, and in the second place college boys of the type who play in the SEC aren't easily tempted. At least, I'll vouch for my 'Cats."

The university's new field house, named Memorial Coliseum in memory of Kentuckians killed in World War II, was dedicated as part of Commencement Week activities that spring. The multipurpose facility, classically simple in design, contains as much space as a seven-story office building covering an entire city block. In addition to a basketball arena seating almost 12,000 persons, it contains a complete plant for the teaching of physical education. Considered near perfect from an acoustical point of view, it also serves as a concert or lecture hall.

An estimated 8,000 fans, second largest crowd ever to see a basketball game in Kentucky, attended the opening game in the new facility and were subjected to a rather drab affair as UK swamped West Texas State, 73-43. The only sophomore in the starting lineup for UK was Frank Ramsey, a 6-foot-3 guard from Madisonville, Kentucky. The other starters were Watson, Spivey, Linville, and Hirsch. Cliff Hagan, who scored a tournament record 41 points in leading Owensboro to the state high school crown over Lafayette, had enrolled at UK in midseason of 1950 and would not become eligible for varsity competition until late January 1951.

The next game, against Purdue, was designated for official dedicatory ceremonies. An estimated 11,000 persons heard Dr. Leo M. Chamberlain, UK vice president, urge that the building "be the home of true sportsmanship, and the source of men of exalted minds, of vigorous bodies, and of great character." The Wildcats won, 70-52.

And then Kansas came to town, focusing national attention on the matchup between Rupp and his old coach Phog Allen and between Jayhawk center Clyde Lovellette and Spivey. Spivey outscored Lovellette, 22-10, and was taken out of the game after the Kansas center fouled out with more than 12 minutes remaining. UK won, 68-39.

Ramsey made a brilliant debut in New York and Linville scored six clutch points midway of the second half to lead the Wildcats over St. John's, 43-37. They then journeyed to New Orleans and the Sugar Bowl, where the UK football team also was part of the festivities, being matched against national champion Oklahoma. Spivey broke a tie against St. Louis with less than two minutes remaining, but the Wildcats lost possession out of bounds with 10 seconds left and St. Louis scored a 43-42 victory. Some gamblers claimed the game was so obviously suspicious that they could not get bets down.

Oklahoma A&M replaced UK in the No. 1 spot nationally, but the Wildcats were back on top after they had won 11 straight, including victories over DePaul and Notre Dame. Hagan had started playing and added strength to the team.

Rupp was ailing practically all of the final five weeks of that season. He was hospitalized eight days in mid-February with a cornea ulcer, had a recurrence of his back pains, and was bothered by high blood pressure. In addition, Vanderbilt ended a 21-game UK winning streak, upsetting the Wildcats, 61-57, in the final game of the SEC tournament. However, that was the first year the SEC championship was decided on the basis of regular season play, and UK was invited to meet Louisville in the opening round of the eastern regional at Raleigh, North Carolina.

Rupp developed such severe pain and swelling that his right leg was put in a cast from the hip to below the knee. The eye ailment also flared up again, causing sportswriters to speculate that he would retire if UK won the championship. The plaster cast was replaced by a laced leather stocking, which covered most of his leg.

Hirsch was declared ineligible for the tournament because he was in his fourth season of varsity play. Hagan replaced him in the starting lineup. Louisville led the Wildcats, 64-60, with less than 10 minutes remaining, but "Skippy" Whitaker hit some clutch baskets to pace UK to a 79-68 victory. St. John's

Celebrating Kentucky's 68-58 victory over Kansas State in the 1951 NCAA championship game are, left to right, standing, front row: Cliff Hagan, trainer Charles Harper, Bill Spivey, Rupp, Lancaster, Frank Ramsey. Rear: C. M. Newton, Bobby Watson, Lou Tsioropoulos, and "Skippy" Whitaker. Shelby Linville kneels in front.

held Spivey to 12 points, but Ramsey scored 15 and Watson 12 as UK beat the Redmen, 59-43.

Spivey came back strong against Illinois, scoring 28 points and grabbing 16 rebounds, but Linville was the UK hero, hitting the deciding goal in a 76-74 victory with only 12 seconds left. He scored 14 points in that game.

Cliff Hagan was on the bench with the flu in the first half of the championship game against Kansas State at Minneapolis, and Spivey had a cold. The Wildcats trailed, 29-27, at halftime. They took control of the game in the second half and won, 68-58. Spivey scored 22 points and had 21 rebounds. Hagan had 10 points.

Rupp was conducting various clinics, and Lancaster was coaching the Greek National Basketball Team when the Wildcat squad, chaperoned by Dale Barnstable, flew to Puerto Rico for a series of six exhibition games that summer. Rupp joined the team at San Juan. The only unpleasant incident occurred when he allegedly accused the Puerto Rican All-Stars of playing dirty and threatened to cancel a game scheduled the following day. Coach Victor Perez said Rupp was the first American coach who had criticized his team's sportsmanship.

Rupp later claimed the six victories in Puerto Rico as part of his all-time total, but the NCAA ruled they were exhibitions and did not count. He would fight a losing battle over the years, trying to get the games sanctioned by that organization.

While he enjoyed the fruits of victory, there were rumblings on other fronts directly affecting his barony. Some Kentucky fans threatened not to purchase tickets if a black player appeared in a game in the Coliseum. New York writers pointed out that St. John's was scheduled to play in Lexington and that relations between the two schools had been strained because the Redman squad would include Solly Walker, a black player. Rupp said the university had arranged for the entire St. John's team to stay in the city's leading hotel, and he had made other arrangements for Walker's comfort.

During the week of August 13, Chicago and New York papers carried hints that an investigation of Kentucky players was under way. Arch Ward wrote in the *Tribune*: "The simmering University of Kentucky basketball scandal will hit the sports pages soon." A Manhattan paper intimated that there might have been something amiss when the "Fabulous Four" lost to Loyola in the opening round of the NIT in 1949.

"We have no reason to believe that any Kentucky player is involved in any way," Shively said. "As far as I know, none of the Kentucky players nor any of Kentucky's games are under investigation."

During an interview in Lincoln, Nebraska, on August 15, Rupp allegedly declared, "The gamblers couldn't get to our boys with a ten-foot pole."

He explained that his team was under "constant and absolutely complete supervision while on the road" and, he added, "Nowhere was that supervision more complete than in New York."

He blamed the gambling outbreak on the immense growth of the game itself. "Basketball is the biggest sport in the nation," he said. "It's the biggest in attendance and is by far our greatest active participation sport. We can't expect it to remain completely untainted."

In New York, District Attorney O'Connor was asked about progress in his investigation. "All I can say," he replied, "is strictly off the record—but Adolph Rupp may be embarrassed by his statement about a ten-foot pole."

Time Out: Bill Spivey

Bill Spivey was one of the best baskctball players ever to appear on the college cage scene, but unlike many other famous players who were practically born with a basketball in their hands, he was 14 years of age before he even picked up a basketball.

"I thought it was a sissy game," the 7-foot former UK All-American (1951) said in the summer of 1975. "I was 6-5 or 6-6 and naturally they asked me to come out for basketball. I didn't try it until the next year, but I quit after a short length of time because I didn't like all that running."

Spivey was born at Lakeland, Florida, and moved to Georgia when he was two years old. He played his first high school basketball at Jordan High in Columbus, Georgia.

"I was 6-7 or 6-8 and a freshman when they talked me into coming out again," he recalled. "I was a substitute center. When our pivotman fouled out against Phenix City (Alabama), I played the entire second half and scored 19 points. They'd lob the ball high to me and I would just turn around and put it in. The newspapers gave me a pretty good buildup the next day and I started getting more attention around the campus, especially from the girls. That more or less convinced me that I'd better take a longer look at this basketball game."

Spivey's father was a civil service worker at nearby Ft. Benning at the time. Before the next season he went to work at an air base near Warner Robins, Georgia, which did not have a high school. Spivey had to go by bus 10 miles to Bon Air, Georgia, where he played basketball.

"We played in a converted old barn with a wood stove at

From the Nashville Banner.

each end of it," he said. "If you weren't careful, you might drive off that red hot stove or stick to it.

"They didn't have any shoes big enough (size 15) to fit me, so I had to play in three pairs of socks. They called traveling on me quite a bit. While trying to catch a pass on the dead run and then stopping, I would slide in those socks. The next season, I got a pair of size 12 and cut the toes out."

Spivey played only half a season at Bon Air. People at Warner Robins had complained so much that a barracks-type building was put up to serve as a high school. Spivey enrolled there, and a basketball team was formed.

"We had a gym that was a USO building, where dances and other functions were held," he said. "It was during my junior year that I learned that you could get a scholarship to go to college if you could play sports good enough. So I'd go any place where I could find a goal and practice as many hours as I could between working at the supermarket and going to school."

Spivey's parents had decided to send him to Lanier High, in Macon, Georgia, that year so he could have qualified teachers instead of the officers' wives who were filling in at Warner Robins. When he did not make the Macon basketball team, he returned to Warner Robins.

There Spivey averaged 22 points his junior year and 29 points as a senior. Rupp heard about him through an article written for the Atlanta newspaper by Ed Danforth. He sent Buddy Parker to see Spivey and invite him to UK for a tryout.

"I wanted to come to UK because I had read about the Fabulous Five and Rupp," Spivey said. "When I read that they had two or three All-Americans sitting on the bench, I didn't understand that at all, except that they had such a powerhouse that you could sit on the bench and become an All-American."

After receiving an invitation to try out for Rupp, Spivey rode a bus to Lexington and joined dozens of other aspirants who were displaying their skills for the UK coach.

"When I went to the gym, my wardrobe was like a pair of bluejeans and a T-shirt," Spivey said. "All the other young men were dressed to the hilt. I was telling them about my long bus ride from Warner Robins to get there and then I found out that all of them had been flown in here and had taken a limousine from the airport. After riding that bus all the way, I had walked from the station to the gym.

"They put me in the Scott Street Barracks. It had holes in the walls. I couldn't imagine that this was the famous school that I had been reading about. I thought about that antique gymnasium and about them putting a so-called high school superstar (in my opinion) up in an old hotel with holes in the loft. Anyway, I was still excited and nervous about the opportunity to work out."

After those tryouts Rupp was asked about Spivey. "His seven feet is interesting," Der Baron said, "but to tell the truth, he doesn't look like very much. He lacks coordination, he is awkward, he doesn't have any shots, and he stands around flat-footed. However, he can run fairly fast, and he seems sincere and very intent in his desire to play for us."

"I understand that Rupp told several people that the only reason he gave me a scholarship was because I could dribble the length of the floor," Spivey said. "After all, I was 6-10½, but I only weighed 170 pounds when I first got on the scales at UK. I didn't have a great range of shots, but I did have a good touch on the ball."

Before Spivey enrolled at UK that summer, Rupp got him a job at Owen Williams' drug store. His first job there was reaching up and plucking the fluorescent lights from the ceiling and cleaning them. He did not need a ladder.

"Rupp put me on a program to fatten me up," Spivey said. "He set me up with free passes to the Ben Ali Theater across from Owen Williams' drug store. Anytime I went to the theater, I was supposed to go into the drug store and drink a malted milk. In addition, I had to take two trays of food through the cafeteria line for each meal. I was eating three or four orders of mashed potatoes and drinking four quarts of milk a day.

"Since Rupp was involved with the Olympics that summer, Harry Lancaster was in charge of my development program. He worked with me, coached me on a personal basis, and we were in that gym all summer long."

Lancaster kept Rupp posted on the progress of Spivey. After the assistant coach triumphantly reported that the player had gained 12 pounds, Rupp wired back: "I know he can eat, but can he play basketball?"

"I got to practice with the Olympians that summer and I was impressed with the hook shots of Vince Boryla and the head fakes of Alex Groza," Spivey said. "I learned a little from Boryla, nothing from Bob Kurland, and a lot from Groza. Of course, I had a whole year after that summer of scrimmaging against the varsity. I was the only freshman who was allowed to scrimmage against them on a daily basis. That was really putting me through two practices, but I was glad to do it. Alex was probably the most clever man I ever played against. He had fantastic moves.

"It seems silly not to use a 7-foot man under the basket, but Rupp had had success with his guard offense, so he put me out there about seven feet from the basket to hand the ball off to these guards running by me. I might have a guy 6-4 guarding me and I could have shot over him all night or just turned around and put it in, but Rupp stuck to his guard offense. He had such good all-round talent that he didn't have to adjust his offense to suit a 7-foot center."

Spivey's biggest thrill was when he first pulled a jersey over his head before a freshman game, looked down and saw KENTUCKY written on it. To a Georgia country boy, playing basketball in Madison Square Garden was also an event to remember.

"We were practicing two days before we were going to New York and I couldn't *buy* a basket," he said. "The rebounds were bouncing off my head and chest and everywhere else. Rupp stopped the scrimmage, came running out there and said, 'Spivey, those New Yorkers up there won't think the Barnum & Bailey Circus has been in town, but they'll think the biggest g.d. clown has.' I thought he had a writer who wrote all those quips, but I found out they just came off the top of his head."

Paul Arizin of Villanova was one of the few pivotmen that Spivey failed to stop. "He was only 6-5, but I had never played with a pivotman who would go out front, in the backcourt, and run a figure 8 pattern with the guards," Spivey said. "I didn't expect him to be able to shoot from there, so I just dropped off eight or 10 feet and let him run that weave. Suddenly he would pop up in the air and shoot a jump shot." UK won that game by one point in overtime.

Remembering his poor showing that year against Art Burrus in Knoxville, Spivey said, "I think I must have been sluggish or in a daze or something. The unfamiliar crowd and the strong rivalry must have rattled me. It was something to be exposed to the band box gym and that roaring crowd and all the abuse. The football team sat right behind our bench and yelled and screamed and cursed Coach Rupp, right in his ear. I just couldn't get my game together.

"When they came to Lexington, I was so fired up at straightening that Burrus guy out that I had a whale of a game. I tore him up."

He outscored Burrus 34-12 as the Wildcats won that game, 79-52.

"CCNY was an unknown type of team the year they beat us in the NIT," Spivey said. "They hadn't any type of impressive record (17-5) and we weren't the least bit concerned, and we waltzed right onto the floor thinking all we had to do was show up. By halftime, we're 25 points down. We cut it to 12, but they got hot again and beat us, 89-50.

Bill Spivey plays defense during UK-Syracuse game in the consolation game of the 1950 Sugar Bowl in New Orleans. UK won, 69-59. Other Wildcats are Frank Ramsey (30), Shelby Linville, and Walt Hirsch (19).

"It developed the following year that one of the big reasons that this team had surprised everybody in winning the NIT and the NCAA was that some of its players had been fixing points all this season, and it made it look like they had a lousy team."

Spivey calls the UK-Kansas game of December 16, 1950, the best game he ever played.

"National publicity played up the duel between me and Clyde Lovellette as one that would decide who was the best big man in the nation," Spivey said. "I guess five or six weeks before the game, Harry or Coach Rupp would put a new clipping praising Lovellette on my locker. Of course, I'd rip it off each day. I kept shooting and looking forward to this contest. When the game time finally came, I felt like they'd thrown open the cage door and let me out.

"I was on my toes pretty well on defense and kept the ball away from my man more than cramming it down his throat. That was my style. I kept slapping it away from Lovellette. I guess the highlight of that game was when I slapped it away from him, picked it up and drove past the guards to the other goal, and slammed it through the basket. That brought the house down."

Lovellette hit only four of 17 shots. Spivey hit nine of 16 and finished with 22 points to 10 for Lovellette. Spivey also slapped 11 passes away from the Kansas ace.

"I was always concerned about Bob Zawoluk of St. John's," Spivey said. "The New York press would take a fair-haired child around the city there and promote him to the high heavens, and they had so many votes they could get him on the All-American lists. I always had respect for Bob, but I knew he had his highs and lows, and I didn't want him to have a high against me." Spivey scored 12 points as the Wildcats defeated the Redmen, 59-43, in NCAA action in Madison Square Garden. He was named All-America and selected as top player in the nation by the Helms Foundation.

"After we returned from a trip to Puerto Rico, the story on the fix scandals hit the newspapers," Spivey said. "It involved some of the UK players who preceded me. That's where a lot of trouble started for my life. The only thing I didn't do was tell Coach Rupp about being approached. It went to a court in New York and I was acquitted by a 9-3 verdict. I later took a lie detector test from the largest agency of that type in the world, John H. Reed & Associates. I wanted to eliminate any thought in anybody's mind about me being involved in fixing basketball games. So I passed the test without any trouble."

Spivey signed a contract to play with the Cincinnati Royals, but other teams in the league objected. They wanted his name put in a hat so that everyone could draw and have a chance to secure his services. When the Royals refused to do that, the league threatened to take away their television rights if Spivey played for them.

"The front office called me in," Spivey said, "and told me they had to back down. So I went and played what you might call second class ball the rest of my career. People coming down here from New York and accusing me of fixing games probably cost me two or three million dollars."

The Darkest Hour

Nicholas "Nick the Greek" Englisis came to the University of Kentucky with five other New York high school football players, saw some first-line duty for coaches A. D. Kirwan in 1944 and B. A. Shively in 1945, and was dropped from the squad after Paul Bryant became head coach in 1946.

If Nick had been a better football player, perhaps he would have shared more in some of the satisfying rewards and bonuses that alumni and boosters were showering upon UK athletes for jobs well done on the field of athletic combat. However, it was his lot to observe the businesslike, almost professional atmosphere of college athletics and to store that knowledge for the day when he would join forces with his brother, Tony, and the gambling element in his native Brooklyn.

Nick met Ralph Beard when Ralph was on the UK football team for a brief spell during Ralph's freshman year in 1945. Nick apparently got to know some other people in the Wildcat basketball program pretty well, so well in fact that a Louisville newspaper ran a photograph of him sitting on the end of the UK bench during an SEC tournament in that city.

So when it came time for Nick to approach the UK basketball players about winning games by a few more points than the "spread" allowed by gamblers, it took only a little friendly persuasion to first bring Groza into the fold, then Beard, then Barnstable.

"The thing about it is that you convince yourself you are doing no harm at the beginning," Barnstable would say later. "You get $15 or $20 from the school for playing a good game and you figure it won't hurt to take some bigger money for winning with something to spare.

"So you take the money (to go over the spread) and then you are offered some real money for 'shaving' (winning by less than the spread) the points. There's a lot of smooth talk and you talk yourself into the idea that it wouldn't hurt you or the school to win by a small score. You are a little confused and you don't know exactly what's going on and the next thing you know you are in it deep—too deep."

"Barney" never knew when he was talking to a would-be fixer. "Everywhere you went, strange people would try to talk to you in hotel lobbies," he said. "They wanted to know if you thought you'd win or if you thought you'd win by 10, and a lot of other things...."

In addition the UK players were attending school in a city that is steeped in the tradition of thoroughbred racing and thoroughly indoctrinated into pari-mutuel wagering. Lexington is historically a gambling town.

The undisputed "king" of Lexington bookmakers at the time was Ed Curd, a nationally known gambling figure who operated in comparative security above the Mayfair Bar on Lexington's Main Street. He was friendly with the "right" persons, made his contributions to charity—Rupp had gone to Curd's home to solicit for the local children's hospital—and operated a 340-acre farm near Lexington. His name was mentioned at least twice in the Senate Crime Committee investigation as Lexington's betting commissioner.

It was Curd to whom Phog Allen referred in 1944, when the Kansas coach charged that headquarters of a nationwide gambling ring was a room above the Mayfair Bar, where a gigantic handbook each Saturday during the football season handled as much as $500,000 on college games. Allen also charged that Lexington was probably the biggest high school and college gambling center in the country and that bookies from race tracks after World War II were moving into the intercollegiate field and the situation was bound to get worse. The Mayfair Bar was only about five blocks from Alumni Gym.

The first game in which UK basketball players were involved with the gamblers was against St. John's, December 18, 1948, in Brooklyn. They were paid for going over the spread in that game and in games against DePaul, Vanderbilt, Notre Dame, Bowling Green, Bradley, and Xavier; and Tulane and St. Louis in the Sugar Bowl. Once they were in that deep, it was easy for Englisis to coerce them into shaving points in a game against Tennessee February 18, 1949, and in an NIT loss to Loyola that year.

Kentucky officially became involved in the gambling scandal on the night of October 20, 1951, when investigators from the office of the New York district attorney seized Barnstable in Louisville and Groza and Beard in Chicago, where Rupp was coaching a team in an all-star game. The first person to break the news to Rupp was Lon Varnell, who was to meet Rupp in their hotel room after Rupp attended a wedding anniversary dinner with a Peoria couple. When Rupp telephoned to say he would be a little late, Varnell said, "Adolph, I have some bad news for you. You had better come over to the hotel as soon as you can."

When Rupp arrived at the hotel and heard the news, he said, "I don't believe it. Call the newspapers and radio stations."

As Rupp paced the room and wrung his hands, Varnell placed the calls.

"It's true," he told Rupp, "every bit of it. And it may be worse than it seems."

"Oh, my God!" Rupp shuddered. He stretched out on the bed and sobbed. It was 3 o'clock in the morning. At 6 o'clock, he called Bernie Shively.

"Shive, what'll I do?" he asked.

"Adolph, you had better get here as quick as you can," Shively said.

Rupp caught a plane within an hour, walked into Shively's office after arriving in Lexington, and was greeted by "Wah Wah" Jones.

"Tough, eh?" Rupp said.

"Sure is, coach. I just feel sorry for them. I've been sick at my stomach all day."

As the judicial process went into action against 31 players from seven schools who were then involved in the spreading scandal, Judge Saul S. Streit in New York called college football and basketball a sordid big business, with commercialization and overemphasis of both rampant throughout the country. He named Maryland, Oklahoma, Texas, Texas A&M, Southern Methodist, Pennsylvania, Tennessee, and Kentucky as examples of schools that were overemphasizing football and basketball.

When investigators from the office of the New York district attorney arrived in Lexington, seeking to question two or more UK athletes who were not members of the current basketball team, attorneys representing the players refused to permit interrogation of their clients, whom they said had violated no laws. After a six-day stay the investigators left, claiming removal of clouds of doubt and suspicion from innocent UK players had been prevented by the refusal of others to submit to questioning.

On the day before Christmas 1951, Bill Spivey requested that his name be omitted from the university's athletic eligibility list until he was cleared of any connection with the scandal. He later told a New York grand jury that he was innocent of any involvement, but that he was approached at a Catskill Mountains resort by a man who said he had arranged fixes with Barnstable and Hirsch, and that the man had later renewed the proposition to him in Lexington. Spivey did not report the incidents because he did not want to get the other players in trouble.

The UK Athletics Board suspended Spivey's eligibility after a four-hour session March 1. Then came that trial and release in New York on the charge of falsifying his testimony when charged with conspiring to fix UK games; then that well-publicized voluntary lie detector test.

Before year's end a New York grand jury would charge Hirsch, Barnstable, and Line with accepting bribes to shave points in the UK-DePaul game (UK won, 49-47) played December 21, 1949, in Louisville, and the UK-Arkansas game (UK won, 57-53) played January 2, 1950, in Little Rock. Neither Kentucky nor Arkansas had laws against bribery in connection with sports events.

The months-long investigation and revelations concerning the scandal definitely had an effect on the Kentucky team that season, but the Wildcats still had some fine moments. While the two New York investigators were in town, the 'Cats defeated St. John's, 81-40, and DePaul, 98-60, in the Coliseum. The loss was the worst suffered by the Redmen in 43 years of basketball. Thirteen thousand fans gave Solly Walker a bigger ovation than any visiting member of the team. The Associated Press reported that he was subjected to no embarrassment during the game or during the visit to Lexington.

Voted No. 1 on Christmas Day, the Wildcats defeated UCLA at home and Brigham Young in the first round of the Sugar Bowl before falling, 61-60, to St. Louis in the champion-

Rupp and Harry Lancaster read the news of UK's involvement in basketball fix scandal.

ship game. A few spectators behind press row kept yelling, "Beat the game-fixers" and "Oh, you little shavers, are you shaving tonight?"

En route to another conference championship, they were subjected at times to rather uncomplimentary remarks. However, Tennessee's Heckler's Row was silent, and the fans applauded when the Kentucky players were introduced. The student newspaper, fraternities, and sororities had conducted a campaign to avert reference to the scandal. Rupp called that one of the finest things he had observed in 30 years of basketball.

Meanwhile during this tense season Hagan, starting at center in the absence of Spivey, virtually rewrote the conference record book and was named to every major All-American team. Against Mississippi in January at Owensboro, he hit 17 of 18 free throws as the Wildcats won, 116-58, breaking their own SEC scoring record of 104 set against Tulane in New Orleans the previous season. The team hit 30 free throws, beating its own record of 25 set in 1948 against Ohio State.

With Hagan scoring 30 points and Ramsey 29 points, they defeated Mississippi State, 110-66, to set a Coliseum scoring record. Hagan left midway of the fourth quarter of a 95-40 victory over Tennessee, after having brought his season's points total to 509, breaking Groza's 1949 record of 508 in 26 games. He also broke Spivey's field goal record of 194 set in 1950. The victory was the Wildcats' twenty-fourth in a regular season schedule of 26 games. The season ended on an exciting note as they defeated DePaul, 63-61, in Chicago after substitute Willie Rouse stole the ball and scored a crip which erased a 61-60 DePaul lead. Ramsey scored 110 points in the conference tournament to break a record held by Pettit.

The absence of a good tall man was felt numerous times that season, but most of all in the second round of the NCAA tournament, where the Wildcats lost to the same St. John's team they had defeated earlier in the season. Bob Zawoluk, 6-foot-6 center, scored 32 points for the Redmen. It is likely that with Spivey the Wildcats would have repeated as national champions.

Before dealing suspended sentences to Beard, Barnstable, and Groza, and placing them on indefinite suspension, Judge Streit issued a 63-page statement detailing the rise of UK in the collegiate athletic world and how its costs for maintaining basketball and football teams jumped far in excess of the normal and average cost of the operation and maintenance of a first-rate professional football or basketball team.

He charged that UK subsidized unqualified athletes in violation of amateur rules, unqualified students got in school through athletic scholarships, and that cribbing by some star athletes was encouraged and tolerated by UK officials. He traced the athletic scandal at Kentucky and the plight of the defendants directly to the inordinate desire by the trustees and alumni of the university for prestige and profit from sports. Eighteen pages of the report were devoted to Rupp, whom Streit accused of aiding and abetting in the immoral subsidization of the players.

In answer, the university did not contend that its record was above criticism. But it affirmed that, in establishing an athletics program, it should be answerable to the people of Kentucky, the NCAA, and to its regional associations, and that its policies would not be dictated by Streit. Disturbed because the attack had not one reference to the organized gambling in New York and the criminals who produced the scandal, it felt the blame for what had happened should be shared by the public that persisted in gambling and in protecting gamblers; by overzealous alumni, real and synthetic, who placed athletic victories above other considerations; by radio stations, newspapers, and magazines that had featured college sports out of all proportions to their importance; and by college and university administrative officials and coaches throughout the land.

The university also felt it was significant that there were no

St. John's Solly Walker, first black to play in Alumni Gym, dribbles around Lou Tsioropoulos as Frank Ramsey watches the action. UK won, 81-40, but lost to St. John's, 64-57, in a rematch in the NCAA Eastern Regional.

basketball fixes in America before the game was featured in Madison Square Garden and that no school, whether located in New York or elsewhere, was ever touched by scandal until its teams had participated in one or more games in that arena.

While the SEC was accepting an invitation to investigate the situation in Lexington, UK officials announced an 11-point plan to slant the athletic program campusward. Basically the university pledged itself to observe strictly all regulations of the SEC and the NCAA and to use every endeavor to see that those regulations were not violated by persons either inside or outside the university. It called upon its coaches to emphasize standards and ideals rather than victories.

The university had expected some disciplinary action from the conference, but it was not quite prepared for an August 11, 1952, Executive Committee decision that ruled the Wildcats out of conference basketball for one year for participating in intercollegiate basketball and in tournaments in violation of conference rules and regulations in the area of subsidizing players during the period between October 1, 1946, and the close of the 1951 basketball season.

Kentucky did not appeal the penalty, but its president, Dr. Herman L. Donovan, said UK was not admitting anything that had not been the practice in other schools and conferences. "The thing that hurt us most was the fact that some of our players took bribes," he said.

Three months after the SEC ruling, the NCAA asked its member schools not to play UK in basketball during the 1952-53 season. The specific violations cited by that body in its ruling were:

1. Members of the 1948 UK basketball team were given $50 each by persons not connected with UK when the team left for the NCAA.

2. Team supporters again gave the players $50 before UK participated in the 1949 NCAA.

3. Six players were given $50 each before playing St. John's in New York in 1950.

4. Several players were given $25 to $50 after the Sugar Bowl games in 1951.

A few days after UK canceled its 21-game basketball schedule, Dr. Donovan told UK alumni he had ordered an investigation of Rupp after the scandals, and that he believed Rupp's woes were due partially to the fact that Rupp was the best basketball coach in the country. Donovan said he and other UK officials knew about and had approved the $50 given to basketball players after two appearances in the Sugar Bowl "because when UK first appeared in football bowls, we learned that it was customary among all schools going to bowls to give their players extraordinary spending money." He said Rupp knew of money given to basketball players after the Sugar Bowl games, but had no knowledge of monthly payments made by alumni to other players.

The punishment meted to UK by the NCAA was far more harsh than any penalty that had been inflicted upon a member for violation of NCAA rules. It amounted to a fine estimated at $100,000. Donovan could have avoided the penalty by dismissing Rupp, but the UK president believed Rupp to be an honorable man, and he refused to make a goat of him.

Deeply hurt by all that had transpired, Rupp said:

"No one has fought for cleaner sports and tried harder to keep them free from gambling than I have, and if anyone had anything on me, I would not be sitting at this desk, and I would not embarrass the university by remaining here."

Pointing to his record he asked: "Now, who has done that before? If I were suspicious, what boys would you trust? What was the guy who wasn't winning—at Northwestern or SMU or some of those other places—thinking about? We walk off with all the trophies they had, and I was supposed to know about it. How stupid can you get?"

Since there was no evidence that Rupp was involved in any way with gambling on games or conspiring to manipulate the final scores, it is obvious that he was completely innocent of such matters. He once said, "I would rather lose a million dollars than lose a basketball game," and he was such a hard loser that it would have been out of character for him to condone manipulation of the point spread; he literally meant it when he once said, "I bleed every time the other team makes a basket." The scandal hurt him so deeply that it would be 20 years before he would speak to those UK players who were involved.

There was some talk of Rupp retiring that year, but he said it was his duty to remain. "The boys needed me worse than ever," he said, "and it would have looked awfully bad if I had walked out on the heels of this thing.

"I'll not retire until the man who said Kentucky can't play in the NCAA hands me the national championship trophy."

Time Out: Cliff Hagan

On July 2, 1975, the day after he became UK athletic director, Cliff Hagan recorded some of his thoughts on the game of basketball:

"I remember the first time I ever saw a basketball. It was in the fourth grade. I had never noticed a goal before that time. There were no goals in my neighborhood. I was down in the grade school gym and I saw the boys playing this game of basketball. 'Gee!' I thought. 'That looks like a lot of fun.'

"We had a young man that came over from the high school adjacent to our campus to conduct practices for the fifth and sixth grades. When I was in the fifth grade and started out for practice, we would play games in the gym and at the YMCA on Saturday morning. I was fairly good size, as large as anybody in my class and larger than most of them, so I immediately had somewhat of an advantage.

"I fell in love with the game right off. I think we won the city grade school championship played in the YMCA gym. The principal at Longfellow Elementary, a lady, wrote ahead of me that she thought I had some kind of outstanding athletic ability at the time. What she meant was that I had a great deal of interest and this might be a way to reach me, which it did.

"When I became six years old, school was already under way for that year. I enrolled in January and went all the way through, from high school to college, that way. Nancy Wilson, a teacher from Mississippi who is now at Oneida Institute, has been a tremendous influence on my life. She had a paddle with little holes in it, sorta like a fraternity paddle, and she would take you back in the cloakroom quick and lay it to you. She ruled with an iron hand, and she had more respect than anybody I know. She encouraged our interest in sports. Our home room won the Central Junior High Basketball Tournament. That was a big thing.

"I guess at that time basketball was the most important thing in my life. I went on to high school, in mid-semester again, at Owensboro, a town of about 20,000 that had grown to about 30,000 by the time I got out of high school. We had two parochial schools and a county school that also played basketball, so there was a lot of basketball competition right there in Owensboro, but none for football since we were the only school with a football team. I really think the YMCA had a lot to do with the success of the Owensboro teams. There was a group that went there just about every night and some older fellows would come down and play. Just this exposure to basketball enabled Owensboro teams year after year to go to the State Tournament.

"I played a half year of freshman ball and joined the varsity in the last semester of that year. I had a lot to learn. Here I was, growing quickly, but I really couldn't do anything, other than what guys my age could do. There were some older guys who I thought were just fantastic, but I don't think any of them went anywhere and played major basketball.

"During my sophomore year, the team made a trip over the Christmas holidays. I got to go along; it was the first time I'd been any place other than maybe to have driven to Lexington with my folks. We were to be gone a week. It was just unbelievable. I knew I wasn't going to be able to contribute to the team, but I guess 'Coach Mac' (Lawrence McGinnis) saw this as a seasoning, getting some experience on the road. It was a highlight of my life. I cheered on the bench, but I didn't get to play in the games. The next year, I stepped into a starting role with Dwayne Morrison, now coach at Georgia Tech, and Bob Watson, now coach at Owensboro. We had a good year. We got beat in the semifinals by Maysville, the toughest team we had ever seen.

"Bobby and Dwayne graduate; I become a senior and I'm growing, about 6-3½ or 6-4, pretty good size for high school. I never really saw anybody larger than I was at that time. If I did run across an opposing center who was taller, he usually was very thin, wasn't real agile, so I didn't have a lot of trouble on defense.

"All I did was play center, but I learned to shoot the jump shot from around the center area. After going over to Western and seeing Bob Lavoy shoot the hook shot, I came home and worked on it. Sometime during that period, I came up to the university and shot around while the 'Cats were practicing. I was watching them when Adolph came over and said, 'Well, boy! When you get ready to come to school, we want you up here.' I was so impressed with that, of course, and that made up my mind right there where I was going to school. I talked a little with Groza. He had a semi-hook, not a full hook shot. He thought it was a very difficult shot to learn, and he really didn't encourage my depending on it or taking it up.

"I went home and worked on it, very dedicatedly, and that became my weapon. Actually, I started shooting it before my junior season; as far as I know, I was really the only player in Western Kentucky using it. I'm sure I wasn't the first high school player to use it, because Bob Lavoy learned it somewhere. I really didn't need it because I was as tall as anybody I played against, but it just wowed me so much the first time I saw it that I just had to learn it, and I did. Coach Mac worked with me a little bit and he saw the value of it.

"We had a good season my senior year. We played in the Louisville Invitational, always a big tournament. We had won it the year before, but Xavier beat us this time. We won the district tournament. I had led the tournament in scoring, but when they announced the All-Tournament team, I wasn't on it. People had been voting for other players, thinking, 'Oh, well, Hagan will get enough votes.' I did make the All-Regional and All-State Tournament teams.

"In the regional final, Henderson came out and held the ball because we had beaten them so badly before. In the first half, it was 5-10. They kept holding the ball and somewhere late in the game it was 19-19. The place was packed. It was exciting. They were holding the ball the last four or five minutes and we couldn't take it away from them. They finally took a shot with about seven seconds to go, we rebounded, came down the court, and one of our guys, Billy Cook, took a long set shot from about 30 feet and made it. We won, 21-19.

"At no time did we think we could win the State Tournament. It's just something up there on a pedestal, too high to be realized by anyone in this lifetime. This is the way I felt about it; that's how big basketball loomed in our lives.

"I remember on all the jump balls beginning each quarter, I would tip the ball down the floor to the top of the circle and we had a little guard who would go in for a layup. It worked game after game. I didn't understand it. We got through the tournament up to the semifinal game and we had to play Xavier. We were scared to death. I got hit in the mouth on the second half tipoff, and I didn't know any of the plays we were calling. Only later did I realize I was out on my feet. We beat them.

"Back at the hotel to rest, I couldn't stand up without getting cramps in my legs. We had played three games in less than three days. I didn't know if I really was going to be able to play that night, and we were playing *Big* Lafayette, big high school from *Big* Lexington. We were a little team from little Owensboro. No way were we going to beat them, we thought, but we were happy to be in the final. Two teammates helped me on my feet so I could leave the hotel room. I had a good game of 41 points, which was unbelievable. I got a long standing ovation. We beat them. It was the biggest moment of my life.

"That final game in Louisville also marked the saddest day of my life. High school basketball was so great for me. It was the end of my world. I cried. They tried to get me on the radio and I didn't have much to say in those days anyway. The less you said the better off you were.

"We rode home on the train. They had a big reception for us at the Sports Center. Immediately afterward, I was flown to Evansville to catch a plane to New York, where UK was playing in the Eastern Regional. I hadn't flown on a plane before. I hadn't been to New York before. Now I was flying to New York. Somebody gave me $20, my first taste of 'friendly' alumni. Frank Ramsey, whose Madisonville team had been beaten earlier, had already gone to New York.

"I didn't get to New York until about 7 a.m. There was no one there to meet me. I went to the Paramount Hotel, found out where Coach Rupp's room was, went up there, knocked on the door, and woke him up. Coach Rupp came to the door. I'm not sure he was expecting me. He told me Ramsey was down the hall. I woke Frank up. Jerome Lederer, owner of Jerry's

Cliff Hagan displays his famous hook shot against Georgia.

Restaurants, showed us around New York—Radio City Music Hall, the Rockettes, all the usual things.

"Watching the games, I remember seeing Tony Lavelli shoot hook shots from 20 feet out, most unbelievable. That just opened my eyes up to all kinds of possibilities. To a high school boy, seeing those teams playing before all those people in Madison Square Garden was just great. So I came back home and still had a semester to go in high school.

"The decision as to where I would attend college wasn't really big for me. I had visited Indiana and stayed in the coach's home there, and "Big Six" Henderson took me to Notre Dame, where Frank Leahy mistook me for a football player. When "Six" told him I was a basketball player, Coach Leahy said he would like for me to come up and play football anyway. I met Leon Hart. He was 6-4, 240, and about the biggest thing I had ever seen.

"When I came to UK, Harry Lancaster was the assistant and coach of a big freshman team. He had been so nice to all of us on our first visit there. But before our first game, we were on the sidelines cutting up a bit, and he got us in the dressing room and he chewed us out about getting serious about what we came there for. That was the first time that side of Lancaster's nature was revealed. Everyone was serious, very quiet. At one time he threw down his chair. This was very enlightening to me, that someone could turn (on us) that fast. It sort of set the stage for the rest of my time at UK.

"For so long a period of time, Kentucky was just a boy's dream. I had reservations about coming to UK, and I think other people gave me those because of my size. I was 6-4, not big enough to play center, not quick enough to play guard. I didn't think I was good enough to play right off, although I was All-America in high school and had scored those 41 points in the state final and averaged 25 points a game my senior year. I didn't have the cocky attitude that a lot of people have about playing immediately. I thought if I could just make the traveling squad and go with the team, perhaps by my junior year I would get to play and I would be happy.

"I played freshman ball that one semester and joined the varsity the second semester. Alumni Gym was packed to the rafters every game. The students were split up into "A" games and "B" games. They were building a new gym, but the building didn't sell me. I was coming to Kentucky—maybe recruiters should remember this, now: you really don't come to play in a facility, you play for a school and all it means.

"There were benches on the end of the floor on either side of the basket. I remember being on the second or third row on either side of the team and really yelling. I remember Kansas coming in to play and seeing Clyde Lovellette, the great hooker. He was the biggest thing next to Spivey. He was 6-8½ and he looked huge because he had wide shoulders. He could stand at the top of the circle and hit set shots. I thought, 'Oh, my goodness!' But he got in foul trouble. When he fouled out, Rupp took Bill out. Bill had beat him badly in the stats, which helped Bill nationally. I remember how the game was built up, the two coaches—teacher and pupil—playing each other.

"I joined the team at mid-year and played behind Hirsch, a great right-hander. I was second banana. We had Shelby Linville and Read Morgan, who is now a TV and movie star. So there were two or three ahead of me before I'd get to play some. Going into the NCAA, Hirsch became ineligible because he had played in three previous NCAA tournaments, and I became a starter.

"I remember the Illinois game in New York, when Linville got hot in the last minute and won for us. Going on to Minnesota to play Kansas State, I got the flu and couldn't start. Early in the first quarter, Coach Rupp asked me if I could play. I thought I could. I remember getting a tip-in from the second position on the foul line immediately after going into the game. That lifted everybody. Spivey was beaten badly by Lou Hitch in the first half, but he came back strong in the second half and we beat them for the NCAA title. 'Gollee!' I thought. 'That's bigger than being the Owensboro champions of Kentucky.' However, it didn't mean more to me, because nothing could be bigger than being Kentucky State Champion.

"All that acclaim focuses attention on you. People watch you, expect certain things out of you. In high school, they knew you. It's not like now, where you move from one city to another and schools are so big, with 1,200 to 2,000 students, and very few know anybody. Coaches like Lancaster and Rupp knew what you were doing. The people in town knew what you were doing. They set guidelines for you. I was always aware of this."

Return Of The 'Cats

Twelve thousand basketball-starved fans sat in hushed anticipation as the wall clock in Memorial Coliseum ticked off the final seconds before 7:30 on the night of December 5, 1953. The scoreboard signs spelled KENTUCKY and TEMPLE. There was only room for two digits beneath the Kentucky sign, contrary to the published reports that Rupp, to make sure there was no shaving of points and to wreak his revenge, was going to run up the score in every game his team played. For that he would need at least three digits, they said.

At the player entrance to the arena, uniformed policemen shielded the runway from a pushing, surging group of youngsters while cheerleaders peered anxiously into the dim hallway. Promptly on schedule a group of tall, angry young men in scanty blue and white uniforms ran from the opening and onto the playing floor. The band struck up "On, On, U of K," the cheerleaders jumped up and down, with pompons waving, and the fans clapped in unison.

It had been almost a year since that scene last was witnessed in the Coliseum. The cheers echoed throughout the arena and into the Kentucky training room, where Rupp, dressed in his best brown suit, finished his silent pregame meditation and prepared for a date with destiny.

As the players ran onto the floor, the team manager quickly tossed basketballs to co-captains Cliff Hagan and Frank Ramsey, who took the first warm-up shots. The others automatically lined up in equal rows on each side of the basket for a series of pregame drills that never varied.

Seconds later Rupp walked down the left side of the hallway as others in his entourage followed in a specific order—assistant coach, trainer, team doctor, etc. He paused until the band quit playing. Then he entered the arena. He turned and waved to a lady seated over the entrance, as he had done in all those better years gone by. She returned the salute and would remain standing until the game began.

A tremendous roar, followed by a "Hello, Adolph" from the student body, greeted him. He smiled, acknowledged the ovation, and sat in his chair. Manager Bobby Moore handed him two sticks of chewing gum and placed a damp towel, blue stripe up, on the floor, so the players could wipe their shoe soles and gain better traction. Before the second half, the white side would be up. Only he was allowed to pick up the towel.

He sat, chin in hand, silently watching the players go through their warm-up paces. Five minutes before game time, players and the entire entourage automatically headed back to the dressing room, via the same route and in the same pecking order as when they entered. After they returned ("all steamed up," as Hagan put it), the band struck up the national anthem, and everyone faced the American flag. Player introductions, with the individuals spotlighted, were followed by the traditional pregame huddle and crossing of hands.

That night Cliff turned in one of the finest performances ever witnessed in the Coliseum. He equalled Temple's output of 20 points in the first half and added 13 more points in the third quarter. Midway of the final period, the crowd realized a record was in sight and began pulling for him to reach the SEC half-century mark held by Bob Pettit. He had made 17 consecutive free throws, but the crowd groaned as he missed two with 43 seconds remaining. Eight seconds later Puckett stole the ball and threw a floor-length pass; Cliff caught it on the run and scored a layup for his 51st point.

"I remember being carried off the floor," Cliff said. "Jess Curry had hold of one leg and Linville Puckett the other."

Described by the *UK Facts Book* as a 6-foot-4 consensus All-American with the "physique of a fabled Greek god and deceiving poetry in motion on the court," Hagan may have been the best player ever to perform for UK, one who had the greatest natural touch in his hands of any player Rupp ever coached.

"He was one of the best 'hookers' I have ever seen," Rupp said. "I was going to break him of that shot, but every time I was about ready to make him stop using that thing, he would make four or five in a row and I'd say to myself, 'I'll break him next week!' After he got most of his 51 points on hookers against Temple, I decided to let him keep it."

Ramsey was an extremely aggressive guard who specialized in driving layups. Especially adept at intercepting passes, he was the floor leader, "a big, powerful kid who would get the ball off the board and bring it down and ram the basket, an intelligent boy who developed every single day," Rupp said.

Lou Tsioropoulos came to the university on a football scholarship and showed up in the old gym when the freshman basketball players started working out there. Bryant asked Rupp if he had seen a football player with his basketball players.

"I don't know, Paul. What's the guy's name?"

"I don't know, Adolph. He's from Lynn, Massachusetts, a big Greek kid with a prominent nose."

Rupp presents the game ball to Cliff Hagan after the Wildcat center scored a record 51 points against Temple in Memorial Coliseum in the opening game of the 1953-54 season.

Rupp checked the impromptu workouts, spotted the football player, called him over, and asked, "Son, what's your name?"

"Tsioropoulos."

"How do you spell it?"

"T-S-I-O-R-O-P-O-U-L-O-S!"

"I never learned to spell that name," Rupp said. "During our first few trips on the road after Lou joined the varsity, I would give the opening lineup to the official scorer. Invariably, the scorer would ask, 'How do you spell that last name?' I had my secretary mimeograph a whole bunch of 'Lou Tsioropoulos' labels that I kept in my pocket to give those scorers."

He started the "Big Three" in every game, alternating the other positions between guards Gayle Rose and Linville Puckett and forwards Bill Evans and Phil Grawemeyer. The reserve group included Willie Rouse, Pete Grigsby, Jerry Bird, Clay Evans, Hugh Coy, Jess Curry, Harold Hurst, Bill Bibb, and Dan Chandler.

Before the season began, four conference schools—Louisiana State, Tulane, Mississippi, and Mississippi State—that were supposed to play in Lexington threatened to boycott Kentucky unless the Wildcats played in their gyms. All but LSU finally played in Lexington. Georgia coach Arbison (Red) Lawson agreed to an extra game to help the Wildcats fill their conference game limit. Rupp always considered Lawson one of his best friends; however, he showed him no mercy on the basketball court, defeating him 106-55 at Lexington and 100-68 at Owensboro that year. Before the second game he told a group at Owensboro that playing Georgia was like kissing your sister.

A rhubarb erupted in St. Louis after Tsioropoulos pointed a finger at a St. Louis player who had fouled him. As the partisan crowd howled, hooted, and called Lou a "greasy Greek," Lancaster struck Pat Hickey, son of the St. Louis coach, for firing the timer's pistol too close to his leg for the second time. The fray was brought quickly under control, but just at the start of the fourth quarter, an unruly spectator took a punch at Shively and a brief flurry followed. When Tsioropoulos was banished on five personal fouls with almost six minutes remaining and the Wildcats leading by 15 points, the crowd cheered wildly. Lou held up his arm in a gesture of triumph and defiance.

A seven-game home stand started with the first University

of Kentucky Invitational Tournament, held during Christmas week to afford the general public an opportunity to purchase tickets of students who were on holiday. The policy was to invite the best teams, beginning with the NCAA and NIT champions, and to split net profits equally among the participating teams. The first tournament netted LaSalle, UCLA, and Duke more than $10,000 each, making it the richest holiday classic in the nation. Kentucky defeated LaSalle for the championship.

Minnesota, Xavier, Georgia Tech, DePaul, and Tulane were easy victims in the Coliseum. Prior to the Tulane game, Rupp had the UK locker room walls plastered with clippings from newspapers of the previous year, especially stories telling about Cliff Wells voting to suspend Kentucky. He told his players:

"He's on the floor now, the man that led the fight against you last year. For every blister, every bruise, every black eye, every tooth knocked out last year, that little runt of a coach owes you. Tonight, you pay them back for all of last year."

Kentucky won that game, 94-43, and easily breezed through the remaining games on the 23-game schedule. En route to Alabama for the final two games, against Auburn and Alabama, Rupp suffered chest pains aboard the team plane and was taken to a Montgomery hospital for an electrocardiogram. The attack was brought on by tension, an attending physician said, and he was advised not to work the following night. He was on the bench for the game.

One of his main antagonists that year was Johnny Dee, a former Notre Dame player who had become head coach of Alabama the preceding year. Taking exception to a Rupp statement that the 1953-54 Wildcats were Kentucky's greatest team, Dee accused him of not playing anyone yet and of calling Georgia names after Lawson did him a favor by scheduling an extra game. Warned that his remarks might incur Rupp's wrath, Dee said it did not make any difference anyway; Rupp was mad enough already.

Dee let his squad race and fire with the Wildcats for only the first seven minutes before waving them into a complete stall and interludes of possession play designed to hold down the scoring. The Wildcats won, 68-43, their lowest scoring total of the season, completing their first undefeated regular season of play since 1934.

Visibly tired, Rupp remained in bed most of the week before a playoff game with Louisiana State for the conference

Cliff Hagan (6) and Frank Ramsey get instructions from an ailing Rupp during time out of a game in the 1953-54 season.

championship. Fortified with a box of pills, he was at courtside in Nashville when the game began, directing UK to a 63-56 victory.

After the game Shively and Lancaster took him snugly by each arm and attempted to help him from the gym. He refused to leave until he shook hands with Harry Rabenhorst and visited the Kentucky locker room. He asked the players if they wanted to participate in the NCAA Tournament without Hagan, Ramsey, and Tsioropoulos, who had been classified as ineligible by the NCAA because they were graduate students. The squad voted 9-3 for playing in the tournament, with the three ineligible players voting negatively.

"I had hoped you would not vote to go and not to put this record in jeopardy," Rupp said. "If we can't play with our full team, we won't allow a bunch of turds to mar the record established in large measure by our three seniors. We are not going to Kansas City."

He was so weak he could not step into a taxi that was waiting at the door. Shively called a policeman to help speed the vehicle through traffic. With siren wailing, the officers escorted the taxi to the hotel. Adolph had another seizure, was helped to the hotel elevator, and taken to bed. The ailment was described as a mild heart attack.

The Wildcats set a national record with a 27.2 average margin of victory, and were selected as the nation's top team in the Associated Press poll of writers. However, they failed to gain the top spot in the United Press poll when three of the participating coaches refused to place them in the Top Ten because of the three "ineligible" players. Some of the writers refused to place either of the "Big Three" on their all-star ballots.

Vengeance had not proved so sweet for Rupp, who, some people thought, should have retired that year. However, he had not fulfilled his mission of being presented the championship trophy by the organization that had suspended his Wildcats, and he had a score to settle with the New York writers, who were primarily responsible for the three stars being ineligible for the playoffs. He had no intention of retiring.

An Upsetting Situation

To say that no one in Kentucky took the Georgia Tech basketball team seriously when the Yellow Jackets lined up to play UK on the night of January 8, 1955, would be putting it mildly.

The Wildcats had won their seven previous games of the season and were rated No. 1 in the nation. Coach John "Whack" Hyder's Yellow Jackets had a 2-4 record to pit against a tradition that had seen UK teams win 129 straight games over a 12-year span in Alumni Gym and Memorial Coliseum. Seventy of those victories were over Southeastern Conference teams.

"This was a game where every UK scrub knew he would see action," substitute Dan Chandler would recall years later, "because Tech was indeed counted upon to be an easy prey."

Tech was so lightly regarded that only 8,000 fans turned out to see the game. UK coaches had not even bothered to scout the Yellow Jackets. They knew about Lenny Cohen and Dick Lenholt, who had played the season before in two lopsided losses to UK, and Bobby Kimmel, a little guard from Valley High near Louisville. Who could get serious about them and a team that had just lost to lowly Sewanee?

Tech was troublesome from the very start, holding UK's high-powered offense in check and building up a surprising five-point halftime lead. "Still no one really doubted the outcome," Dan Chandler said, "but our regulars would have to stop messing around or some of the lowly scrubs might miss getting into action."

Tech built that lead to eight points, 38-30, with 15 minutes remaining, and the startled Wildcats went into an all-court press. They outscored the Yellow Jackets, 16-8, and tied the score at 46-46. They were ahead, 58-55, with 1:12 left when Kimmel sank two free throws.

With UK leading by one point and 18 seconds remaining, Billy Evans took a throw-in from Gayle Rose, turned to face a pressuring Kimmel, and was blind-sided by little Joe Helms, who stole the ball, dribbled to the right, and hit a 12-foot jump shot for a 59-58 Tech lead. Seven seconds remained when Linville Puckett missed a driving shot and Phil Grawemeyer's bat-in attempt missed the mark.

Tev Laudeman called it "the night the mouse ate the cat." Rupp had stronger words of description. In the dressing room

UK's Bob Burrow (50) and Georgia Tech's Dick Lenholt battle for the ball as the Yellow Jackets pull one of basketball's biggest upsets, defeating the Wildcats, 59-58, January 8, 1955, in Memorial Coliseum. UK's Billy Evans and Tech's Bobby Kimmel are at left; Phil Grawemeyer is No. 44; and Jerry Bird is 22 for UK. No. 8 for Tech is Lenny Cohen.

he told his players to go out and purchase the newspapers containing the game write-ups because they undoubtedly would be collectors' items.

"From this time until history is no longer recorded, you will be remembered as the team that broke the string," he said. "Even if you go on to win the NCAA championship, you must carry this scar with you the rest of your lives."

Kentucky had begun that season in the unusual situation of not being ranked among the top five in any preseason poll—"I think I'll buy some ads in the magazines," Rupp said—and not having an established star around whom to fashion the offense.

The best newcomer was Bob Burrow, a 6-foot-7 center who had scored more than 2,000 points in two years at Lon Morris Junior College and had led the Jacksonville, Texas, school to the semifinals of the National Junior College Tournament in the spring of 1954.

Burrow scored only one field goal in a 74-58 victory over LSU, but he got 12 against Xavier and then hit for 27 against Temple. In the UKIT that year the Wildcats had a 67-65 lead over Utah when 6-foot-6 Jerry Bird took the ball on an out-of-bounds play and scored an easy crip shot to preserve the win. Tom Gola and LaSalle were not quite good enough for the Wildcats, losing 63-54 in the final. Burrow had 25 points each in an 82-65 victory over St. Louis and a 101-69 decision over Temple in a rematch. All that transpired before Georgia Tech came to town.

After the shocking loss to Tech, UK defeated DePaul, Tulane, LSU (64-62), Tennessee, and Vanderbilt (75-71) before traveling to Atlanta and a chance to revenge that lone defeat.

Once again "Whack" Hyder used only five men and controlled the game all the way, winning 65-59. Burrow scored 20 points for the Wildcats, but Helms had 24 and Kimmel 20 for Tech. Rupp complained because the Wildcats outscored Tech by seven field goals, but hit only five of 15 free throws while Tech was hitting 25 of 34 from the foul line.

"After that second loss, we all felt fortunate that Rupp let us fly home with him," Dan Chandler said.

The players returned to Lexington during the semester break and decided, against Rupp's rules, to go home overnight. When a student manager reported what was going on to Rupp, he sent someone to check their rooms. When the rooms came up empty, he scheduled a practice for the following day. The players got word of the practice, returned to the campus, met at a service station near the Coliseum, and agreed that if Rupp kicked one of them off the squad, they would all quit.

Rupp called a squad meeting and asked each player where he was the previous night. He got the same answer, "At home." "You couldn't have got home and back," Rupp told one player who lived a long distance from Lexington.

"He said quite positively that he was very upset over what appeared to be a lost set of values," Chandler said. "He said, 'You men don't have winning on your minds.' The punishment—no tickets for the DePaul game the following Saturday."

"These tickets, complimentary to the players, are often purchased at friendly prices by individuals in Lexington," Chandler explained. "At this point Linville Puckett arose and said if he was not given the tickets he was not going to play. Nearly every player echoed his remarks, and they all immediately got up and departed."

That left only Chandler, Rupp, and team captain Billy Evans in the room. Rupp looked at Evans and said, "Go talk to each man, tell them that practice is at 3:15 this afternoon, and that any man who is late today need not bother to clean out his locker room. Harry and I will put his stuff in the middle of Euclid Avenue."

When Evans, who was not in on the revolt, saw Puckett leave the room first, he assumed that Puckett was leading the uprising. The players also were not sure just what had transpired. Evans confronted Puckett outside the gym, and a fight almost ensued. The other players explained to Evans what had happened. They talked to Rupp and Lancaster again. Rupp told them to be on the practice floor at 3:15 if they wanted to play.

Everyone but Puckett and Burrow, who was hospitalized with a sinus infection, reported to the practice, along with six football players. Puckett quit the squad the following day. "I decided after careful consideration to withdraw from the team," his statement said. "I enjoy participating in the game of basketball as much as anyone in the world. However, basketball at Kentucky isn't regarded as a game, but as a matter of life or death, with resemblance of one going to war." From that point on, "He went to war" would be a term of endearment around UK basketball camps.

One of the better on-court battles that season took place

Linville Puckett.

in the Coliseum after Alabama substitute Jim Brogan dared Dan Chandler to cross over the center line while the teams were warming up. The two reserves squared off in a melee that involved several players on both sides before police restored order. So keyed up were the two teams and coaches that on almost every call of an official, either Rupp or Johnny Dee would come bounding off the bench. The Wildcats won, 66-52. They closed the regular season with a 104-61 victory over Tennessee in Lexington. In a special ceremony honoring UK's 50th year of basketball Rupp was presented a blue and white

Cadillac.

In the NCAA tournament at Evanston that year, UK had only two starters left of the five who had started the season. Grawemeyer had suffered a broken leg in a mid-February game with DePaul, Puckett was no longer on the squad, and Evans was not eligible because he was classified as a graduate student. Evans would later win an Olympic gold medal while playing AAU basketball.

John Brewer replaced Grawemeyer, Rose filled Puckett's position, and Calvert, handicapped with a broken finger most of the season, was at the other guard. They stayed even with a fine Marquette team until the final six minutes, then lost, 79-71. They beat Penn State, 84-59, for third place.

Rupp started the 1956-57 season with a slim striking force, but he still had some quality players. The returning seniors—Bird, Burrow, and Grawemeyer—gave him the tallest front line in the conference. He had experienced juniors in Kentuckians Gerry Calvert, Ray Mills, and John Brewer. Up from the freshman team were Kentuckians Abe Collingsworth, Harold Ross, Phil Johnson, Vernon Hatton, John Crigler, Bill Cassady, and Bill Smith, and Ed Beck of Macon, Georgia.

They lost six of 26 games that season, but two of the losses were to Temple and Dayton at home, where they had lost only to Georgia Tech in the previous 13 years, and the other two were to conference foes Vanderbilt and Alabama. Dayton beat them in the UKIT, which they played without Burrow, who was injured the previous night in a victory over Minnesota. After Bird scored 33 points as Burrow's substitute in the pivot, Rupp installed a double pivot offense, marking the first basic change in the offensive pattern since he came to UK. The other loss that year was to DePaul by two points in Chicago. They had beaten DePaul by the same margin earlier in Lexington.

Kentucky natives Clarence Taylor and Al Rochelle scored 51 points between them as Vanderbilt defeated UK for the first time since the 1951 SEC tournament and for the first time in Nashville since 1940. As the final gun sounded, the Commodore fans rushed onto the floor and virtually mobbed the home team. Huston Horn, of the *Tennessean*, describes the reaction:

"Don't stand too near a Vanderbilt man today. You'll get

Bob Burrow.

a button down your throat, it will have popped from the tightest vest in town—a vest swelled and expanded, throbbing with pride in the Commodores.

"They beat the Kentucky Wildcats last night—or do you live in a foreign country and haven't heard?

"It happened in the Vanderbilt gym. Today it's a shrine, a golden palace, an alabaster castle. Take off your shoes before you walk on the floor.

"You know, when you beat Kentucky, you sort of lose your good senses, you hit people on the head and they hit you. You jump up and down and maybe fall down. You may do a cartwheel. You may throw a joint. You may spend the next day in bed."

Kentucky had to beat Alabama in Montgomery that year if it expected to even tie for the conference crown. Johnny Dee's team, featuring a first five players in their fourth year as starters, had a 17-3 record and was undefeated in 10 conference games. With forward Jerry Harper of Louisville scoring 37 points, the Tide won, 101-77, the largest score registered against UK up to that time. Dee left his starting lineup in the game until the last minute, when two players fouled out. It was the first Tide victory over UK since 1943.

After the game Rupp said, "Boys, back when I was playing, we would have taken that ball and eaten it, chewed it up, and swallowed it before we would ever let them score 100 points on us."

Kentucky finished second in the conference and accepted a bid to the NCAA playoffs after Dee refused because Alabama's starters had played varsity ball as freshmen and were not eligible for the tournament.

Rupp took to Iowa City the first UK squad since 1945 to fail to win 20 regular season games, the first since 1951 to lose as many as five scheduled games, and the first to finish out of the nation's Top Ten.

"This team is like a slot machine," Rupp said. "Something is set in there that makes it click or not click. It's played the worst basketball I've seen and some of the best."

Burrow scored 33 points as the Wildcats defeated Wayne University, 84-64, in the opening round of the regional. The Detroit school had lost only one other game that season. Iowa was a different story. The Big Ten champions had defeated

Morehead State, 97-83, after Morehead's Steve Hamilton, a future New York Yankee pitcher, and Dan Swartz fouled out. In addition the partisan Iowa crowd heaped much abuse on both Morehead and UK.

"Go home, Kentucky, and take Adolph Rupp with you," they would yell. "Hey, you hillbillies, pack up and get out." The expletives were accompanied by rolls of toilet paper, programs, and cups of soft drinks thrown at them from the stands.

Grawemeyer was holding Iowa star Carl "Sugar" Cain scoreless during the first 15 minutes when Rupp took him from the game for a rest. Cain hit two quick baskets, and Rupp rushed Grawemeyer back into the game. But it was too late. Cain tallied 34 points, and Iowa won, 89-77.

For the first time in years there was no talk in Lexington about Rupp retiring.

A Highly Competitive Business

Although the 1956 UK basketball team finished with 20 victories, there were signs of weakening in the "House of Rupp," which depended on a steady stream of raw material and sufficient numbers to overcome injuries and fatigue over the long haul of two dozen games or more.

Kentucky natives had come back to "haunt" UK at Georgia Tech, Alabama, and Vanderbilt, and there was a sprinkling of Kentuckians on other Southern teams. Rupp was partly correct in stating that most Kentucky boys from the cradle through high school had a burning ambition to play at UK, but some good ones were swayed in their thinking by the backwash from the scandals, his reputation as an arrogant taskmaster, the Puckett incident, and stepped-up recruiting by in-state and SEC schools. He also had a reputation of being selective, and some boys just did not think they could make the grade under him.

Bobby Watson, a member of the 1951 NCAA championship squad, spoke of the "constant struggle" to make the starting five. "It was the biggest thing on my mind," Bobby said. "I made it after about five games in my sophomore year, but I never knew from one game to the next. It was the same thing every year. Even as a senior I had to make it all over again."

John Lee Butcher, one of 11 candidates on the 1954 freshman squad, transferred to Pikeville College to get away from the "heavy pressure" and to go where he could play "just for the fun of it."

Adrian Smith, a 5-foot-10 guard who was told by Rupp that he was too small for UK, starred at Northeast Mississippi Junior College and then enrolled at UK. "The pressure was stronger, because everybody wanted to knock off Kentucky," he said. "We were under the gun every time we stepped onto the floor. Our practices were tougher, our studies were harder, and when you played for UK you had to be at your best, because if you weren't there were always a couple of guys on the bench ready and capable of taking your place."

In 1952 Rupp claimed, "You can take a boy to the Coliseum, sit him down for five minutes, and if he doesn't want to play at Kentucky after just looking at the place he's too dumb to go to college anyway."

That scene was changing fast as a new breed of conference coaches, every bit as ambitious, ruthless, and talented as he, began to assert themselves on the recruiting scene. In the past all he had to do was sit back and let the good players beat a path to his door. But recruiting had suddenly become an expensive and competitive business, causing many abuses of NCAA regulations and bitterness among the coaches seeking the services of those athletes.

The line was drawn especially fine between Rupp and Everett Case of North Carolina State. Their biggest hassle was over a Brooklyn boy named David Gotkin who chose neither school.

They were also in hot competition for the services of Jackie Moreland, a 6-foot-7 "Mr. Basketball" from Minden, Louisiana. On December 7, 1955, the first day under the SEC rule when scholarship grants could be signed that year, Harry Lancaster signed Moreland to an SEC grant.

"That Mr. Lancaster was a nice fellow, and Mr. (Vic) Bubas (North Carolina State assistant) was too," Mrs. Moreland said. "But I never saw a bunch of people who seemed to hate each other so much."

A very confused Moreland kept changing his mind, all the while assuring Rupp and Lancaster that he intended to honor his commitment to UK. He also committed himself to Texas A&M and Centenary and signed a grant with North Carolina State. The NCAA, reporting that it had found irregularities in the Moreland case, put North Carolina State on probation for four years and denied school officials any voice in NCAA deliberations during that period. The school was ordered to pay a $5,000 fine if Moreland did not complete his four years there. Moreland later left State, played basketball at Louisiana Tech, and then with the professional Detroit team.

Rupp watches a typical UK practice session during the mid-'50s.

The best high school player in Kentucky that year was Kelly Coleman of Wayland, who set a state tournament scoring record. Coleman told Billy Thompson of the *Herald* that he was going to attend West Virginia University because the folks at Morgantown had given him a summer job, and he felt indebted to them.

"I talked with Mr. Rupp, and he said he'd like to have me at Kentucky but he couldn't offer me more than an SEC grant-in-aid," Coleman said. "So I decided to go to West Virginia."

The Mountaineers soon withdrew the scholarship grant but

were placed on probation by the NCAA for alleged recruiting irregularities in the Coleman case. Coleman finally attended Kentucky Wesleyan. West Virginia wrongly blamed UK for reporting the case to the NCAA.

With Moreland and Coleman out of the fold, UK signed E. A. Couch and Bob Shepherd of state champion Carr Creek, "Corky" Withrow of Central City, Roger Newman of Greenville, and Don Mills of Berea. Withrow signed a baseball contract with the Milwaukee Braves and was ineligible under NCAA rules to play for UK. Newman would miss his sophomore and junior years for various reasons. Shepherd would quit after his freshman season, and Couch would not earn a letter at UK.

That one season of recruiting pointed up the problems that had suddenly beset the Wildcat basketball program. Recruiting had long been accepted as a normal part of the UK basketball setup, with coaches, alumni, and others going out and hustling fine high school players. That was part of the game, but it was suddenly a game that a lot of other people were playing, and playing well.

The recruiters were an interesting study themselves. During one battle for a prize prospect in Schenectady, New York, a UK booster set up light housekeeping in town for a week. He attended the player's practices every day, and after a game at the end of the week escorted the player and his parents home. He returned for family chats several times. One night he entered by the front door, and the boy left by the back door in a deliberate attempt to avoid him. When the player returned home at 1 a.m., the UK recruiter was still at the house.

None of the visits from dozens of college scouts were more surprising, however, than one from Rupp. "I was amazed when I walked through the door and saw Mr. Rupp there," the player said. "I was told he never came to visit a boy." Rupp turned on his usual charm and took the family to dinner in the city's finest steak house.

"We never ate so good in our lives as we did when the whole thing was going on," the mother said. "All those fellows always took you out. You know, steaks and all. They were all good fellows, real gentlemen."

The university did not believe in speaking negatively about its competition in recruiting athletes, but some other coaches did resort to innuendos and half-truths to turn kids from UK.

"The South is no place for a Jewish boy," they would say. "What kind of education will your boy get there—fiddle playing?" "Rupp doesn't care for his players. They're like his cattle; if they don't produce, he discards them."

Such competition was new to Rupp, who for years had only to screen the many fine prospects who sought invitations to the Lexington campus. He was convinced that the drawing power of his own image and the Wildcat tradition should be enough to sell a boy on coming to UK, and he hated to humble himself in the field of recruiting. He resented the fact that the boys who were seeking athletic scholarships had become shoppers, spending their time running back and forth and visiting many schools with all expenses paid. However, he had to join the parade to hold his own in what had suddenly become a highly competitive business.

Time Out: Johnny Cox

"I will lift up mine eyes to the hills, from whence cometh my help," Rupp often said, and he was not just quoting the Psalm in jest when it came to Johnny Cox.

Stoop-shouldered and with a loping mannerism, Cox was a deceptive 6-foot-4 forward with a deadly one-hand jump shot and a beautiful hook shot that he could make with either hand. He was one of the most highly sought schoolboy players in the nation after he led Hazard to the 1955 Kentucky State High School Tournament championship.

After Johnny scored a record 127 points in four tournament games—32 of them in a 74-66 victory over Adair County in the final—Rupp walked up to him and asked, "How would you like to run up and down this court for four years?"

Cox thought it was a pretty good idea. So did Rupp. So did UK fans. Since the Hagan-Ramsey-Tsioropoulos team had finished the 1954 season undefeated, two Wildcat squads had compiled a respectable 43-9 record, but they had not gotten beyond the Mideast Regionals in NCAA tournament play. Besides, the Wildcat depth of past years was noticeably missing.

Johnny's trail to basketball glory began in the coal-mining community of Fleming at the headwaters of the Kentucky River in Letcher County. He first had a goal mounted on his house, but that had to go because the constant banging kept his father, a night-shift railroad worker, awake. Johnny moved the goal to another small building in the yard. He developed the hook shot by practicing hour after hour on that goal.

"I started playing organized basketball in grade school," he said, "but my mother didn't know I was playing until I had appendicitis and my coach, who was one of the women teachers, came to see me at the hospital. She told me I had to get out of the hospital or the team was going to lose all its games."

As a ninth grader Johnny was a B-team mainstay who occasionally got in a varsity game for Fleming-Neon High School. He started for the varsity the following year. After hours he could often be found in the little gym, practicing his jump shots and hookers.

Basketball practice had begun in Johnny's junior year when his father moved the family to Hazard, 50 miles to the west. Rather than chance suspension from the KHSAA if he used Cox, Coach Goebel Ritter kept the transfer student out of competition that year. A favorite sport at Hazard was to go by and watch the gangly junior practice his sweeping hooks.

Rupp would remember Johnny as a timid, bashful, skinny, scrawny kid.

"We never had a chance to put any weight on him," Rupp said. "He did not eat a great deal. There was some doubt in Hazard that he could make the grade academically at the university. He came to me that first week and said, 'Coach, I'm in trouble.'"

"What, already?"

"Not that, coach. One of your professors speaks a strange language. He has already assigned 42 pages for tomorrow. I'm not prepared for that, but I'm not going back to Hazard a failure."

"We have tutors, you know?"

"What's that?"

"We got him a tutor," Rupp said. "It helped get his thinking in the right place. He passed every subject."

Since Cox had played center in high school, there was some speculation that he might not be able to make the grade as a UK forward, but he soon dispelled such doubts. He led the freshman team in virtually every department, twice scoring 44 points in a game. Not since Wallace Jones came down from Harlan had a Kentucky mountain lad created so much excitement in the Blue Grass.

As a sophomore Johnny teamed with John Crigler at forward, Ed Beck at center, and Jerry Calvert and Vern Hatton at guard. Before playing in the annual UKIT they defeated Washington & Lee, Miami (Florida), Temple, and Maryland, and lost one-point decisions to St. Louis at home and to Duke at Durham.

After Cox scored 20 points against the Billikens, Coach Ed Hickey called him "the greatest sophomore in the country."

UK led Duke by 15 points at halftime, but the Blue Devils caught up and won, 85-84, after Bucky Allen roughly took the ball from Hatton and scored the winning basket with 20 seconds to play. Rupp questioned that and other decisions of the officials.

The first point of contention came with approximately six minutes remaining and Kentucky leading by five points, with Adrian Smith on the foul line. Before the shot dropped through the net, qualifying Smith for a bonus shot, a Duke substitute ran onto the floor. Atlantic Coast Conference official Phil Fox ruled the goal no try because the shooter did not know Duke had six men on the floor. Smith missed the next try. With one minute remaining Rupp called time out and instructed his players to protect their slim lead. One of the officials ruled that UK's John Brewer took too much time. Duke got the ball and scored on a toss-in.

Center Jim Krebs of Southern Methodist and guard Don Ohl of Illinois were two fine players in the UKIT that year. However, UK's balanced scoring negated Krebs' 25 points for a 73-67 win, and the speedy Ohl was not able to turn the tide as UK beat the previously undefeated Illini, 91-70.

That year Louisiana had passed a new state law banning athletic contests and other such activities involving personal and social contacts between blacks and whites. New Orleans tried and failed to get its Sugar Bowl basketball tournament exempt from the law. Kentucky was scheduled to participate in the tournament with Dayton, Notre Dame, and St. Louis, but the other three teams pulled out. There was talk of a split in the conference because of the rule, since Kentucky, Tennessee, and Vanderbilt were expected to be playing blacks in a few years.

Rupp was pressured to join Dayton and St. Louis in a new Kentucky Invitational Tournament at Louisville, but he chose to remain loyal to the Sugar Bowl, which got a last minute reprieve when Houston, Alabama, and Virginia Tech accepted invitations.

The Gobblers of Coach Chuck Noe apparently had UK beat in an upset of monumental proportions, but John Brewer stole the ball on a throw-in after a UK basket to get the winning goal (56-55) with seven seconds left. Defensive specialist Ed Beck scored 16 points that night and 10 points in a victory over

Coach Rupp and Johnny Cox admire the 1958 NCAA championship trophy. Three other trophies emblematic of NCAA championships are on the table with the 1958 game ball.

Houston (111-76) the following night to earn "Most Valuable Player" honors.

In that win over Houston, UK set five Sugar Bowl records, including all-time high individual team score, highest winning margin, and highest combined team total.

The Wildcats next defeated Georgia Tech, but there was no joy in the UK camp as Hatton underwent an appendectomy. John Brewer took his place. Two weeks after the Sugar Bowl the Wildcats returned to New Orleans and lost, 68-60, to Tulane. It was the Greenies' first victory over UK in 19 years. Yells of derision greeted Rupp as he started his long postgame stroll from the bench to congratulate Tulane's Cliff Wells at the other end of the floor.

Adrian Smith scored 16 points as a substitute guard in a 97-72 victory over Tennessee, replacing Brewer in the lineup. He had 24 against Georgia Tech, 20 against Georgia, and 18 against Florida. Hatton played a few minutes in the Georgia and Florida games, but he did not regain his form until Rupp inserted him into the lineup against Mississippi at Memphis. With 13 minutes remaining and UK trailing, 53-42, Vern stole the ball for a layup and then hit a long shot after Cox hit a one-hander. Vern scored 14 points in the 75-69 UK win.

The Wildcats had a six-game winning streak going when they traveled to Starkville for a game with Mississippi State. Bailey Howell scored 37 points and Jimmy Ashmore chipped in 25 as State beat UK, 89-81, for the first time in 33 years. The Wildcats defeated Loyola, 115-65, in Chicago and won their final four games against SEC competition.

The NCAA Mideast Regional was held in Lexington that year, but the home court did not prove much of an advantage to the Wildcats. They faltered in the second half and had a tough time getting by Pittsburgh, 98-92. Brewer saved that game, hitting eight of eight free throws as a substitute late in the game. UK led Michigan State, 47-35, at halftime, but guard Jack Quiggle scored 22 points, and John Green dominated the rebounding as the Spartans won, 80-68.

Cox capped a brilliant sophomore campaign by gaining a spot on the All-SEC honor five, being picked on the All-NCAA Regional Tournament team and making third team All-America. He scored 544 points, a 19.4 per game average. His best night was against Maryland, when he hit 11 of 21 from the field and 12 of 12 free throws. He got 23 rebounds and scored 32 points in a victory over Tennessee.

With Cox and all starters except Calvert returning the following year, prospects looked bright for the Wildcats.

The Fiddlin' Five

"They might be pretty good barnyard fiddlers," Adolph Rupp said in the fall of 1957, "but we have a Carnegie Hall schedule, and it will take violinists to play that competition."

The basketball maestro was looking over his upcoming schedule and at a Wildcat squad that had four starters—Vern Hatton, Ed Beck, John Cox, and John Crigler—and a fine guard prospect, Adrian Smith, back from the 1956-57 team that had finished 23-5.

Still he was convinced that good players were not enough. What he needed was a Cliff Hagan, or a Frank Ramsey, or a Bill Spivey.

But he did have Cox back from a super sophomore year, Hatton was strong after undergoing an appendectomy late in the preceding season, Crigler was a steady forward, Beck had developed into a fine rebounder and defensive player, and little "Smitty" showed promise of future greatness.

Perhaps it was a barnyard mixture: certainly it was a group composed of many diverse personalities.

Hatton, for instance, was the type of player who gave 100 percent without any prodding, one who would not perform under criticism. The only time Rupp fussed at him was during a defensive drill. Tired of the verbal barrage—"Play defense, play defense, you lazy thing"—Hatton walked to the bench, sat down, and announced that he had quit.

"Vernon, I have been coaching for 30 years," Rupp said, "and this is the first time I ever had a boy quit on me like this."

Crigler was different in that he was motivated by personal criticism and not much else. After John's man scored the tying

basket as halftime ended against Auburn, Rupp said in the dressing room:

"John Lloyd, 150 years from now there will be no university, no field house. There will have been an atomic war, and it will all have been destroyed. But underneath the rubble there will be a monument, which will be inscribed, 'Here lies John Lloyd Crigler, the most stupid basketball player ever at Kentucky, killed by Adolph Rupp,' because, boy, if you don't play better, I'm going to kill you."

With Rupp, left to right, are Adrian Smith, Vernon Hatton, Ed Beck, John Crigler, and Johnny Cox of the 1958 NCAA championship Wildcat team.

Smith went from high school stardom at Farmington to Northeast Mississippi Junior College, which had need for a 5-foot-10, 150-pound guard with skill. In his second season he was the fifth highest junior college scorer in the nation with a 27.2 average.

Beck developed into a fine rebounder and defensive player, leaving the scoring to other members of the squad. He had a personal tragedy when his wife, Billie, died of cancer near the end of the preceding season.

Hatton's finest moment as a Kentucky player came in a triple-overtime duel with Temple in the Coliseum. He made a free throw with 49 seconds to go to send the game into its first overtime. Then with Temple leading by two points with one second remaining, Rupp called time out and sat up an in-bounds play to Hatton.

While Temple defenders backed up to protect against the long pass and with many fans filing out of the arena, Hatton took a throw at midcourt from Crigler and shot with both hands. The horn sounded as the ball swished through the net for the tying points.

Temple tied the score at the end of the next overtime, but fell, 85-83, as Hatton scored six of Kentucky's last eight points.

The following day Hatton asked Rupp for the game ball.

"Give you the game ball?" Rupp snorted. "Just because you scored two points from 47 feet with one second to go. How would I explain that to the Athletic Board, giving away a $35 basketball? What would they think of me spending all that money? If you hadn't scored the basket, one of the other boys would have done the job, because the play was just one we had been practicing for occasions like that."

As Hatton contemplated quitting the team, Rupp reached under his desk, pulled out the game ball, flipped it to him, and said, "Congratulations, son. You're sure tough in the clutch. You may have the ball. Tell your grandchildren about it."

The Temple game was just one of many close contests played by the Wildcats that year. After they lost to Maryland by nine points and to Southern Methodist by one point, both on the road, Rupp said, "This is the greatest record-setting basketball team in the history of the University of Kentucky. It just sets the wrong kind of records."

They returned from Dallas and were defeated by West Virginia in the opening game of the UKIT, marking the first time in 15 years that a UK basketball team had lost two games in a row. Jerry West played superbly as the Mountaineers defeated North Carolina for the championship and ended a 37-game Tar Heel winning streak.

In conference action they lost to Georgia Tech, 71-52, in Atlanta, stalled with the ball more than eight minutes in a 72-62 victory over Mississippi State, defeated Alabama in overtime at

Vernon Hatton scores against Temple with one second remaining to send December 7, 1957, game into first of three overtimes. Guy Rodgers rushes toward Hatton. John Crigler is at right. UK won, 85-83.

Montgomery on a shot by Crigler with two seconds remaining, and lost to Auburn, 64-63. They won the conference title for the 19th time and took a record of 19-6 into the NCAA playoffs.

No team with six losses had ever won the NCAA championship, but the Wildcats had the advantage of playing the regional games on their home floor and the finals at Freedom Hall in Louisville. They got by Miami, Ohio, with ease, but were an underdog against Notre Dame, which had conquered Big Ten champion Indiana.

"I could not rest all that afternoon," Rupp said. "I was in my office and I got ants all over me. I went home. I couldn't brush the ants off. I collected more of them. I told Mrs. Rupp I was going back to the Coliseum."

"But you just came from there," Esther said.

"I know that, but I just can't rest," he said. "I can't do anything."

"Let me fix you something to eat," she said. "Maybe you'll feel better."

"We ate early," Rupp said. "I went to the Coliseum and waited, and waited, and waited. I told the manager, 'As our boys come in, tell them I don't want them to see the first game. I want them to go to the squad room. When they all get there, I want to talk to them.' I changed our strategy, and we beat Notre Dame (89-56)."

When they got to Louisville for the championship games, Temple was working out on the floor. Guy Rodgers came over, shook Rupp's hand, and said, "We're going to beat you this time."

"There's a possiblity of that," Rupp replied.

In 26 games Temple had lost only to UK and Cincinnati.

The Wildcats were down by one point with 24 seconds to go, when Rupp called time out.

"Coach, I believe we can run a back screen and get one of the guards loose," Beck said. "My man has stuck to me and never has switched a single time."

"All right," Rupp said. "We'll run a back screen. But be sure that you don't get caught moving, because these Eastern officials will blow you out of the place."

Hatton took the throw-in pass, dribbled around the screen, and scored with a few seconds remaining on the clock.

In answer to some criticism that he got the points too quickly, Rupp said: "You never get a basket too quick when you are one point behind with seconds to go. I want to be ahead."

He and Lancaster figured Temple would use a double screen to give Rodgers the shot. They guessed right about the screen, but the ball was to go to "Pickles" Kennedy. As Kennedy came around a screen, Rodgers left his feet to throw the pass. The ball was thrown high and was bobbled out of bounds by Kennedy. Time ran out with UK ahead, 61-60. The Wildcats were in the championship game with Elgin Baylor and Seattle, which had defeated Kansas State, 73-51, in the other semifinal game.

Rupp and Lancaster felt that Baylor would guard Beck, who was averaging only 4.8 points a game. However, Crigler had failed to score the night before, so Seattle coach John Castellani switched Baylor to guarding him out on the floor. When Rupp observed that, he told Crigler to drive on Baylor. Crigler drove, got a couple of fouls on Baylor, and at the same time scored a couple of baskets. Seattle loosened up a bit, but by halftime Baylor had three fouls on him.

When Baylor was taken off Crigler and put on the UK centers, Beck and Don Mills, Hatton started to drive the middle, forcing Baylor to switch and pick him up. After Baylor got his fourth foul trying to block a Mills hook shot, Seattle went into a zone defense. Cox started hitting one-hand shots from 20 to 30 feet out on the floor, and Hatton slashed toward the basket where Baylor, because of the foul situation, could only play token defense. Down by 11 points early in the half the Wildcats finally took the lead and won, 84-72, presenting Rupp with his fourth NCAA championship. Hatton was high man with 30 points; Cox had 24.

"Those boys certainly are not concert violinists," Rupp said, "but they sure can fiddle."

Johnny Cox and Adolph Rupp are congratulated after the Wildcats defeat Baylor for the 1958 NCAA crown.

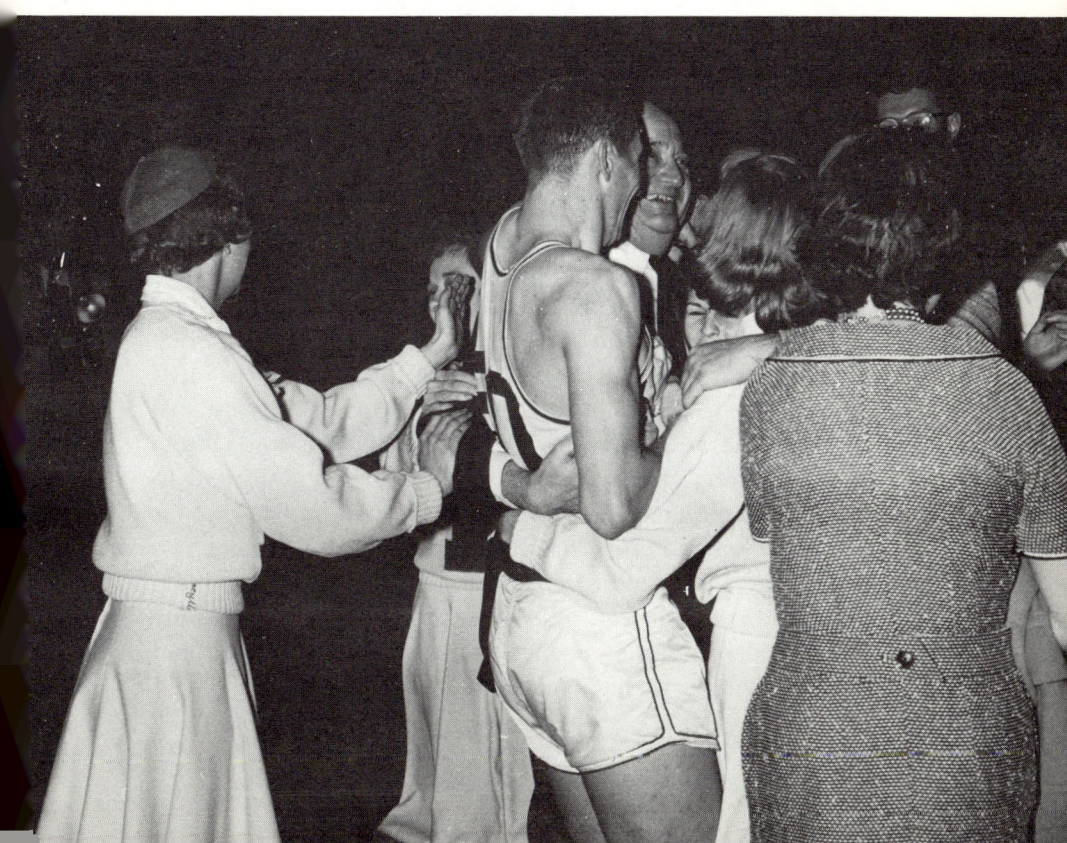

Letter From A "Preacher Man"

When the Rev. Ed Beck wrote the following letter in February 1972, he was pastor of the Warren United Methodist Church in Denver, Colorado. Since then he has returned to the Kentuckiana area and in 1975 was managing a dinner theater in Clarksville, Indiana.

Dear Russ:

I was the first clergyman and may be the last ever to play for Rupp. There was some speculation upon my arrival in September of 1954 that I would not last long because of Adolph's projected gruff manner.

During the freshman season we approached the first Sunday practice, and he called me into his office to state that if in any way practicing basketball on Sunday afternoon was against my religious feelings or sensitivities I would not have to practice and in no way would this hurt my chances with the team. I conveyed to him my feelings that first, it was not in any way against my religious principles and second, that I was a part of the team and wanted to participate when and where they did. I felt if any special consideration was given there might be some harm done. He was appreciative of my feelings but wanted to convey his understanding on whatever position I took.

The second story has to do with Adolph's quickness to change an age-old premise to meet his needs. On more than one occasion at a practice session he would quote the Bible and sometimes change words to communicate and with a twinkle in his eyes he would look at me and say,

"That's what the good book says, doesn't it?"

One day at practice the varsity was running against the freshmen the old bread and butter No. 6 play. One of the forwards, Jerry Bird, instead of running that play ran No. 7, and Adolph rushed out on to the court, throwing his arms up in the air shouting, "Stop! Stop! Stop!" He approached Jerry and said, "Jerry, you have just committed the cardinal sin, you have just broken one of the ten commandments, Thou shalt not be stupid!"

Being the motivational expert that he was he would always use everything that he could to gain the upper hand on the opponent. One time as we played Notre Dame he came in before the game, and he said, "Boys, I don't want you to get upset or feel that you are outnumbered when you see the Notre Dame boys cross themselves before the game or before every free throw. Now don't worry about all those priests that they have on the bench because we have them outnumbered." He said, "We have Ed, and I know he has been praying" and then with that certain grin he pulled out of his pocket a small madonna and said, "The last time I was in Rome the Pope blessed this, and I have put the hex on Notre Dame."

In December of 1956 at the Christmas tournament Kentucky had to play, on successive evenings, the top two teams in the nation, SMU and Illinois. After viewing films on the afternoon of the opening game, much of the discussion had hinged around the fact that both SMU and Illinois had All-American centers and if Kentucky stood a chance I somehow would have to upset these two giants. As he was leaving the team room Adolph called me over to the side and said, "Ed, I hope you are praying a lot because you will need all the help you can get."

The superstitious nature of Adolph is a part of his legend, and we are all familiar with the brown suit, but he has another superstition which is as prevalent as that. It was his obsession on the afternoon and evening of the game to look for hair pins that had fallen on the sidewalk or the playing arena. Depending on the number of hair pins he found he computed that into how well his team was going to play.

One Saturday night in Philadelphia we were to play Temple University with the great Guy Rodgers and Hal

The bouncing ball afforded quite a surprise for UK's Jerry Bird, left, John Crigler (45), and Ed Beck, and for DePaul's Bill Robinzine, Ron Sobieszczyk (21), Kenneth Jaksy (20), and Charles Henry (34) in Alumni Gym December 12, 1955. UK won, 71-69.

Lear. The game was played in the Palestra, which was the auditorium which was used by all kinds of performances. When we walked in the dressing room, they apparently had had some kind of stage show the night before, and our dressing room had been used by females. As Adolph's sharp eyes started perusing the room, he noticed under a table in the corner a box of hair pins that had fallen and scattered. He rushed over to the table, got down on his hands and knees, and started picking them up, and with a grin he turned to Lancaster and said, "Harry, we are going to have a helluva night tonight." And the amazing thing is that we did.

In the spring of 1957 Kentucky traveled to Starkville to play Mississippi State. There was a sophomore on State's team that the scouting report said had potential, but was still a year away. His name was Bailey Howell. I tried to guard him that night, and I think before the game was over he had scored something like 37 points and Kentucky had been defeated. As we moved toward the dress-

ing room, Adolph in disgust turned to me and said, "Ed, you will never make All-American, but you made one tonight." And sure enough the national recognition from that one game started Bailey Howell on his long and glorious career.

Half time pep talks by Adolph are legion, and most of them have long since submerged into the subconscious of the players who really got it. Others are rather difficult to relate because of a language problem, but one sticks indelibly in my mind.

Kentucky was playing the University of Mississippi at Memphis, and at half time we were about six points behind. We had played a miserable game, and Johnny Cox and I were largely responsible for our poor effort. We had gotten mixed up on a number of occasions on definitive assignments, and Mississippi had made easy baskets.

In the dressing room he took the first team one by one and chastised us for our total incompetence, but he saved me for last. I was the only team member from out of the state of Kentucky, and he used that like a surgeon's knife.

After a few preliminary remarks concerning my birthright he said, "Ed, I want you to go to the hotel right now and write me a letter, no, write me a theme, no you better make that a Doctorate Dissertation on this subject, 'Why Adolph Rupp was crazy enough to go to the State of Georgia after the likes of you.'" Then he said, "Ed, you have eaten well at the university over the last two to three years, and I am going to let you play the whole second half no matter how poorly you do and I know it will be poor, but before we go out on the court do you see the corner over there (and with his finger he pointed to the corner of the room)? I want you to go over to that corner and puke up everything you have eaten at the University of Kentucky over the last three years because you have never earned it and at the end of this game I want you to go into that dressing room, look me straight in the eye, and say, 'Coach, I did something in this coliseum tonight, even if it was only over there in that corner.'" The result of the game was that we won handily.

When I was at the university, my wife, Billie, died of cancer in the spring of 1957. There were some strange circumstances surrounding that whole scene which have never probably been pieced together satisfactorily.

I married Billie at the beginning of my sophomore year, and she had cancer even before we were married. She only lived in Lexington about six months but did make periodic visits at other times. She became very close to both Adolph and Harry, and on every occasion that she traveled to Lexington they always made it a point to visit with her.

Approximately a month before she died we were to play at Atlanta, and the team trainer and myself drove from Atlanta to Macon to pick her up at the hospital and to bring her back for the game. Adolph was every bit a gracious host and bent over backwards to make her feel so welcome. He and the team knew quite well that this would probably be the last time they would see her alive.

I guess it is incidental about the extra little things that he did throughout her illness all the way from sending flowers to writing to even calling, but this is a side of the man that not a lot of people know about. One week before she died we played Michigan State for the regional NCAA title. It was a very strange ball game in the sense that we led most of the way, and then after all of their big stars fouled out, including Johnnie Green, we lost the game in the last 30 seconds. If we had won that night we would have gone to Kansas City the next weekend for the title game. As we went to the dressing room, not really knowing what to expect, Adolph made a statement about the game that went something like this as I tried to express my personal displeasure in not bringing the victory home: "Some day we will know the reason why." Harry Lancaster was standing with him and basically repeated the statement.

In the dressing room his statement to the team was rather brief, "Forget about the game. You will never be able to play it again. Just remember one thing. At the start of the season you were the 22nd team in the nation and tonight you are the No. 3 team because you gave me, your coach, more than you actually had. You gave more than your best."

The following Saturday at one o'clock my wife died, and that would have been the afternoon that we would have been playing in Kansas City for the title. When I called Harry Lancaster in Lexington and shared with him the news, his response was, "Now we know the reason why." He also said that he would contact Adolph.

Adolph and Bernie Shively had been to Kansas City for the tournament but according to Bernie, Adolph had become quite dissatisfied with staying in Kansas City and had decided to fly back to Kentucky on Saturday morning. They were unable to get a flight out until the early afternoon. Bernie said he had tried to persuade Adolph to stay at the games, but he refused. Just before they left for the airport Harry called and told them of Billie's death, and so they changed their reservations and flew to Georgia and were with me that evening and the next day for the funeral. On the following Monday at the sports banquet, which I was unable to attend, he gave a glowing tribute to her and shared his feeling about what she meant to him.

Echoes From The '50s

Dr. Frank G. Dickey
(UK President 1956-63)

Dear Russell:

My contacts with Coach Rupp extend back to 1949 when I became dean of the College of Education of the University of Kentucky. I really did not have any close contacts with him, however, until I became president of the University in 1956. During the period from 1956 to 1963 I saw Coach Rupp frequently.

One of my clearest recollections was a discussion we had in my office in 1959 regarding the possibility of make-up exams for members of the basketball squad. Normally, Coach Rupp asked no favors in academic matters for his players, and he received very few such favors. In this instance he was discussing the entire philosophy of examinations. One of his comments made a profound impression on me. He said, "I have never understood why a professor in English, mathematics, history, or science could not give a 'public' examination to his students. In this way the entire community could know what sort of teaching job he had been doing, because my theory is that the success or failure of a student on an examination is just as much determined by the professor as it is by the student." He concluded by saying, "I give my examinations twice a week during the entire season, and these examinations are observed by 10,000 and more interested citizens each time. I'm perfectly willing to have the results of my teaching observed by the public, and I think every professor should be equally willing to place his work on the line."

I feel certain that you have already included one of Coach Rupp's more famous remarks when he was requested to use the Alumni Gym for practice one afternoon in order that Artur Rubenstein could practice for a concert in Memorial Coliseum. Coach Rupp reluctantly agreed to do so, but reminded me that this was really not necessary. He said: "Mr. Rubenstein could miss half a dozen notes tonight and not more than four or five persons would know it, but let one of my players run a play wrong on a Saturday night and the whole damned world will hear about it."

Some of my other recollections of Mr. Rupp and his impact on Kentucky and the nation for that matter deal with subjects other than basketball. One of his interests over the years has been the breeding of Herefords. He has been a forceful element in bringing about more interest in the science of Hereford breeding. Again, one of his more humorous and typical comments was in this context when he said to me at one of the College of Agriculture Animal Husbandry conferences: "I just wish that we could produce basketball players with the same degree of confidence that they will be what I want as I do in breeding my cattle."

Very sincerely yours,

Frank G. Dickey

Hunter Durham
(Mgr. 1961, '62)

Dear Mr. Rice:

One afternoon while I was manager of the UK team someone was walking in the foyer during basketball practice, and I was instructed by Coach Rupp to throw out whoever it was since it was a closed practice.

As I approached toward the individual, I discovered it was Dr. Dickey, then president of the University of Kentucky, and he (Dr. Dickey) asked me what I wanted. I told him that Coach Rupp had given me the instructions to throw out whoever was in the gym but of course since he was the president of the university I assumed that he would have the preference of staying if he wished. Dr. Dickey laughed and said he was leaving anyway and instructed me to tell Coach Rupp that I had thrown him out. Coach Rupp needless to say was very displeased with the fact that we had thrown out the president of the college from the basketball practice. The next day sitting at Coach Rupp's right hand during the practice was Dr. Dickey with a large grin on his face.

        Very truly yours,

        Hunter Durham

       J. T. Denton
       Lexington, Kentucky

Dear Russell:

My mother, Matilda L. Denton (Mrs. J. W. Denton, deceased), was a great supporter of U.K. basketball and football teams.

She was one of the first to receive the Rupp award for support of the team, and attended games from Florida to the N.I.T. in New York and the NCAA in College Park, Maryland.

One year I drove her to Knoxville and upon arrival there Rupp told her he could not get any tickets. He said that since she had driven so far he would take care of her. He told her to get on the bus with the team, ride out to the gym with the boys, go in with them, and she could sit on the bench with the players. This thrilled her to no end. I was left out but contacted J. B. Faulconer. J. B. took me in, and I turned cards for him during the game.

She knew many of the players personally, and considered Bill Spivey the greatest and the Groza-Beard team the greatest.

        Yours truly,
        J. T. Denton

Gayle Rose (1952, '53, and '54)
Lexington, Kentucky

Dear Russell,

We had been practicing for at least two hours one afternoon, and he kept riding me about getting a rebound. Being only six feet tall I was doing my best, but just couldn't get one. Finally, someone stole the ball at midcourt, went in for a wide open crip shot, and missed. I jumped as high as I could and retrieved the rebound. I came trotting down the floor bouncing the ball and obviously proud I had finally gotten a rebound.

At that moment Coach Rupp said, "Rose, you look like a Shetland pony in a stud horse parade. Stop practice and everyone take a shower. I know we are going to have a successful season now. Rose got a rebound."

I remember my senior year around Christmas time I became very discouraged and quit the team. It was after the Christmas tournament, and I refused to go to the banquet and receive my watch, which all the players received for playing in the tournament.

After one miserable week I realized what a mistake I had made. I went to Coach Rupp and asked him to take me back on the team. He agreed and I had a complete change in attitude. I later made the first team and the All-Regional NCAA team along with Bob Burrow. I had played my last game for UK and went up to Coach Rupp after the game and thanked him for taking me back on the team and for helping me to grow up. He gave me a big smile and I started to walk away.

"Wait a minute," Rupp said. When I turned around, he said, "You better stop by the office Monday morning and pick up the watch I've been keeping for you."

Sincerely,

Gayle Rose

Hugh Coy (1954)

Dear Russell,

One night Coach Lancaster showed up in a new navy blue suit looking and feeling very sharp. At this time Herky, who must have been around twelve years old, was our water carrier. We had little trays with Dixie cups of water, and Herky carried them at the home games. Just as we were getting ready to start the game and I had just taken my usual seat on the bench there came a great amount of ugly words out of Coach Lancaster's mouth that could not or should not be repeated. Coach Rupp hearing them turned to Coach Lancaster and said, "What's the matter, Harry?" and Coach Lancaster dripping with water and so mad he was about to explode said, "Ah, hell, Herky poured water all over me." Adolph immediately replied, "He did not. He wouldn't do that." This was said in a tone of voice that assured everyone around that Coach Rupp's little boy was not capable of anything like that. Of course I can't tell the story as funny as it really was, but I would have to say this was the funniest.

Then there was another time when I was a freshman and all we did was practice, as we were suspended that year. We were scrimmaging Memphis State and beating them but not as much as we should have been doing. They were a real scrappy bunch and were giving Hagan and Lou a hard time on the boards. Coach Rupp had some cattlemen from Chicago visiting him that day, and he had invited them out to watch us practice. Well, our style of play did not improve much, and Coach Rupp blew his whistle and turned to the men in the stands and said, "You fellows from Chicago have heard of our great All American Cliff Hagan. Cliff, come over here where they can see you. I'm sure they couldn't tell which one you were by the way you were playing," and Cliff took a bow.

Yours truly,

Hugh Coy

Ken Lehkamp (Mgr. 1956, and '57)

Dear Mr. Rice:

One afternoon early in the 1955-56 season while the players were going through some warm-up drills Coach Rupp very suddenly stopped practice and said in that familiar drawl of his, "Hold everything!" Then as everything got so quiet you could hear a pin drop he turned to Harold Ross, a quiet, easy-going guard from Hickman, Kentucky, who at the time had been whistling while we were going through drills, and said: "Harold, I didn't bring you down here all the way from Hickman to listen to you sing. If you wanted to do that you should have talked to Warren Lutz (U.K. Band Director), and maybe he would have given you a scholarship." This is a good example of how Coach Rupp could be very serious and also very funny at the same time. No one dared crack a smile but all you had to do was look at each player's eyes, and you could see that he was nearly ready to burst.

I was just a green sophomore in my first year as a manager for the U.K. basketball team, and understandably I was quite in awe of Coach Rupp. As the season wore on, every time Coach Rupp wanted me he would yell, "Hey, George" and of course I would always come running. Finally about halfway through the season I finally summoned together all of my courage one day and said something to him besides "Yes, sir." I said, "Sir, my first name is Ken, not George," and his reply was: "Well, I thought your name was George because you always came running when I called you George."

Sincerely,

Ken Lehkamp

(Lowell Hughes earned letters as a football quarterback at UK in 1957, '58, and '59. He also was a member of Adolph Rupp's "Lost Battalion," lettering two years in basketball.)

Dear Russell:

I do not recall the team involved, but the game was a mismatch and Kentucky was ahead by 25 points or so at half-time and as the second half started they immediately increased the lead to put the game all the way out of reach. At this particular time during the season I had been running as the second or third substitute but, because the game seemed to be always somewhat in doubt, had not been getting much playing time.

With about 16 or 17 minutes remaining in the second half the K-Men's section of the Coliseum which was composed basically of the football players began chanting "We want Hughes" and kept this up for an extended period. Coach Rupp began substituting and every time he would substitute the chant would go up again, "We want Hughes," and finally after every substitute was in the game with the exception of myself, and with only about a minute and a half left in the game, Coach Rupp came to me and said, "Hughes you can go in now and you be sure and tell your 'oblong ball players' that I coach this team and that they cost you about fifteen minutes of playing time tonight."

Coach Rupp was always fond, of course, of referring to football players as "oblong ball players." The following day Coach Rupp even took this matter up with Coach Collier for the purpose of assuring that the football players would no longer attempt to contribute to coaching the basketball team.

Sincerely,

Lowell Hughes

After losing to Duke in Durham several years ago, Rupp said: "It's a shame that the University pays me a pretty good salary, spends about $20,000 in scholarships, and then turns our games over to officials to butcher up the play. We work hard two hours every day and then everything we have worked for can be undone by an official in 40 minutes. Entirely too much authority is being given officials. Something must be done. The fans don't come out to ball games to see a free-throw contest, and that is exactly what basketball has boiled down to. I'll finish my coaching career at Kentucky and then I'll retire and raise seeing-eye dogs for officials."

Only At Kentucky

In the summer of 1975 Dicky Parsons could look back on his three years as a University of Kentucky varsity basketball player and figure that a 61-19 record was not so bad, after all.

The 'Cats were 24-3 in his sophomore year (1959), 18-7 his junior year (1960), and 19-9 the year (1961) he served as team captain.

"I'll never forget at the end of that second year how terrible we thought the season was because we had lost seven games," Dicky said. "There is so much tradition, so much pride in basketball at UK that I'll never forget how we felt a little embarrassed and ashamed of ourselves. I'd be glad to have that record today. It turned out that wasn't so bad after all."

At the time of the interview Parsons was chief assistant to Wildcat coach Joe B. Hall, whose 1975 team had just lost to UCLA in the finals of the NCAA Tournament.

Dicky was the smallest—"I never would let them measure me"—player to start for Rupp until Randy Embry came along in 1963. While relaxing in his office in Memorial Coliseum, he briefly recalled how he started playing basketball:

"It began in the little coal mining community of Yancey in Harlan County. Our little gym looked more like a barn than anything else. It had a lot of cracks, no heat, although at one time there was a potbellied stove, and it was so cold in winter that we played in sweat shirts.

"We would play before school, at noon, and after school, and then we'd go home and eat and come back at night. There were some naked lights, so we'd just take two wires and cross them and play until about 9 or 9:30.

The 1961 NCAA-bound Wildcats are, left to right: Carroll Burchett, Billy Ray Lickert, Larry Pursiful, Dicky Parsons, Rupp, Roger Newman, and Ned Jennings. They are celebrating an 88-67 win over Vanderbilt in a playoff at Knoxville.

"That's a lot of basketball, but I felt like that was where I learned some of the fundamentals and style of play that helped me a great deal later on. Our grade school team played on dirt courts along the creeks and up and down the Cumberland River.

"In my senior year at Harlan High I was not recruited by many schools. I had decided to maybe go out of state, but Rupp and Lancaster sent someone down to see me play in a tournament game, and Rupp came in to visit me and Bobby Slusher of Lone Jack. We both eventually signed at UK. I guess if I had known how tough it would be for a small fellow to play at UK, I never would have attended. At the time I was thinking if I couldn't make it there, I could go elsewhere. And when Coach Rupp kept calling me 'Bobby,' thinking I was Bobby Watson, I knew I had it made.

"I was a freshman when UK won the NCAA in 1958. It

was a grand experience. I do not feel it was a great team, but it was a team that played quite well when it was important. We worked a great deal against the varsity, a lot of scrimmage sessions."

Only John Cox, Don Mills and Phil Johnson returned from that championship team. Among the freshmen reporting in 1958-59 was Billy Ray Lickert, who was signed by Rupp shortly after he led Lafayette to the 1957 state high school championship and was named "Mr Basketball" in Kentucky for the annual series with the Indiana All-Stars. He remembered his first meeting with Rupp:

"I went to old Alumni Gym to get his autograph, and when a ball bounced out of bounds during a scrimmage, I shot it. He turned to me and said, 'Get out, kid.'"

Freshmen moving into varsity ranks with Parsons and Lickert were Bob Slusher (6-foot-5), Ned Jennings (6-foot-9) of Harrison County, Carroll Burchett (6-foot-5) of Flat Gap, and Howard Dardeen (6-foot-3) of Terre Haute, Indiana. Rupp also had to indoctrinate into his system junior college graduates Bennie Coffman of Huntington, West Virginia, and Sidney Cohen of Brooklyn.

"Sidney, I want you to meet Johnny Cox of Hazard, Kentucky," Rupp said in practice one day. "He's working over on that side of the court. He's a pretty good basketball player. He just won the national championship for us last year. But he won't have a chance to do it again this year unless you let him feel the ball once in a while."

"Cox was a great leader," Parsons said. "When we were in trouble, we just got the ball in to him. I'll never forget those hook shots and the jumpers he would take. I felt like my role was to get the offense started. I tried to set other people up. I never did shoot a great deal, but I did take a lot of pride in being a good defensive player. I always guarded the opposing guard who was the leading scorer.

"I'll never forget that year because this particular team was not expected to be a very good team. But we seemed to jell. We won our first 11 games and were No. 1 in the nation."

The most thrilling game in that stretch was against Maryland in the Coliseum. The Terrapins were leading by three points with 16 seconds to play when time out was called and UK in possession.

"Coach Rupp told us we would have to drive for the bas-

Ben Coffman made this shot in the closing seconds of a game with Maryland, was fouled by Al Bunge (54), made the free throw, and sent the game into overtime. The Wildcats won, 58-56, December 15, 1958. John Cox (24) is under the basket.

ket and try to make it and draw a foul," Parsons said. "Meanwhile, Coach Bud Milliken was telling his players to be sure and not foul. I took the ball out, threw it in to Bennie, and he took off for the basket. Al Bunge, the Maryland center, fouled him. The ball went in and Bennie made the free throw. We won in overtime."

The streak also included victories over Navy, Illinois, and Georgia Tech. The victory over Illinois was by one point before 18,274 fans in Louisville's Freedom Hall. The Wildcats had a seemingly safe lead, but held on tenaciously after the Illini put on a full-court press in the last minute.

Vanderbilt ended the streak, beating the Wildcats, 75-66, in Nashville. The Commodores were coached by Roy Skinner, a Paducah native filling in for ailing head coach Bob Polk. Jim Henry of New Albany hit 29 points for Vandy. The Wildcats lost one other game, to Mississippi State, in regular season play.

"That game was in Starkville, when Bailey Howell, Babe McCarthy, and all the cowbells were there," Parsons recalled. "It was an experience I'll never forget because the coaches tried to prepare us for what to expect, but there was no way they could prepare us for *that*. I can remember staying on campus the night before the game and some of the students beating on dishpans all night long, trying to keep us awake. They did a pretty good job of it.

"We went out to the old basketball arena about five o'clock, and it was full. We did not take the floor until we saw them take the floor because we did not want to be subjected to all those boos and cowbells. When they went out, we went out; some students would boo, some would cheer, and eventually it would turn to cheers. When they left the playing floor, we threw our basketballs down and just followed them into the locker room and again you'd have some booing and some cheering.

"You just could not hear during a time out. Coach Rupp would yell into each individual player's ear the type of instructions he wanted. It was the loudest place I ever played in. A ruling had been passed that you did not have to shoot free throws as long as they were ringing those cowbells. Cox was at the line once, and he did not shoot, and they kept waiting for the crowd to be quiet. Finally McCarthy went to the mike and told the students, 'Please be quiet. They're gonna miss, anyway.'"

State was leading by 18 points when Bailey Howell fouled out with less than five minutes remaining. Kentucky cut the margin to eight. The students closed the final 15 seconds shouting, "We're No. 1." They carried McCarthy off the floor.

State won the SEC championship, but the school administration refused an NCAA bid because the legislature prohibited its state-supported schools from playing games with teams that had black players. UK ended a 30-game Auburn winning streak, and then Tennessee defeated Auburn. The SEC chose UK to represent it in the NCAA regional at Evanston, Illinois. The Wildcats met Louisville in the opening round.

"We had played good basketball all year, and we were ahead of Louisville by 15 points in the first 10 minutes of play," Parsons said, "but we just seemed to run out of gas. Louisville had a good ball club, and they beat us, 76-61. After we beat Marquette for third place, we sat behind the Louisville bench and cheered for them. It seemed the right thing to do."

Before practice began the following season, potential starter Slusher was dismissed for disciplinary reasons, Dardeen failed to return to school, and Burchett was sidelined by an illness. Former player Roger Newman was declared ineligible because he had participated in a YMCA league, and Coffman was benched temporarily with academic troubles. Jennings and Parsons received injuries at crucial stages of the campaign.

In an opening romp over Colorado State, Herky Rupp, a substitute, tipped in a shot to put the Wildcats over the century mark and received the biggest ovation of his basketball career at UK.

"Then we went to the West Coast," Dicky Parsons said. "None of us will ever forget that trip. We beat John Wooden's UCLA team, 68-66, and lost to Southern Cal, 87-73, the following night. I'll never forget how tired we felt. Travel and the time differential seemed to have sapped our strength. It was hot out there, cold in Lexington.

"After the game with USC, we were down in the dumps and on the team bus coming back to the hotel. A car ran a red light in front of us, and our bus hit the car broadside, pushing it about 30 or 40 feet down the street and wrapping it around a telephone post. Everything happened so suddenly. We could not get the front door of the bus open, and somebody suggested we go out the back. But no one could get the back door open either. Wah Jones, who was along as a radio color announcer, just kicked it off its hinges, and we went out the back door.

"Jim Host (radio announcer) was walking up the aisle of the bus when we made contact with the car. He shot right up the aisle and into the driver's lap; fortunately no one on the bus was injured, but one person in the car was killed and some others seriously injured. Losing a basketball game didn't seem so important.

"We went to Disneyland the next day. Some of us talked Coach Rupp into riding a log flume, which was about 50 or 60 feet in the air. I'll never forget his expression when he came down the flume and hit the water. He said, 'Boy, I'd rather be on that bus than to ride something like this.'"

A highlight of the season was an early victory in Lexington over eventual NCAA champion Ohio State. "That was when Jerry Lucas, John Havlicek, Larry Siegfried, and Mel Noel were sophomores," Parsons said, "and many people said that was the greatest game ever played in the Coliseum."

The Wildcats lost to St. Louis but defeated Kansas, 77-72, in overtime at Lawrence to take a 3-2 record into the UKIT. North Carolina was 3-0 and had defeated Kansas, 60-49, but the Wildcats won, 76-70. West Virginia, with the great Jerry West, came into the tournament undefeated in six games. They disposed of St. Louis and then got a 33-point effort from West, who played with a broken nose, en route to a 79-70 decision over UK. Rupp said West was as good as he had seen.

The worst humiliation was in Atlanta, where Tech defeated them, 65-44, for Hyder's second victory that year over Rupp. UK's point total was the lowest since a 42-40 loss to St. Louis in the 1948 Sugar Bowl. They lost to eventual champion Auburn by one point as Jimmy Fibbe of Frankfort, Kentucky, scored the final two points on free throws. Closing their season with an uninspired loss to Tennessee they placed third in the conference, their lowest finish since 1942.

The low point of the following season came early. Vanderbilt, with eight Kentuckians on the squad, beat them by two points in Nashville; Louisiana State, after 27 frustrating years, won its first game over UK; and Tulane defeated them in New Orleans. They beat Tennessee at home and were seemingly out of the conference race after a 12-foot shot by Roger Kaiser with two seconds to go gave Tech a two-point win in Atlanta. It was the second year in a row that UK had lost as many as four conference games.

They won their next nine games, including a victory over eventual champion Mississippi State at Starkville, where a dead skunk was placed under the UK bench and several obscene and uncomplimentary signs—"See you in hell, Adolph,"—were displayed by the students. Wads of paper, drink cups, ice, and cigar butts were thrown at him.

It was a rare moment when he was carried off the floor by his players after they defeated Vanderbilt, 88-67, in a playoff game at Knoxville for the right to represent the conference in the NCAA.

"The team doctor called me the day of the Vandy game to come up to Rupp's room," team captain Parsons said. "When I arrived I saw Coach Rupp on the bed, looking weak. The doctor said he did not know if Rupp could go to the pre-game meal. I told him I thought that would be all right, and I would explain it to the squad. He said he was not sure if he could make it to the game. I told him not to worry, the team was ready to play. He sat up in the bed and said, 'Heck, I feel better already.' He did make it to the game, but he did not seem as fired up as usual, but we seemed to have the game in good shape throughout.

"After we won he gave me the game ball, and his spirits seemed to have readily improved. We eventually beat a fine Morehead team in the NCAA and lost to Ohio State."

In that regional final Lucas hit 14 of 18 shots, finishing with 33 points. Lickert was selected to the All-Regional team and made All-Conference for the third consecutive year. The 19-9 record was UK's worst in 34 years. Rupp claimed he got everything he could out of the available material.

"I hope God grants me two more wishes before I leave the University of Kentucky," he said. "A fifth NCAA basketball championship and a parking space on this campus." He would come close to getting both those wishes.

"King Cotton"

If Charles "Cotton" Nash had stepped into a telephone booth in downtown Lexington in the fall of 1961, ripped off his street clothes, and emerged decked out in cape and "S" sweater, few UK basketball fans would have been surprised.

The 6-foot-5, 200-pound blond adonis had arrived on campus looking like a hero just out of a comic strip. He reputedly was Wallace Jones, Cliff Hagan, and Frank Ramsey, all rolled in one, a high school wonder boy who could rebound, dribble, pass, and shoot with the best of them.

His Superman antics at Lake Charles High School included scoring 1,412 points in 42 games, unanimous Louisiana all-star selection twice in basketball, and All-State twice in football. He broke the state discus record, hit a baseball so well that some major league scouts tried to sign him, was unanimous choice of the Louisiana Sports Writers Association as the top athlete there in 1960, and was selected as "Homecoming King," earning the nickname "King Cotton" in the process.

A well-traveled young man, Cotton was born in New Jersey in 1942. He did not get interested in basketball until he was 11, after his family had moved to Charlestown, Indiana, where his high school coach for two years was Cliff Barker, a member of UK's "Fabulous Five."

Cotton's father Frank was a former high school basketball coach who had been good enough in baseball to be offered a pro contract while in college. When the duPont firm transferred him to Orange, Texas, Frank moved the family 40 miles into Louisiana at Lake Charles so Cotton could be eligible to play basketball immediately. (Texas regulations required a transfer student to stay out of athletics one year.)

"As a senior at Lake Charles, I really didn't know my best sport," Cotton would recall in the spring of 1975. "I started getting contacts from colleges—Big 10 powers, Eastern powers—and I didn't know whether to stay home and play football (for LSU or Tulane) or go off somewhere and play basketball. I must have visited 15 or 25 colleges. UCLA promised me a date with Jane Fonda if I came back."

As the weeks rolled into months and Cotton still was making his visitations, Frank Nash suddenly stepped in and said, "Son, you'd better make up your mind." They had visited UK and liked what they saw; in fact, Frank later would say, "When we saw the Coliseum, Cotton just seemed to belong there."

"He told me that if I was going to play basketball, Kentucky was the only place," Cotton said. "In Louisiana an assistant football coach usually was the basketball coach and not too knowledgeable about the game, which was mostly an off-season conditioning program for football players. So I signed with UK."

Cotton's timing could not have been more perfect. The Wildcats were still among the nation's basketball elite, but no longer the all-dominating factor on the national scene. UK's big advantage over the years had been first choice of the many fine basketball players from the high school ranks of Kentucky, but that situation had changed since integration of the Kentucky High School Athletics Association in 1955. Skilled black players had made their presence felt immediately, but there was no place for them at UK, where the image of a Kentucky basketball player was still that of the traditional white mountain sharpshooter who exchanged his rifle for a basketball, or in the SEC, which did not allow them to participate.

The best white high school basketball player in Kentucky that year was Jeff Mullins of Lexington Lafayette High School, who enrolled at Duke University. The successful recruiting of Nash helped soften the blow of losing Mullins.

In addition to Nash, UK signed Kentuckians Ted Deeken of state champion Flaget and Tommy Harper of Clark County; Paul Wyatt, 6-foot-8, of Milford, Utah, who would quit after his freshman year; and George Critz of Bellbrook, Ohio, who would letter one year as a seldom used reserve.

"During my first few weeks as a freshman we'd come in a lot of times and sit through varsity practice," Cotton said. "I

"Cotton" Nash.

saw some strange things. I remember when Rupp got so upset at Roger Newman that Roger just took off running and jumped on that iron gate (locked to keep out visitors) and tried to get out. Rupp's methods affected different people in different ways. I sat there wondering if I could take three years of that.

"Basically the thing that impressed me was the efficiency of the operation. There was an old clock on the Coliseum wall that clicked off the minutes. The big hand would lumber over and clump. When it hit 3:14 or 3:15, there was suddenly a different atmosphere. Everybody knew exactly what to do. We didn't practice over one hour and 45 minutes, but we got things done. It was like a well-run business. I enjoyed that part of it most.

"We never came into the dressing room feeling confused or lost. We knew exactly what to do. We were so well prepared that very little was said during a game. During time out it was just a matter of correcting individual play. There was no mass hysteria. Again it was the efficiency of the thing that impressed me. Basically you were on your own before and after practice or a game. If you had problems, you went to Harry."

In 18 freshman games Cotton scored 476 points and rewrote seven first-year marks. What made it all the more impressive was the fact that he was used sparingly. He scored 40 points in two games, hitting 23 of 30 free throws in one of those games and 17 of 26 shots from the floor in the other.

Cotton's chief support as a first-year varsity player came from Larry Pursiful, a sharpshooting guard from Four Mile, Kentucky, whose big fault was a reluctance to shoot, apparently because he was unaccustomed to the quick release required when firing from behind a screen.

"Son, every time you shoot, I think it's going in," Rupp told him. "Fire it up there every chance you get." On another occasion, when the team was leaving a hotel for shooting practice, Rupp told Pursiful, "You might as well stay here, you won't shoot anyway."

"I always felt like I should hit every shot," Pursiful said in 1975. "But if I didn't have a good shot, I would pass it up. As a freshman I always dreaded to play the varsity. I was lucky to get my hands on the ball. I was always getting clobbered. There was no getting any clear shots. I found out that you had to play both ends at UK or you didn't play. It was tough, but it was fair."

Pursiful teamed with Scotty Baesler of Lexington at guard while Roy Roberts, a 6-foot-4 redhead from Atlanta, was at one forward and Allen Feldhaus at the other. Feldhaus eventually yielded the starting position to Carroll Burchett of Flat Gap, but Feldhaus would become a most valuable sixth man. Others seeing action that year were Jim McDonald, Ted Deeken, Charles "Chili" Ishmael, George Atkins, Herky Rupp, Pat Doyle, Tommy Harper, Doug Pendygraft, and George Critz.

With Pursiful gunning from the outside and Nash operating inside, the unranked Wildcats turned in one of the nation's outstanding records, winning 16 consecutive games after an early two-point loss to Southern California in Lexington. After Cotton made three straight bad passes against USC, Rupp pulled him out with 12 minutes to play and kept him out. Cotton had hit four of 11 shots and finished with 12 points.

Cotton remembered another of those early games:

"We were playing Temple in the Coliseum, and they had maybe four black starters. They tried to rattle me by calling me 'poor white trash.' I just lost my head, but I thought I had played a good game. When I looked at the stats sheet and saw I had 30 rebounds, it kinda amazed me. I never came close to that figure again as far as rebounds were concerned."

After the Wildcats defeated Georgia Tech in Atlanta that year, Furman Bisher wrote:

"You will seldom, if ever, see a boy so big with so much grace, so much agility, so much maneuverability and with so soft and velvety a touch as Nash. There were times when Rupp was using this versatile young man to bring the ball down court when Georgia Tech pressed its defense. With his size and his massive hands, Nash gave the impression of a circus giant dribbling an orange."

Another of Cotton's better games was against Notre Dame in Louisville. He hit 12 of 21 shots, including several high, arching 30-footers, and finished with 31 points as the Wildcats romped, 100-53.

The conference showdown game that year was between UK and Mississippi State in Lexington. Babe McCarthy's Bulldogs came to town with an 18-1 record, were ranked ninth in the nation, and had lost to only Vanderbilt in eight SEC encounters. Kentucky had a 17-1 record, was ranked second in the nation behind Ohio State, and was undefeated in conference play.

"I remember their stalling tactics," Cotton said. "They got ahead and put a man in each corner. They would dribble and dribble and work for the crip shot."

State hit 11 of 18 shots in the first half, taking a 28-22 lead, mostly on layups. "Dribble for 15 minutes and play defense for five," McCarthy told his players at halftime. State hit seven of their eight shots in the second half.

When the Wildcats defeated State, 68-62, in Starkville in 1961, someone had placed a wreath with the inscription, "Rest in Peace," on the Bulldog locker room.

"Son, put it away," McCarthy had told a student manager.

"Next year, we take it to Kentucky."

With two seconds remaining and State leading, 49-44, in 1962, Babe pulled the wreath from under his raincoat and passed it to a team manager, who placed it on UK's goal after the final whistle sounded.

A Kentucky cheerleader tearfully tore down the wreath and ripped it to shreds. After Kentucky defeated State, 65-59, in 1964, Wildcat freshmen football players would place a wreath on McCarthy's head.

"I was hoping one of you fellows would ask me how we handled Nash," McCarthy told reporters after the 1962 game. "I was going to tell you my daddy had a cotton gin and I was always good at handling Cotton." Cotton had 23 points in that game.

Kentucky shared the conference title with State and represented the conference in the NCAA after State again refused the bid. Nash scored 23 points and Pursiful 26 in an 81-60 opening victory over Butler in Iowa City. Against Ohio State, Rupp put Burchett in front of Jerry Lucas and slipped Nash behind the Buckeye All-American, but the strategy failed as Lucas scored 33 points, and John Havlicek held Nash to 14 points. Ohio State won, 74-64.

Nash was first team All-America, unanimous All-Conference, "SEC Player of the Year," and All-NCAA Tournament. He was the highest scoring sophomore in UK history, breaking 18 scoring records and becoming the first sophomore in 10 years to capture the conference scoring crown.

The 1962-63 UK basketball facts book featured a cover picture of Rupp and Nash kneeling and smiling over the university's four NCAA championship trophies. By the end of that season neither would be smiling, and the entire Commonwealth would breathe a sigh of relief when the last whistle sounded.

The season began with a three-point loss to upstart Virginia Tech, which administered the first opening setback in Rupp's career. Leland Malear, a graduate of Louisville Manual High School, scored 37 points for the Gobblers and first year

"Land Of Cotton"—Nifty Cotton Nash (44), Kentucky's All-American sophomore, executes a brilliant layup as he outwits three St. Louis Billiken defenders. Left in the lurch as Nash heads up to put in two of his 30 points of the evening are Garry Garrison (41), Dave Harris (23), and Tom Kieffer (35).

coach Bill Matthews. Nash scored 34 points in that game. Other UK starters were Roberts, Don Rolfes, a 6-foot-6 sophomore from Harrison, Ohio, at center, and Scotty Baesler and Sam Harper of Clinton, Kentucky, at guard.

Rupp called his team selfish, a description more polite than some of the verbage he was to use later in the season. They won three games and then lost by two points at home to North Carolina, defeated Iowa and West Virginia in the UKIT, and beat weak Dartmouth and Notre Dame before losing to St. Louis.

Georgia Tech beat them by one point in double overtime in Lexington and later beat them by four points in Atlanta. They beat Vanderbilt, LSU, and Tulane on the road before returning to Lexington and a stunning upset by Tennessee in the Coliseum. The Volunteers, under Bill Gibbs, acting for hospitalized Ray Mears, overcame a 16-point deficit and won by nine points in overtime. After back-to-back losses to Mississippi State at Starkville and Vanderbilt in Lexington, Rupp said that the 'Cats lacked "intestinal fortitude."

They defeated Auburn and Alabama in Lexington and closed the season with a loss to Tennessee in Knoxville as Rupp stayed home with the flu. The 16-9 record was the worst in his coaching career. Some fans actually booed him near the end of the season. Others said he was too old.

Meanwhile, the Southern sports editors were having a field day, writing under such headlines as: "Rupp's Monopoly is Over," "Collapse of An Aristocracy," and "The Baron Of The Blue Grass Becomes One Of The Boys."

Furman Bisher compared Rupp to "an industrious mouse that invents his own better mousetrap."

The faltering "House of Rupp" also was the subject of the following editorial—"Frankenstein Netmen Stalk South"—in the February 2, 1963, issue of the *Lexington Herald*:

> Through the years he (Rupp) has been aiding in the creation of some of these Frankensteins and now sees them blocking his path and wreaking havoc insofar as his own basketball charges are concerned. He has done the job of developing basketball in the South a mite too well.
>
> One consolation: They are letting us relax. After some thirty-five years of tense, spine-tingling, thrilling basketball, it's rather nice just to sit and watch a game

without wondering what effect the outcome will have on our chances to go to the NCAA Tournament for the umpteenth time.

Nash passed 1,000 points in career scoring that season, reaching that plateau quicker than any player in UK history. He made All-America for the second straight year and would make it three in a row the following year. He would finish his career with 1,770 points, bettering the record set by Alex Groza.

It was near the end of Cotton's junior year that the UK ticket office announced that four of the remaining five games were sold out. On the day Wildcat basketball tickets went on sale the following season, lines would stretch more than a block outside the Coliseum. By that night every ticket would be sold except for a few behind-the-basket seats for the Georgia and Dartmouth games. From that point there would be no UK season basketball tickets for sale to the general public.

The "House that Rupp Built" had become "The House that Cotton Filled."

The "Katzenjammer Kids"

The exciting new faces in the University of Kentucky basketball camp during the 1963-64 season were sophomores Larry Conley, Tom Kron, and Micky Gibson, dubbed the "Katzenjammer Kids" by Rupp because "they're always popping off like the kids in the comic strip."

During the annual preseason "Press Day" they put on a dazzling exhibition of ball-handling and then had their picture taken at a piano. It is significant that Conley occupied the seat at the keyboard, because it was he who would develop into a team leader in the future. A 6-foot-4 blond whose father, George, was a well-known basketball official, Larry had led Ashland to the state title and was as adept an off-court charmer as he was an on-court player.

Kron was a 6-foot-5 guard who grew up in Tell City, Indiana, across the river from Owensboro, Kentucky, and always wanted to play for Kentucky. A high-strung young man, it would take him a couple of years to settle into Rupp's disciplined style of play.

Gibson was a stylish left-handed forward who came from Hazard High, the same school that produced John Cox. However, he did not have Cox's staying power, and, due to various disciplinary and academic difficulties, he would never help the Wildcat program.

Lancaster taught the Conley-Kron-Gibson freshman team a 1-3-1 zone press defense that Chuck Noe had used effectively at Virginia Tech. In essence it consisted of one man out front putting pressure on the ball handler, three men forming a second line of defense, and one man guarding the basket. A key to the defense was having a tall guard as the first, or "point" man.

The questionable position was the pivot, which was assigned to John Adams, a likeable, 6-foot-6 junior from Rising Sun, Indiana, after junior Don Rolfes had transferred to the University of Cincinnati.

"John's a nice boy," Rupp said publicly, "but God didn't mean for him to be a basketball player."

Adams was at center, co-captains Nash and Deeken at forward, and Terry Mobley and little Randy Embry at guards for the opening game against Virginia. Nash and Deeken scored 28 points each in that victory. Nash had 33 and Deeken 20 as Texas Tech was beaten, but the significant aspect of that game was the play of Conley, who came off the bench to score 17 points and dazzle fans with his clever feeds to Nash for easy baskets. Before the next game, against Northwestern, Conley had taken Nash's forward spot, and Nash had moved Adams out of the pivot.

Nash was outscored by Billy Cunningham, 32-23, but Deeken got 22, Mobley 21, Ishmael 17, and Conley 15 as the 'Cats beat North Carolina, 100-80, in Lexington. Ishmael was a 6-foot-5 guard who replaced Embry for defensive purposes and finished with eight of 12 shots from the field. The Wildcats beat Baylor and were ranked second in the nation entering their annual holiday tournament.

Bill Bradley scored 33 points in the opening game of the UKIT, but his Princeton team lost to Wake Forest. He made 18 field goals and 47 points, both tournament records, the second night against Wisconsin. UK defeated Wake Forest for the title.

Terry Mobley's best effort for UK came in the Sugar Bowl. He scored only one point in an opening victory over Loyola, but it was his field goal that tied Duke, 79-79, with less than two minutes to go in the championship game. With 47 seconds left and UK in possession, during a time out Rupp instructed Mobley to feed the ball to one of the other players. Mobley dribbled around the keyhole, failed to see an open man, and, in desperation, banked in the winning goal.

Undefeated in 10 games and rated No. 1 nationally, the Wildcats returned home late on a cold, icy night—it even snowed in New Orleans while they were there—and rested only two days before heading south again for games in Atlanta and Nashville.

With the rugged Tech forward wall neutralizing the obviously tired Nash and Deeken and with R. D. Craddock, a dimin-

Spotlighted during the 1963-64 basketball season at UK are, left to right: Scotty Baesler, Roy Roberts, Cotton Nash, Larry Conley, and Ted Deeken.

utive guard from Canmer, Kentucky, hitting at all angles, Tech upset the 'Cats, 76-67.

Two nights later a last-second jump shot from the top of the circle by John Ed Miller gave Vanderbilt a two-point victory over the Wildcats. Nash was scoreless in the first half and hit only four of 20 shots in the game.

A bitter Rupp, clad in his traditional red pajamas, drank bourbon in his hotel room that night and muttered: "How

could they do this to me? How could those boys do this to me?"

Radio announcer Claude Sullivan had seen a similar reaction by Rupp when the Wildcats lost, 89-50, to CCNY in 1950. He recalled that Rupp sat up until dawn, repeating over and over again, "Thirty-damn-nine points. Thirty-damn-nine points."

Rupp sprang a 1-3-1 zone defense in full force against Tennessee and a surprised Ray Mears two weeks later in Lexington.

Mears had come to Knoxville from Wittenberg College the previous year, but sat out the season with an illness. His team was 10-2 and 3-0 in the conference before that fateful night in Memorial Coliseum.

"Harry and I had invented the 1-3-1 trap defense on a trip to Japan," Rupp said. "The first time we used it was against Tennessee."

In order to make the zone more effective Rupp moved Kron out on the point of the defense. It held high-scoring guard Danny Schultz to 11 points. Tall A. W. Davis scored 20 for Tennessee, but UK won, 66-57. Mears remained in his dressing room almost one hour after the game, finally emerged to tell a reporter, "It was a good defense. That's all I'll say."

Rupp had a better answer: "It was a transitional and shifting man-to-man backed by a hyperbolic paraboloid between the ball and the basket.

"What's that?" someone asked.

"You know what a paraboloid is, don't you? It is sort of a cone. And a hyperboloid is one with one of the points cut off it. Stratified means in layers and transitional means changing. So that should explain it."

The Wildcats won 10 conference games in a row before losing to Alabama, 65-59, in Tuscaloosa. Five days later they met Tennessee again, this time in Knoxville for the conference championship. Kron played a magnificent game as point man in the zone, and the Wildcats won, 42-38.

The Wildcats returned home and lost the season finale to St. Louis before participating in the NCAA playoffs at Minneapolis without Gibson, who was dismissed by Rupp after he argued with trainer Joe Brown over the taping of an ankle. Ohio University's black stars Mike Haley, Jerry Jackson, and Don Hilt completely dominated the boards and the game, defeating Rupp's "mountain boys" by 16 points in the opening round of the Mideast Regional. Nash hit only four of 14 shots, scored 10 points, and was booed. The nightmare continued as blacks Les Hunter and Vic Rouse led Loyola of Chicago to a 100-91 victory over UK in the playoff for third place; it was the third time that a Rupp team had lost three games in a row. One bright spot was the fact that the team hit 44.6 percent of its field goal attempts, eclipsing the school record of 43.5 held by the 1961-62 team.

A deficiency of height was evident at the very beginning of

the following season. Adams could have been big enough if his ability had matched his heart and if he had received the help in board control that other Wildcat teams had given their smaller centers. Captain Embry was under 5-foot-10 while Mobley was 6-foot-2, and forwards Pat Riley and Larry Conley each were described as a short 6-foot-4 or a tall 6-foot-3. Kron was almost as tall as Adams, but he was not scheduled to start the opening game against Iowa.

In addition to lack of height the squad was handicapped when Mobley missed two weeks of preseason practice because of an eye injury. As the opening game approached, Rupp kept casting his eye in the direction of Louie Dampier, a quiet, six-foot sophomore guard with a fine eye for the basket.

"Far be it from me to start a little kid like that on my basketball team," Rupp said.

Fortunately for Dampier and the Wildcats he was only kidding.

"I know he is just medium fast," Rupp said, "but he is one of those guys who can go and get a basket when you need it."

Neil Reed, then chief recruiter for Rupp, recalled the first time he saw Louie: "I had gone to look at a player named Rich Jones of Muncie, Indiana, and I was with a bunch of Indianapolis coaches. They told me that without a doubt the boy to get was at South Point. His name was Louie Dampier. I went out to watch him practice, and no one would even tell me which one he was. They thought I was a scout from another high school. Finally I got down to a little guy wearing knee guards, looping the ball in on free throws. After the practice the coach, Blackie Braden, introduced him to me, and I told Louie he had a scholarship at UK."

Louie hit nine of 18 shots in an opening victory over Iowa, but he was replaced in the starting lineup by Kron for a game against North Carolina at Greensboro. After losing to the Tar Heels, Rupp sat alone in his red pajamas, munched a sandwich, and solemnly declared: "We don't have it."

Returning to the lineup Louie scored 30 points in a victory over Iowa State. Kron replaced Embry and scored 31 points in that game. Dave Bing was excellent, but Syracuse fell, 110-77, to the Wildcats. They defeated West Virginia, 102-78, in the UKIT opening round, but the handwriting was on the wall when Skip Thoren operated freely in the pivot to lead Illinois to a 91-86 victory. It was only the fourth time in 12 years that the

Wildcats had failed to win the tournament.

After St. Louis beat them in St. Louis and Notre Dame took their measure in Freedom Hall, a 107-67 victory over weak Dartmouth was most welcome. However, Vanderbilt came into the Coliseum three nights later and defeated the Wildcats, 97-79. Commodore center Clyde Lee scored 41 points, a record for an opposing player in the Coliseum, as the Wildcats suffered their worst home defeat in more than three decades. Louisiana State and Tulane were routine victims, but Tennessee took the 'Cats by 19 points, the worst beating UK had ever taken from the Vols. A grinning Ray Mears displayed a paper proclaiming, "Iconoclastic defense with disharmonious tendencies." Rupp did not think it was very funny.

Mobley called a squad meeting before a game with Auburn in Lexington and urged the players to perform as a team. They won by six points. Five nights later Florida scored its first victory over a Kentucky team in 35 years.

"This is the worst team I've ever had," Rupp told reporters.

At the Holiday Inn in Athens that afternoon Rupp held a series of meetings with individual players. They defeated Georgia, 102-82, and returned home to defeat Florida, Georgia again, Mississippi, and Mississippi State in succession. That season was the last time Babe McCarthy would bring a Mississippi State team to Lexington. He went out in typical style, insisting that his team be seated on the north end of the floor, where the Kentucky team always sat. It was his prerogative as visiting coach to be granted the request, he said. The argument was settled by placing the State bench on the east side of the north basket and the Kentucky team in its customary position on the west side of the goal.

Vanderbilt, Auburn, and Alabama beat them, and for the first time Rupp had lost as many as 10 games in one season.

Dampier was the one bright spot in the dismal season. Louie averaged 17 points a game, connecting on a school record 51.2 percent of his field goal attempts. He hit in double figures in all but one of 25 games. His 37 points against Iowa State were the most ever scored by a UK guard. He was named to the All-Conference team.

One of UK's biggest disappointments that year was Conley, who, as a sophomore, had set a school record in assists (112), shared the team's Most Valuable Player trophy, made the

Tom Kron and Larry Conley, two of the original UK "Katzenjammer Kids," carry off the UKIT trophy after the Wildcats defeated Wake Forest, 98-75, for the championship in the 1963-64 season.

All-Conference and Academic All-American teams, and won a couple of UK awards for effort above and beyond the call of duty. He fell below his sophomore performance in every statistical category, performed erratically, and lost his starting job. He was bothered with tonsillitis throughout the season, but he did not use that as an excuse.

"The truth is, I just didn't play the ball I was capable of playing," he said. "I'm just going to forget about it—I'm not living in the past."

"He's an unselfish boy who has all the basketball talent in the world, but who was sick all year," Rupp said. "There's no doubt in my mind that this will be Larry's year."

It would be Larry's year. And Tommy's year. And Pat's year. And Louie's year. And Adolph's year. And, of course, UK's year.

"Rupp's Runts"

Coming off a "disastrous" 15-10 season in 1964-65, Rupp felt he had all the ingredients for a successful season except that all important good, big man. During a preseason press conference he spoke of the unselfishness of Conley and Kron, the excellent shooting of Dampier, and the strength of Riley.

However, the biggest man among those starters was Kron, and he was a 6-foot-5 guard. Conley and Riley were 6-foot-3, while Dampier was 6-foot-0. The person who would work his way into the opening lineup at the pivot was Thad Jaracz, a left-handed, 6-foot-5 strongboy who had played for a rather mediocre Lafayette High School team.

"Thad was a pleasant surprise," Rupp would say later. "He was a big kid who was not fat exactly, but he had too much weight and he was kinda lazy. I kept telling Harry (Lancaster) to sign him. Harry did not think he could play. We watched him play in the high school tournament. His team got beat some 30 points. 'Get out there and sign him tomorrow,' I told Harry. 'That kid showed me a couple of moves tonight. I believe we can teach him to play basketball.'"

Although Jaracz started at center, Riley jumped center at the opening and halftime tipoffs. Pat would lose only three of 58 taps that season. One of the strongest players to play for Rupp, he had signed with UK after a sensational three-year career at Linton High School in Schenectady, New York. He not only was All-Eastern High School basketball All-American, but was also an All-State football quarterback.

Kron was a strong, hustling guard who played the point on defense, rebounded well, and could score when the occasion

demanded. Born in Owensboro, Kentucky, he had moved to Tell City, Indiana, when he was five years old. He averaged 16 points a game for Tell City and had played against Conley in the 1962 Kentucky-Indiana all-star series. He became a starter at midseason of his sophomore year and was a regular as a junior. He was so enthusiastic as a freshman that Rupp threatened to give him tranquilizers.

"Never have I seen a boy play the point on defense the way he could," Rupp would say later. "He was fast, aggressive, could set up plays, and he never quit." On the practice floor Rupp had a different approach to Kron. "Tommy," he once said, "someday I'm going to write a book on how not to play defense, and a whole chapter will be dedicated to you."

1965-66 team. Seated, left to right: Rupp, Gene Stewart, Pat Riley, Louie Dampier, Bob Tallent, Steve Clevenger, Jim LeMaster, Harry Lancaster. Standing: Tommy Porter, Gary Gamble, Tom Kron, Cliff Berger, Larry Lentz, Brad Bounds, Thad Jaracz, Larry Conley, and manager Carson Harreld.

Dampier was the quiet, introverted type, a deadly shooter who specialized in utilizing a center screen for jump shots around the foul circle. He could play defense when he set his mind to it.

"I went down to watch Louie play in the Indiana high school tournament," Rupp said. "He hit eight shots in the first quarter, all of them on the fast break, where he stopped near the free throw circle, jumped in the air, and let her go. I said to my assistant, 'Sign that kid.'"

Rupp called Conley "a coach on the floor." Larry was the team spokesman, a goodwill ambassador, and complete team player who later would say that the Runts' success was simply due to the fact that they knew each other. He called their uncanny cooperation and coordination "instinct," and he felt that luck had drawn them together.

Looking over that group just before the 1965-66 season got under way, Rupp openly stated, "I honestly believe that man-for-man we just might have in the making a better team than we had in 1958, when we won the national championship." By the time the season opened, the Runts were so perfectly attuned that Rupp would often lean back during routine drills, close his eyes, and listen to the steady pop-pop of the ball being passed from hand to hand.

James Dickenson, of the *National Observer*, observing a practice session, asked Rupp, "Do they always handle the ball like that?"

Rupp's intended reply—"Well, in a 59 minute and 47 second workout..."—was interrupted by Dickenson's laugh.

Rupp glared. Then he continued, "In a 59 minute, 47 second workout, they handle the ball 3,308 times and in a good drill will fumble five times. They fumbled 12 times today."

Two of the fumbles were by a substitute center.

"Son, you have such good hands that we are going to cast them in bronze after you're gone," Rupp said.

The big early surprise was the speed and quickness of the 230-pound Jaracz. He was the only UK player to score in double figures in an opening 83-55 victory over Hardin-Simmons. He scored 22 points and grabbed 13 rebounds in a victory over Virginia and was on the front end of many fast breaks as he scored 32 points in an 86-68 trouncing of Illinois. One opposing coach said, "He looks like a freight train barrelling down the floor on the fast break."

In a victory over Florida that season Jaracz would hit 11 of 15 shots, including some of his special high-looping one-handers from the corner. Gator coach Norm Sloan was high in praise of the UK sophomore. Another sophomore who showed fine promise was Bob Tallent, who entered a game against Texas Tech at Lubbock after Dampier was injured and scored 13 points to spark the Wildcats in a come-from-behind victory.

Sophomore Cliff Berger also had a big moment, hitting four free throws in a double overtime, 69-65, win over Georgia at Athens. Other substitutes that year were Jim LeMaster, Tommy Porter, Brad Bounds, Steve Clevenger, Gary Gamble, Gene Stewart, and Larry Lentz.

Riley had a fine game against Notre Dame in Freedom Hall, scoring 36 points and holding Irish scoring ace Jim Monahan to seven points in a 103-69 UK win.

Dampier's best game was against Vanderbilt at Nashville, where he sizzled the nets for 42 points. He had scored 24 points in an earlier victory over the Commodores.

Nearly everywhere UK played that year, fans who had booed and despised Rupp for years were giving him ovations of respect. That was true even at Vanderbilt, where the fans applauded him after he shook Skinner's hand at the end of a game that eliminated the home team from the conference race and virtually assured UK of a berth in the NCAA tournament. Rupp and Conley walked off the court with arms around each other's shoulders. "I love these boys," Rupp openly stated.

It was easy for him to warm up to them, especially after they won 23 consecutive games, and he pointed with pride to a personal interest in each player.

Hadn't he promised Louie's dying father that he would see to it that the boy got a college education and a good start in life?

Didn't Kron write him while still in grade school and express an interest in playing for UK someday?

Hadn't Conley and Kron agreed before the season began that they would be the unselfish team leaders, passing up shots for themselves in order to set up their teammates?

Hadn't he personally gone to Schenectady to sign Riley after Pat sent word that he wanted to come to UK?

And who had recognized future greatness under all that baby fat when Jaracz was playing at Lafayette High?

Ray Mears wore a brown suit to Lexington that year, but the Vols lost, 78-64, to UK. Rugged Howard Bayne missed that game, but he was back in uniform the following Saturday to help Tennessee break the Wildcat streak at 23 games.

Kentucky finished the season with a victory over Tulane and then traveled to Iowa City to play Dayton in the NCAA regional tournament. The Flyers' 6-foot-11 Henry Finkel scored 36 points and Don May had 16, but UK's balanced attack survived, 86-79. Rupp went to his 1-3-1 zone in the second half to stop Finkel and also switched to a 1-3-1 offense, with Jaracz moving to the top of the circle to set screens for Dampier. UK got 34 points from Dampier and 29 points from Riley.

Riley scored 29 points again as the Wildcats defeated a strong Michigan team, 84-77. Cazzie Russell had 29 points for the Wolverines. Conley said it was the worst beating he ever took in a basketball game. He complained of chest pains and Jaracz suffered from a cold.

"I'm taking a bunch of sick boys to the championship finals," Rupp said as the Wildcats left Lexington to join Duke, Utah, and Texas Western in the playoffs at College Park, Maryland.

Duke had a 25-3 record and was ranked second to the Wildcats when they met in a semifinal round of that tournament. Conley was sick with a cold and only played half of that game, but Duke's Bob Verga also had a cold and saw little action. Jack Marin scored 27 points and Mike Lewis had 21 for the Blue Devils, but the Wildcats won, 83-79. Riley injured the big toe on his right foot in that game, but he did not think it serious enough to merit the attention of the team physician. Texas Western defeated Utah, 85-78, to gain the finals with UK.

Texas Western had 6-foot-7 Dave "Big Daddy" Lattin, a smooth, agile, intimidating center who was probably the best unknown basketball player in the country; rugged forward Nevil Shed, who had been ejected from a regional game against Cincinnati for throwing a right to the chin of Don Rolfes; Willie Cager, who had replaced Shed and helped the Miners win that game in overtime; and Harry Flournoy, who was an excellent rebounder.

The sparkplug of the offense and a fine defensive player was 5-foot-9 Bobby Joe Hill, who specialized in stealing the ball and driving for the basket. He would make two key steals against UK guards in the first half, convert them into easy crips, and set the tone of the game.

Two other little men, Ortis Artis and Willie Worsley, combined with Hill to give the Texans speed and outside shooting to cope with the Kentuckians.

Recruited from the city sidewalks, the Miners featured an all-black starting lineup, with blacks also manning the key reserve posts. That was hardly a startling fact, even then, but it

Larry Conley goes high for a rebound against Duke in the NCAA semifinals at College Park, Maryland, in 1966. Tom Kron watches the action.

is noteworthy because the Miners were meeting all-white Kentucky and Rupp, a combination that spreadeagled both the history and the glory of college basketball. The national final had suddenly become more than a game; it was a contest for racial honors.

After Hill's two goals on steals, the Texans were pretty much in control until UK cut the lead to two points midway of the second half. However, Conley fouled out of the game and Texas Western went on to win, 72-65.

Kentucky scored five more field goals than the Texans, but the game was won and lost on the free throw line, where the Wildcats hit 11 of 13 and Texas Western 28 of 34, including 26 of 27 during one stretch. In the end Hill and Worsley dribbled around until the clock ran out; as the Texans cut the nets, the Wildcats sat with tears in their eyes and accepted the second-place trophy that none of them wanted.

Years later Rupp would say, "I still wake up in the middle of the night wondering what I could have done to help my boys win that game."

The problems the Wildcats are having on the floor against Texas Western in the 1966 NCAA championship game are reflected by, left to right: Tommy Porter, Jim LeMaster, Gary Gamble, Bob Tallent, Rupp, Lancaster, and Elmer Gilb.

A downhearted group of Wildcats wait to accept a second place trophy after the Wildcats were upset by Texas Western in the 1966 NCAA final. Louie Dampier is No. 10.

A key player in his plans the following year was Bob Tallent, a sensitive, intelligent, 6-foot-1 redhead from Langley, Kentucky. "When Red's having a hot night like he did in that second half against Texas Tech," Rupp said, "you could put a lid on the basket and he'd still score. His statistics, which were spotty because he played so much in relief, hid the fact last year that this boy is one of the finest shooters the hills have ever produced."

Tallent accompanied the squad on a 17-game tour of the Middle East that summer. They defeated Warsaw, Cambridge, Salonka, Istanbul, and Warsaw (again) for the championship of the International Universities Tournament in Tel Aviv.

The players returned home tired and weary. Suffering the most was Riley, who had received a back injury in a water skiing spill at Herrington Lake shortly before the trip and had failed to tell Rupp about it. Throughout the ensuing season, the All-American forward was in constant pain. He took pills for relief in the daytime and was strapped with weights and pulleys—in traction—each night. Rupp thought about holding him out of competition, but he needed even a subpar Riley that year.

"Soon as Pat warmed up, he would come over to the bench," Rupp said. "He would say, 'Coach, I haven't got it tonight,' or, 'I'm going to be all right.'"

Tallent described the 1967 season as a real tough situation. "We were 27-2 the previous year and everybody expected us to have a good team," he said, "but we had lost Conley and Kron and that had to be a big blow. Conley was a real team leader. When I came into a game, I asked him what to do."

Tallent replaced Kron, and Gary Gamble, a junior from Earlington, replaced Conley in a starting lineup that included three of the original "Runts"—Dampier, Riley, and Jaracz. Riley scored 23 points and got 11 rebounds as they beat Virginia, 104-84, on the road. "We're better than last year," Riley said.

Two nights later Riley was called for three quick fouls and sat out most of the game as UK lost to Illinois, 98-97, at home in overtime. Riley returned to form and scored the final two points on free throws in a 118-116 UK victory over Northwestern at Evanston. Riley had 33, Dampier 32, Jaracz 23, Tallent 20, and Northwestern's Jim Burns 34 in the shootout. Never had so many points been scored against UK.

The Wildcats returned home to lose to North Carolina and Florida; for the first time, a Rupp team had lost three consecutive home games. They defeated Oregon State and Kansas State in the UKIT, but the season was over for all practical purposes after they lost to Cornell in the Coliseum, beat Notre Dame, 96-85, in Freedom Hall, and then lost to Vanderbilt at home and Florida and Georgia on the road. They beat Auburn, lost to Tennessee in double overtime, and won two each from LSU and Mississippi State before a return match with Tennessee.

Rupp placed much of the blame for the team breakdown on Tallent, who was bothered by an ankle injury. When the Wildcats traveled to Knoxville for a game with Tennessee, Tallent had been replaced in the lineup by sophomore Phil Argento. When the Vols started pulling away, Rupp looked down the bench and yelled, "Red, get in there."

Seconds later Tallent bobbled the ball and was taken from the game. He got another chance, but was ordered from action again after his pass to Dampier went out of bounds. As he walked to his seat, he and Rupp exchanged unpleasantries. They clashed again in the locker room after the game. When Tallent reported for practice the following Monday, his locker was empty, and the equipment manager, on orders from Rupp, refused to issue him any gear.

The student newspaper accused Rupp of disgracing himself, his athletes, and the university community. Its editors questioned the legitimacy of his action, asked for a public apology, and suggested that the university president investigate the situation. Dr. John W. Oswald called Rupp to his office and made it clear that he frowned upon the "public censure" of

Pat Riley, All-American 1966.

Tallent and that such censure should have no place among any member of the staff of the university.

Pat Riley scored 28 points as the Wildcats ended that season with a 110-78 victory over Alabama, giving Rupp a 13-13 season and preserving his record of never having a losing team. As the final gun sounded, a near capacity crowd in Memorial Coliseum gave a standing ovation to Dampier and Riley. Shortly after the season ended, Riley underwent surgery for removal of two slipped discs in his back.

Tallent finished the semester and transferred to George Washington University, where he became a Helms Foundation All-American guard. He was head coach of that university when he sat in the San Diego Arena prior to the UK-UCLA NCAA championship game in 1975 and recalled his brief career at UK.

"We could have had a very good season in 1967," he said. "We lost five or six close games. I'm a coach now, and I know when things start going wrong you want to blame the players. Adolph tried to find someone to blame. He tried to use me after I was injured. I finally lost my temper after something happened and said a few things, and it was all over.

"It wasn't that I was a bad player. It all started with that injury. I was the second leading scorer up to then. He always got after me for losing the ball, but I said I handled it 80 percent of the time. He said when you have to take criticism and can't, go sit on the bench.

"I'll say this, I would love to have a team that could handle the ball like his teams. I may disagree with his handling of players, but his system was great. His game plans were great. We try to copy that at George Washington.

"Kids change and as the years go on it gets a little harder. I would just about do anything my coaches said, but now the kids ask, 'Why?' You've got to come up with reasons. Rupp treated everyone the same. He had no pets. He was just as hard on Riley and Dampier as on the rest of us.

"He put so much pressure on you in practice, if you didn't take it, you weren't tough enough to play for him. That's not a bad philosophy, if you've got the players. Besides, Adolph's players were normally from Kentucky and Indiana. There was no internal friction. They didn't have black athletes. Now, you've got inter-city youths, black kids from the country, Jewish kids, and all mixtures. It takes a lot more today to keep harmony."

A Cruel Blow

Mike Casey was a 6-foot-4, slightly bow-legged, "Peck's Bad Boy" type who was named Kentucky's "Mr. Basketball" after leading Shelby County to the 1966 state tournament championship. UK had no trouble recruiting him, because Mike had decided early in life he wanted to be a Wildcat.

"I remember the 1958 team that won the NCAA Tournament," he said. "I was living down on the farm and listening to the radio. I told daddy I was going to Kentucky."

Mike had a knack for looking bad occasionally, but then he would play brilliantly when the chips were down. "If I had to send my money to Las Vegas to be doubled, I'd send it with Casey," Rupp said in 1969. "He's the best money player I've ever had."

Joining with Casey to form a dynamic trio were fellow sophomores Mike Pratt and Dan Issel. Pratt was a 6-foot-4 forward from Dayton, Ohio, who utilized muscle well around the basket and was a fair shooter. He would make the starting lineup after the fifth game of that season. Issel was the center and anchor man, a 6-foot-8, big-boned blond who got off to a slow start because of an operation to remove a growth from the roof of his mouth. Casey and Issel started the season with seniors Jim LeMaster, Phil Argento, and Steve Clevenger.

In an opening victory at Michigan, Casey scored 28 points and grabbed 14 rebounds, one less than Issel. The Wildcats defeated Florida, Xavier, and Pennsylvania at home before losing to North Carolina, 84-77, at Greensboro. Pratt moved into a starting forward position against Dayton in the UKIT, with Casey shifting back to guard in place of Clevenger. Pratt hit seven of 12 shots and got 15 rebounds in an 88-85 victory over the Flyers. Casey was high with 27 points. Substitutes Tommy Porter and Gary Gamble hit some key baskets the following night to help the Wildcats beat South Carolina, 76-66.

Casey had a fine performance against Notre Dame in Freedom Hall, stealing the ball six times and scoring 26 points to pull UK from behind. He was recipient of the first annual Bernie A. Shively award given to the Most Outstanding Player in the game by the Notre Dame Club of Kentucky.

Rupp claimed that 81-73 victory over the Irish was his 772nd at UK, moving him ahead of Phog Allen as the winningest coach of all time, but the NCAA refused to count the five

Mike Casey.

victories he claimed credit for in the 1966 International Universities Tournament. He officially tied Allen's record that year in Baton Rouge, where the Wildcats defeated LSU, 121-95, in a televised game featuring UK's first encounter with highly touted Tiger sophomore "Pistol" Pete Maravich.

In that game "The Pistol" shot 51 times from the field, an LSU record, and hit 19 of them, eclipsing a record of 17 field goals scored against UK by Jerry Harper of Alabama in 1956. His 52 points were a record for an individual effort against the Wildcats. The combined points total (216) for both teams surpassed the conference mark of 209 established by UK (143) and Georgia (66) in 1956. The two-team field goal total of 90 also beat a record of 85 set in the UK-Georgia game.

During six games against UK in his varsity years Maravich would score a total of 312 points, an average of 52 a game. In his first game at Lexington he would hit 16 of 38 field goal attempts and 12 of 15 free throw attempts for 44 points, most for a UK opponent in the Coliseum. He would score 45 points there in 1969 and 55 points in 1970. His best performance against UK would be a 64-point spree in Baton Rouge in 1970 on 23 of 42 from the field and 18 of 22 from the line. Rupp's policy was to let Pete score his 50 points a game, but to cut off the other players. LSU never beat the Wildcats while Pete was playing there.

In conference play in 1968 UK lost only to Florida, Auburn, and Tennessee, all on the road. The Wildcats won their last 11 games and entered the Mideast playoff at Lexington with a record of 21-4. They were paired with at-large choice Marquette while East Tennessee, the Ohio Valley champion, met Ohio State, winner of a postseason playoff with Iowa for the Big 10 championship, in the other game.

Some friction developed between Rupp and Marquette coach Al McGuire when the latter turned down an invitation to appear on Rupp's television show because Rupp would not pay him for appearing as a guest. At the press dinner the night before the opening games McGuire objected to UK being designated as the home team, with the privilege of wearing white uniforms and occupying the home team's bench.

"There is no such thing as a home team," McGuire contended. "It should be settled by the flip of a coin."

"All right, Al, we'll give you the home uniforms," Rupp said. "It doesn't make any difference to Kentucky. We'll accede to your demands."

"I don't want you to give me anything, coach," McGuire replied. "I've worked for everything I've gotten in life."

UK was designated the home team, in accordance with instructions spelled out in the NCAA Tournament Guide. Issel played one of his best games the following night, scoring 36 points in an easy, 107-89, victory. McGuire vowed to revenge the loss and to get even with what he termed poor treatment by fans and officials at the tournament. Ohio State defeated East Tennessee in the other game that night.

Kentucky's dream of a Mideast championship and playing in the finals in Los Angeles boiled down to the final six seconds of the game, when a missed shot by Ohio State was rebounded and bobbled out of bounds by Casey after Bill Hosket bore down on him from behind. Ohio State coach Fred Taylor called a time out and told Dave Sorenson and Steve Howell to cross and one of them take a close-in shot. The Buckeyes were trailing, 81-80.

In the UK huddle Clevenger asked Rupp if he should foul. The Wildcats had committed only three fouls in the half; another foul would have given Ohio State a tie but almost no chance to win it in regulation because the bonus was not in effect. Rupp told his players not to foul.

Sorenson took the ball on the throw-in and made a medium-range jump shot to give Ohio State the victory, 82-81.

"We were beaten because our defense was not set properly," Rupp said. "It was a zone defense. I really believe we should have set a man-to-man defense at that stage. The boy who scored that shot just threw the ball up in a half-hearted way because he had to get rid of it. It hit clear at the top of the backboard and dropped through. We had all the tickets bought, ready to go to California. We stayed at home."

One of UK's best games the following year was in Philadelphia, where the 'Cats hit their first 11 field goal attempts and first nine free throws, scoring 31 consecutive points without a miss in a 102-78 victory over Pennsylvania in the Palestra.

Issel was named the Most Outstanding Player in the UKIT, after UK beat Michigan and Army, and Phil Argento received the Shively Trophy after scoring 27 points in a 110-90 victory over Notre Dame in Louisville. The Wildcats then traveled to Chicago for a game on New Year's Eve with Wisconsin in the stadium. The temperature dropped to 16 degrees below zero

Rupp cuts the 1,000th victory cake as captain Phil Argento, Tommie Bryant, and Wylie B. Wendt (manager, 1906) await their turn.

and the Wildcats were not much warmer, hitting only 38 percent of their shots and losing by four points. They had lost earlier to North Carolina and were 6-2 entering conference competition.

After defeating Mississippi State at Starkville in January, UK claimed to be the first NCAA school to win 1,000 basketball victories. The NCAA said no, it still was not counting the five victories won by UK in the International Universities Tournament.

"Why the hell not?" Rupp asked. "The NCAA sent us over there to play those other teams, didn't it?"

The UK Sports Information Office dug into old files and discovered four previously unreported games—two victories and two losses—which the NCAA accepted. That tied Kentucky and Kansas with 997 victories each. Oregon State trailed them by five games. The Jayhawks faltered, and UK won three consecutive games, registering its 1,000th win January 13 over Georgia in Lexington. Two weeks later Rupp was one game shy of the personal 800 mark when the Wildcats played Alabama in Tuscaloosa. Before the game he made an unscheduled visit to his motel suite and discovered a large "800th Victory" celebration cake in the bedroom.

"My Gawd!" he exclaimed. "Who put that here? You'll get us beat sure as hell!"

The Wildcats won in overtime after the Tide blew a shot in the closing seconds of regulation play.

After losing at Florida and Vanderbilt, the Wildcats entered the Mideast playoffs with a 22-4 record, meeting Marquette in an opening round rematch in the University of Wisconsin Field House at Madison. Long before the game the fans built their anti-UK feeling to such a frenzy that the overtones were unmistakably racial. Led by black players George Thompson and Dean Miminger, the smaller Warriors won by seven points. UK beat Miami for third place.

Team records were set that season for most points (2,542), highest scoring average (90.8), highest field goal percentage (49.0), and most points allowed (2,199). Issel scored 746 points, beating the 698 scored by Groza in 1949, and his 26.6 points per game average wiped Nash's 24.0 record from the books. Issel also set a record for most field goals, Pratt made a record 53.9 percent of his field goal attempts, and Casey had a record 129 assists.

Kentucky's hopes of winning another national championship were shattered that summer when Casey received a crushed right leg in an automobile accident. "Once again I think fate dealt us a cruel blow," Rupp said. "That was another time we could have won it all, if it had not been for Casey being incapacitated the entire year. Destined to be All-American, no doubt about it, Casey was never able to come back."

The Wildcats still had Issel, Pratt, and Larry Steele around whom to build a team, but it would not seem the same without Casey.

Time Out: Dan Issel

Dan Issel was so disappointed at being a "third round" recruiting choice of UK in the spring of 1967 that he signed a grant-in-aid with the University of Wisconsin. He changed his mind at the proverbial last minute, inked a Wildcat grant, and would become the most prolific scorer in the illustrious history of UK basketball.

En route to that high achievement, he would get a big assist from Rupp, a "thank you," so to speak, for Issel's part in quelling a minor player revolt in the spring of 1971. But let us hear the story from Issel, the ABA champion Kentucky Colonels' superstar, now with the Denver Nuggets, who in the summer of 1975 was dressed in a business suit and occupying an off-season position with the Citizens Fidelity Bank in Louisville:

"I was raised in Missouri, but I didn't play any sports until I got to Batavia (Ill.). It was a small school, where every boy played every sport. In the sixth grade, I was no bigger than the average kid; in the seventh, there were only four guys taller. I was never really that good. I didn't start in junior high.

"I grew four inches, to about 6-6, between my freshman and sophomore years. Don Vandersnick was the coach. He gave me my first real break. He made me work. Before school, I would shoot free throws and jump shots; after school, I would practice one-half hour or 45 minutes on moves under the basket and the outside shot. The fact that he was there made me work harder.

"In the spring of my junior year, I got a letter from the University of Wisconsin. When you get a letter, it makes you take a good hard look. I played football, basketball, baseball and ran track until my senior year. We had a real good basketball team my junior year (27-2) and in my senior year (26-3) we went to the game before the state tournament, which is pretty big when you consider that Illinois has 700 schools playing basketball.

"Then the recruiting started pretty heavy. Joe Hall made a visit or two. I really wasn't interested in Kentucky. I was interested in Wisconsin; my folks wanted me to go to Northwestern.

"I flew into Louisville for a visit to UK. Joe Hall and Phil Argento picked me up at the airport and drove me to Lexington. It was a nice trip. But I picked up the school newspaper and read a story on recruiting. My name was not mentioned. I couldn't help feel I wasn't No. 1. So I went home and signed with Wisconsin.

"My dad still wasn't satisfied. He said, 'Let's take another look at Kentucky.' We made another trip, this time with him paying the expenses. Mr. Logan Gray, the airport manager, had the red carpet rolled out. The stewardesses were running around, wondering who it was for. The big guys UK wanted had signed somewhere else. I changed my mind and signed with UK. Later I learned that I really was their third choice at center.

"In a freshman game with Georgia, Bob Leinhart just ate me alive, and people got on me pretty hard. The thing that a lot of people thought about UK was that basketball was hard core under Harry and Adolph, but the underlying thing is that when it came down to it they could be very nice people and easy to talk to. Lancaster took me aside after that Georgia game and said, 'You just remember one thing. He whipped you here today, but when it's all over, let's sit down and see who got the best ball player.'"

(Issel averaged 20.8 points a game and 17.7 rebounds a game as a freshman.)

"I remember Pat Riley and Louie Dampier used to get on us pretty good because we had some freshman players who were pretty cocky. The varsity was kinda struggling. It didn't take us long after the start of our sophomore year to find out that we weren't as good as we thought.

"I got off to a rocky start that year. I had a tumor removed from the roof of my mouth and the first half of the season was kinda bad. Sophomores played in front of some pretty good seniors, especially in my position. It would have been easy to explain if they had let me sit on the bench."

(Issel scored in double figures the first seven games that year, had only six points against Notre Dame, seven against Vanderbilt, eight against Alabama, 12 against Florida, and was scoreless against Georgia, missing the last 15 minutes of that game after taking a hard fall. In the last 15 games, he would score in double figures except for a nine-point performance against Tennessee. His best performance was 36 points against Marquette in the NCAA.)

"Then the whole world fell in when Sorenson hit that shot for Ohio State. I think half of us already had our bags packed for California. It was a real disappointment."

(In his junior year, Issel averaged 26.6 points and 13.6 rebounds. He scored 41 points against Vanderbilt and hit 36 points in three other games. He hit 53.4 percent of his shots and had scored 1,190 points in two seasons, needing only 581 to break Cotton Nash's career record.)

"The Wisconsin game in Chicago was really a chance for a lot of people who had followed my career to see me close to home. I remember playing absolutely terrible, which happens sometimes when you try too hard. Harry made it a point at halftime to point that out.

"We got a real bad scouting report on Marquette. We had beaten them the year before using our zone in Lexington. We just changed things completely around. They could jump out of the gym, and they were quick. We should never have man-to-manned them. The report was to let Joe Thomas shoot, and the first four they shot hit the cords. They were sky high, especially after we embarrassed them in Lexington the year before. We played at the University of Wisconsin, and you could almost feel the (racial) tension in the crowd. I'm sure that played a big part in the outcome.

"Joe Hall put in a running program the following fall that was really tough. A couple of the guys got together and said it was too hard. We all met in the film room. Mike Pratt and I went down and talked to Joe. He said it was his program, and he wasn't going to call it off. We went back and sat down and waited for Rupp. He sent for me and he said, 'Dan, do you realize that you have an opportunity to be the all-time leading scorer for the University of Kentucky?'

"'Yessir,' I said.

"'Well,' he said, 'You go out there and run today and I will do everything in my power to see that you achieve that.'

"The five freshmen and I went out and ran. Next day everybody was back. He kept his promise because there were games during my senior year where he could have taken me out."

One of those games was at Oxford, Mississippi, where Issel bombarded the nets for 29 points in the first half and then opened the second half with two driving layups. By then the UK bench was cheering him on, and the team manager was keeping a loud, verbal count.

In scoring his 50th and 51st points on a drive to the basket, Issel knocked Tom Butler to the floor, but no foul was called. He scored his 53rd point on a turn-around jump shot with six minutes remaining, beating the UK record of 51 set by Cliff Hagan against Temple December 5, 1953. Issel left the game with five minutes remaining. As Rupp shook his hand, the crowd gave the UK center a standing ovation.

Issel had gotten the season off on a fine note, scoring 34 points in a victory over West Virginia and then moving UK atop the national rankings by scoring 41 points in a victory over North Carolina at Greensboro. During those early games, Rupp used guards Kent Hollenbeck, Bob McCowan, Stan Key, and Bill Busey, forwards Randy Noll and Tom Parker, and Mark Soderberg, a reserve center who played so sparingly that he would quit the squad for a brief spell in midseason. Substitutes Art Laib and Clint Wheeler saw some action in an easy victory over Kansas.

Although the Wildcats ranked No. 1 nationally throughout most of that season, the situation in the basketball camp, where Issel was garnering the points and the accolades, was less than harmonious. Bob McCowan, most valuable player in the UKIT, and substitute Randy Poole were suspended from the team after they and four other substitutes were caught by trainer Claude Vaughan and Joe Hall in a tavern near Starkville on a Sunday afternoon.

"Claude, you may have just cost me the NCAA tournament," Rupp said.

With Issel playing on an injured heel, they fell by eight points to Vanderbilt at Nashville, their only loss of the season. They advanced to the NCAA Mideast Regional at Columbus, Ohio, with independents Notre Dame and Jacksonville and Big Ten champion Iowa.

In the opening five minutes against Notre Dame, four

The 1969 SEC champions are, left to right: Phil Argento, Dan Issel, Larry Steele, Mike Pratt, and Mike Casey.

Kentucky mistakes were converted to field goals; worse yet, no one had passed the ball to Issel. "Look, fellows," Rupp said. "I don't know whether you realize it or not but this boy has on a Kentucky shirt. He's on our side. He's been our bread and butter all season. Now, it would humor me greatly in my advancing years if you would hereafter let him in on our little act."

Issel scored four baskets in less than two minutes and finished with 44 points in a 109-99 victory. Austin Carr scored 52 points for the Irish.

Young Joe Williams' Jacksonville team featured 7-foot blacks Artis Gilmore and Pembrook Burrows—"The biggest team I ever saw," Rupp said. Issel scored 28 points before fouling Vaughn Wedeking and being whistled out of the game with 10 minutes remaining. Both Issel and Rupp thought the foul should be called on Wedeking, who ran in front of Issel. Pratt, Steele, and Mills also fouled out. Kentucky hit 20 of 24 foul shots, and Jacksonville hit 28 of 30 shots. Rupp blamed his team's 106-100 loss on poor officiating and failure of his boys to do what he told them.

"Jacksonville was probably harder than any loss in my college career," Issel said. "The others were against Ohio State in my sophomore year, which we were supposed to win, and Marquette in my junior year, when we still had the next year to go. When Jacksonville beat us, that was the end of my college career.

"The thing that really made me feel bad was because I fouled out with 10 minutes to go. Wedeking stationed himself in front of me. I couldn't become non-aggressive, because if I had, they would have blown us right out of the gym."

Issel bowed out as the most prolific scorer in UK history. He scored 948 points that season, bringing his career total to 2,138 in 83 games. All told, he broke seven individual and two single game records, and he put eight career offensive records on the books.

"I'm as proud of that UK scoring record as of anything I ever accomplished," he said. "When you look down at the list of All-Americans and great basketball players, it really makes you feel proud. I think it will be broken, especially now that players have four years of varsity eligibility. But it is nice to say it is something you accomplished."

Echoes From The '60s

Dear Russell:

Traveling with Coach Rupp we had lots of rituals that we never thought much about. We were in the habit of walking to the table together on our road trips and waiting 'til all the players arrived before we sat down to eat. We were at Auburn in '64 and had just begun to eat in a crowded restaurant. We were quiet, polite—almost formal—that's just the way it always was.

Coach Rupp didn't eat with us but sat with Lancaster and Shively close by. I can imagine he was pleased with the dignified appearance we made.

When all of us had eaten, we stood up in unison, replaced our chairs and filed out. In this particular case as we walked past the cash register, each of us picked up a toothpick. Now usually, we'd go on outside, but this time we just milled around the magazine rack in the motel lobby, casually picking our teeth.

I guess Coach Rupp hadn't taken his eyes off us. This breach of etiquette was too much for him to take. At any rate, he came storming out into the lobby hollering about our bad manners and telling us we were *not* to pick our teeth in public.

He got everyone's attention. The scene he caused seemed to me to be more impolite than our picking our teeth—but nevertheless, we got the point!

Charles F. Ishmael (1963, '64)
(Chili)

Dear Russell:

While en route home by bus after playing Vanderbilt at Nashville, we stopped at a little restaurant across the Kentucky line. We had our UK blazers on and we knew how we were supposed to act. We ate quietly, no ruckus or anything. The owner, an older fellow, watched us. After we had finished, Rupp, Shively and Lancaster went up to pay the bill. The owner complimented them on our attitude and manners. After Rupp thanked him the owner said, "If you ever come this way again, be sure and stop, Mr. Diddle." Rupp didn't say a word all the way home on the bus.

       Sincerely,

       Cotton Nash (1962, '63, and '64)

Dear Russ:

One day in practice we were working on an out-of-bounds play whereby I would get the shot. Coach Rupp was describing each player's assignment such as, you block here and you two other guys will set the screen here. Then he looked at me and said, "Now Mobley, I want you to remain very nonchalant, appear to be very aloof, act like you don't know what's going on and then break behind the screen to get the ball for the shot." Then Coach Rupp hesitated for a second, looked over to me, and said, "Ah hell, just act natural and the play is bound to work."

On another occasion, we had just beaten Temple (December 18, 1962) by a few points at the Palestra in Philadelphia, but played very poorly. Coincidentally, Coach Rupp and I were walking off the floor together when he turned to me and said, "Mobley, would you please go back to the middle of the floor and just sit there until I can get the hell out of this place." My response to him was, "Coach, I always try to do what you say, but I don't quite understand." Coach Rupp quipped back, "I want you to be able to tell the folks back in Lexington that you did something good and constructive here in Philadelphia."

Then there was the day at practice when everything

was going wrong. Coach Rupp, standing in the middle of the floor, raised his head and hands toward the top of the coliseum and prayed, "Dear God, would you please send me someone who is worth a damn?" Immediately, Governor Chandler appeared at practice and Coach Rupp said, "Thank you, God." However, moments later, Governor Chandler laughed aloud at a mistake by one of the players. Coach Rupp, extremely irritated, gave Chandler a good cursing and told him, "I don't care if you are the Governor, either shut up or get out." To say the least, Governor Chandler was very silent the remainder of practice.

I drove Coach Rupp to speak at the Chamber of Commerce banquet in Harrodsburg one evening. One of the points he made was, "Now many mothers and fathers are afraid to let their son play football or basketball because they are afraid he'll get hurt, yet they will buy him a car to speed around in. I tell you, I'd rather my son come home any time with a broken arm, a black eye, or even a broken leg from practice than to come home with a broken character."

Coach Rupp always reiterated during exam week that if any of us needed a tutor, regardless of the hour, to give him a call and he would see that we got what we needed. One night at two a.m. a sophomore from the mountainous area in eastern Kentucky who was having trouble in one of his courses said, "I think I'll find out if Coach Rupp really means what he says." Consequently, he gave Coach Rupp a call and within thirty minutes a tutor was there. Incidentally, the exam and course were passed with flying colors.

During the summer between my Junior and Senior year, I had been on a "goodwill" tour playing ball throughout the Orient. Consequently, I was asked to speak on many occasions. One of those occasions was a Billy Graham crusade in Louisville which had received much publicity. Fall practice had already started and I wasn't about to ask off from practice. I was just going to get there as quickly as possible after practice. About half way through the practice session (fortunately I was having a good day), Coach Rupp came over to me and said, "Harrodsburg, aren't you supposed to speak in Louisville tonight?" I said, "Yes, sir, I am." "Well then, get the hell out of here," Coach Rupp replied. Needless to say, I was surprised, but I saw a sensitivity in him that I did not realize existed.

Sincerely,

Terry B. Mobley (1963, '64, and '65)

Dear Mr. Rice:

One story that always sticks in my mind is to me very characteristic of Coach Rupp. During the 1965-66 season, we were ranked No. 1, and we were playing Mississippi in Oxford, Mississippi. They were one of the weaker teams on our schedule, and this particular game found us playing very well and them playing very poorly. I don't recall the exact score, but it was something like 25-5 after a very short time. Mississippi called a time out, and Coach Rupp found himself in the unusual situation of not knowing exactly what to say. We were playing well, both offensively and defensively, and the game was obviously over already at this early juncture. As the players gathered around for his words of wisdom, Coach Rupp could only scowl, and in his usual gruff manner, stated: "Goddamn, boys; this isn't gonna beat anybody!" Everyone, including Coach Lancaster, laughed. I don't think Coach Rupp ever realized what he said.

I think the above incident is characteristic of Coach Rupp's approach to the game of basketball. In seeking total perfection, I believe that he felt that everyone is always capable of giving a little more or doing a little better. His tongue-lashings and criticisms made players achieve more than they actually wanted to.

Very truly yours,

Gene Stewart (1967)

Russell:

On a fast break early in my sophomore year I laid the ball in the hoop and then twisted to avoid running into Jim LeMaster under the hoop. I failed, and tumbled head over heels into Coach Rupp's feet on the bench. Before I quit rolling Coach was up on his feet yelling, "Get up, Pratt, dammit, your man is already down court." We were up at least twenty at the time!!

Another time we were playing Vandy and I had hit about two in a row and with a third straight one they called time out. At the huddle Coach Rupp said, "Not bad shooting, son—although Chip (Rupp's grandson) probably could have done that, too"—he turned slightly then looked back at me and *smiled* that *grin* and *winked*!!

I'll never forget the day in Columbus after we were beaten by Jacksonville. I was on a bench alone, sweaty and crying. I looked up and there was Coach sitting next to me shaking his head but no words could come out—just the two of us without words!

Mike Pratt (1968, '69, and '70)

Dear Russell:

During one game when I was driving real hard to the basket I missed the shot, got the rebound, missed again, and again and again. The final rebound and shot that I missed on this "hustle" play I got creamed but no foul was called. As a matter of fact I was knocked to the floor and slid right in front of Coach Rupp. Lying on the floor exhausted, hoping for a little compassion from him, he got up to his feet, looked down at me, looked out on the floor and said, "Pat, get your ass up, there goes your man with the ball."

Another memory was the year that we almost won it all and Coach Rupp and I were going up to Schenectady, New York, for "Pat Riley Day" in which he came for nothing. He would always do something for his boys if you ever needed it. I believe he really felt deeply for us all but had to keep this hard shell around himself to maintain discipline. Anyway when we were on the plane he asked me if I needed anything and I said, "No!" He asked if there was anything special he should say at the banquet or to my parents and I said, "No!" He asked me if there was any cash in my pockets and I said, "No!" So knowing Coach Rupp and how he was about any of his boys getting something extra other than what their scholarships called for, I was greatly surprised when he pulled out a $50 bill and said, "Here, in case you have to buy your cronies some Cokes at home." He is a great man.

To show how concerned he was about his players, that "Rupp's Runts" year when they started passing out all-America honors and things like that, the first couple I made 2nd team and 3rd team while Louie made first team. I guess he thought that might bother me because we were just going into the playoffs and maybe I might get down or something like that. After practice one day he got me aside and said, "You know you are going to make 'Look' Magazine's All-America first team," and I said, "No, I was not aware," and then he said, "You know you are going to be named SEC Player of the Year," and I said, "No!" And then he said, "Well anyway I think you're the best goddam player in the nation this year so get your dobber up."

Thank you,

Pat Riley (1965, '66, and '67)

Dear Russell:

Not being one of Coach Rupp's more successful players and being (as one compassionate sportswriter long ago put it) more of a bungler than a bomber, I am not sure that you could use my anecdotes or not. I would like, however, to relate an incident that occurred when I was just a sophomore. I always recall it with a little bit of a smile and since I am now coaching in Illinois it means more to me. I many times answer the same question put to me by players and sportswriters the way Coach Rupp answered me that day.

When I was just a sophomore in 1965, we went on our first southern road trip to play Florida and Auburn. While walking into the Florida Gymnasium to go through a standard, brief workout before the game, Coach Rupp reached down on the floor and picked up a bobby pin. He said, "This means we're going to have good luck, Brad."

I asked him, "Coach, you're not superstitious are you?"

"No," he said, "I learned a long time ago, when I first started coaching in Illinois, that it's bad luck to be superstitious!"

The wit here was buried at first but the more I thought about it the more humorous it became. Since I am now coaching I know exactly what Coach Rupp was trying to tell me.

Sincerely,

Brad Bounds (1966, '67)

Dear Russell:

My first meeting with Coach Rupp occurred when I interviewed for the basketball trainer's position. I will never forget how impressed I was with his office and with his friendly manner. I was also impressed when he asked me if I thought I could do the job for him. When I replied that I would do the best I could, he said, "I don't want to know whether you can do the best you can. I want to know whether you can." My answer was that I could do the job if he gave me enough reins to do so. He put his feet on the desk and said, "You will need a place to live." He picked up the phone and called the head of housing for the university and said to him, "This is Adolph Rupp. I just hired myself a trainer and he needs a place to live so fix him up." I was influenced by his efficiency and the amount of influence he had. He never really waited to see what my answer about the position was going to be....

Rupp used to caution me against spending so much time talking to the football staff. I would tell him I was learning things that would be beneficial to basketball, but I don't think he ever really believed me.

Billy Joe Brown
(Trainer, 1963, '64,
'65, and '66)

The Last Hurrah

The University of Kentucky basketball program was desegregated on June 9, 1969, when Tom Payne, a 7-foot All-American at Shawnee High School, was signed by Rupp to a scholarship at his home in Louisville.

At the time Payne seemed the perfect answer to the black height problem that had been a barrier to UK teams in national competition and to those critics who said a black would never play for one of Rupp's teams.

However, Payne was a calculated risk at best, a rough, unpolished, inexperienced young giant who had not participated in an organized sport until his sophomore year in high school. He had the physical equipment to be a great player, but he was forced to enter the university without benefit of scholarship because of a low test score and was not allowed to practice or play with the freshman team. After his first-year grades met the proper requirements, he was placed on athletic scholarship.

Tom said he chose Kentucky because he thought Rupp could help bring out his potential more than any other coach. Perhaps he was right, but his motivation was wrong. He admitted that he had set his sights on a professional career and that after a certain period of time he was not loving the game anymore. He was trying to look out for himself, and not the team's interest.

Payne's freshman teammates were 6-foot-11 Jim Andrews, 6-foot-3 Steve Penhorwood, and 6-foot-8 Dan Perry, all of Lima, Ohio, and 6-foot-5 Larry Stamper of Lee County. Only Andrews and Stamper would complete their eligibility.

During preseason practice of Payne's sophomore year,

Soderberg broke a bone in his hand, Casey sprained a thumb, and Noll transferred to Marshall because Rupp would not assure him a starting berth ahead of established forwards Larry Steele and Tom Parker.

There was also dissatisfaction at the other positions. While Casey, Dinwiddie, Hollenbeck, Mills, and Key battled for the two guard positions, Andrews dedicated himself to working harder because of Payne's obvious lock on the center position. Soderberg finally quit in early January. Both Noll and Soderberg would later try to get Andrews to transfer to their respective new schools.

Parker and Steele combined for 43 points to carry the team past Northwestern, 115-100, at Evanston. Casey scored only eight points, and there was doubt about the condition of that leg. However, he came back with 25 points as UK defeated Michigan, 104-93, in Lexington. Henry Wilmore hit 17 of 21

Tom Payne has just become the first black to sign a basketball grant-in-aid with the University of Kentucky. That was in the spring of 1969. A pleased Rupp and Payne's parents took part in the ceremony.

field goal attempts and scored 40 points for the Wolverines.

In West Virginia's new 14,000-seat arena, which was designed by Carl Staker, captain of the 1942 UK team, Stan Key hit some clutch baskets in a 106-100 victory. Steele received a broken thumb in practice four days before the Wildcats were to play Indiana and was replaced by Stamper. Parker hit 24 points and UK won, 95-93, in overtime.

DePaul was an easy victim (106-85) in the UKIT, and Purdue was not supposed to be tough; however, the Boilermakers got 27 points from Larry Weatherford and beat UK, 89-83. In the second half of an 84-78 victory over Oregon State, Rupp used a double pivot, with Andrews near the basket and Soderberg (subbing for Payne) in the high post. Soderberg started at forward against Notre Dame at Louisville, but the move failed as UK lost, 99-92. Austin Carr hit 21 of 32 and scored 50 points for the Irish. Larry Steele got nine points and 15 rebounds as a sub.

Steele was back in the lineup as UK beat Ole Miss, 103-95, at Oxford in the conference opener. Johnny Neumann hit 20 of 50 field goal attempts and had 47 points for the Rebels. After not playing in that game or in a 79-71 victory over Mississippi State, Soderberg quit the team. He felt that Rupp tried to bend over for Payne to show that he was not prejudiced.

The Wildcats had lost only to Tennessee in 11 conference games and were 16-3 in early February when Rupp entered the hospital for treatment of a foot ailment. Coached by Joe Hall, UK lost to Florida in Gainesville and then won its remaining SEC games, easily annexing a 26th conference championship. Rupp sat on the bench during a televised game against LSU in the Coliseum, but he returned to the hospital immediately after the game.

Rupp flew to Nashville by chartered plane the following Saturday, but he returned to Lexington as the team traveled to Auburn. Although still a wheelchair patient, he took charge of the team again on March 3 and was on the bench for a closing victory over Tennessee. Payne was ejected from that game for flagrantly fouling Jim Woodall, with whom he had scuffled in an earlier game at Knoxville. UT fans booed Payne and someone had written a racial slur on the bulletin board in the UK dressing room.

In the preliminary game of the Mideast Regional Tournament at South Bend, Western Kentucky, with an all-black starting five, defeated Jacksonville, setting up the first meeting between the Hilltoppers and the Wildcats. Jim McDaniels warned that Western had been waiting 32 years to play Kentucky, and they were going to get the Wildcats. His personal hatred for Rupp stemmed from the preceding year, when he said that pairing Western against Jacksonville in the opposite bracket from Kentucky was just another way of helping Kentucky win the NCAA tournament.

Rupp replied, "I don't doubt that young man said that, but I doubt that he has enough intelligence to comprehend how NCAA brackets are made. You can quote me as saying that Mr. McDaniels isn't smart enough to know about things like that."

Ohio State and Marquette were paired in the semifinal at Athens, Georgia, where the volatile Al McGuire surprised everyone by praising Rupp as probably the finest coach who ever lived, a person who had contributed more to basketball by accident than most coaches had done on purpose. The Hilltoppers were less respectful. With thousands of red-clad followers waving them on, they wiped out Kentucky, 107-83. McDaniels, playing with a high fever after a bout with strep throat, missed seven minutes of the first half after picking up three fouls, but still scored 35 points. With Kentucky trailing 71-48 and 13:22 to go, he walked to the bench with his arms stretched upward in victory.

That was the most humiliating loss of Rupp's career.

"I was thinking about turning this thing over to Joe Hall and taking it easy," he said, "but I can't leave him with a mess like this. They'll think I'm dying on the vine. I can't go out on a sour note like this, not after a game in which not one of our boys would do what I wanted them to do."

In the battle for third place, the listless Wildcats lost, 91-74, to Marquette. Western defeated Ohio State and advanced to the NCAA finals in Houston.

In early April, Rupp again entered the hospital, where he underwent surgery on his ailing foot. He resumed his office duties May 3.

Entering the 1971-72 school year, practically all teams in the Southeastern Conference were integrated. Auburn and Florida each had four blacks on scholarship; Vanderbilt listed three blacks on its rosters; Mississippi, Mississippi State, and Tennessee had two each, and LSU had one. Kentucky had several blacks on the football team, but only Payne in basketball. However, Payne was listed as a "hardship" case with 14 other underclassmen for the National Basketball Association's supplemental draft in September of that year. He signed with the Atlanta Hawks.

The loss of Payne dealt a severe blow to Rupp's plans for another national championship team. He had been told personally by UK president Dr. Otis A. Singletary that he would be retired after the 1971-72 season, but there would be no formal announcement of such action during the season.

That year Hall recruited such fine freshmen as J.D. Conner, Mike Flynn, Bob Guyette, Kevin Grevey, Jerry Hale, G.J. Smith, and Steve Lochmueller. Hollenbeck broke a bone in his foot before the season started, rebroke it during the first week of practice, and then broke it again before the season opened. McCowan received a severe shoulder muscle tear, and Andrews wore a cast several days after spraining an ankle ligament. Rupp warned that the Wildcats were not a good team, and people might as well get used to it.

Lacking depth on the front line, he opened with Andrews at center, senior Tom Parker and junior Larry Stamper at forwards, and senior Stan Key and sophomore Ronnie Lyons at guard. Andrews scored 37 points in an opening victory over Northwestern. They defeated Kansas and Kansas State on the road, but lost to Indiana by one point in double overtime in Louisville after Parker injured an ankle in the first half. Steve Downing scored 40 points and grabbed 25 rebounds for Indiana. Rupp said Payne would never have let that happen.

Without Parker they were upset, 91-85, by Michigan State. Rupp severely criticized his players for lack of talent: "If we had Tom Payne, we'd be undefeated," he said. "The pros don't care whether they destroy a good college team or not. They sure ruined us by drafting my center."

As the freshmen averaged more than 100 points in each of their early games, he openly wondered why such fine material had not been recruited the preceding two years. After the NCAA voted in January to make freshmen eligible for the following season, he complained that the rule was one year too late.

The back-to-back losses to Indiana and Michigan State, coupled with his denunciation of his players—"I had to take them to the woodshed"—brought criticism from some fans, but they were quiet after the Wildcats defeated Missouri and Prince-

Rupp's last coaching staff consisted of Dicky Parsons, Joe B. Hall, and Gale Catlett (far right).

ton in the annual UKIT. McCowan scored 15 points as a substitute against Missouri and seemed to have regained his old form after a year of suspension. Andrews, still reminded often by Rupp of the great loss suffered when Payne turned professional, was named the tournament's most outstanding player.

The Wildcats won their first two conference games, home tilts with Mississippi and Mississippi State, but they were definitely in trouble after losing to Florida and Georgia on the road. They returned home to play Tennessee in the Coliseum. Realizing that the entire season, plus any chance he had of beating the mandatory retirement rule, rested on the outcome of that one game, Rupp was the caustic, critical, sarcastic, and ruthless baron of old, closing his practice sessions and berating his players mercilessly.

"I get letters from your mommas," he said. "Momma wants to know why that nasty old man is mistreating her child."

"Proud of yourself, aren't you?" he said to a player who made a layup. "Guess I ought to give you the rest of the night off for making that one."

Minutes later, "Dammit, you've only made one in the four years you've been here and that was a minute ago."

When they started complaining about the officiating of a manager, he yelled, "Start taking their names down. The next

Rupp's last UK team, seated, left to right: Rupp, Stan Key, Bob McCowan, Kent Hollenbeck, Ray Edelman, Ronnie Lyons, Joe B. Hall. Standing: manager John Ferguson, Gale Catlett, Tom Parker, Dan Perry, Jim Andrews, Rick Drewitz, Larry Stamper, Wendell Lyons, Dick Parsons, and trainer Walt McCombs.

time somebody gripes, it's going to cost him four tickets to the Tennessee game. Boy, I need some tickets to the Tennessee game."

"No need for that," he told a manager who started to wipe a spot where some players fell. "Hell, nobody has worked up a sweat yet. I want to see more people on the floor. That's the first time all day that anybody has dived after the ball."

They defeated Tennessee by two points on a shot by Andrews with two seconds remaining.

After nine more conference victories in a row, the Wildcats

lost to LSU, 88-71, in Baton Rouge (the Tigers' second win over UK in 36 years) and then fell to Alabama, 73-70, at Tuscaloosa. They beat Auburn, 102-67, in Rupp's last coaching appearance in Memorial Coliseum.

The university's farewell celebration for Rupp was staged the night of that Auburn game. When the teams returned to the floor after the National Anthem was played, a single light was spotted in front of the UK bench. Harry Lancaster took over the microphone and said, "Coach Rupp, we want to thank you for what you have done the past 40 years for college basketball. We want you in the spotlight."

Rupp walked into the light and waved to the crowd.

The Wildcats next traveled to Knoxville and beat Tennessee, 67-66, to tie for the SEC championship (14-4 records). On the strength of their two wins over UT, the Wildcats were invited to represent the conference in the NCAA Mideast at Dayton, Ohio, where they were matched once again with Marquette.

Bob Lackey hit seven of 10 shots in the first half for Marquette, but he was held to one shot made in four attempts after Rupp made defensive adjustments at halftime. Kentucky won, 85-69.

For Kentucky, the regional final with Florida State was Texas Western and Western Kentucky all over again. The Seminoles featured an all-black starting five coached by Hugh Durham of Louisville, who in his youth was an avid fan of "The Fabulous Five" and dreamed of playing basketball for Kentucky. He signed a UK football grant with Blanton Collier but changed his mind and attended Florida State in order to play basketball. Kentucky did not offer him a basketball scholarship.

The quickness, superior rebounding ability, and resolute defense of the black Seminoles forced UK into 14 turnovers in the first half and the issue was never in doubt. Florida State won, 73-54.

Rupp told writers at the postgame press conference, "I want to thank you for all your kindness through the years. I'm not nearly the mean old man you fellows have led me to believe I am."

Asked when his retirement would be announced, he said, "In about three or four years."

He had hopes of beating the mandatory retirement rule, but he denied any knowledge of various efforts in his behalf. A major drive to keep him on the job was begun shortly after the season began by Gerry Calvert, a former Rupp player. Dan Issel, Mike Pratt, and Louie Dampier, all of the Kentucky Colonels, also signed a petition urging that he be retained as a coach.

However, after Rupp announced that he might run for a vacant congressional seat, the Athletics Association Board, at a special meeting, voted unanimously to follow the university's established retirement policy. He was retired officially three days later.

During the UK basketball banquet on March 28, 1972, Dr. Singletary said, "There is absolutely no difference of opinion on this—the feeling of appreciation and gratitude that the University of Kentucky and all its friends and all basketball fans share for the really wonderful, really magnificent career of the greatest coach the game of basketball has ever known."

Rupp thanked "all those who have gone down the glory road with me."

In The Shadow Of Rupp

"I wouldn't want to be the man who succeeds Rupp," former basketball coach Ralph Carlisle once said. "I want to be the man who succeeds the man who succeeds Rupp."

The message was simple—the man who stepped into Rupp's shoes would have no way to go but down, and his successor would have to pick up the pieces. John Ed Pierce of the *Courier-Journal & Times* said Joe Hall "seems to be tackling a glacier with an ice pick," but Pierce cautioned that it would be a mistake to write off Hall before he started.

"It's my job now," Hall told Pierce. "I hope to be judged by what I do, not by what someone else did. I expect we will do right well."

Joe's first contact with basketball had come through the Boy Scout troop at Cynthiana, which met in the fire station at City Hall. The boys would get there early and play basketball before the meeting started. "Billy Fitzgerald had a goal on a barn behind his house next to the hospital," Joe would recall in 1975. "We used to play by the light of the hospital parking lots. I got many a licking coming home late from those games. When we got into junior high, we had a window in the school that we'd leave unlocked and slip in and play on weekends. There is something psychological about having it made a little tougher for you."

Joe weighed 87 pounds when he reported for football as a freshman at Cynthiana High, and he only weighed 160 pounds when he graduated. But he earned three letters each in football and basketball, captained both teams his last year, was president of his class all four years, and headed the Beta Club, academic honorary. His grades were the highest of any boy in his class.

"There were only 14 or 15 in my graduating class," he said. "All but about two played both football and basketball, the only sports we had in our school. It was a toss-up to me as to which I liked best. I think there was a time when I would have played football in college rather than basketball. I was a quarterback and linebacker, but I was a little light for college football."

Since his earliest recollection, Joe and his brother Bill had never missed listening to UK games on the radio. "I still have some of the stats we compiled while listening to radio broadcasts of the UK games," Joe said. "I can recollect hearing how All-American 'Wah Wah' Jones trained year-round, how he kept in shape, dieted, and drank a lot of milk."

Joe played with the East-West All-Stars in Alumni Gym in the spring of 1947, meeting Rupp and Lancaster during the week the players practiced on the gym floor. He had also scrimmaged against Hirsch, Townes, Day, Henne, and some other UK players. "When I had the opportunity to try out and make the squad at Kentucky, it was like a dream come true," he said. "I think I was more surprised than anyone when I made the final cut. We worked out two weekends. There were 100 to 150 boys on campus for tryouts, many of whom had been All-State from many parts of the country."

Joe moved into a dormitory with Jim Line and Roger Day. Ralph Beard, "Dutch" Campbell, and Humzey Yessin were in the room under them. "Although he was a senior, Campbell and I became very good friends," Joe said. "He visited my home in Cynthiana on weekends and some of the football players helped me strip bluegrass seed. That was when 'Bear' Bryant was here. I'll never forget when another guy and I forgot to pick up our student passes for one of the games. The man at the gate let us in after I told him I was Joe Hall of the basketball team and the other guy identified himself as Babe Parilli of the football team."

Joe's mother, who opened a florist shop next door to the Hall home in 1945, remembered when Joe came home in the summer of his freshman year at UK and, without telling anyone, went down to the bank and made a note for the money to buy a pickup truck and a hay baler. "Farm labor was hard to get then," she said, "and he made a lot of money that summer, going all over the country, cutting and baling hay. He was just that way."

"My biggest thrill came when I appeared in Alumni Gym with a UK uniform during my sophomore year," Joe said. "I'll never forget that moment when we went out. The band played 'On, On, UK,' and I thought I'd throw my first layup over the basket. I wonder if players today have the same sensation that I had. To really feel like that, you've got to have grown up in Kentucky and to have followed the team, to have them as your heroes way before you dreamed it possible you'd be a player. I'll never forget how fortunate I was to have that opportunity, to be chosen among the many thousands of kids like me who had grown up idolizing Kentucky athletics, both football and basketball."

Joe was used sparingly in his sophomore year, but he did make the traveling squad. One of the big trips was to Boston for a game with Holy Cross and then to Madison Square Garden for a game with St. John's. That was the time the celebrated fight occurred between Crusader fans and "Wah Wah" Jones and Harry Lancaster in Boston Garden.

In New York the Wildcats had a choice of either going to a Willie Pep-Sandy Sadler prize fight or a Broadway show. "Rupp thought we'd seen enough fighting and took us to the show," Joe said. "That was just before Christmas. It was amazing how we'd walk down the streets of New York and people would recognize us as Kentucky basketball players. Kentucky had that kind of reputation in New York."

Joe worked hard at the game, but that was the era of Rupp's great teams and Joe soon tired of riding the bench. During the 1948-49 season he transferred, with Rupp's help, to Sewanee.

"I learned a lot of basketball from Lon Varnell, who was an excellent coach and student of the game," Joe said. "My second game, I set a school scoring record, a modest 28 points, against Millsaps. Upon completing my eligibility, I was given a tryout by the old Chicago Stags. I then toured Europe with Varnell and an all-star team that traveled with the Harlem Globetrotters in the summer of 1951. We were gone two months and played in 14 countries."

Some of Joe's UK credits had not been transferable, and at the end of his senior year he was 12 hours short of his degree. Having exhausted his athletic eligibility and having no more scholarship money, he returned home and became a salesman

Joe B. Hall and Rupp.

for the H. J. Heinz Company. At UK he had met Katharine Dennis, a Harrison County girl who had grown up on a farm, gotten a teaching certificate, and was now teaching in Pendleton County. Within a month after they met again and started dating they were married.

Joe returned to UK in 1953 and received his A.B. degree two years later. He continued to work full-time while Katharine taught in Bourbon County. They commuted to their home in Cynthiana. Joe worked for a while in a manufacturing firm in Cynthiana but quit in the fall of 1956 after his supervisor refused him a transfer to a department where faster advancement seemed likely. The real reason apparently was that Joe's old dream to coach basketball had surfaced.

"He called and asked how I would like to live in Shepherdsville," Katharine Hall recalls, "and I said 'fine.' And then he said he had gotten the job there as coach."

"I really went into the job—at Shepherdsville High School, just south of Louisville—knowing very little about the school, the program, or the schedule," Joe said. "I just wanted to get into coaching. I had made a promise to Katharine that I would stay 10 years in coaching and if we didn't make some progress and if it didn't look like a good decision, I would get out of coaching and go into some form of business or industry."

Joe reported to work the week school started. When the football coach left that week, Joe found himself coaching boys who had never played 11-man football. Powerhouse Elizabethtown swamped them, as did some other teams, and the basketball team did not fare much better. But Joe's second-year cage squad had a 22-6 record and went to the district finals. He was named conference Coach of the Year.

Joe took an assistant's job at Regis College, a small Jesuit college in Denver, guided the freshman squad to a 14-3 season, and then stepped up to the head coaching job for five years, holding the title of athletic director the last three years.

"The Regis job came along at a good time," Katharine Hall would say later. "We had saved a few thousand dollars when I was teaching, but it was about gone. So we loaded what furniture we had in a trailer, put Judy (who had been born in 1955) and Kathy (born in Shepherdsville in 1956) in the back seat, and set out for Denver. And we really loved Denver."

In Joe's second year as head coach, Regis assumed major college status and eventually would defeat such schools as Arizona, Oklahoma State, Oklahoma City, Colorado State, Denver, Air Force Academy, Montana State, Idaho State, and Creighton.

Joe was building his program, having winning seasons, and gaining national prestige for Regis when the school decided to deemphasize basketball by reducing the number of grants-in-aid and cutting financial support. Feeling he had been denied a chance to reap the rewards of a program he had been developing over a five-year period, Joe accepted the job of head coach at Central Missouri State College. He and Katharine loaded the three children—Steven had been born in 1959—in the back seat and headed for Warrensburg. During one year there Joe would compile a 19-6 record, win a conference championship, and represent the league in the NCAA playoffs.

At Regis he had kept in contact with Rupp, sending the UK coach names of players who were out of the possibility of recruiting by Regis. He even made contacts in St. Louis in regard to some players he thought could play for Rupp. As a result Rupp called Joe when a position became open on the UK staff. At the same time Ed Hickey at Marquette had offered Joe an assistant's job, and Joe had turned it down because of the way his program was going at Regis.

"I did not want to go back to Kentucky and be a recruiter on the road because of the travel that would be required," he said. "I told Coach Rupp if he ever wanted a regular full-time coaching assistant, I would be interested." In May 1965, Rupp wanted him in that capacity, and Joe accepted.

"I was to head up the recruiting and handle the paperwork," he said, "but it was to be shared by all three coaches. When I found out there was no recruiting system organized, I talked to other coaches and other recruiters and found out what was being done on a major level. I developed our recruiting program and it was very rewarding in that success was imminent. Kentucky and the Lexington area were easy products to sell to basketball recruits."

That first year Joe brought in such players as Dan Issel, Mike Pratt, Mike Casey, Jim Dinwiddie, and Terry Mills. Another good crop was the one that included Tom Parker, Randy Noll, Stan Key, Mark Soderberg, and Kent Hollenbeck. Some good individual players in "off" years included such performers as Larry Steele, Greg Starrick, Bob McCowan, Larry Stamper, Jim Andrews, Ronnie Lyons, and Tom Payne.

Coach Adolph Rupp discusses the upcoming 1948-49 basketball season with Wildcat sophomores. Left to right are Garland Townes, Walt Hirsch, Joe B. Hall, Coach Rupp, Bob Henne, and Roger Day.

At UK family-man Joe Hall's worst fears came to roost as he found himself more and more on the road in search of basketball players; in addition, there was an element of frustration in a job that seemed to hold no future for him. Rupp was nearing the mandatory retirement age of 70, but the baron showed no signs of accepting retirement unless it was forced on him. It was generally assumed that Harry Lancaster would become head coach when and if Rupp retired. But when Bernie Shively died in December 1967, and Lancaster eventually was named as his successor, Joe was suddenly first in line to succeed Rupp.

The problem was that Joe had no guarantee that he would even be on the UK basketball staff after Rupp retired. Having sought some assurance that he would be chosen to succeed Rupp and having received nothing concrete, he announced on April 2, 1969, that he was accepting the job of head basketball coach at St. Louis University. A week later he was back on the job at UK.

Rupp would later claim that Hall asked to come back to UK, while Hall contends that Rupp asked him to return. "I came back on a weekend after my first week in St. Louis to visit my family," Joe said, "and I was contacted by Coach Rupp through Claude Vaughan (the UK trainer), who said the coach wanted to talk to me. Claude picked me up and we went down and picked up Coach Rupp, and I visited with him in his home, and we talked about St. Louis and what all I had done. And then we rode to the airport together. Claude went in to check the luggage for Coach Rupp, and we sat in the car. At that time Coach Rupp asked me if I would reconsider and get a release from my contract with St. Louis and come back to Kentucky."

After Joe was released from his contract with St. Louis, Rupp said, "There has never been any disagreement between Joe Hall and me." Rupp had told Hall that he would retire in two years (it would be three) and that he would make the recommendation to the Athletic Board that Joe be named his successor. However, those three years would be a hard time for Joe as Rupp showed no inclination to retire, and friends of the old coach circulated a petition and exerted other pressures in his behalf.

The tension broke on March 31, 1972, when the UK Athletic Board, at a luncheon meeting, announced that Joe Hall was the new head basketball coach. Rupp did not attend the ceremony and sent no words of congratulations. He had stalked from his office shortly before the luncheon, announcing curtly that he was "going to the farm."

"I will not attempt to replace Coach Rupp," Hall told the meeting. "I feel he will be part of Kentucky basketball forever. I wish to thank him for giving me my start at the university and for all I have learned from him."

Gentleman Jim

The player in the middle as the Wildcats made the transition from Adolph Rupp to Joe Hall was Jim Andrews, a senior center whose lack of total dedication to the game was a constant irritation to his coaches.

Gary Rawlings of the *Kernel* called Andrews a "split personality," a person whose towering frame intimidated foes but who off the court was just Jim Andrews, the history major who would like to be known as just that.

"I would rather be accepted as a student and have people want to talk to me about things other than basketball," Jim once said. "Talking about basketball is something I do all the time."

On the day of a game, he never took a shower, always shaved, trimmed his toenails and fingernails, sought out the same people to talk with, and avoided his girl friend after 2 p.m. He also kept a little buckeye in the right-hand pocket of his jacket for luck.

Basketball to him was part of his work, a day-to-day job at UK, and he was bothered because people would not accept it for that. His philosophy was pretty well summed up in the middle of the 1973 season when he told a reporter, "Basketball isn't all that important, really."

Whatever his hangups, Andrews was the key to the success or failure of Joe Hall's first Wildcat team, no matter how much was expected of the so-called "Super Frosh" who had just moved up to varsity status. Mike Sullivan of the *Courier-Journal* called Andrews "a big bundle of hope...a leftover...a misfit to be somehow blended in with a flashy, cocky herd of rookies."

With Payne gone to the pros in 1972, Andrews had led the Wildcats in total points scored (602), scoring average (21.5), shooting percentage (57.7), and rebounds (315 for an 11.3 average). Although the big guy was a key factor in the Wildcats' drive to the final game of the NCAA Mideast Regional, Rupp still moaned there was nothing he could do about the center situation "because I just don't have anyone else." In essence Andrews was often a convenient 6-foot-11, 235-pound whipping boy for the retiring baron.

"That stuff didn't bother me," Andrews would say later. "The old man was a great coach, no doubt about it."

What did bother him was the fact that Rupp, Hall, and Gale Catlett all were giving him advice during that 1972 season.

"I was really confused at times," he said. "We had three different coaches and three different philosophies and if you tried to please one, you wouldn't be pleasing the other. Sometimes before a game, one would say, 'Go out there and front this man.' And during a time out, another would say, 'No, do it this way' or 'Do it that way.'"

And what did Andrews do?

"Some games, I just ignored all of them and did what I wanted to do," he said. "Then if something went wrong, I just took the criticism and kept quiet."

The main difference he saw between Rupp and Hall was their temperaments. "Coach Hall was quiet and subtle off the floor and Rupp, off the floor, tended to be a little overbearing and vindictive," Andrews said. "Coach Hall was nothing like that. Of course, everyone has their own little idiosyncrasies, but they both wanted to be the best and they both tried to win. Coach Hall would get excited and none of it would get printed, but Coach Rupp, usually quiet on the court, would wait until he got you in the locker room before telling you what he thought. Then, the next day, every word would be in the newspaper. But both would do just about what they said they would do."

That 1973 season would be one in which Andrews at times seemed to relax and depend too much on his sophomore teammates, then suddenly take control. "What we did was wait around—all of us—wondering who was gonna do it," he said. "We showed great potential against Michigan State, but after that we regressed, laid down, and didn't keep pressure on ourselves."

Jim Andrews.

In that opening game against the Spartans at East Lansing, Hall started Andrews at center, junior Ronnie Lyons and Flynn at guard, and Grevey and Conner at forward.

The 'Cats expanded a 34-27 halftime lead to 58-44 with 8:51 left and then had to hold off a furious Michigan State rally as the Spartans went into a full court press and cut the lead to 62-61 with 4:19 left. Hall inserted super ballhandler Lyons back into the lineup, and the press suddenly became ineffective. Flynn hit two free throws and then hit Conner with a beautiful blind side pass that led to a backdoor layup. UK had a five-point margin with 2:40 left and that was the game. UK won, 75-66.

Andrews hit eight of nine from the field and four of four from the line to lead UK scorers with 20 points. Conner scored 14, including two critical free throws late in the game, and held heralded 6-foot-7 Lindsay Hairston to one field goal in 13 attempts. Defense was the most impressive part of UK's game. Hall used all 12 of his players, a radical departure from Rupp's policy of the past.

Before UK's home opener with Iowa, Hall went into the stands of Memorial Coliseum and gave Rupp, who had just arrived, a box of popcorn. A photographer was conveniently on the scene.

Kentucky took a 6-0 lead and was ahead until the second period, when Iowa forged a 57-48 lead and won, 79-66. Indiana beat UK, 64-58, in Bloomington, and a UK rally fell eight points short (78-70) against North Carolina in Freedom Hall.

In the North Carolina game, Hall stepped completely out of character, jumping continuously to his feet, raving, and at one point throwing his coat to the floor. "Emotional? Sure I got emotional," he said. "Somebody had to get emotional and I did."

Sparked by Lyons, who got all his 15 points in the second half, the Wildcats did not start playing well until the last eight minutes of the game. Hall felt maybe they had turned the corner.

Andrews scored 33 points, grabbed 19 rebounds, and recorded five assists as UK beat Oregon, 95-68, in the final game of the UKIT. He was named most valuable player. Grevey scored 17 points and Andrews had 16 in a 77-71 victory over Kansas. "Digger" Phelps' young Notre Dame squad fell, 65-63, in a game not as close as the score would indicate.

A low point of that season came at Oxford, where Mississippi took an early lead and won, 61-58. It was the first time Ole Miss had beat UK in 45 years. Rebel coach Cob Jarvis called it the school's greatest basketball victory, which it was.

Andrews and Lyons scored 26 points each to lead UK past Mississippi State at Starkville. Andrews had 28, Lyons 17, and Grevey 16 in a 95-65 win over Florida, and Andrews got 27 and

Grevey 22 in an 89-68 trouncing of Georgia.

The Wildcats were 3-1 in the conference and 8-4 overall when they journeyed into Tennessee for games with the Vols and Vanderbilt. Trailing 65-64 in Knoxville, they took the ball out under the UT basket three times in the final pressure-packed nine seconds and were unable to get a shot because the Vols were in a position to foul and not send UK to the free-throw line.

Andrews took the first inbounds pass and was quickly slapped around the wrists. Because UK was not in the bonus, it meant another out-of-bounds play. Five seconds remained. This time Andrews got the toss in the lane, wheeled upward, and received a flurry of Big Orange arms and fingers that knocked him backward. He pushed off a shot before reeling, but the officials said he was not in the act of shooting when fouled. UK had to throw it in again with three seconds left. Before the inbounds pass came to Andrews, he was kicked in the back of the knee and seemed to buckle just before the ball reached him. Larry Robinson stole the ball to preserve the win for Tennessee. Andrews scored 20 points in that game. He was limping throughout practice at Nashville the following afternoon.

With three seconds remaining in Memorial Gymnasium, Joe Ford, a Commodore freshman from Maysville, Kentucky, sank two free throws to give Vanderbilt a 76-75 victory. Kentucky seemed out of the conference race.

Andrews scored 24 and Grevey 22 in an 86-71 win over LSU in Baton Rouge to set up a crucial game with sixth-ranked Alabama five nights later in Tuscaloosa. The Tide had lost only to Wake Forest early in the season, was undefeated in SEC play, and was riding a 12-game win streak. In addition, Coach C. M. Newton's boys had won 28 of their last 33 games and had won 22 straight at home.

Realizing that his regular offense would be ineffective against Alabama's powerful front line, Hall moved Grevey into the high post, where the mobile forward could utilize his one-on-one skills, and put Andrews in the low post. Grevey responded by hitting 15 of 25 from the field and three of three from the line for 33 points, his best varsity production up to that time. Flynn scored 18 points and keyed a second half barrage that lifted the 'Cats from a four-point deficit at 66-62 with 13:35 left. It was Flynn's two free throws that gave UK an insurmountable 95-91 lead in the closing seconds. Johnny Dill's uncontested layup with four seconds to go cut the final margin to 95-93.

Joy was short-lived for the Wildcats, however, as they returned home to lose, 83-76, to Vanderbilt. It was the first home loss in 50 games with SEC teams. Conner scored 27 points and Andrews got 19 rebounds in an 88-57 win over Auburn. An aggressive Andrews was the prime factor in a revenge victory, 88-70, over Ole Miss, and the 'Cats scored a UK record 20 points in overtime to beat Mississippi State, 100-87.

Andrews' clutch shots and Grevey's 24 points help beat Florida, 94-83, at Gainesville, and Grevey had his best night at Athens, scoring 40 points in a 99-86 win over Georgia. Only Bill Spivey, Bob Burrow, Cliff Hagan, Louie Dampier, and Dan Issel had registered as many points for past Wildcat teams.

The Wildcats made it six straight SEC victories as Grevey and Andrews scored 26 points each in a 94-76 win over LSU. Next came Alabama. Before an overflow crowd in Memorial Coliseum, Ray Odums started the scoring by hitting two free throws for the Tide. Conner hit a jump shot to tie the count, and the 'Cats then put together a string of 20 more unanswered points. Grevey scored 29 points as the Wildcats won, 111-95. That victory, plus an upset win by LSU over league-leading Tennessee, put UK right back in the conference race. After the Wildcats beat Auburn, 91-79, Tennessee came to town for the game that would decide the conference championship.

Thirty hours before that game, students began camping on the Avenue of Champions to assure themselves of good seats in their section. They posted such large banners as "Grevey's Gorillas" and "Home of the LOCHness Monster." Just before game time some students started climbing up a large cable leading from a television truck to a window of the Coliseum. One window was broken during the pushing and shoving inside. By tipoff students were crowded into every niche and corner, swelling the crowd to an estimated 13,000.

The Volunteers, utilizing a deadly 58.1 shooting percentage, led 65-61 with 11:07 left. Then Grevey hit four jump shots in a row, one from each corner and two from behind the foul line. The last put UK ahead, 69-67. Grevey finished the game with 13 of 20 from the field and a total of 28 points. UK won, 86-81.

Jim Andrews gets tip over Tennessee's Kosmalski.

For the first time since most anyone present could remember, a UK basketball coach was carried off the floor by his players. The Associated Press named Joe SEC Coach of the Year.

Against Austin Peay in the opening round of the Mideast Regional at Nashville, Larry Stamper scored 10 points, including the final six as the Wildcats held off the quick-pressing entry from the Ohio Valley Conference and won, 106-100, in overtime.

Indiana was leading 45-32 at halftime of the regional final and threatening to make a runaway of the game when UK parlayed a sticky 1-3-1 zone and some awesome inside work by Andrews to forge a short-lived 61-59 lead on Conner's jump shot with 7:35 left. Then four UK shots lapped the tip of the basket, only to fall harmlessly in Hoosier hands.

"Those four shots," Hall would moan later. "If they had only gone in. They were good shots, but they just wouldn't drop. After our comeback, it was kind of a disappointment."

Immediately after the game, IU Coach Bobby Knight looked directly at the UK bench and said, "I've never been so impressed with a bunch of kids as I was with you."

Andrews scored 23 points to share honors with Steve Downing. The big Kentucky center also batted down six Indiana shots and got 10 rebounds. He led the team that season in minutes played, field goal percentage, rebounds, points and point average (19.6), and was third in assists.

His first move after the final whistle of his collegiate career was to fight his way through a sweeping tide of happy Indiana fans and throw his arms around Downing, his adversary and tormentor in three memorable basketball games stretching over two years. Then Andrews walked slowly to the UK bench, sat down with his teammates, and cried.

"I'm not going to worry about it," Andrews said later. "It's not a life or death thing. It's just a ball game and it should be fun."

Time Out: Kevin Grevey

When Kevin Grevey was nine years of age, his father Norman built a goal in the back yard of their Hamilton, Ohio, home, gave Kevin a basketball and a pair of tennis shoes, and said, "Son, I want you to wear these out by the end of the summer. If you do, I'll put you in an organized league."

Norman Grevey had earned All-State honors as a basketball player at Hamilton Catholic High School and had earned basketball letters at Xavier University, so it was a labor of love for him to teach Kevin some shots and to work with the youngster.

"I went ahead and developed my game at an early age, which I think is very important for younger kids who want to be good basketball players," Kevin said shortly after signing a contract with the professional Washington Bullets in the summer of 1975. "I learned all my basketball on the playground, at school, and in my own back yard."

He was "awfully skinny and small," carrying 165 pounds on a 6-foot-2 frame, when he went out for the varsity as a sophomore at Hamilton Taft High, which is noted for its basketball, having won the state tournament twice in Ohio.

"They needed a small forward and I was thrown into that position," Kevin explained. "I developed my game quite fast while playing under a great coach named Marvin McCollum. He developed my skills and showed me the one-on-one techniques that I used in college basketball."

Kevin was twice All-State and a prep All-American at Taft, averaging 32.5 points and 17.1 rebounds his senior year, when he was named Ohio Co-Player-of-the-Year with Ed Stahl. He received scholarship offers from approximately 200 colleges, but the main pressure at home was for him to attend Ohio State or Miami University at Oxford, the latter being only 12 miles from Hamilton. Kentucky came into the picture when Joe Hall, T.L. Plain, and Dicky Parsons visited the Grevey home in early 1971.

"Of course I had read about the national power that was UK and about Adolph Rupp," Kevin said, "but I never did really consider myself as a UK caliber player. I had never seen Kentucky play, but I was just awed by the fact that their coaches would come and talk to me. It was then that I realized that I was a fine high school player, capable of playing with the best. But I had never entertained the thought, never dreamed that I would be playing at UK."

After the UK coaches left, Norman and Kevin talked the situation over and decided to visit UK, along with visits to Ohio State, Miami, Cincinnati, and Tennessee.

"The thing that sold me on UK during my visit to Lexington was the people," Kevin said. "They took a lot of interest in the players and they were really serious about basketball. I went to other schools and there wasn't the enthusiasm and the encouragement in the communities like there was at UK."

He also was sold on the fact that UK had a great tradition and that Hall had recruited such fine players as Mike Flynn, Jimmy Dan Conner, Bob Guyette, and others. He returned home and then visited UK again in the fall. It was during the latter trip that he met Adolph Rupp for the first time.

"Coach Hall took me to Coach Rupp's home," Kevin recalled, "and Coach Rupp opened the door and said, 'Oh, Mike Flynn! Glad to see you. Come on in.'"

That really turned Kevin off. He thought, "Oh, my God! The head coach and he doesn't even know my name. He thinks I'm Mike Flynn." There was no way Kevin was going to UK.

However, Hall explained to Rupp that this was Grevey the recruit and not Flynn the signee. Rupp apologized, and they sat down and talked.

"I found out just sitting there five minutes what kind of a unique individual Coach Rupp was," Kevin said. "In that short length of time, he sold me on the tradition, the type of basketball players they bring in, and what kind of plans they had for me. That was really a terrifying five minutes in my life. Then I went ahead and signed, and of course I have no regrets."

Kevin remembers well the pressures put on the seven "Super Frosh." "The minute I signed, everybody had us touted as national champions," he said. "That included the coach and ourselves."

And were they cocky?

"We were all high school All-Americans," Kevin said. "Mike Flynn thought he was better than Kevin Grevey and Kevin Grevey thought he was better than Jimmy Dan Conner, and we all wanted to prove to each other what type of players we were."

They tried so hard that their practice sessions were super competitive. They would practice three or four hours a day as freshmen, go into the Blue Room, eat a sandwich or two, and then go back out and practice against the varsity. During the scrimmage sessions, Hall would assign Grevey to guard Tom Parker.

"Tom was 6-7, a senior and an all-conference player," Kevin said. "I had never guarded anybody over 6-5. Parker was just eating me alive and Coach Hall would grab me on the sideline and say, 'Kevin, your defense is so terrible, I don't think you could guard your grandmother. You're going to be guarding players like this.' I replied that this guy was all-conference and was supposed to score on me. That's when Coach Hall started making me run up the Coliseum steps."

When Kevin found out that every time Parker scored a bucket, he was going to have to run up those steps, he decided it was a little bit easier to push Tom around.

"So I got myself in a mental state of playing good defense," Kevin said, "and again the practices were so competitive that there was no way you were not going to improve your game, especially with so many good players around."

He gives credit to Hall for getting the freshman together as a unit that went undefeated in 22 games and was ranked No. 1 nationally by a leading basketball magazine.

"People said we would need seven basketballs instead of one because we were all high scorers," Kevin said. "However, we accepted the roles we were to play, realizing that not everybody was going to be the shooter, not everybody was going to

Kevin Grevey.

be the rebounder."

En route to that perfect season, the squad broke 13 Kitten team records, including field goal average (.490), most field goals (890), free throws (428), and rebounds (1,218). Grevey was high scorer with a 22.2 average and a season high of 31 points in games with Furman and Alabama. Conner averaged 19.0, Flynn 15.4, Smith 14.6, Guyette 14.1, Lochmueller 7.6, and Hale 6.7.

"Everybody said there was no way we were not going to go on and be national champion," Kevin said, "but there's a hecka lot more to it than a freshman season. We were fortunate to have Andrews to go along with us."

Grevey had his problems throughout the early part of that season, but he got his game together with a 33-point performance in the 95-93 upset over Alabama at Tuscaloosa. He suffered an ankle injury and saw little action in subsequent games with Ole Miss and Mississippi State. He averaged more than 30 points in UK's last six games, including a 40-point performance against Georgia, tying a 13-year UK single game sophomore mark. He was named SEC Player-of-the-Year with Alabama's Wendell Hudson, first team All-SEC, and SEC Sophomore-of-the-Year.

He played against a touring Russian Olympic team in June, scoring 23 points from the low post, and then was selected the following month to play on a U. S. collegiate team representing the State Department on the first basketball tour of Red China. He was named co-captain of the team, carried the U. S. flag in leading the team onto the floor each game, hit 53 percent of his shots, and averaged 9.8 points in the eight-game series.

The 13-13 record compiled by the 1973-74 Wildcats was not only a disappointment to fans and players alike, but it also tied the worst record (13-13 in 1967) by a UK team since the 1927 team was 3-13.

The season was off to a good start, with Grevey hitting 13 of 26 field goal attempts and three of three from the line in an 81-68 victory over Miami (Ohio), but Kansas beat them, 71-63, in Lawrence, and Indiana and North Carolina beat them in Louisville and Greensboro, respectively. UK led Indiana, 44-39, at halftime, but the third-ranked Hoosiers scored six straight points to take a 45-44 lead. Indiana hit 18 of 22 shots after intermission to win, 77-68. John Laskowski, a 6-foot-5 substitute guard who had scored a total of six points in IU's two previous games, was the Hoosier hero, hitting 11 of 15 shots against the smaller Lyons.

"I just took my man (Lyons) low and our post man set some back picks to set me free," the junior guard said. "He was too little to guard me." Other teams would try to match taller players against the diminutive Lyons.

North Carolina also used superior height to good advantage, getting many layups in a 101-84 victory.

Against Iowa at Iowa City, the 'Cats had a 22-point lead twice but had to hold on to win, 88-80. They defeated Dartmouth, 102-77, and Stanford, 78-77, in the UKIT.

A pressing defense failed to stop Notre Dame as the Irish won, 94-79, in Freedom Hall. John Shumate, 6-foot-9, scored 25 points, got 14 rebounds, and was named Most Valuable Player. Eddie Palubinskas, Collis Temple, and Glenn Hansen combined for 74 points as LSU beat UK, 95-84, in Baton Rouge. Aggressive drives and fine board work by Flynn helped even the record as UK beat Georgia, 80-74. A few hours before the Wildcats played Auburn, Grevey attempted to jump a bicycle, fell, and cut both elbows. He scored 21 points to lead the Wildcats over the Tigers; however, the cuts began to bother him and he had two sore elbows when the Wildcats played Tennessee in Knoxville two nights later.

"I really didn't feel the soreness until the day after the accident," Kevin said. "I couldn't move my arms. When the bus got to Knoxville, somebody had to take my coat off for me. It's no excuse, but I think it was one reason I was so horrible." He hit five of six shots in the first half, but made only one of eight in a low-scoring (19 points) second half for the Wildcats. The Vols won, 67-54.

The painful condition was still a factor a week later, when Grevey scored only six points in an 81-77 loss to Alabama. He scored 35 points as UK beat Florida, 91-82, in Gainesville. Vanderbilt beat them in Lexington, and the 'Cats beat Mississippi State in Starkville behind superb play by Lyons. The squad arrived in Lexington at 2:00 a.m. Sunday morning after a nine-hour bus ride from Starkville. Hall suspended Grevey the following day for a curfew violation. Both would look back on the incident as serious, but somewhat humorous.

"The season was not going too well and Kevin was having a frustrating junior year," Joe would recall. "We had some key early season losses, we were a very small club, and all this added a little bit to his frustration.

"But then when he fell and cut his elbows, it seemed to just put more and more pressure on Kevin. The incident after the Mississippi State game was kind of humorous as you look back on it, because you can laugh about things like that if you handle them good naturedly, and there hasn't been any losing of friendship along the way.

"After that long bus trip, everyone was tired. They had tried to sleep, but it was awful hard to get any rest at all. I came back from the airport to the Coliseum, where we put up the equipment, and I thought I'd go to the dorm and make sure everyone was all right and that we didn't have anyone sick or needing any attention. So as I checked the players in the dorm, Kevin wasn't around."

Joe sat down and waited for Kevin.

"After waiting one-half hour, then 45 minutes," Joe said, "I called my wife and told her I would just wait and see if I could find out where Kevin was and why he was late coming in. As a result, I laid down on his bed and eventually went to sleep."

About every half-hour team captain Ronnie Lyons would come into Kevin's room to see if Hall was still there.

"They called me 'Papa Bear' after that," Joe said. "They said I was sleeping in Little Red Riding Hood's bed. It was funny in a way, but it was very serious in that curfew had been broken, and Kevin was disciplined by being suspended for the following game with LSU. Incidentally, Kevin never came in that morning while I was there. I got up about 6 o'clock, went home, changed clothes, and got back to the office."

Without the high-scoring junior, the Wildcats defeated LSU, 73-70. They defeated Georgia at Athens; lost to Auburn, 99-97, in overtime at Auburn; beat Tennessee, 61-58, at home, and then dropped consecutive games to Mississippi, Alabama, Florida, and Vanderbilt. They closed the season with a 108-69 win over Mississippi State.

Hall said Grevey's elbow injuries were extremely costly to the team. Despite the handicap, Grevey was the team's leading scorer in 18 games and the leading rebounder in eight games. He scored in the 30s three times, in the 20s fourteen times, hit 50.8 percent from the field, and a team-leading 83 percent from the line.

"That year was a big disappointment," Grevey would say later. "Everybody wanted to know what happened. I think there were many things. The loss of Andrews was a big thing because Bob Guyette, who normally is a big forward, had to play center and cope with guys like Leon Douglas and Len Kosmalski.

"After we lost two or three games, people started getting down on us, saying 'You guys are doing this wrong, you're doing that wrong.' We started getting down on ourselves. We also had some internal problems and some jealousies which sorta deteriorated the team. We just found ourselves in a rut, started questioning our ability, questioning each other, and ended up having a demoralizing year. We played like we had never seen a basketball before."

And how did the team feel about being a "loser?"

"We kinda thought we liked the brighter side better," Kevin said. "So we regrouped. Coach Hall organized an overseas trip to Australia and we rejuvenated ourselves right back to our freshman year, where we were playing together like we were capable of playing. Each player played his role. There were no jealousies or animosities toward each other. We became real close because there were only 13 of us over there, and we were the only guys that could party together that knew each other well. We got to telling some stories, and we became real close. We said to each other we could have a real good year if we wanted to. We decided on total dedication. We were to get in shape through our running program, with no playing around, and were to be as serious as we could about the upcoming season."

Kevin felt that the little inner self, the total dedication that each of them brought out, paid off in the long run.

"I think we realized what kind of talent we had and we finally decided to put it all together," he said. "Coach Hall has to take credit for this. He just laid down the law and set rules and regulations we were to follow. It's a real credit to the freshmen who came in, with all the pressures on us, to finally prove to the people of Kentucky that we were what they expected of us when we came in. We weren't a bunch of losers."

Something To Prove

Coming off a 13-13 season in 1974, the Wildcats were determined to prove they were better than the record indicated and that they could live up to the high goals that had been set for them and by them when they were freshmen.

Of the seven players who had compiled a 22-0 record as freshmen, advanced to the Mideast Regional final as sophomores, and then finished with that .500 record in 1974, only Steve Lochmueller was missing. He cast his lot with the football team and then gave that up because of an injury.

The remaining six seniors still had a sentimental attachment to Joe Hall, who in essence was "graduating" with this, his first full class. Sitting in his office in Memorial Coliseum just before the end of the 1975 season, Hall would reflect on how each of those players came to be at UK.

"I first saw Jimmy Dan Conner play for Anderson County in the Central Kentucky Conference Tournament at Danville when he was a 15-year-old sophomore," Hall would recall fondly. "Even then his coolness and maturity on the court impressed me before anything else. In recruiting him, I best remember the day in his senior year when we went fishing and pulled in a nice string of bass and redeye. On that day I felt that UK had landed Jimmy Dan, too. He was a true Kentucky boy. It would have seemed like heresy if he had gone somewhere else."

While Conner was "Mr. Basketball" in Kentucky that year, Mike Flynn of Jeffersonville was his Indiana counterpart. "Mike and J. D. have been running mates ever since," Hall said. "We've seen Mike marry and welcome the arrival of a fine son, Billy Jim

(B. J.)." Hall appreciated the fact that Mike accepted the role of playmaker and subordinated his desire to score. Mike also had become one of the fine defensive players in the nation.

"I started recruiting Kevin Grevey in the summer of 1970," Hall said. "Believe it or not, his biggest worry was that he would not be good enough to play for UK. I had the pleasure of taking him frog-gigging for the first time in his life. He was surprisingly good at it—one of the best left-handed frog-giggers I've ever seen."

G. J. Smith, a 6-foot-8 stringbean from East Kentucky, would become known as the "Kentucky Long Rifle" because of his uncanny outside shooting. Hall called him "one of the most cheered and called-for substitutes in UK history."

Guard Jerry Hale was a youngster at a UK game when a cake-cutting ceremony was held to commemorate some milestone in UK basketball history. He took a piece of the cake back to his New Albany, Indiana, home and still had it in the family freezer when he signed a UK grant-in-aid. Hall called him a "coach's favorite...a 110 percenter who goes all out in every practice."

"I doubt if any player ever contributed more to a team with his attitude," the coach said. "Jerry is a steady, dependable, highly competitive person, and we hope he makes his future home here in Lexington."

Bob Guyette was the last recruit signed by Hall in the spring of 1971. "He came a long way from his home in Ottawa, Illinois, to attend UK," Hall said, "and I think the influence of the other signees and the people of Lexington had a lot to do with his decision to come with us."

Guard Reggie Warford of Drakesboro, Kentucky, was the only junior on that 1975 squad. Up from the jayvee team were guards Larry Johnson of Morganfield and Joey Holland of Charleston, West Virginia, and Merion Haskins of Campbellsville, Kentucky. Holland is a son of Joe Holland, who played with UK's "Fabulous Five" squad of 1948.

"A 13-13 season makes you think," Hall would say later. "I got to looking back at that 1974 season and saw that we'd actually been manhandled by some teams. The problem was that with Conner (6-foot-3) at forward, Guyette (6-foot-8) at center and Lyons (5-foot-9) at guard, there was no way we could match some opponents physically. We were just too small as a team.

"We felt if we were going to play Big 10 teams and others that emphasize the physical part of basketball, we had to branch out and recruit to those needs."

Jack Givens, a 6-foot-4 forward-guard from Bryan Station High School, and James Lee, a 6-foot-5 forward from Henry Clay High School, known as "Mr. Silk" and "Mr. Steel," respectively, in Lexington basketball circles, were only part of what Hall had in mind in filling his most pressing need. But they were two fine basketball players who would strengthen any roster.

Givens had scored 1,777 points, averaging 18.7 points a game, in a three-year career during which Bryan Station compiled a 76-17 record. He was Kentucky's "Mr. Basketball" in 1974. Lee had led Henry Clay to a 65-21 record during a three-year span, setting school marks in scoring (1,671) and rebounding (1,194).

Hall completed one of UK's finest recruiting seasons by signing Dan Hall, a 6-foot-10, 220-pound center from Betsy Layne, Kentucky, who would not turn 18 until September of that year; Mike Phillips, a 6-foot-10, 240-pound center from Manchester High in Ohio; and Rick Robey, a 6-foot-10, 235-pound center from New Orleans.

Phillips had served as captain three straight years for Panther teams that had compiled an 80-10 record during his four-year career. Manchester had gone undefeated (26-0) and won the state AA championship in 1974. Phillips was the most prolific scorer in Ohio schoolboy history, registering 2,573 career points to surpass the 2,460 scored by the famous Jerry Lucas.

Phillips and Robey, who had led Brother Martin High to a 63-10 record in his two years there and to the Louisiana state championship, became good friends when they played together with the victorious all-star team (along with Lee) in the Capital Classic. They decided to attend the same university.

"So there were a lot of players and a lot of size," Hall said. "Each of the signees weighed over 200 pounds. It looked more like a football recruiting year than a basketball recruiting year, but this met our need to have a more physical club that could withstand the intimidation of the strong clubs we were to face."

With either Phillips or Robey capable of starting at the pivot, Hall moved Guyette back to forward and Conner back to his natural guard position. Flynn was at the other guard and Grevey the other forward.

"This gave us much greater size and team strength than

UK's "Super Frosh" of 1971, kneeling: Jerry Hale, Jimmy Dan Conner, and Mike Flynn. Standing: Dick Parsons, Steve Lochmueller, Bob Guyette, G. J. Smith, Kevin Grevey, and Joe B. Hall.

during the 13-13 year," Hall said. "From a very small team, we were able, with the addition of either Robey or Phillips to the lineup, to go to a very good-sized team with good strong guards, the big forward, the quick forward, and the big, powerful post man.

The key to UK's success that season would be team depth that gave Hall the freedom to interchange personnel without sacrificing fine team play. Having three big men at center would allow each to be more aggressive and to give a concentrated

effort without worrying about getting into foul trouble. Moving Guyette to forward also gave the Wildcats a strong one-two punch on the boards and took a lot of pressure off Grevey, allowing him to become a quick forward, almost a swing man, in Hall's offensive system.

The low and high points of that season would center around games with a fine Indiana team led by Kent Benson, a sophomore center whom Hall had followed halfway around the world in an unsuccessful recruiting venture two summers ago.

But before that first eventful meeting with Bobby Knight's Hoosiers, the Wildcats routed Northwestern, 97-70, displaying a "pressure" defense that caused 20 Northwestern turnovers in the first half and 10 in the second. Thirty-two fouls were called against UK. Northwestern coach Tex Winter observed that the Wildcats had the depth to play the physical side of defense. That would become more apparent as the season rolled along, and the big, bruising Wildcats would be accused of playing "karate" defense.

Miami was leading UK, 10-0, at Oxford when Guyette made a three-point play. Kentucky got its game together and won 80-73. Guyette hit five of six from the field and seven of eight from the line to pace the victory.

The humiliating thing about a 98-74 licking by Indiana at Bloomington in early December was not only the score but also the manner in which Benson literally whipped the young Wildcat centers and a courtside incident that had Knight cuffing Joe Hall on the back of the head.

In that game UK had fallen behind, 12-3, at the start, closed it to 14-11, and then had fallen steadily. Benson scored 26 points, got 12 rebounds, and at one point threw a forearm to Robey's jaw. "That's the way it goes," Robey told him. "You're a little older than me. I'm going to learn those tactics."

"He tried to push me around and he's a lot stronger than me," Benson said. "I got tired of it. When I was a freshman, someone taught me a lesson in the same way. I had to get him off my back."

The battle of the big men took a back seat that game to the exchange between Hall and Knight. The incident involving the two coaches occurred in the closing two minutes of the game, when Knight got up and walked in front of the UK bench to protest a foul called on IU sub Steve Ahlfield for charging UK's Hale.

"The start of it was that we were getting beat very badly and had resigned ourselves to that defeat," Hall said. "There was just no way we could get our team back to playing the style of ball they would have to play to be respectable in that game. We were very relaxed on the bench, just waiting for the clock to run out, knowing we would just have to start another day. Many of our starters were on the bench, in foul trouble. The ratio was something like 20 fouls against us to eight against IU.

We felt very much like the game had been called closely against us, and many of the very rough fouls committed by Indiana had been ignored. It was that type of a situation.

"On that particular call against Ahlfield, Bobby came down in front of our bench and told the official to call them at both ends. This seemed to be a very unusual request, since the foul ratio had been so much in their favor. I applauded Bobby's action and told him, 'That's the way to go.' I didn't do it in an aggressive manner or to cause any agitation, but his proximity to me almost called for some kind of statement. When I did this, he turned and told me to coach my team and he would coach his team."

Since he and Knight were good friends on and off the court, Hall stood up and apologized for his actions, telling Knight he (Hall) had no business speaking to him in that manner and that he had meant no harm by it. As Hall turned to walk away, Knight cuffed him on the back of the head.

"As I turned back around," Hall said, "Bobby was smiling and had his hand out. He said, 'I didn't mean anything by that either,' but I felt that it was a situation where I was taken advantage of before the home crowd and that it was not a friendly pat on the head.

"That was a pivotal game. It woke us up to the physical type of play that we were going to face throughout the season and the fact that we had to give the same kind of effort if we were to win. Going into the next game, against North Carolina, we were still a little stunned from the loss to Indiana. It took about 15 minutes for us to find out where we were and what style of ball we were to play the rest of the year."

The Wildcats were down, 31-16, in the North Carolina game when Hall called time out and benched four of his starters. "They sat on the bench," Joe said, "watched what was happening to our team, and finally decided this was not going to be that kind of season. When they returned to the game, Jimmy Dan sparked us with his best game ever."

During the last eight minutes of the first half and the opening minutes of the second half, Conner went on a spree that helped the 'Cats outscore the Tar Heels, 26-3. He finished with 35 points as the Wildcats won, 90-78.

Hall used 14 players in a 100-63 victory over Kansas, with Grevey scoring 29 points. Larry Johnson was the hero of a 113-96 win over Notre Dame, hitting seven of nine shots and playing a fine defensive game during 23 minutes of action.

The Wildcats would tie mighty Alabama for the conference crown, but not without many difficult moments. Tennessee overcame a 14-point deficit in Lexington to deadlock the game at 67-all with 8:29 to play, but UK held the Vols scoreless for six minutes and eventually won, 88-82. Dan Hall, who had played a total of eight minutes in UK games up to that time, saw six minutes of action in the second half, scoring four points, getting four rebounds, and giving Guyette an assist. Givens hit six of eight shots and all six of his free throws and got five rebounds.

Auburn beat UK, 90-85, as freshman Mike Mitchell, a 6-foot-8 forward, scored 31 points and got 15 rebounds at Auburn. Grevey hit three foul shots in the last 22 seconds to lift UK over Alabama, 74-69, and tie the Tide for the conference lead. Conner hit two free throws with five seconds left to give UK a 91-90 win over Vanderbilt in Nashville.

Against LSU in Baton Rouge, UK was leading, 77-76, in the dying seconds when Tiger freshman Doug Saylor's shot from 40 feet dipped in, then popped out of the basket. Grevey hit 15 of 21 from the field, and seven of eight from the line and got 10 rebounds in a revenge victory over Auburn, 119-76, as UK won its ninth game in a row.

A flying orange hit Joe Hall in the back of the head during the second half of a game at Knoxville, but the Vols were rougher than their fans, beating UK, 103-98. It was the first time UT had ever scored 100 points or more against UK. After beating Ole Miss, the Wildcats overcame a 12-point second-half deficit to subdue Alabama, 84-79. Grevey was benched 15 minutes in the first half, but returned to spark the 'Cats to victory.

Florida utilized a series of steals and layups late in the game to beat UK, 66-58, and Alabama beat Georgia that night to regain the conference lead. Phillips scored 26 points in a 109-84 victory over Vanderbilt. Only Mississippi State remained, and UK still trailed Alabama.

"We went into that final game needing a loss by Alabama and a win by us over Mississippi State to tie for the conference championship," Hall recalled. "We were in Starkville in the afternoon of the Auburn-Alabama game, which was on television. Our players were in the motel and, against the orders of the coach, watched the game part of the time. They just could not restrain themselves from sneaking a peek during their rest period late in the afternoon. There was a lot of celebrating in the motel after Auburn beat Alabama that afternoon."

Many Wildcat fans speculated that UK would benefit by losing to Mississippi State and not have to stay in the Mideast and face Marquette and Indiana. However, the Wildcats discounted such talk and played one of their finest games of the entire year, defeating Mississippi State, 118-80.

It was the 29th time UK had won or tied for the league crown. Hall was signed to a four-year extension of his contract through 1980. The Wildcats had more than made up for their dismal showing of the preceding year.

The Slaughterhouse Five

In the Wildcat locker room at Dayton, Ohio, shortly before the tipoff for the 1975 NCAA Mideast Regional championship basketball game against arch-enemy Indiana, the UK players took off their warmup jackets, drank some water, sat down on their benches, and had a brief discussion about defensive assignments and offensive strategy.

Then Joe Hall went to the blackboard and wrote:
NETS!
BUS!
POLICE!
COLISEUM!

As the confused players looked at each other and then back to the board, Hall explained:

"NETS—I want you to be careful that no one gets cut or falls off the ladder as we cut down the nets after the game.

"BUS—We will all ride back on the bus to Lexington.

"POLICE—We will pick up the Kentucky State Police escort as we cross the Ohio River.

"COLISEUM—We will go to the Coliseum for a victory celebration."

The Wildcats that afternoon were facing a Hoosier team that had annihilated and embarrassed them in Bloomington in December and had gone on to finish the regular season undefeated and ranked No. 1 nationally. The Hoosiers had a winning margin of better than 23 points over all foes and were a solid 12-point choice over the Wildcats.

Kentucky had advanced to the regional final by defeating Marquette in Tuscaloosa and Central Michigan in Dayton, while

Indiana had easily disposed of Texas El Paso in Lexington and Oregon State at Dayton.

Before the IU-OSU game, Hall had predicted that the Beavers would beat Indiana, a prognostication that got quite a bit of attention nationwide. He based the prediction on the fact that Oregon State had defeated Indiana the preceding year, and the Beavers had pretty much the same personnel returning. In addition, he felt that the pressure of an undefeated season was building up on the Hoosiers and that they were possibly looking past Oregon State to the finals of the NCAA and even to the national championship.

"Oregon State had the personnel to match Indiana," he said. "It was also a psychological approach on my part to excite the Indiana players, to have them give a psychological effort against Oregon State, and also to let our players know that I didn't feel that Indiana was invincible, that it was possible they could be beaten. I wanted to get that idea in our players' heads at the start."

The UK players had been looking forward to a rematch with Indiana ever since they and their coach had had such a rough time at Bloomington. Hall called it "a great desire on the part of our players to have the game played over and a real desire to redeem our reputation and show that we were deserving of the recognition we had received during the year."

Kevin Grevey said the players who came to UK with him would unanimously agree that the game with Indiana was the most important in their four years at UK. "Many things led up to this," he said. "Kentucky and Indiana has been quite a rivalry, and it just seemed like we could never beat them—in football, basketball, swimming, or anything. (UK beat the Hoosiers in football that fall for the first time since 1918.) That was true up to our senior year. They demolished us in Bloomington and we had to get even for that, and we also had to get by them to go on to the NCAA finals. We knew this, and we wanted to pay them back for what they did to us."

Grevey said that against Indiana the 'Cats had two choices—"Play our game, which we had tried at Bloomington and got beat, or go out there and play their game. I mean rugged defense and playing with reckless abandon, as Coach Hall says quite a bit. This was going to be more important than any game I had ever played."

Hall knew that by the very nature of the players involved,

the game had to be a physical contest. "Indiana is a team that plays with intimidation and we had to meet that intimidation with the same type courage they displayed," he said. "It might even be said that the game would go to the team that maintained its courage and poise."

He explained UK's defensive strategy: "Indiana set a pick on the baseline and ran their good-shooting forwards in behind the screen. If the defense went over the top, sometimes that pick would take a step up, causing you to lose a step or two on your man. He would catch the ball and drive the baseline for an easy basket. If you went baseline side of the pick, the cutter would then turn and come back over the pick and into the middle of the lane to get his shot.

"The main move in defensing this offensive pattern was to avoid that pick. We told our players, 'If it's a moving screen, you have to go on and make contact with it so the referee will call it.' Indiana had four or five offensive picks called against them. It inhibited their offensive screening when they found that the officials would call this pick and we were able to fight over or get to our man."

Grevey said the Wildcats avoided the moving picks by just moving their bodies into the Hoosiers and "checking them like you do in football...You'd go with your arms and check your man in the chest," he said. "Just knock him away. Of course, we were called for this a few times, which let them shoot a few free throws, but over a 40-minute period they weren't going to get their 20 or 25 layups. I'm sure many will say this was probably one of the roughest college basketball games that they had ever seen. I'm sure we can attest to that with all our bruises. I felt I was never more drained after a game, both emotionally and physically. It was one of the roughest I had ever played in. I felt like I was playing for (UK football coach) Fran Curci's Wildcats."

The Indiana defense included great half-court pressure and also a "deep sag," something you do not cope with by coming down and setting up, Hall said. At least, no one all year was able to. That was why he emphasized what he called "our early offenses." This consisted of trying to run out and achieve some penetration before IU was set up on defense, then firing up the open 15-foot shot with the big men going to the boards. Hall's chief concern offensively was in moving the ball away from Indiana's great pressure as the Wildcats ran their patterns.

On the day before the game, Hall had taken Conner and Flynn aside and told them, "You guys just keep on shooting. If you shoot five times and miss, then go out and put up five more shots."

Indiana took an 8-2 lead and later increased that to 38-31, but the Wildcats tied the score, 44-44, at halftime. The Hoosiers had gotten the ball twice in a row with a one-point lead and the chance to go ahead by three but were unable to score. Knight later said that was a vital factor in the game.

Midway in the second half, the lead had changed hands four times in five minutes when Phillips hit a turnaround bank shot to put UK ahead 69-68 at 8:37. Then IU's Benson, who would win most valuable player honors after a magnificent 33-point, 23-rebound performance, was called for a moving pick. Conner put up a 24-footer for a 71-68 UK lead. During the next three and one-half minutes, or until 4:22 remained, UK outscored IU, 14-7, for an 85-75 lead. That spurt included an interception, a defensive rebound, two free throws, and a 12-foot jumper by Robey; two line-drive jumpers by Grevey, and a brilliant driving one-hand flip shot by Johnson, another turnaround by Phillips, and another 25-footer by Conner.

Benson drew an intentional foul for elbowing Robey in the chest, and a technical was called on Green for slapping Johnson on the leg after Johnson had beaten him to a loose ball. Indiana fought back with three baskets and two free throws by Benson and two jump shots by Laskowski. With five seconds remaining, Conner broke open for an inbounds pass, and by the time IU's Wayne Radford could foul him (starting the second of two brief fights in the game), only one second remained. Conner missed the free throw, but time ran out immediately after Indiana rebounded the ball. UK won, 92-90.

Flynn hit six of six field goal attempts in the second half for a team-high 22 points and the honor of cutting the last strand of the net. Conner and Grevey scored 17 points each.

Robert Marcus of the *Chicago Tribune* wrote, "It took the Slaughterhouse Five to end Indiana's dream of glory. The Kentucky Wildcats played like five guys who make their living sledge hammering steers in a stockyard Saturday to earn their greatest basketball victory in a decade.

"It's unlikely that any other team or any other style could have managed the awesome job. There was a touch of madness to Kentucky's method. This was a team driven by anger and

revenge. These twin passions—plus a pair of hot-shooting guards—were too much for even the unbeaten Hoosiers, all year long the top-ranked team in the country and the favorite to win the NCAA crown.

"This was not a typical Kentucky basketball team. You do not expect to get butchered on the boards when you play Kentucky. You expect them to go around and over you, not right through you."

Hall would note later that all the things he wrote on the blackboard before the game had come true. "We were careful and nobody got hurt cutting down the nets," he said. "The Kentucky State Police picked us up as we crossed the Ohio River, then we picked up the Scott County Sheriff's Department escort, then the Metro Police, and finally the UK Campus Police. It was the most exciting ride ever from Dayton to Lexington. The sides of the roads were crowded with people who were waving enthusiastically and holding up signs recognizing our win over Indiana. At the Coliseum, the players were mobbed by fans and autograph seekers."

The NCAA finals and a trip to San Diego were almost an anticlimax after the victory over top-ranked Indiana, so much so that there was concern as to how the UK players would get "up" for the finals.

Kentucky's first foe in San Diego was Syracuse, a very sound ball club with good inside strength, a fine outside shooting guard, and quickness. However, the Orangemen, no match for UK's strength, fell behind, 44-32, at halftime and were out of the game after the Wildcats scored the first 10 points of the second half.

In the other game, UCLA beat Louisville, 75-74, in overtime after a Louisville player missed a foul shot in the dying seconds of regulation time.

The national finals had suddenly become a classic match of tradition and pride between UK and UCLA. The UCLA Bruins had won nine NCAA championships in the past 11 years while the Wildcats had won four, giving the two teams 13 of the 36 titles since NCAA competition began. On the Sunday before the final game between the two teams, Bruin coach John Wooden

Mike Flynn cuts the last strand of the net after UK's big victory over Indiana in the 1975 NCAA Mideast Regional.

announced that he would retire after that game.

"That was a big psychological boost to the UCLA team and their cause," said Joe Hall, who jokingly announced that his seniors—Conner, Flynn, Grevey, Guyette, Hale, and Smith—would retire after the game.

The following morning Wooden made an exception of practicing on the day of a game. He had his players walk through their high post offense, which he planned to substitute for the low post series they had used most of the season. After watching the Wildcats play, Wooden had figured that the UK forwards would be overplaying and leaning on Bruin center Richard Washington. (Washington would score 28 points and earn most valuable player honors.)

"I felt if we moved out to a five-point lead early in the first half," he said, "their leaning would be detected (by the officials) more easily, and we would also have more room to maneuver."

Hall said the "stage was set" in the game with the Bruins when the UK centers picked up some early fouls. "Even though we moved out to a five-point lead early in the first half," he said, "we could see we were headed for trouble as both Robey and Phillips got in early foul trouble. For a long time in the game, we were reduced to our 13-13 squad, with Bob Guyette at center. This made a big difference as UCLA was a very talented as well as a big club with people like Washington (6-9), and Drollinger (7-1), who played very well, and that turned out to be the difference. Andre McCarter was a fine penetrator who got 14 assists."

The Bruins forged ahead by 70-61 with nine minutes to play, but the Wildcats cut it to 74-73. Dave Meyers hit two free throws and Grevey hit a 20-footer with 6:45 to play. Twenty seconds later, Meyers tried an unlikely 20-footer and was called for a foul after coming down on Grevey. The All-American Bruin slapped his palm on the floor and said, "Dammit!" "That's a technical," the official said. Grevey was awarded a one-plus-one; he would shoot the technical foul, and UK would get the ball out of bounds for a possible five-point play.

"Both of Grevey's free throw attempts rimmed in and out, almost in the exact same pattern," Hall noted later, "and on the out-of-bounds series, we were called for an offensive pick on the baseline and didn't get a shot at the basket. So a possible five points dwindled to nothing, and UCLA went down the floor and scored, pulling out to a three-point lead, whereas we could have gone out to a four-point lead at that time. The inability to cash in on that opportunity hurt us quite a bit." Two minutes later, the Bruins built their lead to five points, 82-77, and went on to win, 92-85.

"The game was played hard," Hall said. "I don't think there was any doubt about the tremendous effort our players gave and after we viewed the game on film, we see what a tremendous game they played, and we can only say that UCLA played a better game. They had a great motivation to win, and it was one of the finest games that we had seen them play that season."

Although they had finished second, the Wildcats returned to a hero's welcome in the Coliseum. Signs proclaimed, "Super Play, Super Cats."

"They'll always be No. 1 in our hearts," Harry Lancaster told the gathering. "Right?"

The crowd exploded in agreement.

Joe Hall holds the game ball after UK's victory over Indiana in the 1975 Mideast Regional.

A New Identity

As Eastern Airlines Flight 504, a DC-9 bound for Newark International Airport, took off from Lexington's Blue Grass Field at 8:07 a.m. Tuesday, March 9, 1976, the author leaned back, closed sleep-deprived eyes, hoped for a quick cup of coffee, and let his mind dwell on what had been a most unusual basketball season at the University of Kentucky.

Less than 10 hours earlier, the Wildcats had closed their 25th and final year in Memorial Coliseum with one of the most exciting games ever played in "The House That Rupp Built." The opponent was Mississippi State, whose old crackerbox gym had been laid to rest a year earlier as the Wildcats defeated the Bulldogs, 118-80, in the final game of the regular season for both teams. Kentucky had then advanced to the finals of the NCAA Tournament while State coach Kermit Davis recruited some fine freshmen before moving into sparkling new Humphrey Coliseum and dedicating himself, among other things, to returning the "favor" when the Bulldogs traveled to Lexington the following year.

State brought to that last game in Memorial Coliseum a 13-12 record that included a 77-73 victory over the Wildcats at Starkville. After losing to the Bulldogs, the Wildcats had struggled to a 10-10 record and then won five in a row before meeting the Bulldogs again. Their biggest victory had come on the Saturday before that final game, when they defeated eventual conference champion Alabama, 90-85, in a game televised nationally from the Coliseum and were invited to the NIT.

Considering all factors, it was inconceivable to Kentuckians that Mississippi State could win the final game in an arena where UK teams had won 308 of 346 games. As a reminder of that heritage, the university invited members of the 1951 NCAA championship team, the first team to play in the Coliseum, to attend the game as its guests. Among the players introduced before the State game and applauded by almost 14,000 people were All-Americans Cliff Hagan, Frank Ramsey, and Bill Spivey; All-SEC players Bob Watson and Shelby Linville; and former coaches Rupp and Lancaster, who were invited to sit on the UK bench.

While Wildcat fans settled back for the anticipated slaughter, Mississippi State calmly overcame an early 8-2 deficit, took control in the final minute of the first half, and went to the

Adolph Rupp waves to the crowd after he and members of the 1950-51 UK basketball team are introduced before the final Wildcat game in Memorial Coliseum March 8, 1976. With Rupp (from left) are Cliff Hagan, Frank Ramsey, Bob Watson, Guy Strong, Bill Spivey, Lou Tsioropoulos, Shelby Linville, Dwight Price, Bobby Moore, Harry Lancaster, and Mrs. Bernie E. Shively.

dressing room with a 50-42 lead. Kentucky tried valiantly to catch up, but State led by seven points (82-75) with two minutes remaining and seemed so much in command that three State players were interviewed by the State radio network during a time out. In addition to explaining how MSU had upset the Wildcats, one of the players exclaimed ecstatically, "Hey, Mom! We won!" Cawood Ledford, radio "Voice of the Wildcats," also literally threw in the towel, telling his vast audience at the 1:23 mark that "Kentucky has gone down in flames."

At that point the Bulldogs led, 84-77, and UK was playing without James Lee, who had fouled out, and Mike Phillips, who had been ejected after kicking himself loose from a tangle with a fallen Bulldog. That left the Wildcats with their "runts" lineup of Haskins, Givens, Fowler, Johnson, and Warford, which somehow managed to scrap back and tie the game at 85-85 with seven seconds on the clock. The Bulldogs missed the final shot, and the game went into overtime. Johnson started hitting from long range and made two free throws to give UK a 94-91 lead

UK coach Joe Hall presents the game ball to Adolph Rupp after the Wildcats defeat Mississippi State in the last Wildcat game to be played in Memorial Coliseum.

with 52 seconds left, State got an unchallenged layup, and that was the game—UK 94, MSU 93.

After the crowd departed, Athletics Director Cliff Hagan suggested that the author attend a press conference in Madison Square Garden's Hall of Fame Room at noon of the following day, since Hall would be unable to attend because of recruiting commitments. Arrangements for the early flight out of Lexington were surprisingly easy, and it was just a matter of getting information and pictures together while Jack Perry, the assistant SID who would travel to New York later with the team, and secretary Ann Easterling updated and duplicated the statistics. The press package was completed shortly after midnight.

During the minutes of half sleep as the plane finished its climb and leveled off, the passenger first organized in his mind the chronological events leading up to the trip to New York. From the very beginning, during speeches made throughout the Commonwealth of Kentucky in November and early December, he had warned Wildcat fans not to expect too much of a basketball team that had lost six fine seniors, including starters Grevey, Flynn, Conner, and Guyette, and had also lost a prime signee when Bill Willoughby of New Jersey inked a professional contract with the Atlanta Hawks. That left only newcomers Pat Foschi, a guard from Minnesota who would quit the squad before the season began; Bob Fowler, a high-jumping forward from Michigan; Dwane Casey, a 6-foot-2 guard who had been a teammate of Larry Johnson at Union County High; and Truman Claytor, a late signee at guard from Toledo, to bolster the weakened Wildcats.

The Wildcats lost to Northwestern, 89-77, at Evanston and to North Carolina, 90-77, at Charlotte and defeated Miami at home and Kansas on the road before traveling to Freedom Hall for a game that Indiana had been awaiting eagerly since the undefeated 1975 Hoosiers lost to UK in the Mideast Regional finals at Dayton.

Despite the presence of All-Americans Kent Benson and Scott May and a host of other talented players who would lead the Hoosiers to an undefeated season and the NCAA championship, the Wildcats fought the No. 1-ranked Hoosiers to a standstill and were ahead by two points when Larry Johnson missed a driving shot and Indiana rebounded with seconds left. The Hoosiers got off a quick shot that bounced off the mark, but Benson came through with a miraculous tip at 0:09 that sent the game into overtime. Indiana's superior forces took control, and the Hoosiers won, 77-68, in what Dave Kindred called "possibly the best played game ever in Freedom Hall." Bobby Knight told the Wildcats they were the most aggressive team his Hoosiers had played.

Kentucky defeated Georgia Tech and Oregon State in the UKIT and Notre Dame in Louisville, where Truman Claytor shared MVP honors with Adrian Dantley and took a 4-4 record into the opening conference game in Mississippi State's new arena. Rick Robey received a thigh bruise during that game and then suffered a knee sprain in the second half of a loss to Alabama two nights later in Tuscaloosa. He would miss the next three games, play in two games, and then reinjure the knee in practice and be declared out of action for the season.

Tennessee came to Lexington ranked No. 9 in the nation. The Vols were undefeated in SEC play and seeking their first win in the Coliseum since 1967, the year they won their only outright conference title while UK was having a dismal 13-13 season. Leading them were high-scoring sophomores Ernie Grunfeld (25.3 ppg) at a wing and Bernard King (25.1 ppg) at the high post. Other starters were Doug Ashworth at the low post, freshman John Darden at the point, and Mike Jackson at a wing.

With 9:47 to go in the first half, James Lee was called for fouling Irv Chatman. Grunfeld, at the time the fourth-leading foul shooter in the league, brazenly stepped to the line and made both shots on a bonus situation. Seven minutes later Mike Phillips was called for climbing King's back. As the teams walked to the other end of the floor, Grunfeld engaged King in animated conversation, and Grunfeld wound up with the ball and two more points on free throws as the Vols went into halftime with a 43-42 lead. In the first instance, at least two UK security people—Jim Jones and Dick Derrickson—stationed on or near press row kept telling the referees that the wrong man was shooting the free throws. Hall and his staff did not detect the switches at the time, but a UK fan informed Hall at halftime that Grunfeld had taken shots for Chatman and King. Hall then told the officials, Don Wedge and Red Struthers, that Grunfeld had made free throws that were not due him. Wedge in turn told Grunfeld, who denied the accusation, that he had better not try anything like that again.

Kentucky bounced back and went ahead, 75-61, with

seven minutes to play, but the Vols cut that to four points with 1:36 to go and tied the score, 79-79, after Clark stole the ball from Claytor and hit King on a lead pass for a crip. Tennessee got possession again and went ahead by two after Clark lofted a high pass to King, who caught the ball near the top of the board, fell backward, and flicked the ball upward and into the basket just before his back hit the floor. Haskins scored a layup with one second remaining to send the game into overtime. Kentucky scored first in overtime, but a three-point play by Grunfeld with 3:44 to go gave the Vols a lead they never relinquished. They were ahead by two when Givens missed the final shot of the game.

On his television show the following night, Hall showed film clips of Grunfeld first talking to Chatman and then to King before taking the foul shots not due him. "The evidence is clear and obvious," Hall said. "I thought it should be exposed." During the exchange of charges, denials, and bruised feelings between Lexington and Knoxville, Vols coach Mears added fuel to the fire by saying, "It is not unusual for a taller man to step in on a jump ball or a better foul shooter to go to the line in place of a fellow player." Since a protest in such a case must be made before the shooting team gets its next possession of the ball, UK had nothing to gain except the exposure of Grunfeld's antics.

Between that game and the return meeting with Tennessee at Knoxville, the Wildcats defeated Georgia and Vanderbilt at home and Florida in tough "Alligator Alley" at Gainesville, lost in overtime at Auburn, and defeated Mississippi and LSU at home. In the nationally televised game with Vanderbilt, the Commodores' Jeff Fosnes tied the score, 72-72, with 3:10 to go, and John Sneed put the Commodores ahead with a follow shot 30 seconds later. Larry Johnson scored a three-point play, but Vanderbilt regained the lead at 76-75 on Joe Ford's jumper at 1:40. Thirty seconds remained on the clock when Dicky Keffer swiped a Phillips' pass intended for Warford, ran it down, and, followed by Warford, dribbled downcourt and veered to the right for a crip shot. Warford timed his jump perfectly and got just enough fingernail on the ball to thwart the shot. After Sneed missed a followup, Johnson grabbed the ball, dribbled up court, and hit a 15-foot jump shot with 13 seconds remaining for the UK victory.

The UK-LSU game in the Coliseum was spiced by what

LSU coach Dale Brown offers his coat to official Reggie Copeland and then throws it on the floor during the second half of the UK-LSU game March 1, 1976, in Memorial Coliseum.

Mike Sullivan of the *Courier-Journal* called a "Big Blow-Up" that occurred with 4 minutes and 19 seconds left in the first half and LSU ahead, 29-21. Kenny Higgs had driven for a layup and was fouled by Larry Johnson, which resulted in Johnson drawing a technical foul for giving Higgs a push after they both stumbled out of bounds. Hall exploded off the bench to protest both the absence of an offensive goal-tending call on Bailey and

a signal that the bucket had been credited to Higgs. Hall was issued a technical, and Higgs sank three free throws (one for Johnson's personal foul on the shot, another for Johnson's technical, and a third for Hall's technical) to complete a five-point play and put LSU on top, 34-21.

Kentucky slashed the lead to 44-40 and trailed for the last time in the game at 58-56 with 13:34 to go. In the next six minutes, Phillips scored 10 of his game-high 35 points to help put UK ahead, 71-62, with 6:47 left in the game. It was then that Brown walked to midcourt, offered his suit coat to official Reggie Copeland, and said, "You better coach 'em." When Copeland refused the coat, Brown deposited it in the jump-

Wildcat coach Joe Hall makes a point to an official while LSU coach Dale Brown strikes a pensive expression during the UK-LSU game March 1, 1976, in Memorial Coliseum.

circle at midcourt and returned to his seat, having earned two technicals. After the game Brown went into the officials' dressing room and accused Copeland and Ken Lauderdale of letting themselves be intimidated by Hall. An officer ushered Brown out of the room.

The UK-LSU rhubarb was just a tune-up for the second meeting of the season between Kentucky and Tennessee, this time before regional television cameras at Knoxville. Perhaps Rick Bailey of the *Herald-Leader* best explained what transpired:

> The bizarre became routine. The simple became complicated. The sidelights became highlights.
>
> Tennessee defeated Kentucky 82-75 here yesterday in what was supposed to be a college basketball game. It was, instead, an experiment in pressure for all concerned. Any resemblance of sanity was purely coincidental.
>
> Among the disquieting incidents to challenge the

most discriminating of basketball fans were these:

A semi-fight between UT's Johnny Darden and UK's Truman Claytor. Both left the game with 3:11 to play in the first half. They committed two of the seven technical fouls.

Herald-Leader photographers E. Martin Jessee and Frank Anderson who were ordered from the scene at the same time by irate Knoxville policemen. The cameramen were snapping some of the extra-curricular activities when Anderson was forcibly removed. Jessee followed, shooting pictures of the incident, and was evicted, too.

Kentucky coach Joe Hall calling timeout—and being called for a technical foul by official Reggie Copeland. This came after Mike Phillips was fouled by UT's Bernard King.

Hall drew the technical after he complained to Copeland that Givens had been called for a charge at the UK end of the floor but that the same play had gone uncalled when UT had the ball on their end. Five technicals were called before halftime, two more after that. After one technical each was dealt to freshmen Darden and Claytor for their scuffle, police swarmed around the scorer's table as officials, coaches, and players tried to restore order. Anderson and Jessee were in the middle of the scene, shooting pictures, when the officers began to forcibly evict Anderson. Tennessee officials later vindicated the officers, causing the Knoxville daily newspapers to return their photo passes for the remaining three UT home games. Objections also were raised by such organizations as the Professional Photographers' Association, Associated Press Sports Editors, and the National Press Association.

Other technicals in that game were assessed Hall and Mears because of their vehement objections to the officials' calls, to Grunfeld for protesting a foul call against him, and to Phillips for saying things the referees did not care to hear on two occasions. The game was tied, 48-48, at halftime, with Phillips scoring 18 of the Wildcat points. However, the Vols collapsed their defenses on the big center, held him to a single field goal in the second half, and won, 92-85.

The Wildcats blew a big lead two nights later and were upset by Georgia at Athens. Hall closed practice the remainder of the week and worked the Wildcats hard before taking them to Nashville, where they rallied gamely but lost to Vanderbilt by four points.

"That was the turning point of the season," Jack Givens would say later. "We finally learned after the Vandy game what it took to win. Before that, we'd have some good practices and some bad ones. When the coach got on us, we'd take it personally. But after the Vandy game, our whole attitude changed. We became unselfish and all of a sudden we started to find the open man. We certainly did not want to go down in history as the first Kentucky team in a thousand years to have a losing season."

With no All-Americans or recognized superstars, the Wildcats seemingly had little going for them in New York except tradition and the fact that they were returning to Madison Square Garden for the first time since the university had placed a ban on its teams playing there after some Wildcat players were involved in the gambling scandals of the early 1950s. That ban had been lifted four years earlier, but UK had been involved in the NCAA tournament two of those years and had a record (13-13) that was not attractive to any tournament committee the other year.

The NIT officials and New York seemed glad to have Kentucky back in their basketball midst, but from the very beginning the city belonged to Lee Rose and his previously unheard-of 49ers from the University of North Carolina at Charlotte. Rose had left Lexington only one year earlier to set up housekeeping at Charlotte after a successful career at Transylvania University. At one point in time, when Joe Hall left UK to take the head coaching job at St. Louis, Rupp had placed the name of Rose at the top of his list. Hall reversed his decision after a few days, and Rose preferred to remain at Transylvania rather than be a second assistant coach, as he had once been at the University of Cincinnati. Rose's Kentucky connections went even further. A native of West Irvine, he had learned the game from coaches who played for Rupp, he and Hall both attended Crestview Christian Church in Lexington, and his assistants at Charlotte were former UK star Mike Pratt and former Transylvania star Everett Bass.

During the course of a 21-5 season, the 49ers had defeated such teams as Vanderbilt and Florida. Another strong point in their favor was the fact that North Carolina State had defeated them by only three points and Maryland by only 10 points. The

NIT selection committee also was apparently very impressed with the handsome, personable, straight-talking coach from Charlotte who featured such fine players as Cedric "Cornbread" Maxwell, Melvin "Bionic" Watkins, Bob Ball, and Lew Massey.

While Rose and his team represented a school that had been in existence only a decade, Kentucky offered a direct contrast, bringing to town a tradition that included the most wins by a major college basketball team and the recognized leader in winning percentage over a 50-year period. In addition, Adolph Rupp, "Der Baron" himself, was part of the Kentucky delegation, and it was only natural that the New York press corps would gravitate to Rupp at the beginning, dwelling mostly on the gambling scandals and the reasons Kentucky had not returned to New York sooner.

"I would have come back before," Rupp told them, "if they (the Athletics Board) would have let me." When asked if he would be worried about the gamblers, he answered, "I'm hopeful that everybody realizes how the situation is there. They're going to be aware of it, rather than be caught as coaches were in those days."

In the initial pairings, Kentucky was to open the tournament against Niagara while Providence played Carolina A&T. The winners of those two games were to play seeded teams Kansas State and Louisville, respectively, which meant that the Kentucky-Louisville matchup so desperately sought by some factions in Kentucky could become a reality. The same possibility had existed the previous year, when both UK and UL were in the Final Four in San Diego. However, for the second year in a row, Louisville would lose and miss its chance to play the Wildcats.

The main factors in a 67-61 UK victory over Niagara were Kentucky's 1-3-1 zone defense and James Lee, who scored 20 points and eight rebounds. Kentucky went into the zone within two minutes of the start of the game and used it through the rest of the first half. The Wildcats broke out of a 17-17 tie midway of the period and outscored Niagara, 16-3, within a five-minute span to build a 13-point lead.

After starting the second half in a man-to-man defense, the Wildcats went back to the 1-3-1 when Phillips picked up his fourth personal less than four minutes into the period. Niagara, which trailed by nine points at the half, was within two with 10 minutes to go. But reserves Fowler and Claytor made key offensive plays in succession as UK pulled out to a 15-point lead and held on to win.

Kansas State featured one of the nation's fine guard tandems in Chuckie Williams and Mike Evans, whose bombing from outside led a KSU second-half assault that had UK reeling, 56-47, before Merion Haskins scored a layup to end a five-minute scoring drought. Evans, who hit his 17-point average, had scored one of his long leapers when Hall called for Mike Phillips, who had hurt his ankle with 5:05 left in the first half. Phillips alternated baskets with Johnson as UK roared to 10 straight points while holding State scoreless, slicing the deficit to two points. Phillips and Claytor offset baskets by Williams and Evans, and UK still trailed by one when Williams, the game's top scorer with 27 points, hit a basket at 6:01. He was fouled on the play and missed the gratis toss. Lee pulled down the rebound and later bulled in for two critical baskets, and Phillips added three free throws as UK went on to win, 81-78. Lee led Kentucky with 20 points, Phillips had 17, and Johnson and Givens 15 each. Providence eliminated Louisville, 73-67, that night.

In the semifinal game against Providence, the Wildcats blew to an early 18-point lead and then led twice by 11, but the Friars bounced back each time and finally went ahead, 78-77, with seven seconds to play. Hall called time out and set up a last-ditch play. Warford threw the ball in to Phillips, who stumbled slightly, bobbled the ball a second, and then passed to Johnson, who was cutting toward the free-throw line farthest from the UK basket. According to Hall's instructions, Johnson had the option to find James Lee down low and pass to him. Johnson completely forgot about Lee as he crossed midcourt and reached the top of the free-throw circle with three seconds showing.

"I was looking for white shirts (UK's)," he said, "but I didn't see any, so when I got to the top of the key, I was going all the way. I knew they'd foul me at least. I knew I had to shoot it. I went up (with two seconds remaining) and saw a 'little orange' (color of the rim), but I couldn't see anything else. That dude (Bruce) Campbell (who is six-nine) was up there. So I took it up with two hands. I didn't feel strong enough with just the left hand. Then I shot it with the right. I felt pretty sure it was going in. We've worked on that kind of layup quite a bit."

Although the NIT was playing second fiddle to the NCAA tournaments and drawing its smallest crowds (56,673 for six sessions) since 1940, it was not lacking in excitement. While Kentucky was escaping by the skin of its teeth in the upper bracket, Charlotte was advancing in the same manner in the lower bracket, defeating San Francisco, 79-74; Oregon, 79-72; and North Carolina State by one point to enter a championship game that pitted two teams that no one had expected to be there. Six weeks earlier UK had a 10-10 won-lost record and was looking for ways to avoid its first losing season in 50 years while anonymous Charlotte was on its way to a 21-5 season record. But now UK had won nine straight games, including three in the NIT.

Kentucky had some physical problems entering the game. Phillips' left ankle was still tender from a sprain received five days earlier, and Reggie Warford was wearing a wrap around his ribs for a strained muscle received during pregame warmups in the semifinals. Neither injury was serious. Phillips had played well throughout the tournament, but Warford had failed to score a field goal in any of the games played to date. His total production was three points on free throws.

The stage was set for Warford to bow out in fine style when UK got into serious second-half foul trouble. Givens picked up his fourth foul early in the half, Phillips was charged with his fourth less than a minute later, and Lee was slapped with his fourth violation with 10:37 left. Warford picked up the lag with 10 of his 14 points. His driving left-side layup put UK ahead, 60-59, and his 15-foot jump shot gave the 'Cats a 64-63 advantage, a lead they never relinquished. On that play Maxwell fouled Phillips, who made both free throws.

Melvin Watkins cut the UK lead to 66-65 with 39 seconds left, but two free throws by Johnson restored the three-point edge 17 seconds later. Maxwell again cut the UK lead to a point with 11 seconds remaining. Johnson was fouled two seconds later. His missed free throw bounced to the left and was rebounded and put back in by Phillips, who was fouled on the play. Phillips completed the three-point trip to sew up the championship for the Wildcats.

As the handsome trophy was brought into the UK dressing room, Jack Givens seemed to put things in their proper perspective. "All year long, the press has referred to us as one of the finalists in last season's NCAA Tournament," he said. "Well, the seniors accomplished that, and that's a fact that maybe we've forgotten. Well, this is our own trophy. Now we'll be introduced as the NIT champs. We have an identity of our own."

Appendix

ALL-TIME KENTUCKY CAGE RECORDS
(Revised to Start of 1976-77 Season)
TEAM RECORDS
Season

Most Games Played—39* in 1947-48
    (Regular Season Only—30* in 1946-47)
Most Wins—36*# in 1947-48 (Won 36, Lost 3)
    (Regular Season Only—28* in 1946-47 (Won 28, Lost 2)
    (Conference Play Only—17* in 1969-70
Most Losses—13 in 1926-27 (2-13), 1966-67 (13-13) and 1973-74 (13-13)
    (For Full Season 20 or More Games—13 in 1966-67) and (1973-74)
    (Conference Play Only—10 in 1966-67 (8-10)
Fewest Wins—1 in 1904-05 (Won 1, Lost 4)
    (For Full Season 20 or More Games—13 in 1966-67) and (1973-74)
Fewest Losses—0 in 1911-12 (9-0) and 1953-54 (25-0)
Longest Win Streak—25 in 1953-54 (Won 25, Lost 0)
    (Conference Play Only—14* in 1950-51, 1951-52, 1965-66. Including Play-off Game, Kentucky Won 15 Straight in 1953-54)
Most Consecutive Wins, Conference Play—51* (Jan. 28, 1950-Jan. 8, 1955)
Longest Losing Steak—9 (Jan. 25 to Feb. 23, 1923)
    (Conference Play Only—4 in 1966-67) and (1973-74)
    (Rupp-Coached Teams Have Never Lost More Than 3 in Row)
Most Points—2858 in 31 Games, 1974-75
    Regular Season Only—2523 in 26 Games, 1970-71
    (Conference Play Only—1728* in 18 Games, 1970-71)
    (Most Times 100 or More Points—15 in 1970-71)
    (Two Consecutive Games—244 vs. Georgia and Tennessee, 1956)
Fewest Points—19 in 3 Games, 1903
    (For Full Season 20 or More Games—538 in 22 Games 1924-25)
Greatest Average Scoring Margin—27.2 in 25 Games, 1953-54
    (Including Tournament Play—29.9 in 37 Games, 1946-47)
    (Conference Play Only—35.9* in 14 Games, 1953-54)
Highest Scoring Average—96.8 in 28 Games, 1969-70
    (Regular Season Only—96.7 in 26 Games, 1970-71)
    (Conference Play Only—96.0* in 18 Games, 1970-71)
Lowest Scoring Average—6.3 in 3 Games, 1903
Best Winning Percentage—1.000 in 1911-12 (9-0) and 1953-54 (25-0)
    (Conference Play Only—1.000 in 1932-33 (8-0) and 10 Other Years. Last 14-0 in 1953-54)
Worst Season Percentage—.187 on Record 3-13 in 1926-27
    (20 Games Minimum—.500 (13-13) in 1966-67 and 1973-74)
Most Field Goal Attempts—3645*# in 39 Games, 1947-48
    (Regular Season—2925# in 33 Games, 1947-48)
Most Field Goals Made—1197 in 31 Games, 1974-75
    (Conference Play Only—719* in 18 Games, 1974-75)
Highest Field Goal Pct.—50.6 in 28 Games, 1970-71
    (Regular Season Only—50.8 in 26 Games, 1970-71)
    (Conference Play Only—52.2* in 18 Games, 1970-71)
Most Free Throws Attempted—865 in 32 Games, 1951-52
    (Conference Play Only—425* in 18 Games, 1970-71)
Most Free Throws Made—579 in 28 Games, 1956-57
    (Conference Play Only—320* in 18 Games, 1970-71)

    *Also SEC Record
    **The 1965-66 Wildcat team scored 2,950 points in 25 regular season, four NCAA and five International Universities Tournament games.
    #Recognized As National Record

Highest Free Throw Pct.—76.7 in 26 Games, 1966-67
  (Regular Season Only—76.7 in 26 Games, 1966-67)
Most Personal Fouls—767 in 31 Games, 1974-75
Fewest PF's—307 in 26 Games, 1944-45
Most Points Allowed—2434 in 31 Games, 1974-75
  (Regular Season Only—2175 in 26 Games, 1970-71)
Fewest Points Allowed—(9 Game Min.)—137 in 9 games, 1911-12
  (Conference Play Only—182* in 8 Games, 1934-35)
Most Rebounds—1817* in 32 Games, 1951-52
  (Regular Season Only—1600 in 25 Games, 1950-51)
Best Rebound Average—64.6* in 25 Games, 1953-54
Most Wins in Conference—17* in 1969-70

Single Game

Most Points—143* (Kentucky 143 vs. Georgia 66, Feb. 27, 1956)
  (Conference Play Only—Same)
Most Points, Both Teams—234 Kentucky 118 vs. Northwestern 116 at Evanston, Dec. 10, 1966)
  Conference Play Only—226 (Kentucky 121 vs. LSU 105, Feb. 21, 1970)
Most Points, Home Floor—121 (Kentucky 121 vs. Mississippi 86, Feb. 6, 1971)
Most Points on Opponent's Floor—121 (Kentucky 121 vs. LSU, 95, Jan. 27, 1968; Kentucky 121 vs. LSU, 105, Feb. 21, 1970)
Most Points on Neutral Court—143 (Kentucky 143 vs. Georgia 66, Armory, Louisville, Feb. 27, 1956)
Most Points, One Half—75* (Kentucky 75 vs. Georgia 32, Feb. 27, 1956)
Fewest Points—1 (Kentucky 1 vs. Georgetown 32 in 1903 and vs. Kentucky U 22 in 1905)
  (Conference Play Only—22 Against Tennessee 32, Jan. 18, 1941)
Fewest Points, One Half (Modern)—8 (Kentucky 8, Georgia 6 in First Half, Jan. 16, 1967 Athens)
Fewest Points, Both Teams—17 (State College 5 vs. Kentucky U. 12 in 1904)
Biggest Victory Margin—77* (Kentucky 143 vs. Georgia 66, Feb. 27, 1956)
Smallest Victory Margin—1 (41 One-point Wins. Last, 79-78 Providence (NIT), Mar. 18, 1976
Worst Defeat—68 (Kentucky 19 vs. Centre 87 in 1908-09)
  (CCNY's 39-point Win Over UK in NIT of 1950 Worst Defeat in Modern Records)
Smallest Margin of Defeat—1 (Tennessee 27 vs. Kentucky 26, March 2, 1917)
  (Also on Record are 31 Other One-Point Losses. Last, Ole Miss 61 vs. Kentucky 60, Feb. 18, 1974)
Most Points in Losing Game—100 vs. Jacksonville, 106 (NCAA) March 14, 1970
Fewest Points Allowed—5* (Kentucky 26 vs. Tennessee 5 in 1909-10 and Kentucky 38 vs. Centre 5 in 1916)
  (Conference Play Only—9* Against Tulane, Dec. 20, 1934)
Most Points Allowed—116 (Northwestern 116 vs. Kentucky 118 Dec. 10, 1966)
Most FG Attempted—125* Against Indiana Central, Nov. 29, 1947 (SEC Non-Conference Record); Mississippi, Feb. 8, 1964
  (Conference Play Only—125* Against Mississippi, Feb. 8, 1964)
Most FGA's, Both Teams—209 (Kentucky 125 vs. Mississippi 84, Feb. 8, 1964)
Fewest FG Attempted—39 Against Georgia, Jan. 16, 1967
Fewest FGA One Half—15 (2nd Half) vs. Florida, Jan. 30, 1965
Most Field Goals Scored—60* Against Georgia, Feb. 27, 1956
Most FG's Scored, Both Teams—96 (UK 50 vs. Northwestern 46, Dec. 10, 1966, and UK 50 vs. Austin Peay 46, Mar. 15, 1973)
  Conference Play Only—90* UK 52 vs. LSU 38, Jan. 27, 1968, and UK 48 vs. Alabama 42, Feb. 26, 1973)

  *Also Southeastern Conference Record

Best Field Goal Pct.—65% vs. Florida (H) Feb. 21, 1976 and Auburn (H) Feb. 23, 1976
    (Conference Play Only—65% vs. Florida (H) Feb. 21, 1976 and Auburn (H) Feb. 23, 1976
    (First Half—72.7% vs. LSU, Jan. 24, 1966)
    (Second Half—72.4% vs. Florida (H) Feb. 21, 1976
Lowest Field Goal Percentage—16.3 vs. Ga. Tech (A), Jan. 26, 1960
Most Free Throws Attempted—55* Against Auburn, Feb. 27, 1954. Made 35.
Fewest Free Throws Attempted—2 Against Ga., Feb. 8, 1975.
Most Free Throws Made—48* Against Vanderbilt (A) Jan. 7, 1963. FTA 53.
Fewest Free Throws Made—1 Against Ga., Feb. 8, 1975, in 2 Attempts
Best Free Throw Pct.—1.000 (14 out of 14 vs. Duke, March 3, 1930; 11 out of 11 vs. Alabama, Feb. 1, 1934 and Vanderbilt, Mar. 2, 1974; 9 out of 9 vs. Mississippi, Jan. 4, 1969) 95.5* (21 out of 22 vs. Georgia, Feb. 19, 1973)
Most Rebounds—108* Against Mississippi, Feb. 8, 1964
Most Personal Fouls—41* Against Ohio U., Jan. 12, 1948
    (Conference Play Only—37* (Kentucky vs. Auburn, Feb. 27, 1954)
Most PF's, Both Teams—71* (Kentucky 37 vs. Auburn 34, Feb. 27, 1954)
    (Non-Conference Game—68—Kentucky 41, Ohio U. 27, Jan. 12, 1948)
Fewest PF's Both Teams—17 (Kentucky 7 vs. SMU 10, Dec. 21, 1956)

INDIVIDUAL RECORDS (Season)

Most Points—948 by Dan Issel in 28 Games, 1969-70
    (Regular Season Only—876 by Dan Issel in 26 Games, 1969-70)
    (Conference Play Only—612 by Dan Issel in 18 Games, 1969-70)
    (Soph. Year—608 by Cotton Nash in 26 Games, 1961-62)
Highest Scoring Average—33.9 by Dan Issel in 28 Games, 1969-70
    (Regular Season Only—33.7 by Dan Issel in 26 Games, 1969-70)
    (Conference Play Only—34.0 by Dan Issel in 18 Games, 1969-70)
    (Soph. Year—23.4 by Cotton Nash in 1961-62)
Most Rebounds—528* by Cliff Hagan in 32 Games, 1951-52
    (Regular Season Only—447 by Bill Spivey in 25 Games, 1950-51)
    (Conference Play Only—250 by Cliff Hagan in 14 Games, 1951-52)
Most FG Attempts—667 by Dan Issel in 28 Games, 1969-70
    (Regular Season Only—614 by Dan Issel in 26 Games, 1969-70)
    (Conference Play Only—433 by Dan Issel in 18 Games, 1969-70)
Most Field Goals Made—369 by Dan Issel in 28 Games, 1969-70)
    (Regular Season Only—339 by Dan Issel in 26 Games, 1969-70)
    (Conference Play Only—239 by Dan Issel in 18 Games, 1969-70)
Most Free Throws Attempted—275 by Dan Issel in 28 Games, 1969-70)
    (Regular Season Only—259 by Dan Issel in 26 Games, 1969-70)
    (Conference Play Only—169 by Dan Issel in 18 Games, 1969-70)
Most Free Throws Made—210 by Dan Issel in 28 Games, 1969-70)
    (Regular Season Only—198 by Dan Issel in 26 Games, 1969-70)
    (Conference Play Only—134 by Dan Issel in 18 Games, 1969-70)
    (Consecutive—27 in 6 Games by Louie Dampier, 1966-67)
Highest Field Goal Pct.—57.7 by Jim Andrews in 28 Games, 1971-72
    (Regular Season Only—58.3 by Jim Andrews in 26 Games, 1971-72)
    (Conference Play Only—59.6 by Jim Andrews in 18 Games, 1971-72)
Highest Free Throw Pct.—91.8 by Larry Steele in 23 Games, (45-49) 1969-70
    (Regular Season Only—90.9 by Larry Steele in 21 Games, (40-44) 1969-70)
    (Conference Play Only—90.9 by Kent Hollenbeck in 12 Games (40.44) 1970-71
Most Assists—129 by Mike Casey in 28 Games, 1968-69

    *Also Southeastern Conference Record
    #Recognized As National Record

Single Game

Most Points—53 by Dan Issel (Against Mississippi at Oxford, Feb. 7, 1970)
Most Field Goals Attempted—42 By Bill Spivey (Against Ga. Tech, Feb. 18, 1950. Made 16)
Most Field Goals Made—23 by Dan Issel (Against Mississippi at Oxford, Feb. 7, 1970)
Most Free Throws Attempted—24 By Cliff Hagan (Against Temple, Dec. 5, 1953)
Most Free Throws Made—17 By Cliff Hagan (Against Miss., 1952, and Temple, 1953, and Roger Newman, Ohio State, 1961)
Consecutive Free Throws Made—16* By Cliff Hagan (Against Mississippi, Jan. 2, 1952)
Highest Field Goal Percentage (Min. 10 Made)—Rick Robey 91.7 (11 of 12) against Miami (O.) Dec. 10, 1975
Highest Free Throw Percentage (Min. 10 Made)—1.000 by Louie Dampier (13 of 13 against Florida, Jan. 30, 1965, and 14 of 14 against Oregon State Dec. 22, 1966) 10 other players have 13—1.000% performances. (Min. 15 made)—.944 (17 of 18) by Cliff Hagan against Mississippi, Jan. 2, 1952)
Most Rebounds—34* (SEC non-conference record) by Bob Burrow (Against Temple, Dec. 10, 1955)
Longest Field Goal Made—63 feet, 7½ inches By Cliff Barker (Against Vanderbilt, Feb. 26, 1949 in Alumni Gym). (Other long shots on record include 53 ft., 9½ in. By Ralph Beard Against Tennessee in 1947-48; 53 ft., 6 in. by Linville Puckett Against Miss. State in 1953-54; and 48 ft., 2¼ in. by Red Hagan Against Marquette in 1937-38)

INDIVIDUAL CAREER RECORDS (Varsity Play)

Most Points—2138 by Dan Issel in 83 Games, 1968-70
  (Conference Play Only—1399 by Dan Issel in 54 Games, 1968-70)
Highest Scoring Average—25.7 by Dan Issel, 1968-70
  (Conference Play Only—25.9 by Dan Issel in 54 Games, 1969-70)
Most Games Played—139 by Ralph Beard, 1945-49
  (Conference Play Only—54 by Dan Issel and Mike Pratt, 1968-70, and Jimmy Dan Conner and Mike Flynn, 1972-75)
Most Consecutive Games Started—120 by Alex Groza, Nov. 28, 1946 to March 26, 1949
  (Conference Play Only—54 by Dan Issel and Mike Pratt in 1968-70)
Most Field Goals Attempted—1591 by Dan Issel, 1968-70
  (Conference Play Only—1059 by Dan Issel, 1968-70)
Most Field Goals Made—825 by Dan Issel in 83 Games, 1968-70
  (Conference Play Only—546 by Dan Issel in 54 Games, 1968-70)
Highest FG Pct.—56.3 By Jim Andrews in 80 Games, 1971-73
  (Conference Play Only—56.5 By Jim Andrews in 52 Games, 1971-73
Most Free Throws Attempted—661 by Dan Issel in 83 Games, 1968-70
  (Conference Play Only—405 by Dan Issel in 54 Games, 1968-70)
Most Free Throws Made—488 by Dan Issel in 83 Games, 1968-70
  (Conference Play Only—307 by Dan Issel in 54 Games, 1968-70)
Highest FT Pct.—83.5 by Louie Dampier in 80 Games, 1965-67
  (Conference Play Only—79.3 by Larry Pursiful in 39 Games, 1960-62)
Most Rebounds—1078 by Dan Issel in 83 Games, 1968-70 (No Rebounds kept prior to 1951)
  (Conference Play Only—685 by Dan Issel in 54 Games, 1968-70)
Best Rebound Average—16.1 By Bob Burrow in 51 Games, 1955-56
  (Conference Play Only—17.5 By Bob Burrow in 30 Games, 1955-56)
Most Assists—293 By Larry Conley in 81 Games, 1964-66
Most Personal Fouls—296 By Wallace Jones, 1946-49 (Four Seasons)
  (For 3 Seasons—294 By Pat Riley, 1965-67)

*Also Southeastern Conference Record
#Recognized As National Record

NCAA TOURNAMENT RECORDS

Most Appearances—22# (1942, 1945, 1948, 1949, 1951, 1952, 1955, 1956, 1957, 1958, 1959, 1961, 1962, 1964, 1966, 1968, 1969, 1970, 1971, 1972, 1973, 1975)
Most Points—4184 in 55 Games
Most Games—55#

MISCELLANEOUS RECORDS

Season Opener Consecutive Wins—34
  (Kentucky lost first opening game since 1926 in defeat by Va. Tech, Dec. 1, 1962)
Consecutive Home Floor Wins—129# (Jan. 4, 1943 to Jan. 8, 1955)
  (First 84 wins in Alumni Gym, remainder in Memorial Coliseum)
  (Conference Play Only—70 from Jan. 21, 1939 to Jan. 8, 1955)
  (Overall since 1943, Kentucky has been defeated on its home floor only 38 times)
  (Most losses at home one season—7 in 1966-67)
Longest Winning Streak—32 (Dec. 5, 1953 to Jan. 8, 1955)
Consecutive Conference Wins—51* (Jan. 28, 1950 to Jan. 8, 1955)
  (Excludes tournament and non-SEC games)
Consecutive SEC Losses—4 in 1966-67 and 1973-74 (Lost 3 in row only 11 times, 2 in row only 16 times)
Most SEC Champions—29*
  (12 Titles won in tournament play. Title determined by regular season play since 1951. Tied LSU 1935 and 1954, Miss. State 1962, Tennessee 1972, Alabama 1975)
Consecutive SEC Championships—9*
  (Kentucky held SEC title continuously from 1944 to 1953 when Wildcats were out of competition. The 1952 title represented UK's 6th straight regular season title and 12th win of season race since SEC organized in 1933.)
Attendance Highs—
  One Game—18,833 (UK vs. Morehead, NCAA at Louisville, 1961)
  Regular Season Game—18,274* (UK vs. Illinois at Louisville, 1958)
  Home Game—13,690 (UK vs. LSU, Jan. 24, 1970)
  Two Consecutive Games—31,581 in 1973 (15,581 UK-Austin Peay, 16,000 UK-Indiana, NCAA Mideast Regional, Nashville, Tenn.)
  Complete Season—359,232 in 31 Games, 1974-75
  Home Season—181,295 in 15 Games, 1969-70
Last Overtime Game—Mar. 8, 1976 (UK 94, Miss. St. 93) (H)
  (Last double overtime game—Dec. 11, 1971 (Indiana 90, UK 89) (N)
  (Last three-overtime game—Dec. 7, 1957, Kentucky 85, Temple 83)
Most Players on All-Tournament Team—5 (1947 All-SEC Tournament Team and 1965 UK Invitational Tournament Team)

MEMORIAL COLISEUM RECORDS
(Collegiate-Varsity)
Team—Single Game

Consecutive Wins—45 By Kentucky (Dec. 1, 1950 to Jan. 8, 1955)
  (Part of Overall National Record of 129 Home Floor Victories)
  (Kentucky has lost two in row in Memorial Coliseum only three times and three in row only once—1966-67)
Most Points—121 by Kentucky vs. Mississippi, 86, Feb. 6, 1971
Most Points By UK Opponent—98 (1 OT) By Illinois, Dec. 5, 1966
Biggest Margin of Victory—53 By Kentucky (UK 104 vs. Ga. Tech 51 on Jan. 7, 1956; and UK 108 vs. Georgia 55 on Jan. 29, 1959)

  *Also Southeastern Conference Record
  #Recognized As National Record

Most Points, Both Teams—207 (Kentucky 121 vs. Mississippi 86, Feb. 6, 1971)
Biggest Margin of Defeat For Kentucky—23 (Alabama 94, UK 71, Feb. 23, 1974)
Most Points In One Half—67 By Kentucky in Second Half vs. Auburn, Jan. 29, 1966
Fewest Points—32 By Alabama (Alabama 32 vs. Kentucky 39 on Feb. 23, 1959)
Smallest Margin of Victory—Kentucky 77 vs. UCLA 76 on Feb. 17, 1961; UK 61, Tennessee 60 on Feb. 27, 1965; UK 60, Tennessee 59 on Feb. 12, 1968; Kentucky 78 vs. Stanford 77 on Dec. 22, 1973; Kentucky 77, Vanderbilt 76 on Jan. 17, 1976; Kentucky 94, Miss. St. 93 (OT) Mar. 8, 1976
Smallest Margin of Defeat—1 (Ga. Tech 59 vs. Kentucky 58 on Jan. 8, 1955; St. Louis 71 vs. Kentucky 70 on Dec. 10, 1956; Ga. Tech 86 vs. Kentucky 85 in double overtime on Jan. 5, 1963; Illinois 98 vs. UK 97 (1 OT) Dec. 5, 1966; Ohio State 82, UK 81, March 16, 1968)
Most FGA's, Both Teams—209 (Kentucky 125 vs. Mississippi 84, Feb. 8, 1964)
Most Field Goals Made—54 by Kentucky vs. Mississippi, Feb. 6, 1971
Best FG Pct. (Game)—69.2 (18 of 26) By Miss. State vs. Kentucky, Feb. 12, 1962
Best FG Pct. (First Half)—75.0 (15 of 20) By Ga. vs. UK, Jan. 11, 1971
Best FG Pct. (Second Half)—87.5 (7 of 8) By Miss. State vs. UK, Feb. 12, 1962
Most Free Throws Attempted—50 By Georgia vs. Kentucky, Feb. 4, 1954, and Georgia Tech, Jan. 5, 1957
Most FTA's, Both Teams—89 (Kentucky 39 vs. Georgia Tech 50 on Jan. 5, 1957)
Most FT Made—38 By Kentucky vs. Georgia on Jan. 29, 1959; UK 38 vs. Florida, Jan. 30, 1965
Most Free Throws Missed—23 By Georgia vs. Kentucky on Feb. 4, 1954
Most Rebounds—108 By Kentucky vs. Mississippi, Feb. 8, 1964
Fewest Points, Both Teams—71 (Kentucky 39 vs. Alabama 32 on Feb. 23, 1959)
Most Personal Fouls—34 By Mississippi vs. Kentucky, Feb. 6, 1965
Most PF's, Both Teams—62 (UK 31 vs. Auburn 31, Feb. 5, 1973)
Biggest Crowd—13,690 (Kentucky vs. Louisiana State, Jan. 24, 1970)

Individual—Single Game

Most Points—55 by Pete Maravich, LSU vs. Kentucky, Jan. 24, 1970
Most Field Goals Attempted—53 by Pete Maravich, LSU vs. Kentucky, Feb. 22, 1969
Most Field Goals Made—21 by Pete Maravich, LSU vs. Kentucky, Feb. 22, 1969 and Jan. 24, 1970
Most Free Throws Attempted—24 By Cliff Hagan, Kentucky vs. Temple on Dec. 5, 1953
Most Free Throws Made—17 By Cliff Hagan, Kentucky vs. Temple on Dec. 5, 1953
(Consecutive—14 of 14 By Louie Dampier vs. Oregon State, Dec. 22, 1966)
Most Rebounds—34* (SEC Record Non-Conference Play) By Bob Burrow, Kentucky vs. Temple on Dec. 18, 1954
Longest Field Goal Made—53 ft., 6 in. By Linville Puckett, Kentucky vs. Miss. State on Feb. 15, 1954

HIGHS AND LOWS BY OPPONENTS
(Modern—Since 1930)
Individual—Single Game

Most Points—64 Pete Maravich (LSU) Feb. 21, 1970 at Baton Rouge
Most Rebounds—30 Jerry Lucas (Ohio State) March 18, 1961 (NCAA)
Most Field Goals—23 Pete Maravich (LSU) Feb. 21, 1970 at Baton Rouge
Most Free Throws Made—17 Pete Maravich (LSU) (22 FTA) Feb. 21, 1970 at Baton Rouge

*Also Southeastern Conference Record
#Recognized As National Record

Most FG's Attempted—53 Pete Maravich (LSU) Feb. 22, 1969
Most FT's Attempted—22 Pete Maravich (LSU) Feb. 21, 1970 at Baton Rouge

Team—Single Game

Most Points—116 Northwestern (UK 118) Dec. 10, 1966
  (Conf. Only—110 Vanderbilt, UK 94, March 4, 1967)
Fewest Points—6 Arkansas State (Kentucky 75) Jan. 8, 1945
  (All-Time Record—5 Tennessee 1910, Centre 1916, Ky. Wesleyan 1919)
Biggest Victory Margin—39 CCNY 89-Kentucky 50 in NIT, Mar. 14, 1950
  (All-Time Record—68 Centre 87-Kentucky 19 in 1910)
Smallest Victory Margin—1 Vanderbilt 32, Kentucky 31, Feb. 20, 1932 (28 One-Point Losses since 1930. All-Time, 34 losses) Last by Mississippi 61, Kentucky 60, Feb. 18, 1974.
Most Rebounds—81 Notre Dame, Dec. 29, 1964
(Rebounds not recorded prior to 1951)
Most Field Goals—51 Notre Dame (109 Attempts) Dec. 29, 1964
  (All-Time Record—Same)
Fewest Field Goals—2# Arkansas State Jan. 8, 1945
Most FG's Attempted—109 Notre Dame (Made 51) Dec. 29, 1964
  Field Goal Attempts Not Recorded Prior To 1947)
Most Free Throws Made—35 Auburn (49 Attempts) Feb. 27, 1954
  (All-Time Record—Same)
Fewest Free Throws Missed—0 Georgia Tech (Made 5) Jan. 21, 1946, and Georgia (Made 6) Feb. 19, 1973
Most FT's Attempted)—53 Tennessee (Made 33) March 3, 1956
  (All-Time Record—Same)
Best FT Shooting Percentage—(Minimum 15 FTA) 91.7 (22 of 24) by Notre Dame (N), Jan. 14, 1939
Best FG Shooting Pct.—69.2 By Miss. State, Feb. 12, 1962, at Lexington
  (First Half—75.0% by Georgia (H) Jan. 11, 1971)
  (Second Half—87.5% By Miss. State (H) Feb. 12, 1962)
Lowest FG Shooting Percentage—24.1% Notre Dame Feb. 14, 1959
(Shooting Percentages Not Recorded Prior To 1947)
Most Personal Fouls—36 Iowa Dec. 14, 1973 (A)
  *Also Southeastern Conference Record
  #Recognized As National Record

CITIZENS SAVINGS (HELMS) ATHLETIC FOUNDATION COLLEGIATE BASKETBALL SELECTIONS

College Basketball Hall of Fame

1946—Adolph F. Rupp ..... Coach
1933—Forest (Aggie) Sale ... Player
1964—Carey Spicer .... Player
1966—Cliff Hagan .... Player
1968—Charles (Cotton) Nash Player
1971—LeRoy Edwards ..... Player

Player of the Year

1933—Forest Sale .. Center-Forward
1951—Bill Spivey .... Center
1935—LeRoy Edwards— .... Center
1975—Kevin Grevy ...... Forward

Helms' National Champions

	W	L	Points	Points Against
1933—Kentucky	20	3	1073	630
1948—Kentucky	36	3	2690	1730
1949—Kentucky	32	2	2320	1492
1951—Kentucky	32	2	2540	1783
1954—Kentucky	25	0	2187	1508
1958—Kentucky	23	6	2166	1817

WILDCATS' RECORD AGAINST ALL OPPONENTS

Team	First Meeting	Last Meeting	UK Won	UK Lost
Advent Memorial Club (Cincy)	1909	1909	0	1
Air Force	1965	1065	1	0
Akron	1937	1937	1	0
Alabama	1923	1976	59	16
Alumni	1933	1941	3	0
Arizona	1946	1946	1	0
Arkansas	1946	1950	3	0
Arkansas State	1945	1945	1	0
Army	1969	1969	1	0
Ashland YMCA	1914	1914	1	0
Auburn	1921	1976	36	8
Austin Peay	1973	1973	1	0
Baylor	1946	1963	5	0
Berea	1926	1945	11	0
Bethany	1911	1911	1	0
Bowling Green	1948	1948	1	0
Bradley	1949	1950	2	0
Brigham Young	1951	1951	1	0
Butler	1911	1962	3	0
*Cambridge University	1966	1966	1	0
Carnegie Tech	1931	1943	2	0
Central U.	1906	1913	8	9
Central Michigan	1975	1975	1	0
Centenary	1923	1937	3	1
Centre	1916	1929	18	10
CCNY	1950	1950	0	1
Chattanooga	1914	1935	9	0
Chicago	1932	1935	2	0
Christ Church (Cincinnati)	1906	1913	0	3
Cincinnati U.	1904	1948	21	10
Cincinnati YMCA	1905	1906	0	3
Clemson	1922	1939	11	2
Colorado State College	1959	1959	1	0
Columbia	1948	1948	1	0
Cornell	1966	1966	0	1
Creighton	1930	1948	7	4
Cumberland	1917	1921	4	1
Dartmouth	1942	1973	3	1
Dayton	1947	1967	3	1
De Paul	1943	1970	17	3
DePauw	1910	1944	1	2
Detroit	1938	1938	0	1
Duke	1930	1969	9	2
Eastern Normal	1928	1928	1	0
Florida	1927	1976	37	9
Florida State	1958	1972	2	2
Ft. Benning	1946	1946	1	0
Ft. Knox	1942	1947	7	0
Georgia	1921	1976	54	9
Georgia Tech	1924	1975	50	13
Georgetown (Ky.) College	1903	1938	35	14
Georgetown University	1922	1922	0	1
Great Lakes Navy	1942	1943	0	2
Hardin-Simmons	1965	1965	1	0
Holy Cross	1948	1948	2	0
Houston	1956	1956	1	0
Idaho	1946	1955	2	0
Illinois	1925	1966	8	4
Indiana	1924	1975	6	12

Indiana Central	1946	1949	4	0
Iowa	1956	1973	3	2
Iowa State	1964	1964	1	0
*Instanbul University	1966	1966	1	0
Jacksonville	1970	1970	0	1
Kansas	1950	1975	7	1
Kansas State	1940	1976	7	0
Kentucky Wesleyan	1910	1938	8	2+
La Salle	1953	1954	2	0
Lexington High	1909	1911	1	1
Lexington YMCA	1907	1912	3	4
Long Island U.	1939	1947	2	1
Louisiana State	1933	1976	42	3
Louisville Coliseum	1908	1908	1	1
Louisville U.	1913	1959	8	3
Louisville YMCA	1914	1914	1	0
Louisville YMHA	1914	1914	1	0
Loyola (Chicago)	1949	1964	4	3
Loyola (La.)	1963	1963	1	0
Marietta	1913	1916	2	2
Marquette	1938	1975	7	4
Marshall	1913	1933	6	0
Maryland	1928	1958	4	3
Maryville	1915	1940	5	0
Mercer	1921	1922	1	1
Mexico U.	1933	1942	3	0
Mexico YMCA	1924	1924	1	0
Miami (Florida)	1956	1956	1	0
Miami (Ohio)	1905	1975	16	4
Michigan	1924	1970	4	1
Michigan State	1935	1972	9	6
Minnesota	1951	1957	3	1
Mississippi	1925	1976	46	4
Mississippi State	1921	1976	44	8†
Missouri	1960	1971	2	0
Moores Hill College	1906	1096	1	0
Morehead	1961	1061	1	0
Naval Academy	1928	1969	2	1
Nebraska	1940	1972	2	1
New Albany YMCA	1906	1906	0	1
New York U.	1935	1936	0	2
Niagara	,1976	1976	1	0
North Carolina	1924	1975	6	11
North Carolina Charlotte	,1976	1976	1	0
North Caroline State	1931	1947	2	0
Northwestern	1962	1975	7	1
Notre Dame	1929	1975	24	14
Oglethorpe	1934	1934	1	0
Ohio State	1933	1968	6	7
Ohio University	1944	1964	7	1
Ohio Wesleyan	1911	1911	0	1
Oklahoma A & M State	1944	1974	3	1
Oklahoma U.	1946	1946	1	0
Oregon	1973	1973	1	0
Oregon State	1966	1975	3	0
Otterbein	1911	1911	0	1
Pennsylvania	1967	1969	2	0
Penn. State	1952	1955	2	0
Phillips Oilers	1948	1948	0	1‡
Pittsburgh	1935	1960	4	0
Princeton	1926	1971	1	1
Providence	,1976	1976	1	0
Purdue	1949	1970	2	1

Rhode Island	1946	1946	1	0
Rose Polytechnic	1910	1917	1	1
*Salonika University	1966	1966	1	0
Seattle	1958	1958	1	0
Sewanee	1923	1934	6	0
South Carolina	1928	1967	4	1
Southern California	1959	1961	0	2
St. Andrew	1915	1915	1	1
St. John's	1943	1952	8	3
St. Joseph's	1939	1939	1	0
St. Louis	1948	1966	7	9
Southern Methodist	1956	1958	2	1
Stanford	1973	1973	1	0
Syracuse	1950	1975	3	0
Temple	1944	1962	14	4
Tennessee	1910	1976	96	41
Texas A & M	1941	1946	2	0
Texas Tech	1963	1965	2	0
Texas Western	1966	1966	0	1
Transylvania	1903	1911	6	8#
Tufts	1945	1945	1	0
Tulane	1921	1966	37	5
Tulsa	1947	1948	3	0
UCLA	1951	1975	3	1
Utah	1944	1954	2	1
Utah State	1957	1957	1	0
Vanderbilt	1912	1976	77	27
Vernon College	1906	1906	1	0
Villanova	1949	1949	2	0
Virginia	1914	1966	6	2
Virginia Tech	1924	1962	2	1
VMI	1914	1960	2	2
Wabash	1925	1946	1	1
Wake Forest	1953	1963	2	0
*Warsaw University	1966	1966	2	0
Washington U.	1942	1948	2	0
Washington & Lee	1922	1956	12	1
Washington State	1974	1974	1	0
Wayne	1956	1956	1	0
Western Kentucky	1971	1971	0	1
Western Ontario	1945	1949	4	0
West Texas State	1950	1950	1	0
West Virginia	1924	1970	10	4
Wisconsin	1963	1969	1	1
Wright Field	1944	1944	1	0
Wyoming	1944	1944	1	0
Xavier	1935	1969	37	2
Yale	1961	1961	1	0

†Record includes nine games with Mississippi A&M which later became known as Mississippi State.
‡ Pre-Olympic Games exhibitions not included.
#Record includes 10 games with Kentucky University, which became known as Transylvania in 1909.
*Played in International Universities Tournament at Tel Aviv, Israel, in August, 1966.
+Record does not take in account tie game played between UK and Kentucky Wesleyan Feb. 9, 1918. Unique 21-21 tie resulted from scorer's error which was not discovered until after teams departed.

KENTUCKY'S ALL-TIME RECORD 1903-1976
(73 Seasons — Won 1163, Lost 372, Ties 1)
HOME: Won 645, Lost 109   OTHER: Won 518, Lost 263, Tied 1
(No Schedule Played in 1952-53)
(Losses in Bold Face)

Date	Team	Site	Ky.	Opp.

1903—Won 1, Lost 2.
COACH: Unnamed
STARTERS: (A. C. Bush, B. W. Bush, Houlihan, Smith and Carter)

Date	Team	Site	Ky.	Opp.
Feb. 6	Georgetown	(H)	6	15
Feb. 18	Lexington YMCA	(H)	11	10
Feb. 20	**Kentucky U.**	**(H)**	**2**	**42**
			19	69

1904—Won 1, Lost 4.
COACH: Leander E. Andrus, Mgr.
CAPTAIN: St. John (Guyn, Arnett, St. John, Wurtele, Coons)

Feb. 4	**Georgetown**	(A)	11	26
Feb. 11	**Kentucky U.***	**(A)**	**5**	**12**
Feb. 13	**Georgetown**	**(H)**	**10**	**22**
Feb. 26	**Kentucky U.**	**(A)**	**12**	**14**
Mar. 1	Cincinnati	(H)	25	21
			63	95

* Kentucky University (Transylvania) and Georgetown game at KU was called off because of failure to agree on a referee. State College (University of Kntucky) team was present and agreed to play. The offer was accepted and KU won, 12-5.

1905—Won 1, Lost 4.
COACH:
CAPTAIN: J. M. Coons

Jan. 13	**Georgetown**	**(H)**	**9**	**14**
Jan. 21	**Cincinnati YMCA**	**(H)**	**22**	**43**
Jan. 27	Kentucky U.	(H)	30	29
Feb. 4	**Kentucky U.**	**(H)**	**1**	**22**
Feb. 22	**Kentucky U.**	**(H)**	**23**	**33**
			85	141

1906—Won 4, Lost 9.
COACH: W. B. Wendt (Mgr.)
CAPTAIN: D. P. Branson (Baer, Donan, Barbee, Wilson, Herman)

Jan. 11	Lexington YMCA*	(H)	....	....
Jan. 12	**Miami (Ohio)**	**(H)**	**10**	**15**
Jan. 19	Central U.	(H)	15	14
Jan. 20	**Georgetown**	**(A)**	**9**	**34**
Jan. 26	Central U.	(A)	17	15
Jan. 27	**Cincinnati YMCA**	**(H)**	**16**	**29**
Feb. 3	**Christ Church, Cin.**	**(H)**	**24**	**38**
Feb. 9	**Georgetown**	**(H)**	**22**	**28**
Feb. 12	**New Albany YMCA**	**(A)**	**12**	**29**
Feb. 13	Vernon College	(A)	34	14
Feb. 14	Moores Hill	(A)	32	11
Feb. 15	**Christ Church, Cin.**	**(A)**	**17**	**54**
Feb. 16	**Cincinnati YMCA**	**(A)**	**9**	**38**
Feb. 17	**Miami (Ohio)**	**(A)**	**19**	**29**
			236	328

* W. B. Wendt on Jan. 9, 1969 verified that State College opened the 1906 season against Kentucky U. in the YMCA. Athletic committees of the two schools had cancelled all games after a fight at a football game in November, 1905. Wendt and the Kentucky U. manager agreed to play at the YMCA and list the State College foe as YMCA instead of Kentucky U. State College won but Mr. Wendt didn't remember the score, which he hadn't listed.

1907—Won 3, Lost 6.
COACH: A. M. Kirby (Mgr.)
CAPTAIN: J. M. Wilson (Shanklin, Baer, Bryant, Barbee)

Jan. 16	**Lexington YMCA**	**(H)**	**17**	**25**
Jan. 19	Georgetown	(H)	16	15
Jan. 25	**Central U.**	**(H)**	**22**	**9**
Feb. 12	**Central U.**	**(A)**	**23**	**25**
Feb. 15	Kentucky U.	(H)	16	14
Feb. 21	**Georgetown**	**(A)**	**8**	**19**
Mar. 1	**Lexington YMCA**	**(A)**	**22**	**41**
Mar. 7	**Kentucky U.**	**(A)**	**5**	**19**
Mar. 9	Central U.	(H)	13	15
			142	182

1907-08—Won 5, Lost 6.
COACH: J. S. Chambers (Mgr.)
CAPTAIN: Richard Barbee

Jan. 10	**Lexington YMCA**	**(H)**	**19**	**29**
Jan. 21	Kentucky U.	(H)	20	15
Jan. 25	**Central U.**	**(A)**	**21**	**32**
Feb. 4	Kentucky U.	(H)	20	15
Feb. 8	**Louisville Coliseum**	**(H)**	**29**	**28**
Feb. 11	**Georgetown**	**(A)**	**22**	**30**
Feb. 13	Central U.	(H)	31	20
Feb.15	**Lexington YMCA**	**(H)**	**19**	**23**
Feb. 22	**Louisville Coliseum**	**(A)**	**18**	**30**
Mar. 3	Georgetown	(H)	18	13
Mar. 7	**Central U.**	**(A)**	**10**	**29**
			227	264

1908-09—Won 5, Lost 4.
MGR.: J. S. Chambers
CAPTAIN: W. C. Fox

Jan. 9	Lexington High	(H)	29	9
Jan. 18	**Advent Mem. Club**	**(A)**	**27**	**41**
Jan. 19	**Cincinnati**	**(A)**	**25**	**41**
Jan. 27	Central U.	(H)	24	23
Feb. 6	**Central U.**	**(A)**	**20**	**35**
Feb. 8	Georgetown	(H)	45	32
Feb. 15	Georgetown	(A)	48	19
Feb. 19	**Cincinnati**	**(H)**	**28**	**23**
Feb. 26	**Central U.**	**(H)**	**20**	**26**
			266	249

1909-10—Won 4, Lost 8.
COACH: R. E. Spahr and E. R. Sweetland
CAPTAIN: Bill Rodes

Jan. 8	Kentucky Wesleyan	(A)	14*	12
Jan. 22	Georgetown	(H)	31	11
Jan. 24	**DePauw**	**(H)**	**11**	**24**
Jan. 28	**Central**	**(A)**	**17**	**87**
Feb. 4	**Georgetown**	**(A)**	**16**	**34**
Feb. 7	**Cincinnati**	**(A)**	**17**	**47**
Feb. 9	**DePauw**	**(A)**	**10**	**28**
Feb. 10	**Rose Poly**	**(A)**	**11**	**52**
Feb. 16	Tennessee	(H)	20	5
Mar. 5	**Central**	**(H)**	**13**	**31**
Mar. 8	Georgetown	(H)	24	23
Mar. 11	**Central**	**(A)**	**9**	**51**
			193	405

* Denotes one overtime period.

423

Date	Team	Site	Ky.	Opp.
1910-11—Won 5, Lost 6.				
COACH: H. J. Iddings				
CAPTAIN: J. H. Gaiser				
Jan. 13	**Lexington High**	**(H)**	**29**	**36**
Jan. 20	**Transylvania**	**(H)**	**18**	**23**
Jan. 27	**Ky. Wesleyan**	**(A)**	**19**	**21**
Feb. 4	Bethany	(H)	24	11
Feb. 9	**Ohio Wesleyan**	**(A)**	**19**	**37**
Feb. 10	**Otterbein**	**(A)**	**27**	**41**
Feb. 11	**Cin. Christ's Church**	**(A)**	**21**	**32**
Feb. 17	Georgetown	(A)	47	22
Feb. 23	Butler	(H)	21	16
Feb. 28	Transylvania	(A)	22	19
Mar. 3	Transylvania	(H)	30	24
			277	282
1911-12—Won 9, Lost 0.				
COACH: E. R. Sweetland				
CAPTAIN: W. C. Harrison				
Jan. 5	Georgetown	(H)	38	12
Jan. 12	Central U.	(A)	32	13
Jan. 19	Miami (Ohio) U.	(H)	31	14
Feb. 1	Central U.	(H)	52	10
Feb. 7	Tennessee	(H)	27	15
Feb. 16	Lexington YMCA	(H)	32	20
Feb. 22	Vanderbilt	(H)	28	17
Feb. 23	Vanderbilt	(H)	22	18
Mar. 1	Georgetown	(A)	19	18
			281	137
SOUTHERN CHAMPIONS				
1912-13—Won 5, Lost 3.				
COACH: J. J. Tigert				
CAPTAIN: B. Barnett				
Jan. 24	**Lexington YMCA**	**(H)**	**25**	**27**
Feb. 8	Cincinnati	(H)	20	18
Feb. 13	Marietta	(H)	42	16
Feb. 15	Louisville	(H)	34	10
Feb. 19	**Vanderbilt**	**(H)**	**17**	**24**
Feb. 20	Vanderbilt	(H)	42	29
Feb. 27	Miami (Ohio) U.	(H)	24	16
Mar. 1	**Cin. Christ's Church**	**(H)**	**19**	**30**
			223	170
1913-14—Won 11, Lost 2.				
COACH: Alpha Brumage				
CAPTAIN: William Tuttle				
Jan. 10	Ashland YMCA	(H)	28	15
Jan. 17	Louisville YMCA	(H)	30	21
Jan. 21	Marshall	(A)	46	6
Jan. 20	Ashland YMCA	(A)	30	19
Jan. 22	**Virginia U.**	**(A)**	**23**	**39**
Jan. 24	**Va. Military Inst.**	**(A)**	**18**	**32**
Jan. 31	Louisville YMHA	(H)	59	12
Feb. 7	Louisville	(H)	22	17
Feb. 11	Tennessee	(H)	20	14
Feb. 12	Tennessee	(H)	20	18
Feb. 21	Cincinnati	(H)	20	18
Feb. 23	Chattanooga	(H)	40	7
Feb. 28	Marietta	(H)	19	17
			375	235
1914-15—Won 7, Lost 5.				
COACH: Alpha Brumage				
CAPTAIN: Ralph Morgan				
Jan. 16	Maryville	(H)	37	17
Jan. 22	Louisville	(H)	18	14
Jan. 30	St. Andrews	(H)	35	15
Feb. 4	Maryville	(A)	23	22
Feb. 5	**Tennessee**	**(A)**	**21**	**36**
Feb. 6	**Tennessee**	**(A)**	**22**	**27**
Feb. 12	**Vanderbilt**	**(H)**	**34**	**39**
Feb. 13	Vanderbilt	(H)	36	24
Feb. 17	Tennessee	(H)	22	13
Feb. 18	Tennessee	(H)	20	18
Feb. 26	**St. Andrews**	**(A)**	**25**	**50**
Feb. 27	**Louisville**	**(A)**	**15**	**26**
			308	301
1915-16—Won 8, Lost 6.				
COACH: James Park				
CAPTAIN: K. P. Zerfoss				
Jan. 14	Cincinnati	(A)	39	24
Jan. 18	Georgetown	(A)	29	22
Jan. 31	Georgetown	(H)	30	22
Feb. 4	**Vanderbilt**	**(H)**	**25**	**39**
Feb. 5	**Vanderbilt**	**(H)**	**20**	**23**
Feb. 12	**Louisville**	**(H)**	**22**	**28**
Feb. 15	Centre	(A)	38	5
Feb. 19	Cincinnati	(H)	34	10
Feb. 22	Louisville	(A)	32	24
Feb. 23	**Tennessee**	**(H)**	**17**	**28**
Feb. 26	Maryville	(H)	36	25
Feb. 29	Centre	(H)	38	14
Mar. 3	**Marietta**	**(H)**	**22**	**27**
Mar. 4	**Marietta**	**(H)**	**23**	**27**
			405	318
1916-17—Won 4, Lost 6.				
COACH: W. P. Tuttle				
CAPTAIN: Robert Y. Ireland				
Jan. 17	Centre	(H)	31	21
Jan. 27	**Georgetown**	**(A)**	**19**	**22**
Jan. 30	Rose Polytechnic	(H)	33	12
Feb. 9	**Tennessee**	**(H)**	**20**	**23**
Feb. 10	**Tennessee**	**(H)**	**19**	**22**
Feb. 16	**Centre**	**(A)**	**24**	**28**
Feb. 21	Georgetown	(H)	32	18
Mar. 1	Cumberland	(A)	48	20
Mar. 2	**Tennessee**	**(A)**	**26**	**27**
Mar. 3	**Tennessee**	**(A)**	**10**	**30**
			262	223
1917-18—Won 9, Lost 2, Tied 1.				
COACH: S. A. Boles				
CAPTAIN: Patrick Campbell				
Jan. 9	Ky. Wesleyan	(H)	23	13
Jan. 17	**Centre**	**(A)**	**21**	**29**
Jan. 24	Georgetown	(A)	22	18
Feb. 7	Tennessee	(H)	33	26
Feb. 8	Tennessee	(H)	40	12
Feb. 9	Ky. Wesleyan	(A)	21	21
(This unique tie game resulted from scorer's error which was not discovered until after teams' departures. The contest was re-scheduled but never played for unknown reasons.)				
Feb. 14	Georgetown	(A)	25	16
Feb. 21	Centre	(H)	22***20	
Feb. 28	Cumberland	(A)	42	21
Mar. 1	Tennessee	(A)	29	18
Mar. 2	Tennessee	(A)	32	20
POST-SEASON GAME (For State Championship)				
Mar. 9	**Centre**	**(N1)**	**12**	**22**
			322	236
*** Denotes 3 overtime periods.				
(N1) Louisville				
1918-19—Won 6, Lost 8.				
COACH: Andrew Gill				
CAPTAIN: J. A. Dishman				
Jan. 13	Ky. Wesleyan	(H)	46	5
Jan. 18	**Georgetown**	**(H)**	**30**	**32**
Jan. 25	**Centre**	**(A)**	**30**	**38**
Jan. 31	**Cincinnati**	**(A)**	**18**	**28**
Feb. 6	Chattanooga	(A)	28	25
Feb. 7	**Tennessee**	**(A)**	**22**	**40**
Feb. 8	Cumberland	(A)	22	21
Feb. 14	**Vanderbilt**	**(H)**	**26**	**36**

Date	Team	Site	Ky.	Opp.
Feb. 15	Georgetown	(A)	18	22
Feb. 21	Cincinnati	(H)	34	21
Feb. 22	Ky. Wesleyan	(H)	18	13
Feb. 24	Centre	(H)	10	21
Feb. 28	Tennessee	(H)	30	14
Mar. 8	Miami (Ohio) U.	(H)	14	38
			346	354

1919-20—Won 5, Lost 7.
COACH: George C. Buchheit
CAPTAIN: J. C. Everett

Date	Team	Site	Ky.	Opp.
Jan. 17	Cincinnati	(A)	11	13
Jan. 22	Maryville	(H)	27	16
Jan. 31	Georgetown	(H)	25	14
Feb. 5	Tennessee	(H)	24	29
Feb. 7	Tennessee	(H)	26	27
Feb. 14	Centre	(A)	15	44
Feb. 17	Georgetown	(A)	28	16
Feb. 21	Ky. Wesleyan	(H)	43	13
Feb. 26	Cumberland	(A)	21	30
Feb. 27	Tennessee	(A)	25	28
Feb. 28	Tennessee	(A)	36	25
Mar. 6	Centre	(H)	18	*20
			299	275

1920-21—Won 13, Lost 1.
COACH: George C. Buchheit
CAPTAIN: Basil Hayden

Date	Team	Site	Ky.	Opp.
Jan. 12	Ky. Wesleyan	(H)	38	13
Jan. 15	Cumberland	(H)	37	21
Jan. 18	Georgetown	(H)	38	23
Jan. 21	Chattanooga	(H)	42	10
Jan. 26	Cincinnati	(A)	26	19
Jan. 29	Auburn	(H)	40	25
Feb. 8	Centre	(A)	27	29
Feb. 15	Georgetown	(A)	56	11
Feb. 18	Centre	(H)	20	13
Feb. 22	Vanderbilt	(H)	39	18

SIAA TOURNAMENT (Atlanta, Ga.)

Date	Team	Ky.	Opp.
Feb. 25	Tulane	50	28
Feb. 26	Mercer	49	24
Feb. 28	Mississippi A & M	28	13
Mar. 1	Georgia (championship)	20	19
		510	266

1921-22—Won 10, Lost 6.
COACH: George C. Buchheit
CAPTAIN: R. E. Lavin

Date	Team	Site	Ky.	Opp.
Jan. 14	Georgetown	(H)	17	26
Jan. 17	Louisville	(A)	38	14
Jan. 18	Vanderbilt	(A)	12	22
Jan. 21	Louisville	(H)	29	22
Jan. 26	Miss. A & M	(H)	28	21
Jan. 27	Marshall	(H)	34	12
Feb. 4	Centre	(A)	27	21
Feb. 6	Georgetown	(A)	26	17
Feb. 8	Washington & Lee	(A)	21	20
Feb. 9	Va. Military Inst.	(A)	32	37
Feb. 11	Georgetown U.	(A)	23	28
Feb. 13	Virginia	(A)	30	32
Feb. 16	Clemson	(H)	38	14
Feb. 20	Centre	(H)	40	23

SIAA TOURNAMENT (Atlanta, Ga.)

Date	Team	Ky.	Opp.
Feb. 24	Georgetown	41	21
Feb. 25	Mercer	22	35
		457	361

1922-23—Won 3, Lost 10.
COACH: George C. Buchheit
CAPTAIN: Fred Fest

Date	Team	Site	Ky.	Opp.
Jan. 13	Georgetown	(A)	24	13
Jan. 20	Tennessee	(A)	26	30
Jan. 22	Chattanooga	(H)	25	18
Jan. 25	Alabama	(H)	35	45
Jan. 27	Centre	(H)	14	21

Date	Team	Site	Ky.	Opp.
Feb. 3	Georgia	(H)	19	23
Feb. 5	Cincinnati	(A)	24	33
Feb. 7	Centenary	(H)	21	38
Feb. 10	Tennessee	(H)	23	28
Feb. 14	Centre	(A)	10	17
Feb. 15	Clemson	(H)	17	30
Feb. 19	Georgetown	(H)	21	48
Feb. 23	Sewanee	(H)	30	14
			289	348

1923-24—Won 13, Lost 3.
COACH: G. C. Buchheit
CAPTAIN: A. T. Rice

Date	Team	Site	Ky.	Opp.
Jan. 1	Vanderbilt	(H)	33	13
Jan. 8	Mexico YMCA	(H)	25	14
Jan. 12	Georgetown	(A)	32	24
Jan. 14	Miss. A & M	(H)	16	17
Jan. 15	Sewanee	(H)	50	15
Jan. 18	Tennessee	(A)	13	20
Jan. 19	Chattanooga	(A)	24	23
Feb. 4	West Virginia	(H)	24	21
Feb. 9	Centre	(A)	27	18
Feb. 11	Georgetown	(H)	39	35
Feb. 13	Clemson	(H)	38	13
Feb. 14	Virginia	(H)	29	16
Feb. 19	Virginia Tech	(H)	36	14
Feb. 21	Centre	(H)	38	24
Feb. 23	Georgia Tech	(H)	33	27

SIAA TOURNAMENT (Atlanta, Ga.)

Date	Team	Ky.	Opp.
Feb. 29	North Carolina	20	41
		477	335

ALUMNI GYM ERA (1924-1950)

1924-25—Won 13, Lost 8.
COACH: C. O. Applegran
CAPTAIN: James McFarland

Date	Team	Site	Ky.	Opp.
Dec. 13	Cincinnati	(H)	28	23
Dec. 18	Indiana	(H)	18	20
Dec. 20	Michigan	(H)	11	21
Jan. 3	Cincinnati	(A)	20	24
Jan. 5	Illinois	(A)	26	36
Jan. 6	Wabash	(A)	11	57
Jan. 9	Mississippi	(H)	26	23
Jan. 10	Georgetown	(H)	25	17
Jan. 17	Centre	(H)	33	26
Jan. 30	Washington & Lee	(H)	28	22
Feb. 2	West Virginia	(H)	29	19
Feb. 5	Alabama	(A)	15	24
Feb. 6	Georgia Tech	(A)	18	16
Feb. 7	Georgia	(A)	24	28
Feb. 9	Tennessee	(A)	35	22
Feb. 12	Tulane	(A)	29	22
Feb. 14	Georgetown	(A)	36	21
Feb. 18	Tennessee	(A)	26	21
Feb. 21	Centre	(H)	39	10

SOUTHERN CONF. TOUR. (Atlanta, Ga.)

Date	Team	Ky.	Opp.
Feb. 27	Mississippi A&M	31	26
Feb. 28	Georgia	31	32
		539	510

1925-26—Won 15, Lost 3.
COACH: Ray Eklund
CAPTAIN: Burgess Carey

Date	Team	Site	Ky.	Opp.
Dec. 19	DePauw	(H)	29	38
Jan. 5	Indiana	(A)	23	34
Jan. 9	Berea	(H)	37	23
Jan. 12	Georgetown	(A)	36	21
Jan. 16	Georgia Tech	(H)	25	24
Jan. 22	Centre	(H)	45	25
Jan. 30	Georgetown	(H)	25	20
Feb. 1	Alabama	(H)	27	16
Feb. 4	Centre	(A)	46	19
Feb. 5	Washington & Lee	(H)	44	34
Feb. 8	Auburn	(H)	35	26

Date	Team	Site	Ky.	Opp.
Feb. 12	Tennessee	(A)	51	17
Feb. 15	Georgia	(A)	22	18
Feb. 18	Tennessee	(H)	27	21
Feb. 20	Vanderbilt	(H)	30	20

SOUTHERN CONF. TOUR. (Atlanta, Ga.)

Date	Team	Site	Ky.	Opp.
Feb. 26	Va. Military Inst.		38	25
Feb. 27	Georgia		39	34
Mar. 1	**Mississippi A&M**		**26**	**31**
			605	446

1926-27—Won 3, Lost 13.
COACH: Basil Hayden
CAPTAIN: Paul Jenkins

Date	Team	Site	Ky.	Opp.
Dec. 18	**Cincinnati**	**(H)**	**10**	**48**
Dec. 21	**Indiana**	**(H)**	**19**	**38**
Dec. 29	**Cincinnati**	**(A)**	**23**	**51**
Dec. 31	**Princeton**	**(H)**	**26**	**30**
Jan. 3	Florida	(H)	43	36
Jan. 10	**Ky. Wesleyan**	**(A)**	**25**	**31**
Jan. 15	**Vanderbilt**	**(H)**	**32**	**48**
Jan. 21	**Tennessee**	**(A)**	**14**	**19**
Jan. 22	**Georgia Tech**	**(A)**	**16**	**48**
Jan. 29	Centre	(H)	27	25
Feb. 1	**Georgetown**	**(A)**	**19**	**26**
Feb. 4	**Washington & Lee**	**(H)**	**34**	**36**
Feb. 7	**West Virginia**	**(H)**	**26**	**44**
Feb. 11	**Mississippi**	**(H)**	**17**	**37**
Feb. 12	**Centre**	**(A)**	**22**	**16**
Feb. 19	**Tennessee**	**(H)**	**21**	**30**
			374	563

1927-28—Won 12, Lost 6.
COACH: John Mauer
CAPTAIN: Paul Jenkins

Date	Team	Site	Ky.	Opp.
Dec. 16	Clemson	(H)	33	17
Dec. 20	**Miami (Ohio) U.**	**(H)**	**31**	**36**
Jan. 4	Berea	(H)	37	16
Jan. 9	Centre	(A)	36	25
Jan. 14	Vanderbilt	(H)	43	23
Jan. 16	Virginia	(A)	31	28
Jan. 18	**Naval Academy**	**(A)**	**26**	**32**
Jan. 19	**Maryland**	**(A)**	**7**	**37**
Jan. 28	Tennessee	(H)	48	18
Feb. 3	Washington & Lee	(H)	34	28
Feb. 4	**Indiana**	**(A)**	**29**	**48**
Feb. 8	**Vanderbilt**	**(A)**	**54**	**29**
Feb. 9	**Tennessee**	**(A)**	**43**	**16**
Feb. 11	**Georgia Tech**	**(H)**	**31**	**35**
Feb. 18	Centre	(H)	30	20

SOUTHERN CONF. TOUR. (Atlanta, Ga.)

Date	Team	Site	Ky.	Opp.
Feb. 24	South Carolina		56	40
Feb. 25	Georgia		33	16
Feb. 27	**Mississippi**		**28**	**41**
			630	505

1928-29—Won 12, Lost 5.
COACH: John Mauer
CAPTAIN: Lawrence McGinnis

Date	Team	Site	Ky.	Opp.
Dec. 15	Eastern Normal	(H)	35	10
Dec. 21	Miami (Ohio) U.	(H)	43***	42
Jan. 4	**North Carolina**	**(H)**	**15**	**25**
Jan. 12	Notre Dame	(A)	19	16
Jan. 16	**Georgia Tech**	**(A)**	**19**	**33**
Jan. 17	Tennessee	(A)	35	29
Jan. 19	Tennessee	(H)	27	22
Jan. 26	**Alabama**	**(H)**	**26**	**27**
Feb. 1	Mississippi A&M	(H)	25	23
Feb. 2	Mississippi A&M	(A)	32	14
Feb. 3	**Tulane**	**(A)**	**22**	**34**
Feb. 8	Washington & Lee	(H)	31	30
Feb. 13	Centre	(H)	47	11
Feb. 22	Mississippi	(H)	35	30
Feb. 23	Mississippi	(H)	32	24

SOUTHERN CONF. TOUR. (Atlanta, Ga.)

Date	Team	Site	Ky.	Opp.
Mar. 1	Tulane		29	15
Mar. 2	**Georgia**		**24**	**26**

*** Denotes 3 overtime periods.   496   411

1929-30—Won 16, Lost 3.
COACH: John Mauer
CAPTAIN: Paul McBrayer

Date	Team	Site	Ky.	Opp.
Dec. 14	Georgetown	(H)	46	9
Dec. 20	Miami (Ohio) U.	(H)	35	20
Dec. 31	Berea	(H)	29	26
Jan. 3	Clemson	(H)	31	15
Jan. 10	**Creighton**	**(H)**	**27**	**28**
Jan. 11	Creighton	(H)	25	21
Jan. 18	Tennessee	(H)	23	20
Jan. 24	Mississippi A&M	(H)	43	17
Jan. 25	Mississippi A&M	(H)	20	14
Jan. 31	**Tennessee**	**(A)**	**26**	**29**
Feb. 1	Georgia	(A)	22	21
Feb. 3	Clemson	(A)	34	20
Feb. 8	Georgia Tech	(H)	39	19
Feb. 14	Georgia	(H)	36	23
Feb. 18	Ky. Wesleyan	(H)	32	20
Feb. 22	Washington & Lee	(H)	28	*26

SOUTHERN CONF. TOUR. (Atlanta, Ga.)

Date	Team	Site	Ky.	Opp.
Feb. 28	Maryland		26	21
Mar. 1	Sewanee		44	22
Mar. 3	**Duke**		**32**	**37**
			599	408

* Denotes overtime period.

ADOLPH RUPP ERA

1930-31—Won 15, Lost 3.
COACH: Adolph Rupp
CAPTAIN: Carey Spicer

Date	Team	Site	Ky.	Opp.
Dec. 18	Georgetown	(H)	67	19
Dec. 27	Marshall	(H)	42	26
Dec. 31	Berea	(H)	41	25
Jan. 3	Clemson	(H)	33	21
Jan. 10	Tennessee	(A)	31	23
Jan. 16	Chattanooga	(H)	55	18
Jan. 21	Vanderbilt	(A)	42	37
Jan. 31	Tennessee	(A)	36	*32
Feb. 6	Washington & Lee	(H)	23	18
Feb. 9	Georgia Tech	(H)	38	34
Feb. 13	**Georgia**	**(A)**	**16**	**25**
Feb. 14	**Clemson**	**(A)**	**26**	**29**
Feb. 16	Georgia Tech	(A)	35	16
Feb. 20	Vanderbilt	(H)	43	23

SOUTHERN CONF. TOUR. (Atlanta, Ga.)

Date	Team	Site	Ky.	Opp.
Feb. 27	North Carolina State		33	28
Feb. 28	Duke		35	30
Mar. 1	Florida		56	36
Mar. 3	**Maryland (finals)**		**27**	**29**
			679	469

* Denotes overtime period.

1931-32—Won 15, Lost 2.
COACH: Adolph Rupp
CAPTAIN: Ellis Johnson

Date	Team	Site	Ky.	Opp.
Dec. 15	Georgetown	(H)	66	24
Dec. 18	Carnegie Tech	(H)	36	34
Dec. 23	Berea	(H)	52	27
Dec. 30	Marshall	(H)	46	16
Jan. 2	Clemson	(H)	43	24
Jan. 14	Clemson	(A)	30	17
Jan. 15	Sewanee	(A)	30	20
Jan. 16	Tennessee	(A)	29	28
Jan. 21	Chattanooga	(H)	51	17
Jan. 30	Washington & Lee	(H)	48	28
Feb. 6	Duke	(H)	37	30
Feb. 8	Alabama	(H)	50	22
Feb. 10	Vanderbilt	(A)	61	37
Feb. 13	Tennessee	(H)	41	27
Feb. 20	**Vanderbilt**	**(H)**	**31**	**32**

SOUTHERN CONF. TOUR. (Atlanta, Ga.)

Date	Team	Site	Ky.	Opp.
Feb. 26	Tulane		50	30
Feb. 27	**North Carolina**		**42**	**43**
			743	456

Date	Team	Site	Ky.	Opp.

1932-33—Won 20, Lost 3.
COACH: Adolph Rupp
CATAIN: Forest Sale

Date	Team	Site	Ky.	Opp.
Dec. 12	Georgetown	(H)	62	21
Dec. 17	Marshall	(N1)	57	23
Dec. 20	Tulane	(H)	53	17
Dec. 21	Tulane	(H)	42	11
Dec. 30	Chicago	(A)	58	26
Jan. 2	**Ohio State**	**(H)**	**30**	**46**
Jan. 6	Creighton	(A)	32	26
Jan. 7	**Creighton**	**(A)**	**22**	**34**
Jan. 10	South Carolina	(H)	44	36
Jan. 14	Tennessee	(A)	42	21
Jan. 16	Clemson	(H)	67	18
Jan. 28	Tennessee	(H)	44	23
Jan. 31	Vanderbilt	(A)	40	29
Feb. 1	Clemson	(A)	42	32
Feb. 2	**South Carolina**	**(A)**	**38**	**44**
Feb. 6	Mexico U.	(H)	81	22
Feb. 11	Georgia Tech	(H)	45	22
Feb. 13	Alabama	(N2)	35	21
Feb. 18	Vanderbilt	(H)	45	28

SEC TOURNAMENT (Atlanta, Ga.)

Feb. 25	Mississippi		49	31
Feb. 26	Florida		48	24
Feb. 27	L.S.U.		51	38
Feb. 28	Mississippi State		46	27
	(championship)			
SEC CHAMPIONS			1073	630

(N1) Ashland, Ky.   (N2) Birmingham

1933-34—Won 16, Lost 1.
COACH: Adolph Rupp
CAPTAIN: John DeMoisey

Dec. 5	Alumni	(H)	53	20
Dec. 9	Georgetown	(H)	41	12
Dec. 14	Marshall	(H)	48	26
Dec. 16	Cincinnati	(H)	31	25
Dec. 21	Tulane	(A)	32	22
Dec. 22	Tulane	(A)	42	29
Jan. 12	Sewanee	(A)	55	16
Jan. 13	Tennessee	(A)	44	23
Jan. 20	Chattanooga	(H)	47	20
Jan. 27	Tennessee	(H)	53	26
Feb. 1	Alabama	(N1)	33	28
Feb. 3	Vanderbilt	(A)	48	26
Feb. 8	Alabama	(H)	26	21
Feb. 10	Georgia Tech	(H)	49	25
Feb. 15	Sewanee	(H)	60	15
Feb. 17	Vanderbilt	(H)	47	27

SEC TOURNAMENT (Atlanta, Ga.)

Feb. 24	**Florida**		**32**	**38**
			741	399

(N1) Birmingham

1934-35—Won 19, Lost 2.
COACH: Adolph Rupp
CO-CAPTAINS: Dave Lawrence and Jack Tucker

Dec. 10	Alumni	(H)	61	10
Dec. 13	Oglethorpe	(H)	81	12
Dec. 20	Tulane	(A)	38	9
Dec. 21	Tulane	(A)	52	12
Jan. 2	Chicago	(H)	42	16
Jan. 5	**New York U.**	**(A)**	**22**	**23**
Jan. 18	Tulane	(H)	63	22
Jan. 19	Tulane	(H)	55	12
Jan. 22	Chattanooga	(H)	66	19
Jan. 26	Tennessee	(H)	48	21
Feb. 1	Alabama	(N1)	33	26
Feb. 2	Vanderbilt	(A)	58	22
Feb. 5	Xavier	(A)	40	27
Feb. 9	Georgia Tech	(H)	57	30
Feb. 11	Alabama	(H)	25	16
Feb. 13	**Michigan State**	**(A)**	**26**	**32**

Feb. 16	Tennessee	(A)	38	36
Feb. 22	Creighton	(H)	63	42
Feb. 23	Creighton	(H)	24	13
Mar. 2	Vanderbilt	(H)	53	19
Mar. 7	Xavier	(H)	46	29

SEC CO-CHAMPIONS   991   448

(N1) Birmingham

1935-36—Won 15, Lost 6.
COACH: Adolph Rupp
CAPTAIN: Milerd Anderson

Dec. 6	Georgetown	(H)	42	17
Dec. 17	Berea	(H)	58	30
Dec. 23	Pittsburgh	(H)	35	17
Jan. 8	**New York U.**	**(A)**	**28**	**41**
Jan. 14	Xavier	(A)	36	32
Jan. 17	Tulane	(H)	49	24
Jan. 18	Tulane	(H)	39	21
Jan. 21	Michigan State	(H)	27	19
Jan. 25	Tennessee	(H)	40	31
Feb. 1	**Vanderbilt**	**(A)**	**23**	**32**
Feb. 3	Alabama	(A)	32	30
Feb. 7	Alabama	(H)	40	34
Feb. 10	**Notre Dame**	**(A)**	**20**	**41**
Feb. 11	Butler	(A)	39	28
Feb. 15	**Tennessee**	**(A)**	**28**	**39**
Feb. 18	Xavier	(H)	49	40
Feb. 21	Creighton	(H)	68	38
Feb. 22	**Creighton**	**(H)**	**29**	**31**
Feb. 24	Vanderbilt	(H)	61	41

SEC TOURNAMENT (Knoxville, Tenn.)

Feb. 28	Mississippi State		41	39
Mar. 1	**Tennessee**		**28**	**39**
			812	664

1936-37—Won 17, Lost 5.
COACH: Adolph Rupp
CAPTAIN: Warfield Donohue

Dec. 9	Georgetown	(H)	46	21
Dec. 12	Berea	(H)	70	26
Dec. 15	Xavier	(A)	34	28
Dec. 21	Centenary	(H)	37	19
Jan. 2	Michigan State	(H)	28	21
Jan. 5	**Notre Dame**	**(N1)**	**28**	**41**
Jan. 8	Creighton	(H)	59	36
Jan. 14	**Michigan State**	**(A)**	**23**	**24**
Jan. 16	Akron U.	(N2)	32	22
Jan. 23	Tennessee	(H)	43	26
Jan. 30	Vanderbilt	(A)	41	26
Feb. 1	Alabama	(N3)	38	27
Feb. 3	**Tulane**	**(A)**	**28**	**35**
Feb. 4	Tulane	(A)	28	25
Feb. 8	Mexico U.	(H)	60	30
Feb. 10	**Alabama**	**(H)**	**31**	**34**
Feb. 13	**Tennessee**	**(A)**	**24**	**26**
Feb. 20	Vanderbilt	(H)	51	19
Feb. 22	Xavier	(H)	23	15

SEC TOURNAMENT (Knoxville, Tenn.)

Feb. 26	Louisiana State		57	37
Feb. 28	Georgia Tech		40	30
Mar. 1	Tennessee (championship)		39	25
SEC CHAMPIONS			860	593

(N1) Louisville (N2) Cincinnati (N3) Birmingham

1937-38—Won 13, Lost 5.
COACH: Adolph Rupp
CAPTAIN: J. Rice Walker

Dec. 5	Berea	(H)	67	33
Dec. 18	Cincinnati	(H)	38	21
Dec. 22	Centenary	(H)	35	25

Date	Team	Site	Ky.	Opp.
	SUGAR BOWL TOURNAMENT			
	New Orleans, La.			
Dec. 29	Pittsburgh (championship)		40	29
Jan. 8	**Michigan State**	**(A)**	**37**	**42**
Jan. 10	**Detroit**	**(A)**	**26**	**34**
Jan. 15	**Notre Dame**	**(A)**	**37**	**47**
Jan. 22	Tennessee	(H)	52	27
Jan. 29	Vanderbilt	(A)	42	19
Jan. 31	Alabama	(N1)	57	31
Feb. 5	**Xavier**	**(A)**	**32**	**39**
Feb. 7	Michigan State	(H)	44	27
Feb. 12	Alabama	(H)	27	21
Feb. 14	Marquette	(H)	35	33
Feb. 17	Xavier	(H)	45	29
Feb. 21	Vanderbilt	(H)	48	24
Feb. 26	Tennessee	(A)	29	26
	SEC TOURNAMENT (Baton Rouge, La.)			
Mar. 3	**Tulane**		**34**	**36**
			725	541

(N1) Birmingham

1938-39—Won 16, Lost 4.
COACH: Adolph Rupp
CAPTAIN: Bernard Opper

Date	Team	Site	Ky.	Opp.
Dec. 2	Georgetown	(H)	39	19
Dec. 10	Ky. Wesleyan	(H)	57	18
Dec. 17	Cincinnati	(H)	44	27
Dec. 21	Washington & Lee	(H)	67	47
Jan. 4	**Long Island**	**(A)**	**34**	**52**
Jan. 6	St. Joseph's	(A)	41	30
Jan. 14	**Notre Dame**	**(N1)**	**37**	**42**
Jan. 21	**Tennessee**	**(H)**	**29**	**30**
Jan. 28	**Alabama**	**(N2)**	**38**	**41**
Jan. 30	Vanderbilt	(A)	51	37
Feb. 4	Marquette	(H)	37	31
Feb. 8	Xavier	(A)	41	31
Feb. 11	Alabama	(H)	45	27
Feb. 13	Mississippi State	(H)	39	28
Feb. 18	Tennessee	(A)	36	**34
Feb. 21	Xavier	(H)	43	23
Feb. 25	Vanderbilt	(H)	52	27
	SEC TOURNAMENT (Knoxville, Tenn.)			
Mar. 2	Mississippi		49	30
Mar. 3	Louisiana State		53	34
Mar. 4	Tennessee (championship)		46	38
			878	646

SEC CHAMPIONS
(N1) Louisville (N2) Birmingham
** Denotes 2 overtime periods

1939-40—Won 15, Lost 6.
COACH: Adolph Rupp
CAPTAIN: Layton Rouse

Date	Team	Site	Ky.	Opp.
Dec. 9	Berea	(H)	74	24
Dec. 16	**Cincinnati**	**(H)**	**30**	**39**
Dec. 21	Clemson	(A)	55	31
	SUGAR BOWL (New Orleans, La.)			
Dec. 27	Ohio State (championship)		36	30
Jan. 1	Kansas State	(H)	53	26
Jan. 6	Xavier	(A)	42	41
Jan. 8	West Virginia	(H)	47	38
Jan. 13	**Notre Dame**	**(A)**	**47**	**52**
Jan. 20	Tennessee	(H)	35	26
Jan. 27	**Alabama**	**(N1)**	**32**	**36**
Jan. 29	**Vanderbilt**	**(A)**	**32**	**40**
Feb. 3	Marquette	(A)	51	45
Feb. 10	Alabama	(H)	46	18
Feb. 12	Xavier	(H)	37	29
Feb. 13	Mississippi State	(H)	45	37
Feb. 17	**Tennessee**	**(A)**	**23**	**27**
Feb. 19	**Georgia Tech**	**(A)**	**39**	**44**
Feb. 24	Vanderbilt	(H)	43	38
	SEC TOURNAMENT (Knoxville, Tenn.)			
Feb. 29	Vanderbilt		44	31
Mar. 1	Tennessee		30	29
Mar. 2	Georgia (championship)		51	43
			892	724

SEC CHAMPIONS
(N1) Birmingham

1940-41—Won 17, Lost 8.
COACH: Adolph Rupp
CAPTAIN: Lee Huber

Date	Team	Site	Ky.	Opp.
Dec. 7	Alumni	(H)	62	25
Dec. 12	West Virginia	(H)	46	34
Dec. 13	Maryville	(H)	53	14
Dec. 18	**Nebraska**	**(A)**	**39**	**40**
Dec. 19	**Creighton**	**(A)**	**45**	**54**
Dec. 20	Kansas State	(A)	28	25
Dec. 27	Centenary	(H)	70	18
	SUGAR BOWL (New Orleans, La.)			
Dec. 30	**Indiana**		**45**	**48**
Jan. 4	**Notre Dame**	**(N1)**	**47**	**48**
Jan. 9	Xavier	(A)	48	43
Jan. 11	**West Virginia**	**(A)**	**43**	**56**
Jan. 18	**Tennessee**	**(A)**	**22**	**32**
Jan. 20	Georgia Tech	(A)	47	37
Jan. 25	**Xavier**	**(H)**	**44**	**49**
Feb. 1	Vanderbilt	(A)	51	50
Feb. 3	Alabama	(A)	38	36
Feb. 8	Alabama	(H)	46	38
Feb. 10	Mississippi	(H)	60	41
Feb. 15	Tennessee	(H)	37	28
Feb. 17	Georgia Tech	(H)	60	41
Feb. 24	Vanderbilt	(H)	58	31
	SEC TOURNAMENT (Louisville, Ky.)			
Feb. 27	Mississippi		62	52
Feb. 28	Tulane		59	30
Mar. 1	Alabama		39	37
Mar. 2	**Tennessee**		**33**	**36**
			1182	943

(N1) Louisville

1941-42—Won 19, Lost 6.
COACH: Adolph Rupp
CAPTAIN: Carl Staker

Date	Team	Site	Ky.	Opp.
Dec. 6	Miami (Ohio) U.	(H)	35	21
Dec. 13	**Ohio State**	**(A)**	**41**	**43**
Dec. 16	Nebraska	(H)	42	27
Dec. 22	South Carolina	(H)	64	25
Dec. 30	Texas A&M	(H)	49	29
Jan. 2	Washington & Lee	(H)	62	32
Jan. 10	Xavier	(A)	40	39
Jan. 17	**Tennessee**	**(A)**	**40**	**46**
Jan. 19	Georgia	(A)	51	26
Jan. 20	Georgia Tech	(A)	63	53
Jan. 24	Mexico	(H)	56	26
Jan. 31	Georgia	(H)	55	38
Feb. 2	**Alabama**	**(A)**	**35**	**41**
Feb. 7	**Notre Dame**	**(A)**	**43**	**46**
Feb. 9	Alabama	(H)	50	34
Feb. 14	Tennessee	(A)	36	33
Feb. 16	Georgia Tech	(H)	57	51
Feb. 21	Xavier	(H)	44	36
	SEC TOURNAMENT			
	Louisville, Ky.			
Feb. 26	Florida		42	36
Feb. 27	Mississippi		59	32
Feb. 28	Auburn		40	31
Mar. 1	Alabama (championship)		36	34

SEC CHAMPIONS
POST SEASON GAME (Louisville, Ky.)

Date	Team	Site	Ky.	Opp.
Mar. 14	**Great Lakes**		**47**	**58**

Date	Team	Site	Ky.	Opp.
NCAA TOURNAMENT (New Orleans, La.)				
Mar. 20	Illinois		46	44
Mar. 21	**Dartmouth**		**28**	**47**
			1161	928

1942-43—Won 17, Lost 6.
COACH: Adolph Rupp
CAPTAIN: Melvin Brewer

Date	Team	Site	Ky.	Opp.
Dec. 12	Cincinnati	(H)	61	39
Dec. 19	Washington	(H)	45	38
Dec. 23	**Indiana**	**(N1)**	**52**	**58**
Jan. 2	**Ohio State**	**(H)**	**40**	**45**
Jan. 4	Ft. Knox	(H)	64	30
Jan. 9	Xavier	(A)	43	38
Jan. 16	Tennessee	(A)	30	28
Jan. 18	Georgia	(A)	60	28
Jan. 19	Georgia Tech	(A)	38	36
Jan. 23	Notre Dame	(N1)	60	55
Jan. 26	Vanderbilt	(H)	39	38
Jan. 30	**Alabama**	**(A)**	**32**	**41**
Feb. 1	Vanderbilt	(A)	54	43
Feb. 6	Alabama	(H)	67	41
Feb. 8	Xavier	(H)	48	36
Feb. 13	Tennessee	(H)	53	29
Feb. 15	Georgia Tech	(H)	58	31
Feb. 20	**De Paul**	**(A)**	**44**	**53**

SEC TOURNAMENT
Louisville, Ky.

Date	Team	Site	Ky.	Opp.
Feb. 25	Tulane		48	31
Feb. 26	Georgia		59	30
Feb. 27	Mississippi State		52	43
Feb. 28	**Tennessee**		**30**	**33**

POST-SEASON GAME (N1)

Date	Team	Site	Ky.	Opp.
Mar. 6	**Great Lakes**		**39**	**53**
			1124	887

(N1) Louisville

1943-44—Won 19, Lost 2.
COACH: Adolph Rupp
CAPTAIN:

Date	Team	Site	Ky.	Opp.
Dec. 1	Ft. Knox	(H)	51	18
Dec. 4	Berea (Naval V-12)	(H)	54	40
Dec. 11	Indiana	(N1)	66	41
Dec. 13	Ohio State	(A)	40	28
Dec. 18	Cincinnati	(H)	58	30
Dec. 20	**Illinois**	**(A)**	**41**	**43**
Dec. 28	Carnegie Tech	(A)	61	14
Dec. 30	St. John's	(A)	44	38
Jan. 8	Notre Dame	(N1)	55	54
Jan. 15	Wright Field	(H)	61	28
Jan. 31	Ft. Knox A.R.C.	(H)	76	48
Feb. 5	DePauw	(H)	38	35
Feb. 7	Illinois	(H)	51	40
Feb. 12	Cincinnati	(A)	38	35
Feb. 26	Ohio U.	(H)	51	35

SEC TOURNAMENT (Louisville, Ky.)

Date	Team	Site	Ky.	Opp.
Mar. 2	Georgia		57	29
Mar. 3	Louisiana State		55	28
Mar. 4	Tulane (championship)		62	46

SEC CHAMPIONS

NATIONAL INVITATION TOUR. (New York)

Date	Team	Site	Ky.	Opp.
Mar. 20	Utah		46	38
Mar. 22	**St. John's**		**45**	**48**
Mar. 26	Oklahoma A&M (consolation)		45	29
			1095	745

(N1) Louisville

1944-45—Won 22, Lost 4.
COACH: Adolph Rupp
CAPTAIN:

Date	Team	Site	Ky.	Opp.
Dec. 2	Ft. Knox	(H)	56	23
Dec. 4	Berea	(H)	56	32
Dec. 9	Cincinnati	(H)	66	24
Dec. 16	Indiana	(N1)	61	43
Dec. 23	Ohio State	(H)	53	*48
Dec. 26	Wyoming	(N2)	50	46
Dec. 30	Temple	(A)	45	44
Jan. 1	Long Island	(A)	62	*52
Jan. 6	Ohio U.	(H)	59	46
Jan. 8	Arkansas State	(H)	75	6
Jan. 13	Michigan State	(H)	66	35
Jan. 20	**Tennessee**	**(A)**	**34**	**35**
Jan. 22	Georgia Tech	(A)	64	58
Jan. 27	**Notre Dame**	**(N1)**	**58**	***59**
Jan. 29	Georgia	(H)	73	37
Feb. 3	Georgia Tech	(H)	51	32
Feb. 5	**Michigan State**	**(A)**	**50**	**66**
Feb. 17	Tennessee	(H)	40	34
Feb. 19	Ohio U.	(A)	61	38
Feb. 24	Cincinnati	(A)	65	35

SEC TOURNAMENT (Louisville, Ky.)

Date	Team	Site	Ky.	Opp.
Mar. 1	Florida		57	35
Mar. 2	Louisiana State		68	37
Mar. 3	Alabama		52	41
Mar. 3	Tennessee (championship)		39	35

SEC CHAMPIONS

NCAA TOURNAMENT (New York)

Date	Team	Site	Ky.	Opp.
Mar. 20	**Ohio State**		**37**	**45**
Mar. 21	Tufts (consolation)		66	56
			1464	1042

* Denotes overtime period.
(N1) Louisville
(N2) Buffalo, N. Y.

1945-46—Won 28, Lost 2.
COACH: Adolph Rupp
CAPTAIN: Jack Parkinson

Date	Team	Site	Ky.	Opp.
Dec. 1	Ft. Knox	(H)	59	36
Dec. 7	Western Ontario	(H)	51	42
Dec. 8	Western Ontario	(H)	71	28
Dec. 15	Cincinnati	(H)	67	31
Dec. 18	Arkansas	(H)	67	42
Dec. 21	Oklahoma	(A)	43	33
Dec. 29	St. John's	(A)	73	59
Jan. 1	**Temple**	**(A)**	**45**	**53**
Jan. 5	Ohio U.	(H)	57	48
Jan. 7	Fort Benning	(H)	81	25
Jan. 12	Michigan State	(A)	55	44
Jan. 14	Xavier	(A)	62	36
Jan. 19	Tennessee	(A)	50	32
Jan. 21	Georgia Tech	(A)	68	43
Jan. 26	**Notre Dame**	**(N1)**	**47**	**56**
Jan. 28	Georgia Tech	(H)	54	26
Feb. 2	Michigan State	(H)	59	51
Feb. 4	Vanderbilt	(A)	59	37
Feb. 9	Vanderbilt	(N2)	64	31
Feb. 16	Tennessee	(H)	54	34
Feb. 19	Ohio U.	(A)	60	52
Feb. 23	Xavier	(H)	83	40

SEC TOURNAMENT (Louisville, Ky.)

Date	Team	Site	Ky.	Opp.
Feb. 28	Auburn		69	24
Mar. 1	Florida		69	32
Mar. 2	Alabama		59	30
Mar. 2	Louisiana State (championship)		59	36

SEC CHAMPIONS

POST-SEASON GAME
Louisville, Ky.

Date	Team	Site	Ky.	Opp.
Mar. 9	Temple		54	43

NATIONAL INVITATION TOUR. (New York)

Date	Team	Site	Ky.	Opp.
Mar. 16	Arizona		77	53
Mar. 18	West Virginia		59	51
Mar. 20	Rhode Island (Championship)		46	45
			1821	1198

(N1) Louisville
(N2) Paducah, Ky.

Date	Team	Site	Ky.	Opp.
1946-47—Won 34, Lost 3.				
COACH: Adolph Rupp				
CAPTAIN: Ken Rollins				
Nov. 28	Indiana Central	(H)	78	36
Nov. 30	Tulane	(H)	64	35
Dec. 2	Ft. Knox	(H)	68	31
Dec. 7	Cincinnati	(A)	80	49
Dec. 9	Idaho	(H)	65	35
Dec. 12	De Paul	(N1)	65	45
Dec. 14	Texas A&M	(H)	83	18
Dec. 16	Miami (Ohio) U.	(H)	62	49
Dec. 21	St. John's	(N2)	70	50
Dec. 23	Baylor	(H)	75	34
Dec. 28	Wabash	(H)	96	24
SUGAR BOWL (New Orleans, La.)				
Dec. 30	**Oklahoma A&M**		**31**	**37**
Jan. 4	Ohio U.	(H)	46	36
Jan. 11	Dayton U.	(H)	70	29
Jan. 13	Vanderbilt	(A)	82	30
Jan. 18	Tennessee	(A)	54	39
Jan. 20	Georgia Tech	(A)	70	47
Jan. 21	Georgia	(A)	84	45
Jan. 25	Xavier	(H)	71	34
Jan. 27	Michigan State	(H)	86	36
Feb. 1	Notre Dame	(N1)	60	30
Feb. 3	Alabama	(A)	48	37
Feb. 8	**De Paul**	**(A)**	**47**	**53**
Feb. 10	Georgia	(H)	81	40
Feb. 15	Tennessee	(H)	61	46
Feb. 17	Alabama	(H)	63	33
Feb. 19	Xavier	(A)	58	31
Feb. 21	Vanderbilt	(A)	84	41
Feb. 22	Georgia Tech	(H)	83	46
SEC TOURNAMENT (Louisville, Ky.)				
Feb. 27	Vanderbilt		98	29
Feb. 28	Auburn		84	18
Mar. 1	Georgia Tech		75	53
Mar. 1	Tulane (championship)		55	38
SEC CHAMPIONS				
POST-SEASON GAME (Louisville)				
Mar. 8	Temple		68	29
NATIONAL INVITATION TOURNAMENT New York, N. Y.				
Mar. 17	Long Island		63	62
Mar. 19	North Carolina State		60	42
Mar. 24	**Utah**		**45**	**49**

(N1) Louisville 2533 1416
(N2) Mad. Sq. Gar., Record Crowd, 18,493

1947-48—Won 36, Lost 3.
COACH: Adolph Rupp
CAPTAIN: Kenneth Rollins

Date	Team	Site	Ky.	Opp.
Nov. 29	Indiana Central	(H)	80	41
Dec. 1	Ft. Knox	(H)	80	41
Dec. 5	Tulsa U.	(H)	72	18
Dec. 6	Tulsa U.	(H)	71	22
Dec. 10	De Paul	(N1)	74	50
Dec. 13	Cincinnati	(A)	67	31
Dec. 17	Xavier U.	(H)	79	37
Dec. 20	**Temple U.**	**(A)**	**59**	**60**
Dec. 23	St. John's	(A)	52	40
Jan. 2	Creighton	(A)	65	23
Jan. 3	Western Ontario	(H)	98	41
Jan. 5	Miami (Ohio)	(A)	67	53
Jan. 10	Michigan State	(A)	47	45
Jan. 12	Ohio U.	(A)	79	57
Jan. 17	Tennessee	(A)	65	54
Jan. 20	Georgia Tech	(A)	71	56
Jan. 20	Georgia	(A)	88	51
Jan. 24	Cincinnati	(H)	70	43
Jan. 31	De Paul	(A)	68	51
Feb. 2	**Notre Dame**	**(A)**	**55**	**64**
Feb. 5	Alabama	(A)	41	31
Feb. 5	Washington U.	(N2)	69	39
Feb. 9	Vanderbilt	(A)	82	51
Feb. 14	Tennessee	(H)	69	42
Feb. 16	Alabama	(H)	63	33
Feb. 20	Vanderbilt	(H)	79	43
Feb. 21	Georgia Tech	(H)	78	54
Feb. 24	Temple	(N1)	58	38
Feb. 28	Xavier	(A)	59	37
SEC TOURNAMENT (Louisville, Ky.)				
Mar. 4	Florida		87	31
Mar. 5	Louisiana State		63	47
Mar. 6	Tennessee		70	47
Mar. 6	Georgia Tech (championship)		54	43
SEC CHAMPIONS				
NCAA TOURNAMENT (New York)				
Mar. 18	Columbia		76	53
Mar. 20	Holy Cross		60	52
Mar. 23	Baylor (championship)		58	42
NATIONAL CHAMPIONS				
OLMPYIC TRIALS (New York)				
Mar. 27	Louisville		91	57
Mar. 29	Baylor		77	59
(Championship—Collegiate Bracket)				
Mar. 31	**Phillips Oilers**			
	(AAU Champs)		**49**	**53**

(N1) Louisville 2690 1730
(N2) Memphis

OLYMPIC TEAM
EXHIBITION GAMES
Kentucky vs. Phillips Oilers

6-30-48 — Tulsa, Okla.			52	60
7- 2-48 — Kansas City, Mo.			70	**69
7- 9-48 — Lexington, Ky.			50	56

†OLYMPIC GAMES (London, England)

July 30	Switzerland		86	21
Aug. 2	Czechoslovakia		53	28
Aug. 3	Argentina		59	57
Aug. 4	Egypt		66	28
Aug. 6	Peru		61	33
Aug. 9	Uruguay		63	28
Aug. 11	Mexico		71	40
Aug. 13	France (championship)		65	21

WORLD CHAMPIONS

** Denotes two overtime periods.
† Kentucky participated as part of U.S. basketball entry.

1948-49—Won 32, Lost 2.
COACH: Adolph Rupp
CAPTAIN:

Date	Team	Site	Ky.	Opp.
Nov. 29	Indiana Central	(H)	74	38
Dec. 8	De Paul	(N1)	67	36
Dec. 10	Tulsa U.	(H)	81	27
Dec. 13	Arkansas	(H)	76	39
Dec. 16	Holy Cross	(A)	51	48
Dec. 18	St. John's	(A)	57	30
Dec. 22	Tulane	(N1)	51	47
SUGAR BOWL (New Orleans, La.)				
Dec. 29	Tulane		78	47
Dec. 30	**St. Louis**		**40**	**42**
Jan. 11	Bowling Green	(N2)	63	61
Jan. 15	Tennessee	(A)	66	51
Jan. 17	Georgia Tech	(A)	56	45
Jan. 22	De Paul	(A)	56	45
Jan. 29	Notre Dame	(N1)	62	38
Jan. 31	Vanderbilt	(A)	72	50
Feb. 2	Alabama	(A)	56	40
Feb. 3	Mississippi	(N3)	75	45
Feb. 5	Bradley	(N4)	62	52
Feb. 8	Tennessee	(H)	71	56
Feb. 12	Xavier	(H)	96	50
Feb. 14	Alabama	(H)	74	32
Feb. 16	Mississippi	(H)	85	31
Feb. 19	Georgia Tech	(H)	78	32

Date	Team	Site	Ky.	Opp.
Feb. 21	Georgia	(H)	95	40
Feb. 24	Xavier	(A)	51	40
Feb. 26	Vanderbilt	(H)	70	37

SEC TOURNAMENT (Louisville, Ky.)

Mar. 3	Florida		73	36
Mar. 4	Auburn		70	39
Mar. 5	Tennessee		83	44
Mar. 5	Tulane (championship)		68	52

SEC CHAMPIONS

NATIONAL INVITATION TOUR. (New York)

Mar. 14 Loyola of Chicago 56 67

NCAA TOURNAMENT
(Eastern Regionals)
New York, N. Y.

Mar. 21	Villanova		85	72
Mar. 22	Illinois		76	47

NCAA FINALS (Seattle, Wash.)

Mar. 26	Oklahoma A&M (championship)		46	36
			2320	1492

NATIONAL CHAMPIONS

(N1) Louisville (N3) Memphis
(N2) Cleveland (N4) Owensboro, Ky.

1949-50—Won 25, Lost 5.
COACH: Adolph Rupp
CAPTAIN: Dale Barnstable

Dec. 3	Indiana Central	(H)	84	61
Dec. 10	Western Ontario	(H)	90	18
Dec. 15	**St. John's**	**(A)**	**58**	**69**
Dec. 21	De Paul	(N1)	49	47
Dec. 25	Purdue	(A)	60	54

SUGAR BOWL (New Orleans, La.)

Dec. 29	Villanova		57	*56
Dec. 30	Bradley (championship)		71	66
Jan. 2	Arkansas	(A)	57	53
Jan. 4	Mississippi State	(N2)	87	55
Jan. 9	North Carolina U.	(H)	83	44
Jan. 14	**Tennessee**	**(A)**	**53**	**66**
Jan. 16	Georgia Tech	(A)	61	47
Jan. 17	**Georgia**	**(A)**	**60**	**71**
Jan. 21	De Paul	(A)	86	53
Jan. 23	**Notre Dame**	**(A)**	**51**	**64**
Jan. 26	Xavier	(A)	58	47
Jan. 28	Georgia	(H)	88	56
Jan. 30	Vanderbilt	(A)	58	54
Feb. 2	Alabama	(A)	66	64
Feb. 4	Mississippi	(N3)	61	55
Feb. 11	Tennessee	(H)	79	52
Feb. 13	Alabama	(H)	77	57
Feb. 15	Mississippi	(H)	90	50
Feb. 18	Georgia Tech	(H)	97	62
Feb. 23	Xavier	(H)	58	53
Feb. 25	Vanderbilt	(H)	70	66

SEC TOURNAMENT (Louisville, Ky.)

Mar. 2	Mississippi State		56	46
Mar. 3	Georgia		79	63
Mar. 4	Tennessee (championship)		95	58

SEC CHAMPIONS

NATIONAL INVITATION TOUR. (New York)

Mar. 14 City Col. of N. Y. 50 89

			2089	1696

(N1) Louisville
(N2) Owensboro
(N3) Memphis

* Denotes overtime period.

MEMORIAL COLISEUM ERA

1950-51—Won 32, Lost 2.
(Including exhibition games, Kentucky won 39½ games and lost 2.)
COACH: Adolph Rupp
CAPTAIN: Walt Hirsch

Dec. 1	West Texas State	(H)	73	43
Dec. 9	†Purdue	(H)	70	52
Dec. 12	Xavier	(A)	67	56
Dec. 14	Florida	(H)	85	37
Dec. 16	Kansas	(H)	68	39
Dec. 23	St. John's	(A)	43	37

SUGAR BOWL (New Orleans, La.)

Dec. 29	**St. Louis**		**42**	***43**
Dec. 30	Syracuse (consolation)		69	59
Jan. 5	Auburn	(H)	79	35
Jan. 8	De Paul	(H)	63	55
Jan. 13	Alabama	(H)	65	48
Jan. 15	Notre Dame	(H)	69	44
Jan. 20	Tennessee	(A)	70	45
Jan. 22	Georgia Tech	(A)	82	61
Jan. 27	Vanderbilt	(A)	74	49
Jan. 29	Tulane	(A)	104	68
Jan. 31	Louisiana State	(A)	81	59
Feb. 2	Mississippi State	(A)	80	60
Feb. 3	Mississippi	(N1)	86	39
Feb. 9	Georgia Tech	(H)	75	42
Feb. 13	Xavier	(H)	78	51
Feb. 17	Tennessee	(H)	86	61
Feb. 19	De Paul	(A)	60	57
Feb. 23	Georgia	(H)	88	41
Feb. 24	Vanderbilt	(H)	89	57

SEC CHAMPIONS

SEC TOURNAMENT (Louisville, Ky.)

Mar. 1	Mississippi State		92	70
Mar. 2	Auburn		84	54
Mar. 3	Georgia Tech		82	56
Mar. 3	**Vanderbilt**		**57**	**61**

POST-SEASON GAME

Mar. 13	Loyola of Chicago	(H)	97	61

NCAA TOURNAMENT
(First Round—Raleigh, N. C.)

Mar. 20	Louisville		79	68

(Eastern Regional—New York N.Y.)

Mar. 22	St. John's		59	43
Mar. 24	Illinois		76	74

(National Finals—Minneapolis, Minn.)

Mar. 27	Kansas St. (championship)	68	58

NATIONAL CHAMPIONS   2540 1783

EXHIBITION GAME

Apr. 27	Ky. All-Stars	(H)	92	49

PUERTO RICO EXHIBITION TOUR

Aug. 25	San German Athletics		86	38
Aug. 26	Ponce Lions		83	43
Aug. 27	San Turce		93	40
Aug. 29	Univ. of Puerto Rico		91	44
Sept. 2	U. S. Navy		52	23

(Called at half on account of rain)

Sept. 3	Puerto Rico All-Stars		75	46

† Memorial Coliseum Dedication Game.
* Denotes overtime period.
(N1) Owensboro, Ky.

1951-52—Won 29, Lost 3.
COACH: Adolph Rupp
CAPTAIN: Robert Watson

Dec. 8	Washington & Lee	(H)	96	46
Dec. 10	Xavier	(A)	97	72
Dec. 13	**Minnesota**	**(A)**	**57**	**61**
Dec. 17	St. John's	(H)	81	40

Date	Team	Site	Ky.	Opp.
Dec. 20	De Paul	(H)	98	60
Dec. 26	U.C.L.A.	(H)	84	53
	SUGAR BOWL (New Orleans, La.)			
Dec. 28	Brigham Young		84	64
Dec. 29	**St. Louis**		**60**	**61**
Jan. 2	Mississippi†	(N1)	116	58
Jan. 5	Louisiana State	(H)	57	47
Jan. 7	Xavier	(H)	83	50
Jan. 12	Florida	(A)	99	52
Jan. 16	Georgia	(N2)	95	55
Jan. 19	Tennessee	(A)	65	56
Jan. 21	Georgia Tech	(A)	96	51
Jan. 26	Alabama	(A)	71	67
Jan. 28	Vanderbilt	(A)	88	51
Jan. 30	Auburn	(A)	88	48
Feb. 2	Notre Dame	(N3)	71	66
Feb. 4	Tulane	(H)	103	54
Feb. 6	Mississippi	(H)	81	61
Feb. 9	Georgia Tech	(H)	93	42
Feb. 11	Mississippi State	(H)	110	66
Feb. 16	Tennessee	(H)	95	40
Feb. 21	Vanderbilt	(H)	75	45
Feb. 23	De Paul	(A)	63	61

SEC CHAMPIONS

	SEC TOURNAMENT (Louisville, Ky.)#			
Feb. 28	Georgia Tech		80	59
Feb. 29	Tulane		85	61
Mar. 1	Tennessee		81	66
Mar. 1	Louisiana State (championship)		44	43

	NCAA TOURNAMENT (Eastern Regionals) Raleigh, N. C.			
Mar. 21	Penn. State		82	54
Mar. 22	**St. John's**		**57**	**64**
			2635	1774

† Not counted as SEC game.
(N1) Owensboro, Ky.
(N2) Louisville
(N3) Chicago
Tournament abandoned after 1952.

1952-53—No Schedule.
(Under suspension by NCAA)
Intra-Squad Scrimmage Results
COACH: Adolph Rupp
CO-CAPTAINS: Cliff Hagan and Frank Ramsey

Dec. 13	Varsity	76	Freshmen	45
Jan. 19	Ramseys	71	Hagans	50
Feb. 4	Hagans	68	Ramseys	55
Feb. 28	Blues	49	Whites	47
		264		197

1953-54—Won 25, Lost 0.
COACH: Adolph Rupp
CO-CAPTAINS: Cliff Hagan and Frank Ramsey

Dec. 5	Temple	(H)	86	59
Dec. 12	Xavier	(A)	81	66
Dec. 14	Wake Forest	(H)	101	69
Dec. 18	St. Louis	(A)	71	59
	UK INVITATIONAL TOURNAMENT			
Dec. 21	Duke		85	69
Dec. 22	LaSalle (championship)		73	60
Dec. 28	Minnesota	(H)	74	59
Jan. 4	Xavier	(H)	77	71
Jan. 9	Georgia Tech	(H)	105	53
Jan. 11	De Paul	(H)	81	63
Jan. 16	Tulane	(H)	94	43
Jan. 23	Tennessee	(A)	97	71
Jan. 30	Vanderbilt	(A)	85	63
Feb. 2	Georgia Tech	(N1)	99	48
Feb. 4	Georgia	(H)	106	55
Feb. 6	Georgia	(N2)	100	68
Feb. 8	Florida	(A)	97	55
Feb. 13	Mississippi	(H)	88	62
Feb. 15	Mississippi State	(H)	81	49
Feb. 18	Tennessee	(H)	90	63
Feb. 20	De Paul	(A)	76	61
Feb. 22	Vanderbilt	(H)	100	64
Feb. 27	Auburn	(N3)	109	79
Mar. 1	Alabama	(A)	68	43

	SEC PLAYOFF (Nashville, Tenn.)			

(Playoff game to determine SEC champion and representative in NCAA Tournament. Kentucky and LSU tied for league title due to a schedule disagreement. Kentucky won but declined NCAA.)

Mar. 9	Louisiana State		63	56
			2187	1508

SEC CHAMPIONS
(N1) Louisville
(N2) Owensboro, Ky.
(N3) Montgomery

1954-55—Won 23, Lost 3.
COACH: Adolph Rupp
CAPTAIN: Bill Evans

Dec. 4	Louisiana State†	(H)	74	58
Dec. 11	Xavier	(A)	73	69
Dec. 18	Temple	(H)	79	61
	UNIVERSITY OF KENTUCKY INVITATIONAL TOURNAMENT Lexington, Ky.			
Dec. 21	Utah		70	65
Dec. 22	LaSalle (championship)		63	54
Dec. 30	St. Louis	(H)	82	65
Jan. 1	Temple	(A)	101	69
Jan. 8	**Georgia Tech**	**(H)**	**58**	**59**
Jan. 10	De Paul	(H)	92	59
Jan. 15	Tulane	(A)	58	44
Jan. 17	Louisiana State	(A)	64	62
Jan. 22	Tennessee	(A)	84	66
Jan. 29	Vanderbilt	(A)	75	71
Jan. 31	**Georgia Tech**	**(A)**	**59**	**65**
Feb. 3	Florida	(H)	87	63
Feb. 5	Mississippi	(N1)	84	66
Feb. 7	Mississippi State	(A)	61	56
Feb. 9	Georgia	(H)	86	40
Feb. 14	Xavier	(H)	66	55
Feb. 19	De Paul	(A)	76	72
Feb. 21	Vanderbilt	(H)	77	59
Feb. 26	Auburn	(A)	93	59
Feb. 28	Alabama	(H)	66	52
Mar. 5	Tennessee	(H)	104	61

SEC CHAMPIONS

	NCAA TOURNAMENT (Eastern Regionals) Evanston, Illinois			
Mar. 11	**Marquette**		**71**	**79**
Mar. 12	Penn State		84	59
			1987	1588

† Game not counted in SEC standings.
(N1) Memphis

1955-56—Won 20, Lost 6.
COACH: Adolph Rupp
CAPTAIN: Phil Grawemeyer

Dec. 3	Louisiana State†	(A)	62	52
Dec. 10	**Temple**	**(H)**	**61**	**73**
Dec. 12	De Paul	(H)	71	69
Dec. 15	Maryland	(A)	62	61
Dec. 17	Idaho	(H)	91	49
	UK INVITATIONAL TOURNAMENT			
Dec. 20	Minnesota		72	65
Dec. 21	**Dayton**		**74**	**89**

432

Date	Team	Site	Ky.	Opp.
Dec. 28	St. Louis U.	(A)	101	80
Jan. 7	Georgia Tech	(H)	104	51
Jan. 12	Tulane	(H)	85	63
Jan. 14	Louisiana State	(H)	107	65
Jan. 21	Tennessee	(A)	95	68
Jan. 28	**Vanderbilt**	**(A)**	**73**	**81**
Jan. 30	Georgia Tech	(A)	84	62
Feb. 1	Duke	(H)	81	76
Feb. 4	Auburn	(N1)	82	81
Feb. 6	Florida	(A)	81	70
Feb. 11	Mississippi	(H)	88	49
Feb. 13	Mississippi State	(H)	86	65
Feb. 18	**De Paul**	**(A)**	**79**	**81**
Feb. 20	Vanderbilt	(H)	76	55
Feb. 25	**Alabama**	**(N1)**	**77**	**101**
Feb. 27	Georgia	(N2)	143	66
Mar. 3	Tennessee	(H)	101	77

NCAA TOURNAMENT
(Kentucky represented the SEC in NCAA when champion Alabama declined the bid.)
(Eastern Regionals) Iowa City, Iowa

Mar. 16	Wayne U.	(A)	84	64
Mar. 17	**Iowa**	**(A)**	**77**	**89**
			2197	1802

† Game not counted in SEC standings.
(N1) Montgomery
(N2) Louisville

1956-57—Won 23, Lost 5.
COACH: Adolph Rupp
HONORARY CO-CAPTAINS:
Ed Beck and Gerry Calvert

Date	Team	Site	Ky.	Opp.
Dec. 1	Washington & Lee	(H)	94	66
Dec. 3	Miami (Fla.)	(H)	114	75
Dec. 8	Temple	(A)	73	58
Dec. 10	**St. Louis**	**(H)**	**70**	**71**
Dec. 15	Maryland	(H)	76	55
Dec. 18	**Duke**	**(A)**	**84**	**85**

UK INVITATIONAL TOURNAMENT

Dec. 21	Southern Methodist		73	67
Dec. 22	Illinois (championship)		91	70

SUGAR BOWL (New Orleans, La.)

Dec. 28	Virginia Tech		56	55
Dec. 29	Houston (championship)		111	76
Jan. 5	Georgia Tech	(H)	95	72
Jan. 7	Loyola (Chicago)	(H)	81	62
Jan. 12	Louisiana State	(A)	51	46
Jan. 14	**Tulane**	**(A)**	**60**	**68**
Jan. 19	Tennessee	(A)	97	72
Jan. 26	Vanderbilt	(A)	91	83
Jan. 28	Georgia Tech	(A)	76	65
Jan. 30	Georgia	(H)	84	53
Feb. 2	Florida	(H)	88	61
Feb. 8	Mississippi	(N1)	75	69
Feb. 11	**Mississippi State**	**(A)**	**81**	**89**
Feb. 15	Loyola (Chicago)	(A)	115	65
Feb. 18	Vanderbilt	(H)	80	65
Feb. 23	Alabama	(H)	79	60
Feb. 25	Auburn	(H)	103	85
Mar. 2	Tennessee	(H)	93	75

SEC CHAMPIONS

NCAA TOURNAMENT
(Midwest Regional) Lexington, Ky.

Mar. 15	Pittsburgh		98	92
Mar. 16	**Michigan State**		**68**	**80**
			2357	1953

(N1) Memphis

1957-58—Won 23, Lost 6.
COACH: Adolph Rupp
HONORARY CAPT.: Ed Beck

Date	Team	Site	Ky.	Opp.
Dec. 2	Duke	(H)	78	74
Dec. 4	Ohio State	(A)	61	54
Dec. 7	Temple	(H)	85***	83
Dec. 9	**Maryland**	**(A)**	**62**	**71**
Dec. 14	St. Louis	(A)	73	60
Dec. 16	**Southern Methodist**	**(A)**	**64**	**65**

UK INVITATIONAL TOURNAMENT

Dec. 20	**West Virginia**		**70**	**77**
Dec. 21	Minnesota		78	58
Dec. 23	Utah State	(H)	92	64
Dec. 30	Loyola (Chicago)	(H)	75	42
Jan. 4	Georgia Tech	(H)	76	60
Jan. 6	Vanderbilt	(A)	86	81
Jan. 11	Louisiana State	(H)	97	52
Jan. 13	Tulane	(H)	86	50
Jan. 18	Tennessee	(H)	77	68
Jan. 27	**Georgia Tech**	**(A)**	**52**	**71**
Jan. 29	Georgia	(N1)	74	55
Jan. 31	Florida	(A)	78	56
Feb. 8	Mississippi	(H)	96	65
Feb. 10	Mississippi State	(H)	72	62
Feb. 15	**Loyola (Chicago)**	**(A)**	**56**	**57**
Feb. 17	Vanderbilt	(H)	65	61
Feb. 22	Alabama	(N2)	45	*43
Feb. 24	**Auburn**	**(N3)**	**63**	**64**
Mar. 1	Tennessee	(A)	77	66

SEC CHAMPIONS

NCAA TOURNAMENT
(Mideast Regional) Lexington, Ky.

Mar. 14	Miami (Ohio)		94	70
Mar. 15	Notre Dame		89	56

(FINALS)
Louisville, Ky.

Mar. 21	Temple		61	60
Mar. 22	Seattle (championship)		84	72
			2166	1817

NATIONAL COLLEGIATE CHAMPIONS
FOR RECORD FOURTH TIME

*** Three overtime periods.
* One overtime period.
(N1) Atlanta   (N3) Birmingham
(N2) Montgomery

1958-59—Won 24, Lost 3.
COACH: Adolph Rupp
HONORARY CAPT.: Johnny Cox

Date	Team	Site	Ky.	Opp.
Dec. 1	Florida State	(H)	91	68
Dec. 6	Temple	(A)	76	71
Dec. 8	Duke	(A)	78	64
Dec. 11	Southern Methodist	(H)	72	60
Dec. 13	St. Louis	(H)	76	57
Dec. 15	Maryland	(H)	58	*56

UK INVITATIONAL TOURNAMENT

Dec. 19	Ohio State		95	76
Dec. 20	W. Virginia (championship)		97	91
Dec. 29	Navy	(H)	82	69
Dec. 30	Illinois	(N1)	76	75
Jan. 3	Georgia Tech	(H)	72	62
Jan. 6	**Vanderbilt**	**(A)**	**66**	**75**
Jan. 10	Louisiana State	(A)	76	61
Jan. 12	Tulane	(A)	85	68
Jan. 17	Tennessee	(H)	79	58
Jan. 26	Georgia Tech	(A)	94	70
Jan. 29	Georgia	(H)	108	55
Jan. 31	Florida	(H)	94	51
Feb. 7	Mississippi	(N2)	97	72
Feb. 9	**Mississippi State**	**(A)**	**58**	**66**
Feb. 14	Notre Dame	(N3)	71	52
Feb. 18	Vanderbilt	(H)	83	71
Feb. 21	Auburn	(H)	75	56
Feb. 23	Alabama	(H)	39	32
Feb. 28	Tennessee	(A)	69	56

NCAA TOURNAMENT
(Kentucky represented the SEC in NCAA when champion Miss. State declined the bid.)
(Mideast Regional) Evanston, Ill.

Mar. 13	**Louisville**		**61**	**76**

Date	Team	Site	Ky.	Opp.
Mar. 14	Marquette		98	69
			2126	1737

* Denotes overtime period.
(N1) Louisville (N3) Chicago, Ill.
(N2) Jackson, Miss.

1959-60—Won 18, Lost 7.
COACH: Adolph Rupp
CO-CAPTS.: Bill Lickert and Don Mills

Date	Team	Site	Ky.	Opp.
Dec. 1	Colorado State	(H)	106	73
Dec. 4	UCLA	(A)	68	66
Dec. 5	**So. California**	**(A)**	**73**	**87**
Dec. 12	**St. Louis**	**(A)**	**61**	**73**
Dec. 14	Kansas	(A)	77*	72

UK INVITATIONAL TOURNAMENT

Dec. 18	North Carolina		76	70
Dec. 19	**West Virginia**		**70**	**79**
Dec. 20	Temple	(N1)	97	92
Dec. 28	Ohio State	(H)	96	93
Jan. 2	**Georgia Tech**	**(H)**	**54**	**62**
Jan. 5	Vanderbilt	(A)	76	59
Jan. 9	Louisiana State	(H)	77	45
Jan. 11	Tulane	(H)	68	42
Jan. 16	Tennessee	(A)	78	68
Jan. 25	**Georgia Tech**	**(A)**	**44**	**65**
Jan. 27	Georgia	(N2)	84	60
Jan. 29	Florida	(A)	75	62
Feb. 6	Mississippi	(H)	61	43
Feb. 8	Mississippi State	(H)	90	59
Feb. 13	Notre Dame	(H)	68	65
Feb. 16	Vanderbilt	(H)	68	60
Feb. 20	**Auburn**	**(A)**	**60**	**61**
Feb. 22	Alabama	(N3)	75	55
Feb. 27	**Tennessee**	**(H)**	**63**	**65**
Mar. 5	Pittsburgh	(H)	73	66
			1838	1642

* Denotes overtime period.
(N1) Louisville (N3) Montgomery, Ala.
(N2) Columbus, Ga.

1960-61—Won 19, Lost 9.
COACH: Adolph Rupp
CAPTAIN: Dick Parsons

Dec. 1	Va. Military Inst.	(H)	72	56
Dec. 3	**Florida State**	**(H)**	**58**	**63**
Dec. 7	Notre Dame	(N1)	68	62
Dec. 13	North Carolina	(N2)	70	65
Dec. 17	**Temple**	**(A)**	**58**	**66**

UK INVITATIONAL TOURNAMENT

Dec. 21	Illinois		83	78
Dec. 22	**St. Louis**		**72**	***74**
Dec. 31	Missouri	(H)	81	69
Jan. 2	Miami (Ohio)	(H)	70	58
Jan. 7	Georgia Tech	(H)	89	79
Jan. 9	**Vanderbilt**	**(A)**	**62**	**64**
Jan. 13	**Louisiana State**	**(A)**	**59**	**73**
Jan. 14	**Tulane**	**(A)**	**70**	**72**
Jan. 21	Tennessee	(H)	83	54
Jan. 30	**Georgia Tech**	**(A)**	**60**	**62**
Feb. 4	Florida		89	68
Feb. 7	Georgia	(H)	74	67
Feb. 11	Mississippi	(N3)	74	60
Feb. 13	Mississippi State	(A)	68	62
Feb. 17	UCLA	(H)	77	76
Feb. 21	Vanderbilt	(H)	60	59
Feb. 25	Alabama	(H)	80	53
Feb. 27	Auburn	(H)	77	51
Mar. 4	Tennessee	(A)	68	61

SEC PLAYOFF (Knoxville, Tenn.)

(To determine SEC representative in NCAA Tournament after champion Miss. State declined bid. Second place Kentucky and Vanderbilt each had 10-4 records.)

Date	Team	Site	Ky.	Opp.
Mar. 9	Vanderbilt		88	67
Mar. 11	**Marquette**	**(N4)**	**72**	**88**

NCAA TOURNAMENT
(Mideast Regional) Louisville, Ky.

Mar. 17	Morehead		71	64
Mar. 18	**Ohio State**		**74**	**87**
			2027	1858

(N1) Louisville, Ky.
(N2) Greensboro, N. C.
(N3) Jackson, Miss.
(N4) Chicago, Ill.
* Denotes one overtime period.

1961-62—Won 23, Lost 3.
COACH: Adolph Rupp
CAPTAIN: Larry Pursiful

Dec. 2	Miami (Ohio)	(H)	93	61
Dec. 4	**So. California**	**(H)**	**77**	**79**
Dec. 11	St. Louis	(H)	86	77
Dec. 16	Baylor	(H)	94	60
Dec. 18	Temple	(H)	78	55

UK INVITATIONAL TOURNAMENT

Dec. 22	Tennessee		96	69
Dec. 23	Kansas St. (championship)		80	67
Dec. 27	Yale	(H)	79	58
Dec. 30	Notre Dame	(N1)	100	53
Jan. 2	Virginia	(H)	93	73
Jan. 6	Georgia Tech	(H)	89	70
Jan. 8	Vanderbilt	(A)	77	68
Jan. 12	Louisiana State	(H)	84	63
Jan. 15	Tennessee	(A)	95	82
Jan. 29	Georgia Tech	(H)	71	62
Jan. 31	Georgia	(N2)	86	59
Feb. 2	Florida	(A)	81	69
Feb. 10	Mississippi	(H)	83	60
Feb. 12	**Mississippi State**	**(H)**	**44**	**49**
Feb. 19	Vanderbilt	(H)	87	80
Feb. 24	Alabama	(A)	73	65
Feb. 26	Auburn	(A)	63	60
Mar. 5	Tulane	(H)	97	72
Mar. 10	Tennessee	(H)	90	59

SEC CO-CHAMPIONS

NCAA TOURNAMENT
(Mideast Regional) Iowa City, Iowa

Mar. 16	Butler		81	60
Mar. 17	**Ohio State**		**64**	**74**
			2141	1704

(N1) Freedom Hall, Louisville
(N2) Ga. Tech Coliseum, Atlanta

1962-63—Won 16, Lost 9.
COACH: Adolph Rupp
CAPTAIN: Scotty Baesler

Dec. 1	**Virginia Tech**	**(H)**	**77**	**80**
Dec. 8	Temple	(A)	56	52
Dec. 12	Florida State	(H)	83	54
Dec. 15	Northwestern	(H)	71	60
Dec. 17	**North Carolina**	**(H)**	**66**	**68**

UK INVITATIONAL TOURNAMENT

Dec. 21	Iowa		94	69
Dec. 22	West Va. (Championship)		79	75
Dec. 27	Dartmouth	(H)	95	49
Dec. 29	Notre Dame	(N1)	78	70
Dec. 31	**St. Louis**	**(A)**	**63**	**87**
Jan. 5	**Georgia Tech**	**(H)**	**85**	****86**
Jan. 7	Vanderbilt	(A)	106	82
Jan. 11	Louisiana State	(A)	63	56
Jan. 12	Tulane	(A)	81	72
Jan. 19	**Tennessee**	**(H)**	**69**	***78**
Jan. 26	Xavier	(H)	90	76
Jan. 28	**Georgia Tech**	**(A)**	**62**	**66**
Jan. 31	Georgia	(H)	74	67
Feb. 2	Florida	(H)	94	71

434

Date	Team	Site	Ky.	Opp.
Feb. 9	Mississippi	(N2)	75	69
Feb. 11	**Mississippi State**	**(A)**	**52**	**56**
Feb. 18	**Vanderbilt**	**(H)**	**67**	**69**
Feb. 23	Auburn	(H)	78	59
Feb. 25	Alabama	(H)	80	63
Mar. 2	**Tennessee**	**(A)**	**55**	**63**
			1893	1697

(N1) Louisville   (N2) Jackson
* Denotes overtime periods

1963-64—Won 21, Lost 6.
COACH: Adolph Rupp
CO-CAPTS.: Cotton Nash and Ted Deeken

Date	Team	Site	Ky.	Opp.
Nov. 30	Virginia	(H)	75	64
Dec. 2	Texas Tech	(H)	107	91
Dec. 7	Northwestern	(A)	95	63
Dec. 9	North Carolina	(H)	100	80
Dec. 14	Baylor	(H)	101	65

UK INVITATIONAL TOURNAMENT

Dec. 20	Wisconsin		108	85
Dec. 21	Wake Forest		98	75
	(Championship)			
Dec. 28	Notre Dame	(N1)	101	81

SUGAR BOWL (New Orleans, La.)

Dec. 30	Loyola (La.)		86	64
Dec. 31	Duke (Championship)		81	79
Jan. 4	**Georgia Tech**	**(A)**	**67**	**76**
Jan. 6	**Vanderbilt**	**(A)**	**83**	**85**
Jan. 10	Louisiana State	(H)	103	84
Jan. 11	Tulane	(H)	105	63
Jan. 18	Tennessee	(H)	66	57
Jan. 25	Georgia Tech	(H)	79	62
Feb. 1	Florida	(A)	77	72
Feb. 3	Georgia	(A)	103	83
Feb. 8	Mississippi	(H)	102	59
Feb. 10	Mississippi State	(H)	65	59
Feb. 17	Vanderbilt	(H)	104	73
Feb. 22	Auburn	(N2)	99	79
Feb. 24	**Alabama**	**(A)**	**59**	**65**
Feb. 29	Tennessee	(A)	42	38
Mar. 2	**St. Louis**	**(H)**	**60**	**67**

SEC CHAMPIONS

NCAA TOURNAMENT
(Mideast Regional)
Minneapolis, Minn.

Mar. 13	**Ohio University**		**69**	**85**
Mar. 14	**Loyola (Chicago)**		**91**	**100**
			2326	1954

(N1) Louisville
(N2) Montgomery, Ala.

1964-65—Won 15, Lost 10.
COACH: Adolph Rupp
CAPTAIN: Randy Embry

Date	Team	Site	Ky.	Opp.
Dec. 4	Iowa	(H)	85	77
Dec. 7	**North Carolina**	**(N1)**	**67**	**82**
Dec. 9	Iowa State	(H)	100	74
Dec. 12	Syracuse	(H)	110	77

UK INVITATIONAL TOURNAMENT

Dec. 18	West Virginia		102	78
Dec. 19	**Illinois**		**86**	**91**
Dec. 22	**St. Louis**	**(A)**	**75**	**80**
Dec. 29	**Notre Dame**	**(N2)**	**97**	**111**
Jan. 2	Dartmouth	(H)	107	67
Jan. 5	**Vanderbilt**	**(H)**	**79**	**97**
Jan. 9	Louisiana State	(A)	79	66
Jan. 11	Tulane	(A)	102	72
Jan. 16	**Tennessee**	**(A)**	**58**	**77**
Jan. 18	Auburn	(A)	73	67
Jan. 23	**Florida**	**(A)**	**68**	**84**

Date	Team	Site	Ky.	Opp.
Jan. 25	Georgia	(A)	102	82
Jan. 30	Florida	(H)	78	61
Feb. 1	Georgia	(H)	96	64
Feb. 6	Mississippi	(H)	102	65
Feb. 8	Mississippi State	(H)	74	56
Feb. 16	**Vanderbilt**	**(A)**	**90**	**91**
Feb. 20	Auburn	(A)	69	88
Feb. 22	**Alabama**	**(A)**	**71**	**75**
Feb. 27	Tennessee	(H)	61	60
Mar. 1	Alabama	(H)	78	72
			2109	1914

(N1) Charlotte, N. C.
(N2) Louisville, Ky.

1965-66—Won 32, Lost 2.
COACH: Adolph Rupp
HON. CAPT.: (None)

Dec. 1	Hardin-Simmons	(H)	83	55
Dec. 4	Virginia	(A)	99	73
Dec. 8	Illinois	(A)	86	68
Dec. 11	Northwestern	(H)	86	75

UK INVITATIONAL TOURNAMENT

Dec. 17	Air Force		78	58
Dec. 18	Indiana (Championship)		91	56
Dec. 22	Texas Tech	(A)	89	73
Dec. 29	Notre Dame	(N1)	103	69
Jan. 3	St Louis	(H)	80	70
Jan. 8	Florida	(A)	78	64
Jan. 10	Georgia	(A)	69	**65
Jan. 15	Vanderbilt	(H)	96	83
Jan. 24	Louisiana State	(H)	111	85
Jan. 29	Auburn	(H)	115	78
Jan. 31	Alabama	(H)	82	62
Feb. 2	Vanderbilt	(A)	105	90
Feb. 5	Georgia	(H)	74	50
Feb. 7	Florida	(H)	85	75
Feb. 12	Auburn	(A)	77	64
Feb. 14	Alabama	(A)	90	67
Feb. 19	Mississippi State	(A)	73	69
Feb. 21	Mississippi	(A)	108	65
Feb. 26	Tennessee	(H)	78	64
Mar. 5	**Tennessee**	**(A)**	**62**	**69**
Mar. 7	Tulane	(H)	103	74

SEC Champions

NCAA TOURNAMENT
(Mideast Regional—Iowa City, Iowa)

Mar. 11	Dayton		86	79
Mar. 12	Michigan		84	77

(Finals—College Park, Md.)

Mar. 18	Duke		83	79
Mar. 19	**Texas Western**		**65**	**72**
			2519	2028

INTERNATIONAL UNIVERSITIES
TOURNAMENT
Tel Aviv, Israel

Aug. 3	Warsaw Univ.		67	58
Aug. 4	Cambridge Univ.		104	45
Aug. 6	Salonika Univ.		91	60
Aug. 10	Instanbul Univ.		82	36
Aug. 11	Warsaw Univ.		87	57
	(Championship)			
			2950	2284

(N1) Louisville
** Double overtime

1966-67—Won 13, Lost 13.
COACH: Adolph Rupp
HON. CAPT.: (None)

Dec. 3	Virginia	(H)	104	84
Dec. 5	**Illinois**	**(H)**	**97**	***98**
Dec. 10	Northwestern	(A)	118	116
Dec. 13	**North Carolina**	**(H)**	**55**	**64**

435

Date	Team	Site	Ky.	Opp.
Dec. 17	**Florida**	**(H)**	**75**	**78**
	UK INVITATIONAL TOURNAMENT			
Dec. 22	Oregon State		96	66
Dec. 23	Kansas St. (Championship)		83	79
Dec. 28	**Cornell**	**(H)**	**77**	**92**
Dec. 31	Notre Dame	(N1)	96	85
Jan. 5	**Vanderbilt**	**(H)**	**89**	***91**
Jan. 14	**Florida**	**(A)**	**72**	**89**
Jan. 16	**Georgia**	**(A)**	**40**	**49**
Jan. 21	Auburn	(H)	60	58
Jan. 23	**Tennessee**	**(H)**	**50**	****52**
Jan. 28	Louisiana State	(H)	102	72
Jan. 30	Mississippi	(H)	96	53
Feb. 4	Louisiana State	(A)	105	84
Feb. 6	Mississippi	(A)	79	70
Feb. 11	**Mississippi State**	**(H)**	**72**	***77**
Feb. 13	**Tennessee**	**(A)**	**57**	**76**
Feb. 18	Mississippi State	(A)	103	74
Feb. 20	Georgia	(H)	101	76
Feb. 25	**Alabama**	**(A)**	**71**	**81**
Feb. 27	**Auburn**	**(A)**	**49**	**60**
Mar. 4	**Vanderbilt**	**(A)**	**94**	**110**
Mar. 6	Alabama	(H)	110	78
			2151	2012

(N1) Louisville
* Overtime   ** Double Overtime

1967-68—Won 22, Lost 5.
COACH: Adolph Rupp
CAPTAIN: Thad Jaracz

Date	Team	Site	Ky.	Opp.
Dec. 2	Michigan	(A)	96	79
Dec. 4	Florida	(H)	99	76
Dec. 6	Xavier	(H)	111	76
Dec. 9	Pennsylvania	(H)	64	49
Dec. 12	**North Carolina**	**(N1)**	**77**	**84**
	UK INVITATIONAL TOURNAMENT			
Dec. 22	Dayton		88	85
Dec. 23	South Carolina		76	66
	(Championship)			
Dec. 30	Notre Dame	(N2)	81	73
Jan. 6	Vanderbilt	(A)	94	78
Jan. 8	Alabama	(A)	84	76
Jan. 13	**Florida**	**(A)**	**78**	**96**
Jan. 15	Georgia	(H)	104	73
Jan. 20	**Auburn**	**(A)**	**73**	**74**
Jan. 22	**Tennessee**	**(A)**	**59**	**87**
Jan. 27	Louisiana State	(A)	121	95
Jan. 29	Mississippi	(A)	85	76
Feb. 3	Louisiana State	(H)	109	96
Feb. 5	Mississippi	(H)	78	62
Feb. 10	Mississippi State	(A)	92	84
Feb. 12	Tennessee	(H)	60	59
Feb. 17	Mississippi State	(H)	107	81
Feb. 19	Georgia	(A)	106	87
Feb. 24	Alabama	(H)	96	83
Feb. 26	Auburn	(H)	89	57
Mar. 2	Vanderbilt	(H)	85	80
	SEC Champions			
	NCAA TOURNAMENT			
	MIDEAST REGIONAL			
	Lexington, Ky.			
Mar. 15	Marquette		107	89
Mar. 16	**Ohio State**		**81**	**82**
			2400	2103

(N1) Greensboro, N.C.   (N2) Louisville

1968-69—Won 23, Lost 5.
COACH: Adolph Rupp
CAPTAIN: Phil Argento

Date	Team	Site	Ky.	Opp.
Nov. 30	Xavier	(H)	115	77
Dec. 2	Miami	(A)	86	77
Dec. 7	North Carolina	(H)	77	87
Dec. 14	Pennsylvania	(A)	102	78
	UK INVITATIONAL TOURNAMENT			
Dec. 20	Michigan		112	104
Dec. 21	Army		80	65
	(Championship)			
Dec. 28	Notre Dame	(N1)	110	90
Dec. 31	**Wisconsin**	**(N2)**	**65**	**69**
Jan. 4	Mississippi	(A)	69	59
Jan. 6	Mississippi State	(A)	91	72
Jan. 11	Florida	(H)	88	67
Jan. 13	Georgia	(H)	88	68
Jan. 18	Tennessee	(A)	69	66
Jan. 25	Louisiana State	(A)	108	96
Jan. 27	Alabama	(A)	83	*70
Feb. 1	Vanderbilt	(H)	103	89
Feb. 3	Auburn	(H)	105	93
Feb. 8	Mississippi	(H)	104	68
Feb. 10	Mississippi State	(H)	91	69
Feb. 15	**Florida**	**(A)**	**81**	**82**
Feb. 17	Georgia	(A)	85	77
Feb. 22	Louisiana State	(H)	103	89
Feb. 26	Alabama	(H)	108	79
Mar. 1	**Vanderbilt**	**(A)**	**99**	**101**
Mar. 3	Auburn	(A)	90	86
Mar. 8	Tennessee	(H)	84	69
	SEC Champions			
	NCAA TOURNAMENT			
	MIDEAST (Madison, Wisc.)			
Mar. 13	**Marquette**	**(N)**	**74**	**81**
Mar. 15	Miami	(N)	72	71
			2542	2199

(N1) Louisville; (N2) Chicago

1969-70—Won 26, Lost 2.
COACH: Adolph Rupp
CO-CAPTAINS: Dan Issel and Mike Pratt

Date	Team	Site	Ky.	Opp.
Dec. 1	West Virginia	(H)	106	87
Dec. 6	Kansas	(H)	115	85
Dec. 8	North Carolina	(N1)	94	87
Dec. 13	Indiana	(H)	109	92
	UK INVITATIONAL TOURNAMENT			
Dec. 19	Navy		73	59
Dec. 20	Duke		98	76
	(Championship)			
Dec. 27	Notre Dame	(N2)	102	100
Dec. 29	Miami (Ohio)	(H)	80	58
Jan. 3	Mississippi	(H)	95	73
Jan. 5	Mississippi State	(H)	111	76
Jan. 10	Florida	(A)	88	69
Jan. 12	Georgia	(A)	72	71
Jan. 17	Tennessee	(H)	68	52
Jan. 24	Louisiana State	(A)	109	96
Jan. 26	Alabama	(H)	86	71
Jan. 31	**Vanderbilt**	**(A)**	**81**	**89**
Feb. 2	Auburn	(A)	84	83
Feb. 7	Mississippi	(A)	120	85
Feb. 9	Mississippi State	(A)	86	57
Feb. 14	Florida	(H)	110	66
Feb. 16	Georgia	(H)	116	86
Feb. 21	Louisiana State	(A)	121	105
Feb. 23	Alabama	(A)	98	89
Feb. 28	Vanderbilt	(H)	90	86
Mar. 2	Auburn	(H)	102	81
Mar. 7	Tennessee	(A)	86	69
	SEC Champions			
	NCAA TOURNAMENT			
	MIDEAST (Columbus, Ohio)			
Mar. 12	Notre Dame	(N3)	109	99
Mar. 14	**Jacksonville**	**(N3)**	**100**	**106**
			2709	2253

(N1) Charlotte, N.C.; (N2) Louisville;
(N3) Columbus, Ohio

1970-71—Won 22, Lost 6.
COACH: Adolph Rupp
HON. CO-CAPTAINS: Mike Casey and Larry Steele

Date	Team	Site	Ky.	Opp.
Dec. 1	Northwestern	(A)	115	100
Dec. 5	Michigan	(H)	104	93
Dec. 7	West Virginia	(A)	106	100
Dec. 12	Indiana	(A)	95	93

UK INVITATIONAL TOURNAMENT

Dec. 18	De Paul		106	85
Dec. 19	**Purdue**		**83**	**89**

(Championship)

Dec. 22	Oregon State	(H)	84	78
Dec. 29	**Notre Dame**	**(N1)**	**92**	**99**
Jan. 2	Mississippi	(A)	103	95
Jan. 4	Miss. State	(A)	79	71
Jan. 9	Florida	(H)	101	75
Jan. 11	Georgia	(H)	79	66
Jan. 16	**Tennessee**	**(A)**	**71**	**75**
Jan. 23	Louisiana State	(A)	82	79
Jan. 25	Alabama	(A)	86	73
Jan. 30	Vanderbilt	(H)	102	92
Feb. 1	Auburn	(H)	114	76
Feb. 6	Mississippi	(H)	121	86
Feb. 8	Miss. State	(H)	102	83
Feb. 13	**Florida**	**(A)**	**65**	**74**
Feb. 15	Georgia	(A)	107	95
Feb. 20	Louisiana State	(H)	110	73
Feb. 22	Alabama	(H)	101	74
Feb. 27	Vanderbilt	(A)	119	90
Mar. 1	Auburn	(A)	102	83
Mar. 6	Tennessee	(H)	84	78

SEC Champions

NCAA TOURNAMENT
MIDEAST REGIONAL (Athens, Ga.)

Mar. 18	Western Ky. (N2)		83	107
Mar. 20	**Marquette (N2)**		**74**	**91**

			2670	2373

(N1) Louisville; (N2) Athens, Ga.

1971-72—Won 21, Lost 7.
COACH: Adolph Rupp
HON. CO-CAPTAINS: Stan Key and Tom Parker

Dec. 1	Northwestern	(H)	94	85
Dec. 4	Kansas	(A)	79	69
Dec. 6	Kansas State	(A)	71	64
Dec. 11	**Indiana**	**(N1)**	**89**	****90**
Dec. 13	**Michigan State**	**(H)**	**85**	**91**

UK INVITATIONAL TOURNAMENT

Dec. 17	Missouri		83	79
Dec. 18	Princeton		96	82

(Championship)

Dec. 28	Notre Dame	(N1)	83	67
Jan. 8	Mississippi	(H)	93	82
Jan. 10	Mississippi State	(H)	104	76
Jan. 15	**Florida**	**(A)**	**70**	**72**
Jan. 17	**Georgia**	**(A)**	**73**	**85**
Jan. 22	Tennessee	(H)	72	70
Jan. 24	Vanderbilt	(H)	106	80
Jan. 29	Louisiana State	(H)	89	71
Jan. 31	Alabama	(H)	77	74
Feb. 5	Vanderbilt	(A)	85	*80
Feb. 7	Auburn	(A)	78	72
Feb. 12	Mississippi	(A)	90	82
Feb. 14	Mississippi State	(A)	63	55
Feb. 19	Florida	(H)	95	68
Feb. 21	Georgia	(H)	87	63
Feb. 26	**Louisiana State**	**(A)**	**71**	**88**
Feb. 28	**Alabama**	**(A)**	**70**	**73**
Mar. 6	Auburn	(H)	102	67
Mar. 9	Tennessee	(A)	67	66

SEC Co-Champions (Earned NCAA bid by beating Tennessee twice)

NCAA TOURNAMENT
MIDEAST REGIONAL (Dayton, Ohio)

Mar. 16	Marquette	(N2)	85	69
Mar. 18	**Florida State**	**(N2)**	**54**	**73**

			2311	2093

(N1) Louisville; (N2) Dayton, Ohio

JOE HALL ERA
1972-73—Won 20, Lost 8.
COACH: Joe B. Hall
HON. CAPTAIN: Jim Andrews

Nov. 29	Chilean NAT (Exh)*	(H)	125	62
Dec. 2	Michigan State	(A)	75	66
Dec. 4	**Iowa**	**(H)**	**66**	**79**
Dec. 9	Indiana	(A)	58	64
Dec. 11	**North Carolina**	**(N1)**	**70**	**78**

UK INVITATIONAL TOURNAMENT

Dec. 15	Nebraska		85	60
Dec. 16	Oregon		95	68

(Championship)

Dec. 23	Kansas	(H)	77	71
Dec. 30	Notre Dame	(N1)	65	63
Jan. 6	**Mississippi**	**(A)**	**58**	**61**
Jan. 8	Mississippi State	(A)	90	81
Jan. 13	Florida	(H)	95	65
Jan. 15	Georgia	(H)	89	68
Jan. 20	**Tennessee**	**(A)**	**64**	**65**
Jan. 22	**Vanderbilt**	**(A)**	**75**	**76**
Jan. 27	Louisiana State	(A)	86	71
Jan. 29	Alabama	(A)	95	93
Feb. 3	**Vanderbilt**	**(H)**	**76**	**83**
Feb. 5	Auburn	(H)	88	57
Feb. 10	Mississippi	(H)	88	70
Feb. 12	Mississippi State	(H)	100	*87
Feb. 17	Florida	(A)	94	83
Feb. 19	Georgia	(A)	99	86
Feb. 24	Louisiana State	(H)	94	76
Feb. 26	Alabama	(H)	111	95
Mar. 3	Auburn	(A)	91	79
Mar. 8	Tennessee	(H)	86	81

SEC Champions

NCAA TOURNAMENT
MIDEAST REGIONAL (Nashville, Tenn.)

Austin Peay	(N2)	106	*100
Indiana	**(N2)**	**65**	**72**

		2341	2098

(N1) Louisville; (N2) Nashville, Tenn.
* Not counted in win or pts. total.

1973-74—Won 13, Lost 13.
COACH: Joe B. Hall
CAPTAIN: Ronnie Lyons

Dec. 1	Miami (O.)	(H)	81	68
Dec. 3	**Kansas**	**(A)**	**63**	**71**
Dec. 8	Indiana	(N1)	68	77
Dec. 10	**North Carolina**	**(N2)**	**84**	**101**
Dec. 14	Iowa	(A)	88	80

UK INVITATIONAL TOURNAMENT

Dec. 21	Dartmouth		102	77
Dec. 22	Stanford		78	77

(Championship)

Dec. 29	Notre Dame	(N1)	79	94
Jan. 5	**Louisiana State**	**(A)**	**84**	**95**
Jan. 7	Georgia	(H)	80	74
Jan. 12	Auburn	(H)	79	58
Jan. 14	**Tennessee**	**(A)**	**54**	**67**
Jan. 19	Mississippi	(H)	93	64
Jan. 21	**Alabama**	**(A)**	**77**	**81**
Jan. 26	Florida	(A)	91	82
Jan. 28	**Vanderbilt**	**(H)**	**65**	**82**
Feb. 2	Mississippi State	(A)	82	70
Feb. 4	Louisiana State	(H)	73	70
Feb. 9	Georgia	(A)	86	72
Feb. 11	**Auburn**	**(A)**	**97**	***99**
Feb. 16	Tennessee	(H)	61	58
Feb. 18	**Mississippi**	**(A)**	**60**	**61**
Feb. 23	**Alabama**	**(H)**	**71**	**94**
Feb. 25	Florida	(H)	65	75
Mar. 2	**Vanderbilt**	**(A)**	**69**	**71**
Mar. 4	Mississippi State	(H)	108	69

(N1) Louisville; (N2) Greensboro, N.C.

Date	Team	Ky.	Opp.
	1974 AUSTRALIAN EXHIBITION TOUR		
	(Not Counted in Won-Lost Record)		
May 13	Tahitian National Team	116	62
May 17	**Australia**	**87**	**97**
May 18	Newcastle	90	78
May 19	N.S.W. All Stars	123	67
May 21	Illawarra Hawks	115	57
May 22	N.S.W. All Stars	106	50
May 23	A.C.T.	96	69
May 25	Bulleen Heidelberg	88	83
May 26	St. Kilda Business House	80	67
May 27	Nunawading	99	82
May 28	**Melbourne**	**79**	**86**
May 30	Gippsland All Stars	127	74
May 31	Bulleen Heidelberg	72	71
June 1	Laker All Stars	111	83
June 3	So. Australian All Stars	109	96
June 4	So. Australian All Stars	110	81
June 5	So. Australian All Stars	111	84
June 6	Coburg	108	82
June 7	St. Kilda Business House	96	85
		1923	1454

1974-75—Won 26, Lost 5
COACH: Joe B. Hall
CAPTAIN: Jimmy Dan Conner

Date	Team		Ky.	Opp.
Nov. 25	Ath. In Action*	(H)	103	65
Nov. 30	Northwestern	(H)	97	70
Dec. 2	Miami (O.)	(A)	80	73
Dec. 7	**Indiana**	**(A)**	**74**	**98**
Dec. 9	North Carolina	(N1)	90	78
	UK INVITATIONAL TOURNAMENT			
Dec. 20	Washington State		97	75
Dec. 21	Oklahoma State		90	65
	(Championship)			
Dec. 23	Kansas	(N1)	100	63
Dec. 28	Notre Dame	(N1)	113	96
Jan. 4	L. S. U.	(H)	115	80
Jan. 6	Georgia	(A)	96	77
Jan. 11	**Auburn**	**(A)**	**85**	**90**
Jan. 13	Tennessee	(H)	88	82
Jan. 18	Mississippi	(A)	85	82
Jan. 20	Alabama	(H)	74	69
Jan. 25	Florida	(H)	87	65
Jan. 27	Vanderbilt	(A)	91	90
Feb. 1	Mississippi State	(H)	112	79
Feb. 3	L. S. U.	(A)	77	76
Feb. 8	Georgia	(H)	75	61
Feb. 10	Auburn	(H)	119	76
Feb. 15	**Tennessee**	**(A)**	**98**	**103**
Feb. 17	Mississippi	(H)	108	89
Feb. 22	Alabama	(A)	84	79
Feb. 24	**Florida**	**(A)**	**58**	**66**
Mar. 1	Vanderbilt	(H)	109	84
Mar. 8	Mississippi State	(A)	118	80
	SEC Co-Champions			

Date	Team	Site	Ky.	Opp.
	NCAA TOURNAMENT			
	Mideast Regional			
	(Tuscaloosa, Ala., and Dayton, O.)			
Mar. 15	Marquette	(N2)	76	54
Mar. 20	Central Michigan	(N3)	90	73
Mar. 22	Indiana	(N3)	92	90
	Finals (San Diego, CA.)			
Mar. 29	Syracuse	(N4)	95	79
Mar. 31	**UCLA**	**(N4)**	**85**	**92**
			2858	2434

* Exhibition—Not counted in won-lost record.
(N1) Louisville; (N2) Tuscaloosa, Ala.; (N3) Dayton, O.; (N4) San Diego, CA.

1975-76—Won 20, Lost 10
COACH: Joe B. Hall
CAPTAIN: Jack Givens

Date	Team		Ky.	Opp.
Nov. 22	Yugoslavia (EXH.)*	(H)	75	74
Dec. 1	**Northwestern**	**(A)**	**77**	**89**
Dec. 8	**North Carolina**	**(N1)**	**77**	**90**
Dec. 10	Miami	(A)	91	69
Dec. 13	Kansas	(A)	54	48
Dec. 15	**Indiana**	**(N2)**	**68**	***77**
	UK INVITATIONAL TOURNAMENT			
Dec. 19	Georgia Tech		66	64
Dec. 20	Oregon State		82	74
	(Championship)			
Dec. 30	Notre Dame	(N2)	79	77
Jan. 3	**Mississippi State**	**(A)**	**73**	**77**
Jan. 5	**Alabama**	**(A)**	**63**	**76**
Jan. 10	**Tennessee**	**(H)**	**88**	***90**
Jan. 12	Georgia	(H)	92	76
Jan. 17	Vanderbilt	(H)	77	76
Jan. 24	Florida	(A)	89	82
Jan. 26	**Auburn**	**(A)**	**84**	***91**
Jan. 31	Mississippi	(H)	89	81
Feb. 2	Louisiana State	(H)	85	71
Feb. 7	**Tennessee**	**(A)**	**85**	**92**
Feb. 9	**Georgia**	**(A)**	**81**	**86**
Feb. 14	**Vanderbilt**	**(A)**	**65**	**69**
Feb. 21	Florida	(H)	96	89
Feb. 23	Auburn	(H)	93	82
Feb. 28	Mississippi	(A)	94	87
Mar. 1	Louisiana State	(A)	85	70
Mar. 6	Alabama	(H)	90	85
Mar. 8	Mississippi State	(H)	94	*93
	NATIONAL INVITATION TOURNAMENT			
	New York, N.Y.			
Mar. 13	Niagra		67	61
Mar. 16	Kansas State		81	78
Mar. 18	Providence		79	78
Mar. 21	U.N.C. Charlotte		71	67
	(Championship)			
			2415	2345

* Exhibition—Not counted in won-lost record.
(N1) Charlotte, N.C.; (N2) Louisville.

WILDCAT MASCOTS HAD COLORFUL NAMES

Over the years, Kentucky athletic teams have been spurred on in efforts toward victory by numerous colorfully-named wildcat mascots. Records indicate the first animal was given to the University in 1921. Named "Tom," this live Kentucky wildcat died quickly from being in captivity and was replaced with "TNT." Other live mascots followed—including "Whiskers," "Hot Tamale," and "Colonel"—only to pass from the scene due to death or being turned loose in the mountains after they did not thrive out of their native habitat.

KENTUCKY COACHES THROUGH THE YEARS

Years at UK	Name	Tenure	Won	Lost	Pct.	Best Season
1903-09	W. W. H. Mustaine and Others+	7	21	35	.375	
1910	E. R. Sweetland & R. E. Spahr	1	4	8	.333	
1911	H. J. Iddings	1	5	6	.454	5-6 in 1911
1912	E. R. Sweetland	1	9	0	1.000	9-0 in 1912
1913	J. J. Tigert	1	5	3	.625	5-3 in 1913
1914-15	Alpha Brumage	2	18	7	.720	11-2 in 1914
1916	James Park	1	8	6	.571	8-6 in 1916
1917	W. P. Tuttle	1	4	6	.400	4-6 in 1917
1918	S. A. Boles	1	9	2-1*	.791	9-2-1 in 1918
1919	Andrew Gill	1	6	8	.428	6-8 in 1919
1920-24	George Buchheit	5	44	27	.619	13-1 in 1921
1925	C. O. Applegran	1	13	8	.619	13-8 in 1925
1926	Ray Eklund	1	15	3	.833	15-3 in 1926
1927	Basil Hayden	1	3	13	.187	3-13 in 1927
1928-30	John Mauer	3	40	14	.740	16-3 in 1930
1931-72	Adolph Rupp	42#	880	190	.822	25-0 in 1954
1973	Joe B. Hall	4	79	36	.687	26-5 in 1975

18 Coaches in 73 Seasons—Record 1534 Games: Won 1163, Lost 372, Tied 1—75.8%

*Unique tie game resulted from scorer's error discovered after game.
#No schedule played in 1953—Rupp's record for 41 seasons.
+Basketball at UK reportedly started when W. W. H. Mustaine called together some students, took up a collection totaling $3 for a ball and told them to start playing. There was no official coach from 1903 until 1910. Managers ran the team.

ON THE TRAIL OF TITLES — NCAA CHAMPIONS

1939	Oregon	1952	Kansas	1965	UCLA
1940	Indiana	1953	Indiana	1966	Texas Western
1941	Wisconsin	1954	LaSalle	1967	UCLA
1942	Stanford	1955	San Francisco	1968	UCLA
1943	Wyoming	1956	San Francisco	1969	UCLA
1944	Utah	1957	North Carolina	1970	UCLA
1945	Oklahoma A&M	**1958**	**Kentucky**	1971	UCLA
1946	Oklahoma A&M	1959	California	1972	UCLA
1947	Holy Cross	1960	Ohio State	1973	UCLA
1948	**Kentucky**	1961	Cincinnati	1974	N.C. St.
1949	**Kentucky**	1962	Cincinnati	1975	UCLA
1950	CCNY	1963	Loyola (Chicago)	1976	Indiana
1951	**Kentucky**	1964	UCLA		

HOME FLOOR LOSSES SINCE 1943

(Total of 38)

Date	Opponent	Score	Margin
Jan. 8, 1955	Georgia Tech	59-58	1
Dec. 10, 1955	Temple	73-61	12
Dec. 21, 1955	Dayton (UKIT)	89-74	15
Dec. 10, 1956	St. Louis	71-70	1
Mar. 16, 1957	Michigan State (NCAA)	80-68	12
Dec. 20, 1957	West Virginia (UKIT)	77-70	7
Dec. 19, 1959	West Virginia (UKIT)	79-70	9
Jan. 2, 1960	Georgia Tech	62-54	8
Feb. 27, 1960	Tennessee	65-63	2
Dec. 3, 1960	Florida State	63-58	5
Dec. 22, 1960	St. Louis (UKIT)	74-72*	2
Dec. 4, 1961	Southern California	79-77	2
Feb. 12, 1962	Mississippi State	49-44	5
Dec. 1, 1962	Virginia Tech	80-77	3
Dec. 17, 1962	North Carolina	68-66	2
Jan. 5, 1963	Georgia Tech	86-85**	1
Jan. 19, 1963	Tennessee	78-69*	9
Feb. 18, 1963	Vanderbilt	69-67	2
Mar. 2, 1964	St. Louis	67-60	7
Dec. 19, 1964	Illinois (UKIT)	91-86	5
Jan. 5, 1965	Vanderbilt	97-79	18
Dec. 5, 1966	Illinois	98-97*	1
Dec. 13, 1966	North Carolina	64-55	9
Dec. 17, 1966	Florida	78-75	3
Dec. 28, 1966	Cornell	92-77	15
Jan. 5, 1967	Vanderbilt	91-89*	2
Jan. 23, 1967	Tennessee	52-50**	2
Feb. 11, 1967	Mississippi State	77-72*	5
Mar. 16, 1968	Ohio State (NCAA)	82-81	1
Dec. 7, 1968	North Carolina	87-77	10
Dec. 19, 1970	Purdue (UKIT)	89-83	6
Dec. 13, 1971	Michigan State	91-85	6
Dec. 4, 1972	Iowa	79-66	13
Feb. 3, 1973	Vanderbilt	83-76	7
Jan. 28, 1974	Vanderbilt	82-65	17
Feb. 23, 1974	Alabama	94-71	23
Feb. 25, 1974	Florida	75-65	10
Jan. 10, 1976	Tennessee	88-90*	2

*One overtime period.   **Double overtime.   Average loss margin—6.8

(Kentucky's home floor winning streak started against Ft. Knox on Jan. 4, 1943, following a loss to Ohio State two nights earlier. Before Ga. Tech snapped the string, the Wildcats had posted a national record 129 consecutive victories. All told, since the Ohio State loss, the Wildcats have won 392 and lost only 38 at home. Since Memorial Coliseum became the home floor at the start of the 1950-51 season, the record is 308-38.)

ALL-SOUTHEASTERN CONFERENCE
(54 Players Chosen 96 Times)

Ellis Johnson (G) 1933	Shelby Linville (F) 1951
Forest Sale (C) 1933	Bobby Watson (G) .... 1951, '52
John DeMoisey (F) ..... 1933, '34	Frank Ramsey (G) . 1951, '52, '54
Bill Davis (G) 1934	Cliff Hagan (C) .... 1952, '54
Leroy Edwards (C) 1935	Bill Evans (G-F) 1955
Dave Lawrence (F) 1935	Bob Burrow (C) ...... 1955, '56
Ralph Carlisle (F) ...... 1936, '37	Johnny Cox (F) ... 1957, '58, '59
Warfield Donohue (G) 1937	Vernon Hatton (G) 1958
Bernie Opper (G) ...... 1938, '39	Don Mills (C) 1960
Layton Rouse (G) 1940	Bill Lickert (F-G) .. 1959, '60, '61
Lee Huber (G) 1941	Larry Pursiful (G) 1962
James King (C) 1941	Cotton Nash (C-F) . 1962, '63, '64
Marvin Akers (F) ...... 1941, '43	Ted Deeken (F) 1964
Ermal Allen (F) 1942	Tommy Kron (G) ..... 1965, '66
Melvin Brewer (C) 1943	Pat Riley (F) .... 1965, '66
Bob Brannum (C) 1944	Thad Jaracz (C-F) 1966
Jack Parkinson (G) .. 1944, '45, '46	Larry Conley (F) 1966
Jack Tingle (F) . 1944, '45, '46, '47	Louie Dampier (G) . 1965, '66, '67
Kenton Campbell (C) 1945	Mike Casey (G) ... 1968, '69, '71
Ralph Beard (G) . 1946, '47, '48, '49	Dan Issel (C) ..... 1968, '69, '70
Wallace Jones (F) 1946, '47, '48, '49	Mike Pratt (F) .... 1969, '70
Joe Holland (F) 1947	Larry Steele (F) 1971
Alex Groza (C) .... 1948, '49	Tom Parker (F) ...... 1971, '72
Kenny Rollins (G) ...... 1947, '48	Tom Payne (C) 1971
Jim Line (F) 1950	Jim Andrews (C) ..... 1972, '73
Bill Spivey (C) .... 1950, '51	Kevin Grevey (F) .. 1973, '74, '75
Walt Hirsch (F) 1951	Jack Givens (F) .... ,1976

KENTUCKY ACADEMIC ALL-AMERICANS

Louie Dampier	Guard	1966-67
Dan Issel	Center	1970
Mike Pratt	Forward	1970
Mike Casey	Guard	1971
Bob Guyette	Forward	1975
Jimmy Dan Conner	Guard	1975

ALL-NCAA TOURNAMENT

*Alex Groza (C) .... 1948, '49	Johnny Cox (F) 1958
Bill Spivey (C) 1951	Pat Riley (F) 1966
Shelby Linville (F) 1951	Louie Dampier (G) 1966
Vernon Hatton (G) 1958	Kevin Grevey (F) 1975

*Chosen Most Valuable Player 1948, '49.

(REGIONAL)

Larry Pursiful (G) 1962	Cotton Nash (C-F) 1962
*Alex Groza (C) .... 1948, '49	*Pat Riley (F) 1966
Bill Spivey (C) 1951	Louie Dampier (G) 1966
Bob Burrow (C) .... 1955, '56	Mike Casey (G) 1968
Vernon Hatton (G) 1958	Dan Issel (C) ..... 1968, '69, '70
Johnny Cox (F) .... 1957, '58, '59	Jim Andrews (C) ..... 1972, '73
Bill Lickert (F) 1961	Mike Flynn (G) 1975
	Jimmy Dan Conner (G) 1975

*Chosen Most Valuable Player.

ALL-SOUTHERN CONFERENCE

Paul Jenkins (G) 1926	George Yates (G) 1931
Carey Spicer (G) ...... 1929-'31	Ellis Johnson (C-F) 1932
Louis McGinnis (F) 1931	

TOP ALL-TIME KENTUCKY SCORERS—VARSITY CAREER

(The 1,000 Point Club)

Player—Pos.	Years	Points	Games	Average
1. Dan Issel (C)	3 (1968-70)	2,138	83	25.7
2. Kevin Grevey (F)	3 (1973-75)	1,801	84	21.4
3. Cotton Nash (C-F)	3 (1962-64)	1,770	78†	22.69
4. Alex Groza (C)	4 (1945, 47-49)	1,744	120	14.4
5. Louie Dampier (G)	3 (1965-67)	1,575	80	19.7
6. Mike Casey (G)	3 (1968-69-71)	1,535	82	18.7
7. Ralph Beard (G)	4 (1946-49)	1,517	139	10.8
8. Cliff Hagan (C)	2½ (1951-52, 54)	1,475	77	19.2
9. Pat Riley (F)	3 (1965-67)	1,464	80	18.3
10. Johnny Cox (F)	3 (1957-59)	1,461	84	17.3
11. Mike Pratt (F)	3 (1968-70)	1,359	81	16.8
12. Frank Ramsey (G)	3 (1951-52, 54)	1,344	91	14.7
13. Jim Andrews (C)	3 (1971-73)	1,320	80	16.5
14. Tom Parker (F)	3 (1970-72)	1,238	80	15.5
15. Bill Spivey (C)	2 (1950-51)	1,213	63	19.2
16. Vernon Hatton (G)	3 (1956-58)	1,154	76	15.1
17. Wallace Jones (F)	4 (1946-49)	1,151	98*	....
18. Bill Lickert (F-G)	3 (1959-61)	1,076	73	14.7
19. Jim Line (F)	4 (1947-50)	1,041	100*	....
20. Bob Burrow (C)	2 (1955-56)	1,023#	51	20.0
21. Jimmy Dan Conner (F-G)	3 (1973-75)	1,009	85	11.9
22. Bobby Watson (G)	3 (1950-52)	1,001	96	10.4

* No record for number of games played in 1947.
† Achieved membership in club earliest of any Wildcat, hitting 1,000th point in the 19th game of junior year.
# Kentucky career totals only. Junior College total of 2,191 points not included.

TOP REGULAR SEASON SCORERS

Player—Pos.	Year	Games	FG	FT	TP	Ave.
Dan Issel (C)	1970 (Sr.)	26	339	198	876	33.7
Dan Issel (C)	1969 (Jr.)	26	269	159	697	26.8
Cotton Nash (C-F)	1964 (Sr.)	25	233	149	615	24.6
Kevin Grevey (F)	1975 (Sr.)	26	265	99	629	24.2
Cliff Hagan (C)	1954 (Sr.)	25	234	132	600	24.0
Cotton Nash (C-F)	1962 (Soph.)	24	205	161	571	23.8
Jim Andrews (C)	1972 (Jr.)	26	224	120	568	21.9
Kevin Grevey (F)	1974 (Jr.)	25	232	83	547	21.9
Pat Riley (F)	1966 (Jr.)	25	225	91	541	21.6
Louie Dampier (G)	1966 (Jr.)	25	211	99	521	20.8
Cliff Hagan (C)	1952 (Jr.)	26	206	128	540	20.8
Jack Givens (F)	1976 (Soph.)	26	216	105	537	20.7
Louie Dampier (G)	1967 (Sr.)	26	219	99	537	20.6
Cotton Nash (C-F)	1963 (Jr.)	25	176	162	514	20.6
Mike Casey (G)	1968 (Soph.)	25	215	76	506	20.2
Mike Pratt (F)	1970 (Sr.)	26	208	96	512	19.7
Alex Groza (C)	1949 (Sr.)	26	188	134	510	19.6
Jim Andrews (C)	1973 (Sr.)	26	217	75	509	19.6
Mike Casey (G-F)	1969 (Jr.)	26	220	65	505	19.3

KENTUCKY ALL-AMERICANS
(27 Players Chosen 40 Times)
*Consensus; †Second Team Consensus

BASIL HAYDEN
Forward—1921

BURGESS CAREY
Guard—1925

CAREY SPICER
F—1929-31

PAUL McBRAYER
Guard—1930

FOREST SALE
C-F—1932-33

ELLIS JOHNSON
Guard—1933

JOHN DeMOISEY
Center—1934

LeROY EDWARDS
Center—1935

BERNARD OPPER
Guard—1939

LEE HUBER
Guard—1940-41

BOB BRANNUM
Center—1944

JACK PARKINSON
Guard—1946

RALPH BEARD
G—47-48*-49*

ALEX GROZA
C—47-48†-49*

WALLACE JONES
Forward—1949†

BILL SPIVEY
Center—1951*

CLIFF HAGAN
C—1952*, 54*

FRANK RAMSEY
G—1952, 54†

BOB BURROW
Center—1956†

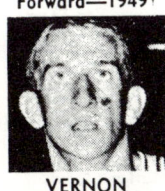
VERNON HATTON
Guard—1958

JOHNNY COX
Forward—1959*

COTTON NASH
C-F—62†-63†-64*

PAT RILEY
Forward—1966

LOUIE DAMPIER
Guard—1966†

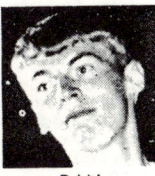
DAN ISSEL
C—1969-70*

KEVIN GREVEY
Forward—74-75

JACK GIVENS
Forward—1976

WILDCAT CAGE LETTERMEN

— A —

John Adams (63, 64, 65)
Earl Adkins (55, 57, 58)
Don Adkins (Mgr.)(74,75)
Marvin Akers (41, 42, 43)
Charles Alberts (25, 26)
Abramson Allan (44) (Mgr.)
Ermal Allen (40, 41, 42)
Ed Allin (45)
Carl Althaus (43)
H. M. Amoss (04)
Milerd Anderson (34, 35, 36)
Jim Andrews (71, 72, 73)
Lee Andrus (03, 04)
Phil Argento (67, 68, 69)
R. H. Arnett (04)
Jay Atkerson (Mgr.) (57, 58, 59)
Paul Adkins (21, 22)

— B —

H. A. Babb (Mgr.) (11)
Adrian Back (42)
Stanley Baer (05, 06, 07)
Scotty Baesler (62, 63)
Richard C. Barbee (06, 07, 08, 09)
Cliff Barker (47, 48, 49)
Bill Barlowe (43)
B. Barnett (11, 12, 13)
Dale Barnstable (47, 48, 49, 50)
Bobby Barton (Mgr.) (67)
Ralph Beard (46, 47, 48, 49)
Ed Beck (56, 57, 58)
Cecil Bell (31)
Cliff Berger (66, 67, 68)
Henry Besuden (26)
Bill Bibb (54)
Arthur Bicknell (40)
Doug Billips (Mgr.) (69,70)
Jerry Bird (54, 55, 56)
Crittenden Blair (34)
Harry Bliss (35)
Ralph Boren (24)
Brad Bounds (66, 67)
Bob Brannum (44, 47)
D. P. Branson (05, 06)
John Brewer (55, 56, 57)
Leo Brewer (08)
Melvin Brewer (41, 42, 43)
G. C. Bridges (10)
Jake Bronston (30, 31)
T. R. Bryant (05, 06, 07)
Nathanial Buis (44)
Carey Burchett (34) (Mgr.)
Carroll Burchett (60, 61, 62)
L. S. Burnham (19, 20, 22, 23)
Bob Burrow (55, 56)
Bill Busey (68)
Kirk Byars (Mgr.) (63)

— C —

Gerry Calvert (55, 56, 57)
Patrick Campbell (17, 18)
George Campbell (35) (Mgr.)
Kenton Campbell (45, 46)
Burgess Carey (25, 26)
Ralph Carlisle (35, 36, 37)
Armiel Carman (Mgr.) (16)
Dwane Casey (76)
Mike Casey (68, 69, 71)
Billy Ray Cassady (56, 57, 58)
J. S. Chambers (Mgr.) (09)
Truman Claytor (76)
Steve Clevenger (66, 67, 68)
Marion Cluggish (38, 39, 40)
Bennie Coffman (59, 60)
Sid Cohen (59, 60)
Lincoln Collinsworth (56, 57, 58)
Carl Combs (40)
Cecil Combs (28, 29, 30)
Charles Combs (38)
Larry Conley (64, 65, 66)
Jimmy Dan Conner (73, 74, 75)
Joe Coons (05)
Johnny Cox (57, 58, 59)
Hugh Coy (54)
John Crigler (56, 57, 58)
George Critz (64)
Larry Crosby (65) (Mgr.)
John S. Crosthwaite (10)
Albert Cummins (47)
Fred Curtis (37, 38, 39)

— D —

Louie Dampier (65, 66, 67)
Darrell Darby (31, 32, 33)
Howard Dardeen (59)
Berkley Davis (34)
Bruce Davis (36)
Mulford Davis (43, 46, 47)
Robert Davis (37)
William Davis (33, 34)
Ted Deeken (62, 63, 64)
Claire Dees (27, 28, 29)
John DeMoisey (32, 33, 34)
Truitt DeMoisey (44)
Harry Denham (39)
Jim Dinwiddie (69, 70, 71)
J. A. Dishman (18, 19)
Mike Dolan (Mgr.) (52, 54)
A. L. Donan (06)
Warfield Donohue (35, 36, 37)
H. H. Downing (08)
Pat Doyle (63)
Rick Drewitz (72, 73, 74)
Hunter Durham (Mgr.) (61, 62)
James Durham (45)

— E —

Ray Edelman (72, 73, 74)
Leroy Edwards (35)
Russell Ellington (35, 36)
Randy Embry (63, 64, 65)
Kenneth England (41, 42)
Bill Evans (52, 54, 55)
William Evans (42) (Mgr.)
J. C. Everett (19, 20)

— F —

H. L. Farmer (12, 13)
Keith Farnsley (39, 40, 41)
J. B. Faulconer (Mgr.) (39)
Allen Feldhaus (60, 61, 62)
John Ferguson (71) (Mgr.)
Fred Fest (23)
Garrett Fitzpatrick (41) (Mgr.)
Chigger Flynn (56) (Mgr.)
Mike Flynn (73, 74, 75)
Bob Fowler (76)
W. C. Fox (07, 08, 09)

— G —

J. H. Gaiser (10, 11, 12)
Gary Gamble (66, 67, 68)
Elmer Gilb (29)
Jack Givens (75, 76)
Max Glickman (18)
James Goforth (35, 36, 37)
James Goodman (38, 39)
Phil Grawemeyer (54, 55, 56)
Kevin Grevey (73, 74, 75)
William Griffin (Mgr.) (29)
Alex Groza (45, 47, 48, 49)
George Gumbert (14, 15, 16)
Bob Guyette (73, 74, 75)
J. White Guyn (04)

— H —

Cliff Hagan (51, 52, 54)
Joseph Hagan (36, 37, 38)
Jerry Hale (73, 74, 75)
Dan Hall (75)
Philip Haring (36, 38) (Mgr.)

444

Sam Harper (63, 64)
Tom Harper (64)
Carson Harreld (65, 66) (Mgr.)
W. C. Harrison (11, 12)
D. W. Hart (11, 12, 16)
Merion Haskins (75, 76)
Vernon Hatton (56, 57, 58)
Basil Hayden (20, 21, 22)
Elmo Head (37, 38, 39)
G. Foster Helm (25, 27)
J. H. Herman (06)
Walter Hirsch (49, 51)
Walter Hodge (37)
Joey Holland (76)
Joe Holland (46, 47, 48)
Kent Hollenbeck (70, 71, 72)
Dick Howe (57, 58)
Lee Huber (39, 40, 41)
C. T. Hughes (24, 25)
Lowell Hughes (58, 59)
Harry Hurd (62)

— I —

Robert Y. Ireland (16, 17) (Mgr.)
Charles Ishmael (63, 64)
Dan Issel (68, 69, 70)

— J —

Ralph Jackowski (38)
Thad Jaracz (66, 67, 68)
Irvine Jeffries (28)
Paul Jenkins (26, 27, 28)
Ned Jennings (59, 60, 61)
Herbert Jerome (34)
Ellis Johnson (31, 32, 33)
Larry Johnson (74, 75, 76)
Phil Johnson (56, 58, 59)
Walter Johnson (44)
Wallace Jones (46, 47, 48, 49)
James Jordan (47, 48)

— K —

...... Kelly (05)
William P. Kemper (Mgr.) (05)
Ron Kennett (64)
Stan Key (70, 71, 72)
James King (40, 41, 42)
William King (21, 22, 24)
A. M. Kirby (07)
William Kleiser (32)
Edwin Knadler (27)
Howard Kreuter (32, 33)
Tommy Kron (64, 65, 66)

— L —

Bob Ladin (20, 21, 22)
Art Laib (68)
Ed Lander (43)
Phil Latham (Trn.)(74, 75)
Dave Lawrence (33, 34, 35)

Roger Layne (51)
James Lee (75, 76)
Ken Lehkamp (Mgr.) (56, 57)
Jim LeMaster (66, 67, 68)
Larry Lentz (66)
Morris Levin (31) (Mgr.)
Garland Lewis (34, 35, 36)
Bill Lickert (59, 60, 61)
James Line (47, 48, 49, 50)
Shelby Linville (50, 51, 52)
Ercel Little (32)
Steve Lochmueller (73, 74)
Ronnie Lyons (72, 73, 74)

— M —

F. L. Marx (10, 11)
B. G. Marsh (18)
James Mathewson (42)
Charles Maxson (33) (Mgr.)
Jack May (35, 36) (Mgr.)
Paul McBrayer (28, 29, 30)
Bob McCowan, (69, 72)
Jim McDonald (60, 61, 62)
James McFarland (24, 25, 26)
Lawrence McGinnis (28, 29, 30)
Louis McGinnis (29, 30, 31)
James McIntosh (37)
James McKinney (36, 37) (Mgr.)
C. F. Meadors (12)
Hub Metry (64, 65) (Mgr.)
Don Mills (58, 59, 60)
Rav Mills (55, 56, 57)
Terry Mills (69, 70, 71)
Stanley Milward (28, 29, 30)
Will Milward (24, 25)
Terry Mobley (63, 64, 65)
Gayle Mohney (26)
Bob Moore (Mgr.) (50, 51, 52)
Ralph Morgan (13, 14, 15)
Tom Moseley (44)

— N —

Cotton Nash (62, 63, 64)
Alonzo Nelson (45)
Roger Newman (61)
C. M. Newton (51)
Tommy Nichols (36)
Paul Noel (43)
Randy Noll (70)

— O —

Dan Omlar (64) (Mgr.)
Bernard Opper (37, 38, 39)
Harp Owens (28, 29)
Hays Owens (30)

— P —

Harold Park (45) (Mgr.)
James Park (14)
Clyde Parker (43)
Ed Parker (Mgr.) (19)
J. Ed Parker (45, 46, 47)
Tom Parker (70, 71, 72)
Jack Parkinson (44, 45, 46, 48)
Dick Parsons (59, 60, 61)
Tom Payne (71)
Bart Peak (17)
Leonard Pearson (50)
Doug Pendygraft (62)
E. S. Penick (43)
Dan Perry (72)
George Perry (54)
Mike Phillips (75, 76)
Frank Phipps (27)
Wayne Plummer (09)
William Pogentz (21, 23)
Randy Pool (68, 69)
Tommy Porter (66, 67, 68)
Shelby Post (08, 09)
Sam Potter (34)
Mike Pratt (68, 69, 70)
R. C. Preston (11, 12, 13, 14)
Linville Puckett (54)
Larry Pursiful (60, 61, 62)

— R —

Frank Ramsey (51, 52, 54)
Lloyd Ramsey (41-42)
Tripp Ramsey (Mgr.) (76)
Robert Reynolds (32)
A. T. Rice (23, 24)
S. H. Ridgway (20, 21)
Carl Riefkin (23, 24)
Pat Riley (65, 66, 67)
R. N. Roark (04)
Roy Roberts (62, 63)
Rick Robey (75, 76)
Al Robinson (59)
William "Doc" Rodes (17)
William Rodes (09, 10)
Karl Rohs (25)
Don Rolfes (63)
Kenneth Rollins (43, 47, 48)
Van Buren Ropke (27)
Gayle Rose (52, 54, 55)
Harold Ross (56, 57, 58)
Ben Roth (Mgr.) (15)
Layton Rouse (38, 39, 40)
Willie Rouse (54)
Herky Rupp (62)

— S —

Forest Sale (31, 32, 33)
Charles Schrader (14, 17)
Wilbur Schu (44, 45, 46)
Herschel Scott (13, 14, 15)
Jim Server (15, 16)
Evan Settle (33, 34)
A. P. Shanklin (18)

Shelby Shanklin (08)
James Sharpe (27)
Glenn Sims (73) (Mgr.)
George Skinner (33)
Bobby Slusher (59)
Adrian Smith (57, 58)
Bill Smith (56, 57, 58)
G. J. Smith (73, 74, 75)
G. K. Smith (21, 23)
Mark Soderberg (70)
Carey Spicer (29, 30, 31)
Bill Spivey (50, 51)
Vincent Splane (42)
Carl Staker (40, 41, 42)
Larry Stamper (71, 72, 73)
Larry Steele (69, 70, 71)
Gene Stewart (67)
Bobby Stilz (36)
C. P. St. John (04)
N. Stone (08)
John Stough (45, 48)
Guy Strong (50)
William Sturgill (45, 46)
Bill Surface (Mgr.) (55)

— T —

Bob Tallent (66)
Bob Taylor (35)
Alan Theobald (Mgr. 68)
H. C. Thomas (18, 19)
Homer Thompson
 (37, 38, 39)

Tommy Thompson (Mgr.)
 (60)
Milton Ticco
 (41, 42, 43)
E. J. Tierney (35)
Jack Tingle
 (44, 45, 46, 47)
Garland Townes (50)
Bill Trott (31)
Lou Tsioropoulos
 (51, 52, 54)
Jack Tucker (33, 34, 35)
Paul Turrell (35)
William P. Tuttle
 (12, 13, 14, 15)

— U —

Lovell Underwood
 (24, 25, 26)

— V —

Arthur Vastin (18)
George Vulich (44, 45)

— W —

J. Rice Walker
 (36, 37, 38)
Reggie Warford (76)
L. B. Waters (05)
Robert Watson
 (50, 51, 52)

A. J. Weisenberger (13)
Wylie B. Wendt (06)
Leo Wenkley (Mgr.) (30)
Clint Wheeler (71)
Lucian Whitaker
 (50, 51, 52)
Waller White
 (40, 41, 42)
Don Whitehead (44)
E. Wilheling (21)
W. G. Wilkinson (23)
Maury Wilson
 (06, 07, 08)
W. C. Wilson (13)
Charles Worthington
 (31, 32)
H. J. Wurtele (04)

— Y —

George Yates
 (30, 31, 33)
Humzey Yessin (Mgr.)
 (46, 47, 48, 49)
Rudy Yessin (44)

— Z —

George Zerfoss
 (16, 18)
Karl Zerfoss
 (13, 14, 15, 16)
Tom Zerfoss (14)

WHO WERE THE 'FABULOUS FIVE'?

The most frequently asked question tossed at basketball historians and sports authorities is "Who were the 'Fabulous Five' of Kentucky?" The answer is Alex Groza (center), Ralph Beard and Kenny Rollins (guards), Wah Wah Jones and Cliff Barker (forwards). This famous 1948 team, captained by Rollins, won 36 and lost 3 while sweeping to Kentucky's first NCAA title and went on to participate as a unit in the Olympic Games—helping the USA team capture the world championship. Rollins graduated after the '48 season, but the remaining foursome continued to play havoc with collegiate basketball and copped another NCAA title for Kentucky in 1949 on a record of 36-2.

IN RECOGNITION OF OUTSTANDING ACHIEVEMENTS IN THE FIELD OF ATHLETIC ENDEAVOR, THE UNIVERSITY OF KENTUCKY ATHLETICS ASSOCIATION HAS RETIRED THE JERSEYS OF THE FOLLOWING FORMER WILDCAT BASKETBALL PLAYERS

"THE FABULOUS FIVE" 1948
NATIONAL CHAMPIONS - OLYMPIC GOLD MEDALISTS

12 RALPH BEARD 1946-47-48-49   15 ALEX GROZA 1945-47-48-49   22 CLIFF BARKER 1947-48-49   26 KENNETH ROLLINS 1943-47-48   27 WALLACE JONES 1946-47-48-49

UNDEFEATED NATIONAL CHAMPIONS 1954

6 CLIFF HAGAN 1951-52-54   16 LOU TSIOROPOULOS 1951-52-54   20 GAYLE ROSE 1952-54-55   22 JERRY BIRD 1954-55-56

30 FRANK RAMSEY 1951-52-54   42 BILLY EVANS 1952-54-55   44 PHIL GRAWEMEYER 1954-55-56

This handsome plaque is on display in the east concourse trophy case of Memorial Coliseum.

In a 10-year period from 1963-1973, Kentucky's 87.88 point scoring average ranked third nationally, topped only by Houston's 88.36 and Oklahoma City's 87.89. The Wildcats' 48.2 per cent marksmanship for the same period ranked fourth behind North Carolina's 49.2, Davidson's 48.7, and UCLA's 48.6.